CINDERELLA ARMY:
THE CANADIANS IN NORTHWEST EUROPE
1944–1945

In his controversial and award-winning 2003 book *Fields of Fire*, Terry Copp offered a stunning reversal of accepted military history, challenging the conventional view that the Canadian contribution to the Battle of Normandy was a failure. *Cinderella Army* continues the story of the operations carried out by the First Canadian Army in the last nine months of the war, and extends the argument developed in *Fields of Fire* that 'the achievement of the Allied and especially the Canadian armies ... has been greatly underrated while the effectiveness of the German army has been greatly exaggerated.' Copp supports this argument with research conducted on numerous trips to the battlefields of France, Belgium, Holland, and Germany. His detailed knowledge of the battlefield terrain, along with contemporary maps and air photos, allows Copp to explore the defensive positions that Canadian soldiers were required to overcome, and to illustrate how impressive their achievements truly were.

Except for a brief period during the Rhineland battle, the First Canadian Army was the smallest to serve under Eisenhower's command. The Canadian component never totalled more than 185,000 of the four million Allied troops serving in Northwest Europe. It is evident, however, that the divisions of 2nd Canadian Corps played a role disproportionate to their numbers. Their contribution to operations designed to secure the channel ports and open the approaches to Antwerp together with the battles in the Rhineland place them among the most heavily committed and sorely tried divisions in the Allied armies. By the end of 1944 3rd Canadian Division had suffered the highest number of casualties in 21 Army Group with 2nd Canadian Division ranking a close second. In the armoured divisions, 4th Canadian was at the top of the list as was 2nd Canadian Armoured Brigade among the independent tank brigades. Overall Canadian casualties were 20 per cent higher than in comparable British formations. This was a direct result of the much greater number of days that Canadian units were involved in close combat.

As passionately written and compellingly argued as its precursor, *Cinderella Army* is both an important bookend to Copp's earlier work, and stands on it's own as a significant contribution to Canadian military history.

TERRY COPP is a professor emeritus in the Department of History at Wilfrid Laurier University, and director of the Laurier Centre for Military Strategic and Disarmament Studies.

CINDERELLA ARMY

The Canadians in Northwest Europe 1944–1945

TERRY COPP

UNIVERSITY OF TORONTO PRESS
Toronto Buffalo London

© University of Toronto Press Incorporated 2006
Toronto Buffalo London
Printed in Canada

Reprinted 2006, 2007

Reprinted in paperback 2007

ISBN 978-0-8020-3925-5 (cloth)
ISBN 978-0-8020-9522-0 (paper)

Printed on acid-free paper

Library and Archives Canada Cataloguing in Publication

Copp, Terry, 1938–
    Cinderella army : the Canadians in northwest Europe, 1944–1945 / Terry Copp.

    Includes bibliographical references and index.
    ISBN 978-0-8020-3925-5 (bound)   ISBN 978-0-9522-0 (pbk.)

    1. Canada. Canadian Army – History – World War, 1939–1945.
    2. World War, 1939–1945 – Campaigns – Western Front.   I. Title.

D768.15.C656 2006   940.54'21   C2006-900970-8

Cover photographs: (front) Personnel of C Company, North Shore Regiment, 7 April 1945 / Zutphen, Netherlands / Donald I. Grant / Library and Archives Canada / PA130059; (back) Canadian soldiers marching toward Veen, 22 March 1945, courtesy Western Canada Pictorial Index. Tinted by John Beadle

University of Toronto Press acknowledges the financial assistance to its publishing program of the Canada Council for the Arts and the Ontario Arts Council.

University of Toronto Press acknowledges the financial support for its publishing activities of the Government of Canada through the Book Publishing Industry Development Program (BPIDP).

Contents

Illustrations follow pages 84 and 196

List of Maps

Don Bain

Preface

This book is a sequel to *Fields of Fire: The Canadians in Normandy*, but it may be read as a stand-alone account of the operations carried out by First Canadian Army in the last nine months of the war. The metaphor in the book's title reflects the challenges that army faced in October 1944, when it was depleted of resources and burdened with a multitude of tasks. It also reflects the challenges the Canadians faced in fighting a series of low-priority actions on a long left flank. *Cinderella Army* extends the argument developed in *Fields of Fire* that 'the achievement of the Allied and especially the Canadian armies ... has been greatly underrated while the effectiveness of the German army has been greatly exaggerated.'

This approach has been influenced by my many trips to the battle-fields of France, Belgium, the Netherlands, and Germany. Military historians need to have a detailed knowledge of the battlefield terrain, and I have been able to explore – with the aid of contemporary maps and air photos – the defensive positions that Canadian soldiers were required to overcome. I remain in awe of what they achieved.

In writing this book I have relied on a wide variety of archival sources, especially on War Diaries and Message Logs and on the Historical Officer interviews collected by the Library and Archives of Canada, to be found today in Record Group 24. The reports of No. 2 Operational Research Section and of its parent organization the Army Operational Research Group have continued to prove of great value, and I am grateful to the scientists who served in both organizations – David Hill, David Baley Pike, Tony Sargeant, Ronnie Shephard, Omand

Solandt, and Michael Swann – for providing personal papers and for patiently answering questions over a period of several years.

The battles of October 1944 and February–March 1945 produced a very large number of battle exhaustion casualties, and having reviewed my files on military psychiatry, I must again acknowledge the debt I owe to Drs Travis Dancey, Jack Griffin, Burdett McNeel, Clifford Richardson, and John Wishart, all of whom served as army psychiatrists. The veterans of the Regina Rifles who shared their experiences with me while I was preparing *Look to Your Front ... Regina Rifles* have added greatly to my knowledge of the actions at the Leopold Canal, Moyland Wood, and Emmerich. In this regard I must especially thank my co-author on that book, Lieutenant-Colonel Gordon Brown. I am similarly grateful to the veterans who helped me research *The Brigade: The Fifth Canadian Infantry Brigade 1939–1945*. They are acknowledged in that book.

Other veterans of the campaign in Northwest Europe who have directly contributed to this project include Cliff Chaderton, Harry Knox, Douglas Copp, Ernest A. Coté, W.A.B. Anderson, Leslie Chater, S. Radley Walters, Michel Gauvin, Roland Reid, Denis Whitaker, George Pangman, Don Learment, Trevor Hart Dyke, Hugh McVicar, Richard Hilborn, and Bill Whiteacre.

The first stage of my research on the campaign in Northwest Europe was carried out in partnership with my mentor, colleague, and friend, the late Robert Vogel. The thousands of pages of documents, notes, and drafts we worked with during the writing of the last three volumes of the *Maple Leaf Route* series, published between 1984 and 1988, have been re-examined for this study, and I have not hesitated to borrow material I wrote for these or other previously published books.

A number of my former students have undertaken research for me in the United Kingdom and the Netherlands. Here, I have drawn from notes and Xeroxes compiled by Marc de Waard, Oliver Haller, Kathleen Hynes, and Mike Bechthold. Major Kevin Connor, 52nd Lowland Regiment, provided documents relating to 52nd Lowland Division and much good advice. I wish to thank Rod Suddaby and the staff of the Imperial War Museum for their help over a period of many years and for their willingness to allow me to acquire microfilm copies of the Montgomery Papers. David Keogh at the United States Army Historical Institute in Carlisle, Pennsylvania, has been consistently helpful to me over the past two decades. The Staff at the Directorate of History and Heritage, Department of National Defence, have provided assistance and good council over a number of years.

My present and former colleagues at the Laurier Centre for Military, Strategic, and Disarmament Studies and at the Canadian Battlefields Foundation – Mike Bechthold, Mike Boire, Angelo Caravaggio, Doug Delaney, Serge Durflinger, Ralph Dykstra, Michelle Fowler, Geoff Hayes, Mark Humphries, Andrew Iarocci, Andrew Jankowski, Roman Jaramowycz, Marc Kilgour, Whitney Lackenbauer, John Maker, Marc Milner, Jeff Nilsson, David Patterson, Brian Rawding, Evert Steiber, Ralph Trost, Randy Wakelam, and Lee Windsor – provided both challenges and inspiration. The final version of the manuscript benefited from the comments of three anonymous reviewers and a number of my colleagues, especially Mike Bechthold, Kevin Connor, Doug Delaney, Andrew Jankowski, and David Patterson. Jeffrey Williams, author of *The Long Left Flank* and a veteran of the campaign, also read the manuscript and offered helpful comments. I alone am responsible for errors, omissions, and opinions. My thanks to Gail Corning, Mark Humphries, and Michelle Fowler for assistance in preparing earlier drafts of the manuscript. I am especially grateful to Brandey Barton, who worked closely with me in the preparation of the final draft, and to Mike Bechthold for his fine maps.

CINDERELLA ARMY:
THE CANADIANS IN NORTHWEST EUROPE
1944–1945

Introduction

On 6 June 1944 the Allies launched one of the most complex operations in the history of war – an assault landing on a defended coast. Its planners, remembering Gallipoli and Dieppe, made certain they took every conceivable measure to improve the odds of victory, but when D-Day arrived, poor weather limited the contributions of naval gunnery, airpower, and artillery. For that reason the enemy defences were substantially intact when the infantry touched down. The courage and determination of combat soldiers won the day for the Allied forces, and by midnight they had established a shallow bridgehead. This forced the Germans to establish a new defensive perimeter, on high ground inland from the beaches. All available German reserves were drawn into battle, and they met each Allied advance with determined resistance and aggressive counter-attacks. But the bloody seven-week stalemate that resulted did not prevent an Allied breakout that forced the remnants of forty German divisions to retreat from Normandy and ultimately from all of France.

General Bernard Law Montgomery, who commanded the American, British, and Canadian armies, stage-managed a cautious campaign, relying on a series of set-piece attacks designed to wear down the enemy. The Canadians played a major role in five of these large operations: Charnwood, the battle for Caen; Atlantic, the Canadian phase of Operation Goodwood; Spring, the holding attack at Verrières Ridge; and the two armoured thrusts towards Falaise, Totalize and Tractable. Canadian casualties in these battles were 18,444, including 5,021 killed in action – large in proportion to the troops engaged and a reflection of the heavy fighting on the Canadian front in late July and August. Overall Allied casualties exceeded 250,000 men, making Normandy a more costly battle than the infamous First World War killing ground at Passchendaele.[1]

Seventy per cent of these casualties, as well as most of the thousands evacuated as a result of battle exhaustion, were suffered by less than 15 per cent of the total force – that is, by those who served in the infantry rifle companies.[2] The Americans' replacement system was able to handle this level of losses; unfortunately, the British and Canadian military planners, ignoring the evidence from the Italian Campaign, had failed to address the critical question of how to supply trained reinforcements to their rifle companies. In the short term, the British dealt with this problem by disbanding an infantry division and several brigades to fill the ranks of depleted units; but the Canadians had only two infantry divisions in France and would not consider this option. As a consequence, many Canadian infantry battalions were forced to carry on at much diminished strength until a conversion program could retrain soldiers from other branches.[3]

Casualties among junior officers and NCOs were especially heavy, and by late August very few of the original section and platoon commanders were still with their regiments. The loss of well-trained combat leaders was a serious problem. The newly promoted NCOs had already stood the test of battle and won the respect of their fellow soldiers; unfortunately, this could not be said of the new platoon commanders. The Canadian Army had failed to adopt a policy of battlefield promotion and was relying instead on a steady stream of replacement lieutenants who were recent graduates of Officer Training Schools. Many of these young men had served in the ranks and had been selected for officer training because of their educational background or higher scores on the Army's M Test, but none of those who joined battalions in August had combat experience.[4] They were simply told to listen to their platoon sergeants until they found their feet.

The 3rd Division had suffered a high proportion of its casualties in June and July. At the time, there was still an adequate supply of trained infantry replacements, so it was able to maintain the strength of its battalions. As of 27 August 1944 that division was just 604 men under its authorized strength.[5] The division's command structure had also survived the experience of Normandy. When Major-General Rod Keller was wounded during Operation Totalize, the senior brigadier, Kenneth Blackader, assumed command of the division until a newly promoted thirty-one-year-old veteran of the Italian campaign, Dan Spry, arrived to take over. Spry, a Permanent Force infantry officer who had commanded a brigade for six months,[6] was a quick learner who had the sense to listen to his experienced staff. By August 1944, Lieutenant-Colonel Don Mingay, the senior staff officer (GSO 1) for operations, and Lieutenant-Colonel Ernest Coté, in charge of logistics and administration, were supervising a highly proficient, smooth-running staff. The other key figure in the division, Brigadier Stanley Todd, the senior gunner (CRA), possessed outstanding leadership and command skills.

With Blackader back in command of 8th Brigade, the dynamic Jock Spragge from the Queen's Own Rifles promoted to lead 7th Brigade, and John Rockingham, the most promising young brigadier in the army, taking over 9th Brigade, the leadership of the division was in excellent shape. Much the same could be said for 3rd Division's battalions. The post-Spring shake up in 9th Brigade had removed two competent veterans, but the new COs proved to be capable officers who quickly bonded with their regiments. When the Canadian Scottish Regiment and Queen's Own Rifles learned that their COs had been promoted, they correctly assumed that both would be succeeded by the experienced regimental officers serving as second-in-command. The other battalions continued under tested leadership.

The situation in 2nd Division was very different. The army had been unable to provide the 1,500 to 2,000 replacements required to restore the division's combat power, and this placed an extraordinary burden on the infantry battalions. For Major-General Charles Foulkes, who continued in command, the manpower shortage was just one of many challenges. His new senior staff officer (GSO 1), Lieutenant-Colonel C.M. 'Bud' Drury, had great potential but limited experience. The division was also plagued by administrative difficulties, partly because it had fought without a break between 19 July and 19 August.[7]

Problems at Divisional Headquarters were complicated by command difficulties in all three brigades. The casualties in July included Brigadier Sherwood Lett, a highly regarded officer slated for future divisional command. His immediate replacement was Lieutenant-Colonel Fred Clift, CO of the South Saskatchewan Regiment, who had been recommended for promotion to brigadier; but Foulkes wanted Clift to rebuild his devastated battalion before taking up a higher appointment. Lieutenant-Colonel J.E. Ganong, then serving as GSO 1 at 4th Division Headquarters, assumed command on 3 August, just before Operation Totalize. This decision, which must have adversely affected 4th Division on the eve of its first battle without adding much to 4th Infantry Brigade, is just one of the many examples of the failure of the Canadian Army's senior leadership to prepare for the consequences of attritional warfare. Ganong had few opportunities to demonstrate his leadership skills before he was removed from command in late August.[8] Ganong's replacement, Fred Cabeldu, the young, accomplished CO of the Canadian Scottish Regiment, commanded the brigade effectively for the balance of the war. Two of 4th Brigade's three battalions, the Essex Scottish and Royal Regiment of Canada, had suffered very heavy losses at Verrières Ridge and were struggling to rebuild throughout August. The Royal Hamilton Light Infantry was in better shape, but the loss of two commanding officers – Denis Whitaker to wounds and John Rockingham to promotion – did not help the command situation.

Bill Megill continued to lead 5th Brigade – as he would throughout the war – but his position was weakened by the festering resentment of Black Watch veterans, who blamed him for the losses suffered in Operation Spring. Megill in turn was unhappy with the Black Watch and sought unsuccessfully to impose on the battalion an officer from outside the regiment. He was also concerned about the command situation in the Calgary Highlanders, but after the battalion 2IC, Major Vern Stott, was wounded, no change was made. The Maisonneuves were now commanded by Julien Bibeau, who was proving to be an outstanding leader, but the battalion was still at half-strength with little prospect of obtaining enough French-speaking replacements to reconstitute a four-company battalion.[9]

Brigadier Hugh Young, like Megill a Permanent Force signals officer, failed to provide leadership during Operation Atlantic, and his determined efforts to blame battalion commanders for the debacle won him few friends.[10] Young was promoted on 25 August and transferred to a staff position in Ottawa. His successor, Fred Clift, might well have provided a new kind of leadership had he avoided the mortar fire that wounded him three days later. Clift was replaced by Jacques Gauvreau, the CO of the Fusiliers Mont-Royal, who commanded effectively until he was wounded in October. All three 6th Brigade battalions were commanded by first-rate men, but the shortage of replacements placed a terrible strain on everyone, especially after the fighting in the Fôret de la Londe squandered much of what had been accomplished earlier in August.

The regiments of 2nd Canadian Armoured Brigade that fought alongside the infantry had also suffered considerable casualties, but all three COs and most of the squadron commanders had survived to lead their regiments out of Normandy. With the enemy's anti-tank screen shattered and most of its armoured vehicles destroyed or abandoned, the

Sherman tanks' notorious vulnerability mattered less than their speed and mechanical reliability.

The 4th Canadian Armoured Division had been in action for little more than two weeks when it was faced with the challenge of blocking the exodus of the German army from lower Normandy. Despite the best efforts of 10th Infantry Brigade, large numbers of Germans escaped through the Trun–Chambois gap. Simonds was dissatisfied with the performance of the divisional commander, George Kitching, and replaced him with Harry Foster, an infantry brigadier, just as the division was preparing to join the pursuit to the Seine. Simonds told Foster to rely on a newly promoted twenty-six-year-old, Robert Moncel, one of the most promising armoured corps officers in the army, who had just left his job on Simonds's staff to take over the armoured brigade.[11]

The 4th Armoured Brigade was in rough shape. The British Columbia Regiment had been virtually destroyed at Hill 140, and both the Grenadier Guards and the Governor General's Foot Guards had been reduced to squadron-sized regiments in the August battles. The brigade's motorized infantry battalion, the Lake Superior Regiment, was in much better condition, but the brigade was badly in need of rest and reorganization. Brigadier Jim Jefferson, a veteran of the Italian campaign, continued to lead 10th Infantry Brigade. The rifle companies of his three infantry battalions were at little better than half-strength, but the Lincs and Algonquins had new, effective COs, while Lieutenant-Colonels Dave Stewart and G.D. 'Swotty' Wotherspoon continued to provide the Argyll and Sutherland Highlanders and South Alberta Regiment with outstanding leadership. If used properly, 10th Brigade was still capable of effective action.

Also attached to 2nd Canadian Corps was the 1st Polish Armoured Division, which was to play a leading role in the pursuit from the Seine to the Scheldt. The division suffered heavy losses in the August battles, especially in the infantry battalions, which were reduced to less than half-strength. Prisoners from the German army were the main source of replacement soldiers of Polish ethnicity. They were integrated into the Polish battalions in the last ten days of August, but the division remained chronically understrength.[12]

By the end of the Normandy campaign there were good reasons to be optimistic. The General Officer Commanding (GOC) 2nd Canadian

Corps, Lieutenant-General Guy Granville Simonds, was an innovative leader who approached each operation in a problem-solving mode. Simonds was a firm believer in artillery-based battle doctrine, which called for bite-and-hold tactics to destroy the enemy in a 'battle of counter-attacks,'[13] but he did not hesitate to modify that doctrine and improvise new methods. The British and Canadian armies had been trained to fight during daylight hours, when artillery observation as well as air and armoured support would be most effective. Simonds revised this basic concept after his first battle, when it became evident that in the open terrain of the Caen-Falaise plain, good visibility favoured the enemy. His next two corps-level operations were carried out at night and the third under the reduced visibility of a smoke screen. His decision to transform self-propelled guns into armoured personnel carriers also had a profound effect on tactics. Simonds was much less effective at managing the last stages of the Normandy battle, but so was every other Allied commander.

This brief overview of the strengths and weaknesses of the Canadian formations committed to battle in late August 1944 is intended to serve as a reminder of how difficult it is to generalize about large, complex organizations. Recently the British popular historian Max Hastings, drawing on limited evidence from two of 2nd Canadian Division's battalions, dismissed the entire Canadian Army 'as a weak and flawed instrument because of chronic manning problems.'[14] Hastings did not offer a statistical comparison with the strength of British or American units, nor did he attempt to distinguish between Canadian divisions. Hastings ought to have known that the combat power of divisions, brigades, and battalions in the Allied and German armies varied widely over time. While some Canadian battalions were seriously understrength in September and October 1944, all were at full strength in the battles of 1945, when many British and American units were experiencing serious shortages. Furthermore, the actual strength of a battalion is only one of the variables that must be considered when combat effectiveness is assessed. The battles fought by the Allies in the last nine months of the campaign to liberate Northwest Europe were shaped by such a wide variety of factors that each action needs to be carefully examined before the historian can hope to offer a rough approximation of what happened and why it happened that way.

This account of the experience of the Allies' Cinderella Army offers a discussion of the strategic direction of the campaign insofar as it affected the Canadians. The focus then shifts to corps- and divisional-level operational planning. Information about the effectiveness of weapons systems – especially tactical air power and artillery – is presented using data from operational research reports. The soldiers' experience of war at the battalion and company level is then examined in some detail so that the nature of close combat and its costs may be fully understood. The documents reproduced in the appendices offer further evidence of the professionalism of Canada's citizen army and of the sacrifices this country's soldiers made for the liberation of Europe and the hope of a better world.

1

Normandy to the Scheldt

The Battle of Normandy is usually said to have ended in the third week of August, when the Trun–Chambois gap east of Falaise was finally closed. After just seventy-six days the Allies had destroyed the offensive combat power of two German armies, and what was left of both was in full retreat. In retrospect, this achievement has seemed less than complete because a large number of enemy soldiers escaped encirclement. At the time, though, the battle appeared to be a decisive victory that might bring the immediate collapse of the Nazi state. It was like the summer of 1918 all over again, except this time there was no separate peace on the Eastern Front. This optimistic view was especially evident in London and Washington, where intelligence analysts were insisting that 'no German recovery was now possible.' At Eisenhower's headquarters, SHAEF intelligence officers declared that 'the August battles have done it; have brought the end of the war in Europe in sight, almost within reach.'[1]

The mood at 21 Army Group headquarters was equally euphoric. General Bernard Montgomery, who was still responsible for coordinating the land campaign, paid little attention to the battle raging in the Trun–Chambois gap or the evidence of an organized enemy withdrawal. On 17 August he met with his American counterpart, General Omar Bradley, to discuss strategy 'after crossing the Seine.' His proposal to employ 'a solid mass of some 40 divisions' to advance through Antwerp and Brussels with their 'right flank on the Ardennes' was based on his belief that such a single thrust would meet little resistance and set the stage for a German surrender.[2] Bradley was even less concerned with the remnants of the German armies in Normandy and was developing his own plan for a rapid advance to the east. The Supreme Commander, General Dwight D. Eisenhower, shared this attitude. On 19 August he announced that he intended to assume direct command of the ground forces on 1 September and outlined proposals for the approach to Germany. He expressed no concern about the remnants of the German army still south of the Seine.[3]

While the senior commanders focused their planning on ending the war, the leading elements of 15th U.S. Corps reached the Seine at Mantes-Gassicourt, forty-eight kilometres west of Paris and sixty-four kilometres east of Rouen. This was the corps that General George Patton had turned towards the Seine after he was denied permission to

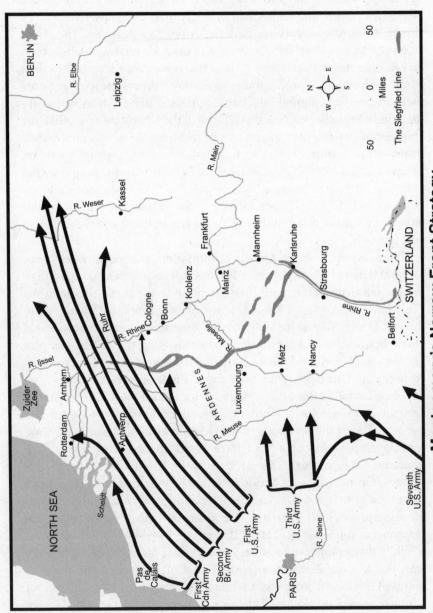

Montgomery's Narrow Front Strategy

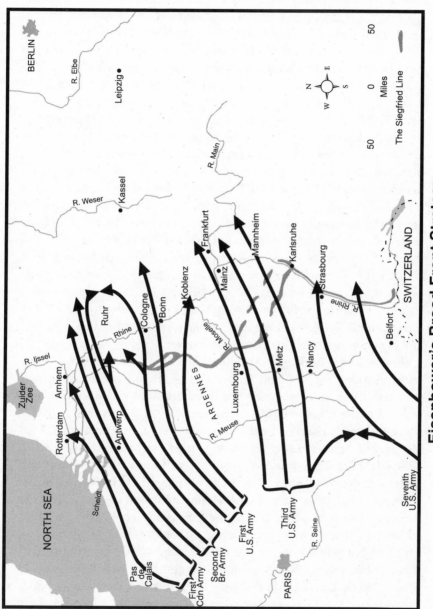

Eisenhower's Broad Front Strategy

send it from Argentan to Falaise. Patton had instead ordered Major-General Wade Haslip to begin the so-called long envelopment advancing along the south bank of the river to cut off the German retreat.[4]

News of the rapid progress of 15th Corps prompted Montgomery to focus briefly on the immediate problem of the German withdrawal. The next day, 20 August, he issued a directive calling for 'the complete destruction of enemy forces' in Normandy followed by an advance north 'with a view to the eventual destruction of all enemy forces in north-east France.' This was to be accomplished by surrounding the enemy with troops of U.S. 12 Army Group to the north and the Canadian Army to the south. The Americans were to advance 'to Elbeuf and beyond,' blocking the enemy's 'lines of withdrawal across the Seine.'[5]

Had these orders been implemented, most of the estimated 75,000 men and 250 armoured vehicles still south of the river[6] might have been captured or destroyed, but it was not to be. When Haslip reported that there was nothing to prevent his corps from crossing the Seine, Patton and Bradley allowed him to send his only infantry division, the 79th, across the river 'to establish a springboard for future operations.'[7] Patton wanted to exploit this bridgehead by thrusting to the west to start a double envelopment of the German forces, but Bradley, who was looking east, overruled his army commander.[8]

On the south bank, 5th Armoured Division, hampered by heavy rains, morning fog, difficult terrain, and scattered enemy resistance, was making limited progress. The three divisions of 19th U.S. Corps ordered to assist were slow to get underway, and then their advance was temporarily checked by the intervention of mobile elements of 1st SS Panzer Corps.[9] Bradley was preoccupied with plans to lay siege to Brest while finding resources to support a drive towards Germany, and he was no longer interested in an envelopment at the Seine. On the morning of 23 August he met with Montgomery and suggested that the Americans stop in place so that the U.S. Army could begin a rapid advance eastwards. Montgomery wanted the American 'right hook' to continue, but before a decision could be made, 19th Corps reported that it had broken through the German line and was 'well on its way to Elbeuf.' Bradley decided to allow the corps to take Elbeuf before handing over the area to 21 Army Group and so informed Montgomery.[10] Unfortunately, it took three days to reach Elbeuf, and by then most of

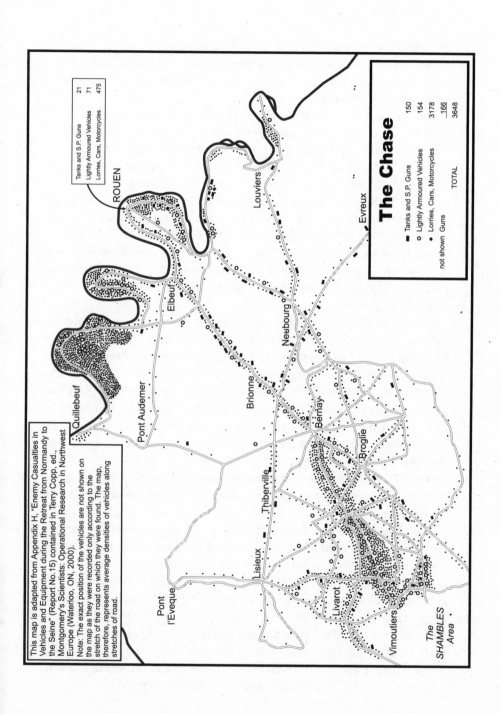

The Chase

This map is adapted from Appendix H, "Enemy Casualties in Vehicles and Equipment during the Retreat from Normandy to the Seine" (Report No.15) contained in Terry Copp, ed. Montgomery's Scientists: Operational Research in Northwest Europe (Waterloo, ON, 2000).

Note: The exact position of the vehicles are not shown on the map as they were recorded only according to the stretch of the road on which they were found. The map, therefore, represents average densities of vehicles along stretches of road.

Tanks and S.P. Guns	21
Lightly Armoured Vehicles	71
Lorries, Cars, Motorcycles	475

ROUEN

Quillebeuf

Pont Audemer

Pont l'Eveque

Lisieux

Thiberville

Livarot

Vimoutiers

The SHAMBLES Area

Broglie

Bernay

Brionne

Neubourg

Elbeuf

Louviers

Evreux

■	Tanks and S.P. Guns	150
o	Lightly Armoured Vehicles	154
•	Lorries, Cars, Motorcycles	3178
	not shown Guns	166
	TOTAL	3648

the enemy were across the river and heading north. Those who remained were concentrated in the heavily forested loops of the Seine
south and east of Rouen, where improvised ferries were still operating
in the hours of darkness.

The Allies' failure to exploit their third opportunity to encircle the
enemy in Normandy suggests that the difficulties of coordinating coalition forces were systemic, given the personalities of the senior commanders.[11] Montgomery, who in this instance advocated decisive action,
weakened his case by insisting that 2nd British Army not become
involved at the Seine. When Bradley offered to transport British troops
forward so that they could carry out the advance to the coast, his offer
was rejected.[12] The 2nd British Army, which had stayed out of the last
stages of the battle to close the Trun-Chambois gap, was preparing for a
dash to the Somme, and neither Montgomery nor his Army Commander, General Miles Dempsey, wanted any part of the messy job of
blocking a German retreat.

The Allied commanders rationalized their reluctance to commit resources by claiming that the tactical air forces were interdicting the
river and successfully attacking the retreating columns. There was some
truth in this assertion. When operational research teams examined the
area between Vimoutiers and the Seine, they identified 364 pieces of
abandoned or destroyed motorized military equipment, including 150
tanks and self-propelled guns. The hundreds of horse-drawn vehicles
were not counted. Direct air attack and the interdiction imposed in
daylight hours at the Seine were responsible for almost all of these
losses.[13] The huge numbers of prisoners taken between 23 August and 1
September – more than 45,000 – also seemed to vindicate the emphasis
on air power.[14]

The Operational Research Section went on to examine evidence of
how much equipment had got across the Seine during the withdrawal.
It reported back that as many as '40,000 items of motor transport and
250 tanks and SP guns could have crossed the river.' This estimate was
based on interviews with French civilians and was considered greatly
exaggerated, but no precise numbers could be determined. The civilians reported that the Germans 'had travelled chiefly at night but that
in the vitally important week there were three days when the visibility
was very poor and during which they were able to ferry much traffic
across in daylight without any great interference from the RAF.'[15]

After his meeting with Bradley on the morning of 23 August, Montgomery returned to his tactical headquarters to prepare for the arrival of the Supreme Commander. Montgomery was determined to press his idea of a single, strong northern advance and to persuade Eisenhower to leave command of the land battle in his hands. 'The Supreme Commander,' Monty argued, 'must sit on a very lofty perch ... to take a detached view of the whole intricate problem - which involves land, sea, air, civil control, political problems, etc.'[16] Eisenhower listened quietly but stuck with his announced intention to assume direct control of both British and American army groups on 1 September. He did agree to order the left flank corps of 1st U.S. Army to support the advance to Antwerp, and he gave Montgomery the authority to coordinate operations between 2nd British Army and 'Bradley's left wing.'[17]

On 26 August, Montgomery issued a new directive – one that, whatever his private feelings, faithfully reflected Eisenhower's decisions. The tasks of 21 Army Group were 'to destroy enemy forces in N.E. France and Belgium,' 'to secure the Pas-de-Calais and the airfields in Belgium,' and 'to secure Antwerp as a base.' The directive ordered First Canadian Army to free the ports of Dieppe and Le Havre and destroy 'all enemy forces in the coastal belt up to Bruges.' The 2nd British Army, now rested and ready to make a largely unopposed crossing of the Seine, was to drive on with all speed through northern France into Belgium.[18] Montgomery underestimated the degree of enemy resistance likely at the Seine below Rouen and ignored the presence of large, well-organized enemy forces on the Channel coast, presumably because he thought the war would be won by a rapid thrust to the Rhine.

First Canadian Army's pursuit began on 15 August, when 1st British Corps started offensive operations on the coastal flank of the Normandy bridgehead. The story of 1st British Corps' role in the campaign to liberate Northwest Europe has never been examined in any detail. Except for 1st Canadian Parachute Battalion, part of 6th Airborne Division, the corps was an entirely British formation, one that served for most of the war in First Canadian Army. The corps was commanded by Lieutenant-General Sir John Crocker, who was not one of Montgomery's disciples but who was sufficiently well regarded that he had been assigned to command the D-Day landings at Sword and Juno. Shortly after D-Day the corps was committed to the thankless task of defending the bridgehead north of Caen and south of the Orne. The one major set-piece battle fought under Crocker, Operation Charnwood, was a solid achievement, but as the bridgehead expanded the corps was ordered to limit its role to holding the increasingly long left flank. Montgomery left Crocker with three divisions, which for various reasons were seen as suitable for this limited role. The airborne division, understrength and poorly equipped for conventional land warfare, was to return to England to rebuild as soon as it could be spared. The two infantry divisions, 49th (West Riding) and 51st (Highland), had both been criticized for their performance in Normandy, and Montgomery was content to leave them in a defensive role until it was evident that a German withdrawal had begun. He then assigned 7th Armoured Division, another much criticized formation, to provide armoured support for their advance.[19]

It took the corps ten days to reach the Seine, a rate of progress that has confirmed the opinion of critics. To the troops on the ground, the pace of the pursuit seemed to be determined by the orders of high command and the strength of enemy resistance rather than by problems at the sharp end. The German army's 86th Corps, made up of 711th, 346th, and 272nd Infantry Divisions, may not have retained any offensive capability, but its half-strength infantry regiments were backed by substantial artillery and anti-tank gun assets[20] and were able to establish well-sited blocking positions that could only be overcome by painstaking flanking movements.

Along the coastal road to Honfleur, 6th Airborne Division, with 4th Commando Brigade under command, had little transport available, so the men walked most of the forty-five miles to the River Risle. The enemy occupied a series of canal and river positions, with strongpoints originally built as part of the Atlantic Wall, and Major-General Richard Gale was determined to avoid taking casualties in overcoming these obstacles. His orders were to maintain contact with a retreating enemy, mopping up isolated pockets of resistance. The 3rd Para Brigade, which included the Canadians, was warned that it was 'to advance if and when it is certain the enemy were withdrawing.'[21]

Gale's casualty conservation measures were dictated by the knowledge that the men would soon be returning to England to form the core of a revitalized division available for future airborne operations. Unfortunately, this sensible decision influenced the pace of other formations, especially on the flank, where 49th Division was ordered 'to conform to the general speed of the advance.'[22] The deliberate nature of the corps' approach to the Seine was further evident when the Highland Division, after fighting against a stubborn enemy defending Lisieux, was ordered to secure the town and then go into reserve. This pause provided an opportunity to absorb much-needed reinforcements, but it left the pursuit to 7th Armoured Division with its one badly understrength infantry brigade.[23] On 25 August, when leading elements of the British divisions reached the Risle, 2nd Canadian Corps caught up and took over the lead in the final drive to the Seine.

The Canadian advance began on 21 August, when 2nd Canadian Infantry Division handed over its responsibilities in Falaise to the British and joined the pursuit. By the following morning 5th Brigade had established a bridgehead across the River Touques. The 6th Brigade, transported through the bridgehead by Service Corps transport companies, met no significant resistance before reaching Orbec late the next day. Here, for the first but not the last time in the pursuit, the mobility of the divisional recce regiment proved decisive. The 14th Canadian Hussars (8th Recce Regiment) had been operating in front of the division, scouting the route north and searching for river crossings. When the Cameron Highlanders were held up in front of Orbec, the enemy was attacked from the rear by the Hussars, who crossed the river to the west and circled back to attack the town. Orbec was cleared, at which point the Fusiliers Mont-Royal took the vanguard role, capturing St-Germain-la Campagne in a fierce night action.[24] The French-Canadian regiments were greeted with special fervour in the villages of the Seine Valley. In a letter to his family, Lieutenant-Colonel Julien Bibeau wrote: 'La réception qui nous fut faite est indescriptible. Tout le monde était réuni sur la grande place nous attendant, les cloches de l'église sonnaient a toute volée. Nous avons comtés de fleurs, de vin ...'[25]

It had rained on 24 August, but the next day 'was perfectly beautiful with bright sunshine and warm wind.' The Black Watch occupied Brionne, leaving the rest of the brigade just west of the town around a village named St-Cyr-de-Salerne. Shortly before midnight the sky above the village was illuminated by a ring of parachute flares. The Calgaries, who were scheduled to move out and lead the next stage of the advance, were caught in the open while waiting to load the trucks. The Luftwaffe attacked in two waves, and the Calgary casualties were appalling: fifteen dead and seventy-two wounded, the worst day for the regiment since Tilly-la-Campagne.[26]

The plight of the Calgaries meant that the Black Watch would have to resume the lead. Brigadier Megill arranged for additional trucks from the Royal Canadian Army Service Corps, and Lieutenant-Colonel Frank Mitchell organized the battalion into four battlegroups for the advance. The carrier platoon led the column, followed by a squadron of Sherbrooke Fusilier tanks. Then came the four rifle companies, each with its own anti-tank guns, mortars, and engineers. Mitchell rode with the forward rifle company, and this battlegroup, together with the carrier platoon and tanks, moved straight through into Bourgtheroulde without meeting any opposition. The rest of the battalion was not as lucky. As the column approached a wood just 3 kilometres short of the objective, 'a German infantry battalion, hidden in the forest, attacked from all sides. For thirty minutes a life-and-death battle was fought with infantrymen and RCASC personnel fighting viciously in the semi-darkness with a determined enemy.'[27]

In Bourgtheroulde, Mitchell's contingent was moving through the village when orders to consolidate and establish a firm base were received. The battlegroup established itself northeast of the main square and began to draw fire from all directions. Mitchell later wrote: 'The initial phase of the battle in the village resembled an individual battle in which every man carried on his own private war, firing in any direction he heard shots coming from, taking his own prisoners and not knowing in the confusion where to send them.'[28] As the other companies entered the village, they came under fire from snipers and a 75 mm anti-tank gun, which fired on the column at point-blank range. Mitchell decided it would be impossible to coordinate what was becoming an intense and highly confused battle unless he could concentrate the battalion. He ordered the three companies held up on the southern edge of the village to join him.[29]

The Black Watch had run into a significant blocking force of German troops, who fortunately had not had time to fully organize their defences. Mitchell's decision to regroup his men outside the village and attack back into the objective was a bold move – one that, as he later explained, was 'justified by the surprise achieved.' However, the battalion took losses that day - fifteen killed and thirty-six wounded, not counting casualties in the RCASC transport companies and the RCE platoon, both of which had suffered heavily. The Maisonneuves reached the outskirts of Bourgtheroulde in the afternoon while the fighting in the village still raged. They mounted a small-scale, set-piece attack with an artillery barrage and tank support and quickly cleared out the last area of German resistance on the high ground east of the village.[30]

On 26 August, while the Black Watch was waging its unusual battle in Bourgtheroulde, Lieutenant-General Henry Duncan Crerar issued new orders: 'The enemy no longer has the troops to hold any strong positions - or to hold any positions for any length of time if it is aggressively outflanked or attacked. Speed of action and forcible tactics are therefore required from commanders at every level in First Canadian Army. We must drive ahead with utmost energy. Any tendency to be slow or "sticky" on the part of subordinate commanders should be quickly and positively eliminated.'[31]

Crerar's optimism was no doubt due to the rapid progress of the 3rd and 4th Divisions, which reached the Seine on 26 August. The 4th Division's advance north began on 23 August, 'about an hour behind' the corps' armoured car regiment. The Manitoba Dragoons soon encountered the enemy, losing several Staghound armoured cars. Lieutenant-Colonel J.A. Roberts reported that they had located the enemy line of resistance; his squadrons then drew back, waiting for the 'other arms' to take over. The 4th Division had been trained in the use of all-arms battlegroups and had successfully employed them earlier in the month; but for reasons that have never been explained, the advance to the Seine began with the tanks of the British Columbia Regiment (BCR) as the sole element of the vanguard. When Roberts called for other arms, he meant infantry and a Forward Observation Officer (FOO) who could direct artillery fire. Instead, a squadron of BCR Shermans appeared. After the two lead tanks were lost, the squadron commander worked out a flanking attack, but before this could be teed up, Brigadier Robert Moncel ordered the BCRs to press ahead. A second squadron was sent forward, and soon 'the BCRs were short seven more tanks.' A company of the Lake Superior Regiment arrived, but before they could put in an attack, a heavy rain and nightfall put an end to the action. The

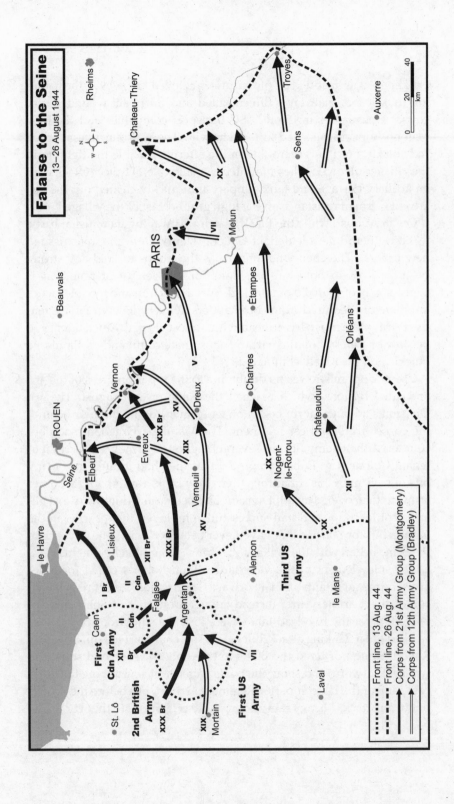

Falaise to the Seine
13–26 August 1944

Rheims

Château-Thiery

Troyes

Auxerre

XX

Sens

VII

Melun

PARIS

Étampes

Beauvais

Orléans

Vernon

Chartres

ROUEN

Seine

Elbeuf

V

Dreux

XV

XXX Br

Evreux

XIX

Verneuil

XV

Nogent-
le-Rotrou

Châteaudun

le Havre

Lisieux

XII Br

XXX Br

XX

XII

St. Lô

Caen

First
Cdn Army

II
Cdn

I Br

XII

II
Cdn

Falaise

Br

Argentan

2nd British
Army

XXX Br

XIX

Mortain

V

Alençon

Third US
Army

XX

First US
Army

VII

le Mans

Laval

N
W E
S

40

20

0   km

Front line, 13 Aug. 44

Front line, 26 Aug. 44

Corps from 21st Army Group (Montgomery)

Corps from 12th Army Group (Bradley)

next morning the enemy was gone, leaving a Tiger and two anti-tank guns behind.[32] Moncel and Major-General Foster had been with the division for only a few days and were under pressure to move quickly, but this does not excuse a serious command failure. The following day Foster reorganized the division, placing the vanguard under Lieutenant-Colonel R.A. Keane of the Lake Superiors. 'Keane Force' comprised two armoured regiments, the entire motor battalion, and an infantry regiment (the Argyll and Sutherland Highlanders), as well as engineers and self-propelled guns. The force moved forward with orders to reach the Seine that day.[33]

As each element of the division arrived at Bernay, a large town left undefended by the retreating enemy, crowds of cheering citizens filled the streets to welcome their liberators – and slow their advance. The infantry brigade's historian captured the mood:

> Will Bernay ever be forgotten? Bernay where the people stood from morning to night, at times in the pouring rain, and at times in the August sun. Bernay where they never tire of waving, of throwing fruit and flowers, of giving their best wines and spirits to some halted column. Bernay where the local schoolmistress and her children line along the main street singing in unison and in English 'Thank you for liberating us.' It was the Brigade's first large crowd, and many a hardened lad from Caen and Falaise felt his eyes fill as he witnessed the joys, the smiles, the tears of wild gratitude and triumph all around him. These were the days of tremendous confidence and realization that maybe it was worth while and that those boys left along the hedges, in the grain fields, in the casualty posts of Normandy had not fallen in vain.[34]

The Manitoba Dragoons, who were the first to run the gauntlet of flowers and wine, continued on to the Risle, where they found the main road impassable due to a blown bridge. A patrol found an alternative route with an intact bridge, but Foster 'did not choose to change the Green centre line' and sent his engineers forward to repair the main route.[35] The next morning the advance began again, but by mid-morning units of the U.S. 2nd Armoured Division were encountered withdrawing directly across the Canadian line of march. A monumental traffic jam developed, and the division was forced to stand down to let the Americans pass. Movement on 26 August was still hampered by traffic congestion. The division finally reached the Seine later that day.

One 4th Division battlegroup, comprising the Lincoln and Welland Regiment, a squadron of South Alberta tanks, a platoon of New Brunswick Rangers, and a troop of the 8th Light Anti-Aircraft Regiment, occupied Criquebeuf-sur-Seine without opposition. The town soon came under artillery fire from the hills across the river. Despite this, a patrol from the Lincs' scout platoon crossed the Seine in a borrowed boat, paddled with shovels. They returned to report no sign of the enemy near the riverbank. Lieutenant-Colonel Cromb decided that was too good an opportunity to miss and ordered 'D' Company to cross the river and occupy the village of Freneuse. By dark the men were dug in across the Seine.[36]

The Lincs remember acting on their own initiative, but in fact they were carrying out specific orders. First Canadian Army had been developing plans for the Seine crossing for more than a year. The assumptions of Operation Axehead, an assault crossing of the Seine, were now out of date, but an enormous reserve of engineering equipment and bridging material had been gathered, and there was scarcely a yard of the riverbank that had not been studied. The area Criquebeuf–Pont de l'Arche had been assigned to 4th Division with the injunction that the division 'will, by coup-de-main, seize a bridgehead on the north bank of the Seine.'[37]

The 3rd Division had even less difficulty reaching the Seine, and 7th Brigade followed the recce regiment into Elbeuf on the afternoon of 26 August. The Americans had cleared the town before withdrawing to the east, and the enemy was not attempting to defend the low-lying ground across the river, so the engineers were able to ferry the Reginas to the north bank and begin building a bridge without significant interference. With two bridgeheads across the Seine, the corps commander ordered immediate exploitation. Both Spry and Foster were told to continue the advance by sending the rest of the infantry brigades across the river without waiting for bridges. Simonds also ordered 2nd Division to move troops towards Rouen through a heavily wooded area known as the Fôret de la Londe. Simonds assumed that 'it would probably be a non-tactical move and that no, or very few, enemy would be encountered.'[38] Major-General Foulkes ordered 4th Brigade forward that night to provide flank protection for the main corps crossing at Elbeuf. The Royal Hamilton Light Infantry (RHLI) took the lead, reaching the outskirts of Port du Gravier, where the convoy took a wrong turn and ran into heavy mortar and machine gun fire while the troops were still in the vehicles. The RHLI withdrew. The Essex Scottish, routed through Elbeuf, moved along the left bank of the Seine towards Port du Gravier, stopping under intense albeit inaccurate fire some 500 metres short of the town. The Royal Regiment, in brigade reserve, pulled up in Orival at the foot of a three-hundred-foot cliff, which 'C' Company was ordered to climb. As dawn broke on 27 August, the brigade had its first look at the battlefield. The neck of land in the meander was some 5000 metres wide. Two railway lines roughly 500 metres apart ran across the neck, the further line disappearing into openings tunnelled into the heavily forested hills of the peninsula. The highest feature, which bordered the river, controlled the narrow road to Oissel. The main highway to Rouen ran between this promontory and a second hill, which was soon to be designated 'Maisie.'[39]

Brigadier J.E. Ganong came forward at 0900 hours and dismissed the possibility of a further advance until the riverside position had been outflanked. He ordered the Royals to undertake a wide flanking movement aimed at capturing 'Maisie.' The battalion set off through the dense woods. By mid-afternoon they had come across a company of the Fusiliers Mont-Royal, who had followed a somewhat circuitous route on the right flank of 6th Brigade's advance. With the FMRs under command, the Royals were now told to rendezvous with the Essex Scottish, who were to support the attack. The Royals did not find the Essex, but both they and the Essex Scottish found the enemy, who easily pinned down the two battalions.

It is quite evident that Brigadier Ganong had no real knowledge of either the enemy's dispositions or his own. In a signal to divisional headquarters he reported: 'Attack bogged down entirely in thick wood. Have ordered units concerned back to the south.' Unfortunately, the units were badly scattered and out of touch. The Royals, without food or water, waited out the night near the La Londe railway station. The two Essex companies were not able to withdraw back to Port du Gravier until morning.[40]

Over on the west side of the forest the South Saskatchewan Regiment occupied the high ground south of La Bouille, while the Queen's Own Cameron Highlanders of Canada moved along the left flank closer to the river, encountering enemy mortar and machine gun fire as they approached the railway tunnel. By nightfall on 27 August the two battalions were dug in and awaiting further orders. No one could make any sense of the available maps, which seemed to bear little relationship to the actual ground.[41] Shortly before midnight on 27 August, Foulkes met with Ganong and informed him that 3rd Division was across the Seine and that the corps required 2nd Division to push on to Rouen. An early-morning attack was ordered, with both the Essex Scottish and the Royals required to renew the assault. It was hoped that they would make contact with 6th brigade along the way.[42]

The situation that confronted the Royal Regiment was not a happy one. Their lead companies had gone to ground in dense underbrush. Ahead of them 'the ground dipped slightly beyond the railway track, then rose steeply up to the forest which was unbroken as far as could be seen. The steep slope was bare for about 60 yards and the enemy positions were just inside the tree line. Directly across the brush from the lead platoon was a chalk pit with a perpendicular face and a post on the top.' This hill was held by the enemy, which had observation over all the surrounding low ground. The Royals first tried to capture what they called Chalk Pits Hill by a pincer movement, but the right-hand platoon was caught in a hail of small arms fire and forced to withdraw. Despite this check, a battalion attack was set for 1130 hours, even though complete artillery support could not be arranged owing to uncertainty as to the whereabouts of 6th Brigade units. The attack soon faltered, with the lead companies pinned down in front of Chalk Pits Hill. They were to spend the night there, cut off from the rest of the battalion.[43]

On the Essex Scottish front, two companies were ordered to attack through Port du Gravier behind an intensive artillery barrage. They moved forward until they reached a steep slope, which they had to slide down in full view of the enemy. This feat was accomplished, but enemy fire forced them to dig in and wait for darkness.[44] Foulkes now ordered a night march by the RHLI to the Royals' position; from there, an attack on 'Maisie' was to be launched under cover of darkness. Both battalion commanders protested this order, to no avail. The RHLI set off at midnight; at daybreak they were approaching the Royals' position when they came under machine gun and mortar fire. 'D' Company, moving out behind smoke, attempted to outflank this position, only to come under fire from yet another direction. At 1326 hours the battalion reported: 'Situation with us as follows – 3 companies involved suffered heavy casualties – 2 companies have been pulled back 400–500 yards and are still under heavy machine gun and mortar fire. Sunray [the CO] feels that it is impossible to proceed with original plan and that position must be taken from another direction.' [45]That night the RHLI and the Royals were withdrawn.

On the left flank the South Sasks' lead company (total strength thirty-five) was allowed to get half its men across the railway before machine guns raked the troops. Two flanking attacks were tried before the remaining thirteen men (there were no officers left) were withdrawn. A second attack following an artillery barrage made some progress before resistance was met. In the dark, heavily wooded forest, where 30 metre gullies with 45 degree slopes cut through the landscape, the 'enemy was so close that only small bits of bush' separated the combatants. The battalion combat element, now only slightly larger than a full-strength rifle company, 'stood to' throughout the night. At first light the battle started up again until a message – later assumed to have come over the wireless from the Germans – ordered withdrawal![46]

The Camerons, who had spent the day exchanging mortar and artillery fire with the enemy, were ordered to assist the South Sasks, with the Calgary Highlanders coming up to take over the firm base. Their move was made on a pitch-black night after a hasty Orders Group conducted with the aid of the only available map. Moving behind the South Sasks, the Camerons came under continuous mortar and artillery fire. The next morning the withdrawal of the South Sasks caused some of the Camerons to panic, and a disorderly retreat was the result. What was left of the lead companies – one hundred Camerons and fifty South Sasks – were grouped in and around a quarry. Order was restored, and the CO of the Saskatchewans moved his men back up the road to their previous positions. With the support of five tanks, the situation was stabilized. Foulkes now ordered the brigade to hold its position regardless of the casualties, to the last round and the last man. On this absurd note, 6th Brigade's battle came to an end, for the Germans were withdrawing, having completed their task.

Two brigades of 2nd Canadian Infantry Division had been roughly handled during the three-day battle in the Fôret de la Londe, suffering

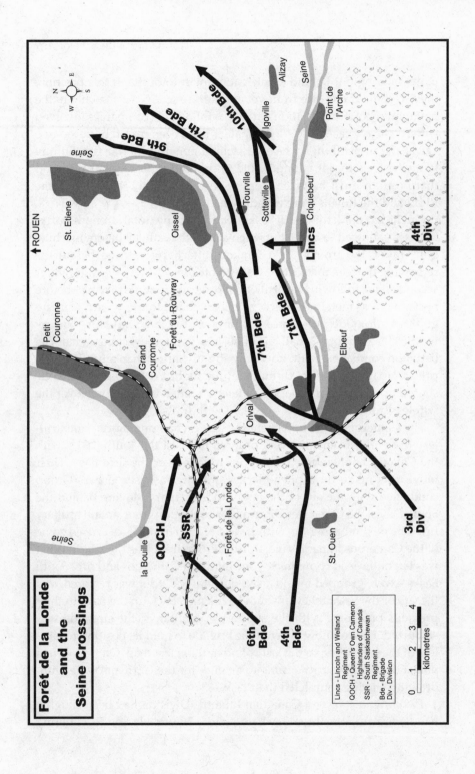

Forêt de la Londe
and the
Seine Crossings

N
E
W
S

↑ ROUEN

Seine

St. Etiene

Petit
Couronne

Grand
Couronne

Forêt du Rouvray

Oissel

9th Bde
7th Bde
10th Bde

Seine

Igoville

Alizay

Seine

Sotteville

Tourville

Criquebeuf

Point de
l'Arche

Lincs

7th Bde

7th Bde

4th
Div

Elbeuf

Orival

la Bouille

Seine

QOCH

SSR

Forêt de la Londe

St. Ouen

3rd
Div

6th
Bde

4th
Bde

Lincs - Lincoln and Welland
         Regiment
QOCH - Queen's Own Cameron
         Highlanders of Canada
SSR - South Saskatchewan
         Regiment
Bde - Brigade
Div - Division

0   1   2   3   4
      kilometres

577 casualties.[47] They had come up against a well-organized enemy force under orders to buy time for other German units, struggling under air attack, to get across the Seine. The 331st Infantry Division, reinforced with a battlegroup from 6th Paratroop Regiment and elements of 2nd SS Panzer Division, had fulfilled their mission. But what was the mission of 2nd Canadian Division? With 3rd and 4th Divisions across the Seine on 27 August, the decision to order 2nd Division to continue fighting a costly infantry action for three more days simply made no sense. Given the serious manpower shortages in 2nd Division before the battle, the further battering of five of its infantry regiments seems especially difficult to understand.

Much the same could be said for the initial decision to rush the attack on the high ground in 4th Division's sector. The Algonquin Regiment was ordered to cross the river at 0230 hours on 27 August, then advance through the shallow bridgehead to seize Sotteville and a hill, Point 88, beyond the village. The plan called for a pause at a railway embankment, with the guns of 15th Field Regiment supporting a one-company advance across four hundred yards of open ground. Sotteville was taken, but the enemy inflicted a heavy price during the advance and also during the counter-attack, which employed a self-propelled gun and armoured half-tracks. Consolidation was only possible when a 'well placed PIAT bomb' knocked out the assault gun.[48]

The Argylls, who were to pass through to seize Igoville and Point 88, crossed the startline at 0930 hours under continuous fire. The battalion's command group, less the CO, were 'misdirected down the main road' to Igoville, where they were captured. The history of the regiment, *Black Yesterdays*, provides a detailed picture of the confusion that almost overwhelmed one of the best led battalions in the corps. By nightfall the Argylls had suffered seventy-five casualties and had been unable to move beyond Igoville.[49] During the night Brigadier Jefferson wisely decided to wait until a South Alberta squadron had been ferried across the river and a new fire plan involving the full divisional artillery had been developed. This time the co-ordinated advance of two battalions supported by armour and a proper artillery programme brought quick results.

The operations conducted by 2nd Canadian Corps in the pursuit to the Seine were carried out without adequate planning and preparation.

The basic reason for this was a complete misunderstanding of the enemy's intentions and capabilities. The German high command (OKW) responded to the collapse of the front in Normandy with instructions to organize the defence of the Seine and Paris, in order to gain time to construct a new defensive position along the Somme. The Seine position was hopelessly weak around Paris,[50] but from Vernon downstream, Fifth Panzer Army deployed what was left of 2nd SS Panzer Corps and both 81st and 86th Infantry Corps. On 26 August, 81st Corps, which had resisted the American advance to Elbeuf, was across the Seine and withdrawing to the Somme.[51] Strong rearguards from 17th Luftwaffe Field Division were posted on the high ground above Elbeuf to prevent rapid pursuit, and it was these battlegroups that checked the advance of 10th Brigade. The corps also provided the troops committed to the Fôret de la Londe. Lieutenant-General Walter Steinmeuller, who commanded the force, described the 331st Division as 'well-officered with young troops of good morale, training and equipment.'[52] No Canadian soldier who fought at Fôret de la Londe would disagree.

When General Crerar, in his orders of 26 August, stated that 'the enemy no longer has the troops to hold any strong positions or to hold any positions for any length of time if it is aggressively outflanked or attacked,' he was seriously underestimating the enemy. Guy Simonds, the Corps Commander, seems to have done so as well. So in fact did the intelligence officers of army, corps, and division, which advanced the same view as both men in simplistic, 'cheerleader' terms. Consequently the tired, terribly understrength units of 2nd Canadian Division were sent blindly forward into the Fôret de la Londe. The same optimism prompted Simonds to order the infantry battalions of 4th Division to seize the high ground in their sector without waiting for the armour to cross or for proper reconnaissance. It is important to understand the context in which such command decisions are made; but it is equally valid to point out that brigade and divisional commanders have responsibilities to the men under their command as well as to their superior officers. On the 4th Division front, Foster and Jefferson were slow to revise plans to seize the high ground, but they did act. In the Fôret de la londe, in the pursuit of a meaningless victory, Foulkes overrode protests from battalion and brigade commanders. He then blamed Brigadier Ganong for all the problems that 4th Brigade encountered and insisted on replacing him. Simonds and Crerar agreed to remove Ganong, through a better case could have been made for reliving Foulkes.[53]

While the Canadians were fighting their way across the Seine, Eisenhower issued his first directive as land force commander. From his perspective the most urgent problem facing the Allies in early September was the rapidly deteriorating supply situation. Despite all the Allied victories, only one major port, Cherbourg, had been opened. With the supply lines stretching farther and farther from the Normandy beaches, the problem of providing the advancing troops with gasoline, food, and ammunition was rapidly becoming unmanageable. With the French railway system still in chaos, almost all supplies had to be brought forward by truck, and there were simply not enough trucks to bring the 650 tonnes per day each active division was thought to require. Any advance to Germany would mean the grounding of ancillary units and of a number of divisions. Trucks would have to be stripped from these units to allow the others to move.[54]

The supply situation made the decision about how to pursue the Germans difficult. The only port with both the capacity and the location to satisfy the needs of the advancing Allied armies was Antwerp. Eisenhower was also concerned about the V-1 problem and about intelligence reports regarding the V-2. An advance along the Channel coast into Holland had to have first call on Allied resources, as that would put an end to the V-1 threat and force the V-2 out of range. Consequently, Eisenhower issued a directive that satisfied none of his subordinates but that did address the major issues. The 'Northern Group of Armies' was to operate west of the Amiens–Lille line, seize the Pas-de-Calais ports and launching sites, establish airfields in Belgium, and 'secure a base at Antwerp.' The 'Central Group of Armies' was to advance east of the Amiens-Lille line, with Montgomery authorized 'to effect ... any necessary coordination between his own forces and the left wing of Central Group of Armies.'[55]

Eisenhower saw the advance along the northeast corridor to secure Antwerp as the principal operation for early September. He confirmed this commitment by allotting his strategic reserve, First Allied Airborne Army, to Montgomery 'to ensure the destruction of the retreating en-

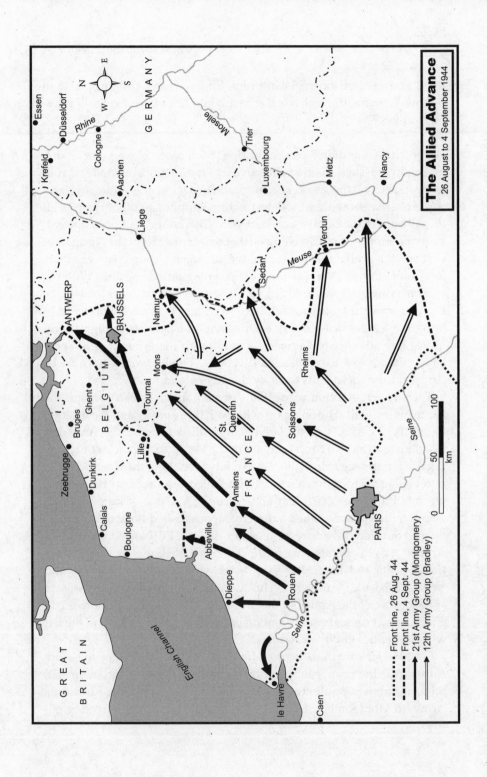

The Allied Advance
26 August to 4 September 1944

Legend:
········· Front line, 26 Aug. 44
- - - - - Front line, 4 Sept. 44
⬛ 21st Army Group (Montgomery)
⬜ 12th Army Group (Bradley)

Scale: 0 — 50 — 100 km

GREAT BRITAIN

English Channel

GERMANY

BELGIUM

FRANCE

Essen
Düsseldorf
Krefeld
Cologne
Aachen
Rhine
Liège
ANTWERP
BRUSSELS
Namur
Sedan
Meuse
Trier
Luxembourg
Moselle
Metz
Nancy
Verdun
Rheims
Soissons
St. Quentin
Mons
Tournai
Lille
Ghent
Bruges
Dunkirk
Zeebrugge
Calais
Boulogne
Abbeville
Amiens
Dieppe
Rouen
Seine
le Havre
Caen
PARIS
Seine

N E S W

emy' and the seizure of the Pas-de-Calais ports. Eisenhower had not accepted Montgomery's single thrust to the Ruhr, but he had placed priority on the coastal ports – especially Antwerp – as a necessary preliminary to a broad front approach to the Rhine. Unfortunately, he changed his mind.

Hitler also revised his command structure in early September, reappointing Field Marshal Gerd von Rundstedt as Commander-in-Chief West. Field Marshal Walther Model, who had been filling this post as well as commanding Army Group B, was now to focus on operational matters while von Rundstedt took over the large headquarters responsible for theatre logistics, the training of new formations, and the rebuilding of the Westwall defences. Von Rundstedt's message to his 'soldiers of the Western Army,' dated 3 September, was designed to reassure exhausted warriors that the Führer's secret weapons would turn the tide:

> As your new Commander-in-Chief I direct this call to your honour as soldiers.
>
> We have lost a battle, but I tell you, we shall win the war! I cannot say more now, although I know that there are many questions burning on the troop's lips. Despite everything that has happened do not allow your firm, confident faith in Germany's future to be shaken ... [We must] gain the time the Fuhrer needs to bring into operation new troops and new weapons.[56]

Von Rundstedt's immediate problem was to find reserves to reinforce his threatened left flank, where Patton's army was driving for the Rhine. Two Panzer Grenadier divisions transferred from Italy were joined by three of the battered Normandy divisions: 21st Panzer, Panzer Lehr, and 17th SS, rebuilt with SS troops from training divisions in Denmark. Most of the new Peoples Grenadier formations were also sent to this sector.[57]

While the Germans concentrated on stopping Patton's advance, 2nd British Army and the left wing of General Courtney Hodges's 1st U.S. Army charged ahead. General Brian Horrocks's 30th Corps reached Amiens early on 31 August, breaching the Somme 'line' and moving off for Belgium. On their right, two U.S. corps were converging on Tournai and Mons, where on 3 September some 25,000 Germans were trapped.[58] The British reached Brussels that same day. Opposition was negligible, and as the Belgian cities were liberated, the leading armoured divisions seemed to be almost on a victory parade rather than a battlefield. On 4 September, 11th Armoured Division burst into Antwerp. There was virtually no German garrison, and the few security troops could do little to stop the well-organized Belgian resistance from seizing control of the vital docks. Antwerp, the largest port in Europe, had fallen into Allied hands without a major battle and without damage to the port. Surely the Third Reich was all but finished.[59]

The capture of Antwerp created a new situation for both sides. The German commanders had to solve three separate but closely related problems if they hoped to minimize the impact of Antwerp's sudden fall. First, they needed to improvise some defences along the river and canal systems of northern Belgium and southern Holland; second, they needed to somehow extricate their 15th Army, which was pinned to the coast and cut off from all land routes to Germany; and third, they needed to deny the Allies the use of as many deep-water ports as possible – but particularly Antwerp itself.

The task of blocking a further British advance north from Antwerp fell to Lieutenant-General Kurt Chill, who had assumed command of 85th Infantry Division, which at that point was a regiment-sized battlegroup incorporating elements of 84th, 85th, and 89th Divisions, all of which had suffered heavy losses in Normandy. Chill, described as 'an officer of great skill and uncommon energy,' reinforced his battalions with 'German police, security forces, and stragglers' and occupied a position from Merxem east along the Albert Canal.[60] At the urging of Belgian resistance leaders, Major-General G.P.B. Roberts, commander of 11th Armoured Division, ordered an advance across the Albert Canal to seize the suburb of Merxem. One of his three infantry battalions, the King's Shropshire Light Infantry (KSLI), sent three companies into a 'ghastly factory area, one mass of small streets, lanes, passages, walls, walls within walls, piles of iron and waste of every description.' The Germans deployed tanks in support of their infantry, squeezing the KSLI's bridgehead and forcing them to withdraw to a single factory on the north bank of the canal. Exploiting a damaged railway bridge, Roberts sent across two companies of the Monmouthshires with a squadron of tanks. This attempt to take the pressure off the KSLI failed, and Roberts decided to withdraw the battalion before it was 'shot to pieces.'[61] He had little choice.

Montgomery's orders to hand over the defence of Antwerp and move east for the advance to the Rhine were issued late on 6 September, and the transfer to 53rd Division was soon underway.[62] By then, 719th Division had arrived from the Dutch coast to thicken the defences; regimental battlegroups of two divisions, the 346th and 711th – among the first formations to cross the Scheldt – were also reinforcing the positions along the Albert and Escaut canals.[63]

The actions fought by 11th Armoured Division at the Albert Canal suggest that postwar statements by Horrocks that Roberts could have bypassed Antwerp, cut off the Beveland Isthmus, and prevented 15th Army from employing its divisions north of Antwerp are incorrect.[64] Nothing short of a major commitment by several infantry divisions could have breached the German defences and reached South Beveland. It is also necessary to point out that if more German divisions had been trapped on Walcheren and Beveland, the campaign to clear the approaches to Antwerp would have been even more difficult than it actually was. Under such circumstances Antwerp might not have been available until 1945.

The early arrival of divisions from 15th Army indicated just how smoothly the withdrawal across the Westerschelde was going. Even before von Rundstedt issued orders to evacuate the army through Breskens and Terneuzen there had been a good deal of northbound traffic, with the Dutch car ferries *Queen Wilhelmina* and *Queen Emma* carrying the equivalent of two divisions to Flushing and Hansweert. Once German naval officers arrived, scores of other ships, both Dutch and German, were used to transport men, animals, and equipment in daylight, with little interference from the Allied air forces. The original Dutch ferry crews were replaced with German sailors, and anti-aircraft guns were concentrated at the crossing points. There was sufficient time to stage an unhurried withdrawal; units were taken across with all their vehicles 'repacked so as to make the most efficient use of space.'[65]

The first Allied air attack took place on 11 September; it closed the harbour at Breskens until the next morning. But on 12 September the RAF was occupied elsewhere, and some seventy-five craft of varying sizes helped the large ferries make the forty-minute journey, carrying more than 10,000 men with all their equipment. Terneuzen was attacked on 13 September and was out of action for twenty-four hours, but another 10,000 men crossed from Breskens to Flushing and via a new small-boat route to Ellewoutsdjk on the southern tip of South Beveland. The Allied air forces bombed Flushing on 15 September; the next day they attacked troop-carrying ships in the estuary. However, by 21 September, when the Polish Armoured Division reached Terneuzen, the evacuation was essentially over.[66] Not all of 15th Army reached the mainland. General Gustav von Zangen had been ordered to reinforce the garrisons of Boulogne, Calais, and Dunkirk and to assign divisions to defend what Hitler called Fortress North Scheldt, Walcheren Island, and Fortress South Scheldt – the area north of the Leopold Canal soon to be known to Canadians as the Breskens Pocket.

Hitler and the German army's high command had responded to the loss of Antwerp with measures designed to minimize the consequences of this potentially disastrous blow. Yet the capture of Europe's largest port brought no comparable changes to Allied conceptions of the campaign. The day before the seizure of Antwerp, Eisenhower issued a directive that began: 'Enemy resistance on the entire front shows signs of collapse.' The directive assigned new missions to both army groups. Montgomery's forces were to 'secure Antwerp, breach the sector of the Siegfried Line covering the Ruhr and then seize the Ruhr' with the assistance of 1st U.S. Army. The remainder of Bradley's forces – essentially 3rd U.S. Army – were 'to occupy the sector of the Siegfried Line covering the Saar and then to seize Frankfurt.' The 1st Airborne Army was still assigned to Montgomery, but now it could be used 'up to and including the crossing of the Rhine.' This was a very different set of tasks than those described in the directive of 29 August and clearly reflected the mood of optimism at Supreme Headquarters.[67]

Montgomery did not differ from Eisenhower in his appreciation of the state of the enemy. However, Montgomery was convinced that there 'were not enough resources for two full-blooded thrusts.' He told Eisenhower that 'we have now reached a stage where one really powerful and full-blooded thrust toward Berlin is likely to get there and thus end the German war.' Eisenhower replied the same day, 5 September, reiterating his intention 'to occupy the Saar and the Ruhr and by the time we have done this, Havre and Antwerp should be available to maintain one or both thrusts you mention. In this connection I have always given and still give priority to the Ruhr ... Please let me know at once your further maintenance requirements for the advance to and occupation of the Ruhr.'[68]

Montgomery was quite unpersuaded. He wrote back on 7 September: 'I submit with all respect ... that a reallocation of our resources of every description would be adequate for one thrust to Berlin.' Eisenhower was anxious not to see the dispute aggravated, especially since it was only a week since he had taken over the ground command. On 10 September he flew to see Montgomery in Brussels. Only two other men were present at the meeting: the Deputy Commander, Air Chief Marshal Arthur Tedder, and Montgomery's supply officer, Major-General M.W.A.P. Graham. It is not quite clear what was said, but by the end of the meeting Eisenhower had agreed to an ambitious airborne operation with Arnhem as its immediate objective. The Supreme Commander had not granted Montgomery's demand for absolute priority in maintenance, nor had he accepted notions about thrusts to Berlin, but he had given priority to a major operation that had nothing to do with the problem of Antwerp.[69]

The next day Montgomery signalled to say he would have to postpone the agreed-upon attack because he did not have enough supplies. Eisenhower's Chief of Staff, General Walter Bedell Smith, flew up to see Montgomery, and as a result of this meeting, Eisenhower promised to deliver 500 tonnes of supplies daily by aircraft as long as the aircraft were not involved in an airborne operation, plus 500 tonnes daily obtained by grounding three newly arrived U.S. infantry divisions. The 1st U.S. Army, on Montgomery's right flank, would be assured full maintenance, and Montgomery would be able to communicate directly with Hodges, its commander. This was tantamount to being given full control of the most important part of the front – certainly the only one that was likely to see major action.[70] Montgomery was jubilant. He wrote to Crerar on 13 September: 'Since last meeting you we have had a great victory with SHAEF and the main weight of maintenance is now diverted to the northward thrust against the Ruhr.'[71]

The attack that Montgomery planned and that Eisenhower agreed to, Operation Market Garden, was to send 30th British Corps northwards on roads that led to Eindhoven, Nijmegen, and Arnhem, with the help of three airborne divisions, which were to seize the bridges over six major water obstacles. Arnhem lay beyond the northernmost point of the German fortifications known as the Westwall; thus, if the British reached Arnhem in strength they could turn east and enter Germany without facing any major obstacles. In ideal circumstances, 30th Corps could also move north and occupy Apeldoorn and Zwolle, thus cutting off all the German troops in southern and western Holland. The Canadian Army, coming up on the left flank, would then take Rotterdam and Amsterdam. At the same time, 1st U.S. Army would move directly eastwards, advance to the Rhine, occupy Cologne and Bonn, and meet with the British troops, thereby surrounding the entire Ruhr.[72]

It was an ambitious plan, and one that depended entirely on accurate intelligence estimates that a German collapse was imminent. The difficulties were clear. The 1st U.S. Army would be attacking eastwards, and 2nd British Army northwards, the two at right angles to each other; thus, the faster they advanced the bigger the gap between them would grow. The second major difficulty involved the path that 2nd British Army would be attempting to follow into Germany; the SHAEF planners had initially rejected it as too difficult owing to limited roads and the number of rivers and canals.

On the positive side, the Allies could finally use their strategic reserve, the airborne divisions, as General George Marshall and others had been urging them to do. Though the corridor of the proposed advance was narrow, three divisions would be dropping from the sky and occupying the roads and bridges, in effect creating a magic carpet over which the advancing units could roll. It was an exciting prospect, and during the very short week between Eisenhower's agreement on 10 September and the actual launching of Market Garden on 17 September, there was much to do, and as a consequence the matter of Antwerp received less attention than it deserved.

The Allied naval command was much more alert to the problems of Antwerp. The day it fell, Admiral Bertram Ramsay signalled SHAEF and 21 Army Group headquarters to warn that Antwerp would be useless until the Scheldt Estuary had been cleared of the enemy. He went to see Eisenhower the next day and stayed at SHAEF headquarters for several days. Eisenhower's worries over Antwerp apparently increased during this time, but with the intelligence reports as optimistic as they were in the first weeks of September, it seems to have been impossible for ground force commanders to think of giving up a major advance for the sake of clearing the Scheldt.[73] The Combined Chiefs, meeting in Quebec City, drew Eisenhower's attention to 'the necessity for opening the northwest ports, Antwerp and Rotterdam in particular, before the bad weather sets in,' but they also approved priority for the advance to Germany.[74]

Eisenhower certainly realized that Market Garden would postpone the clearing of the Scheldt. He wrote to Marshall on 14 September: 'I have sacrificed a lot to give Montgomery the strength he needs ... Our main effort for the moment ... It should be successful in carrying Montgomery up to and across the Rhine; thereafter it is absolutely imperative that he quickly capture the approaches to Antwerp, so that we may have use of that port.'[75] But how did Eisenhower envisage the capture of the approaches to Antwerp? He seems to have left the timing of this task entirely in Montgomery's hands, and for the field marshal it was the Rhine, not the Scheldt, that mattered.

Operation Market Garden was to become one of the most controversial battles of the Second World War, but on 10 September it appeared to be a feasible plan that might bring about the end of the war in 1944. The Rhine had long loomed large in the imaginations of the staff officers at SHAEF and 21 Army Group, so a proposal to employ airborne troops to secure a bridgehead across the river won initial support from almost everyone. As always, the devil was in the details, and as the Market Garden plan took shape doubts began to grow. There was not enough airlift to transport all three divisions on the first day, and logic dictated that there was no point in seizing the bridge at Arnhem unless the other crossings were secure. The 101st U.S. Airborne was therefore allotted 100 percent of its necessary lift and the 82nd Division 50 percent, leaving 1st British Airborne with just one-third of the aircraft necessary to transport its troops. Much would therefore depend on good weather over Holland. There was also concern about the limited road network between the start line and Arnhem. The single two-lane highway, and the local roads as well, were generally built on top of dykes, which could easily be blocked, so the planners justified their estimates that the land forces could relieve the airborne divisions after seventy-two hours by assuming that 'once the crust of resistance had been broken the German Army would be unable to concentrate any other troops in sufficient strength to stop the breakthrough.'[76]

This assumption, like so much else in the plan, was based on an interpretation of the available intelligence that in retrospect proved to be deeply flawed. Historians have focused particular attention on the ULTRA decrypts and on other intelligence that revealed the presence of 2nd SS Panzer Corps in the Arnhem area.[77] But the real problem was not at Arnhem; the 1st British Airborne Division held a bridgehead there for six days waiting for the ground forces to reach them. The German battlegroups that defended the other river and canal crossings, thus slowing the British armoured advance, were barely mentioned in ULTRA, and all levels of Allied intelligence consistently underestimated their capacity to interfere. ULTRA did reveal the arrival of divisions from 15th Army that had crossed the Scheldt,[78] but British army intelligence thought that these formations were unlikely to be able to intervene in a three-day advance and that they could be left to 12th British Corps, which had been assigned to protect and expand the western flank of the salient. When the formal orders for Market Garden were issued on 14 September, those who believed it might succeed greatly outnumbered the doubters.

During the first two weeks of September, First Canadian Army was engaged in a very different war from the one experienced by the British and Americans. On the left flank of the Allied advance the enemy deployed a well-organized army with a number of full-strength divisions that had not been involved in the bloodletting in lower Normandy. The new commander of 15th Army, General Gustav von Zangen, arrived from the Eastern Front in late August to discover that despite the rout of the German armies now retreating across the Seine, his forces were still deployed to defend the coast from invasion. Von Zangen quickly ordered an immediate withdrawal of his southernmost corps while 226th Volksgrenadier Division sent a reinforced regiment to Le Havre. Von Zangen decided to abandon the defences of Dieppe and moved the horse-drawn 245th Division north while it was still able to withdraw in good order. He later recalled that in the absence of clear orders, 'there was no longer any sense in staying at the Channel.' So after ensuring that Boulogne, Calais, and Dunkirk were adequately garrisoned, he assembled forces in the Arras area 'to build up a deep front.' This task was carried out by 84th Corps employing three recently created infantry divisions. A third corps headquarters, with two infantry divisions – 331st and 346th – was subordinated to 15th Army on 2 September, and preparations were made to break out across the path of Allied forces and withdraw to Germany east of Antwerp. When further Allied pressure made this impossible, the only option left was to evacuate the army across the Scheldt to Walcheren and South Beveland, and plans were made for a staged withdrawal to the ports of Breskens and Terneuzen. In his memoir, von Zangen wrote that he was surprised when no serious attack was launched on his vulnerable eastern flank; instead, the Allies allowed him to withdraw his divisions to a series of east–west canal lines without fear of encirclement.[79]

First Canadian Army crossed the Seine with very clear instructions about its limited responsibilities. Montgomery told Crerar to secure the port of Dieppe and proceed quickly with 'the destruction of all enemy forces in the coastal belt up to Bruges' while 1st British Corps captured the port of Le Havre. Both 6th Airborne Division, returning to England, and 7th Armoured Division, restored to 2nd British Army, would no longer be available, and for logistical reasons 1st British Corps would remain on the Le Havre peninsula after it had secured the area.[80]

North of the Seine, 2nd Canadian Corps faced a featureless stretch of open country, the Caux district. There was a dense network of roads and no significant obstacles until the wide, marshy valley of the Somme was reached. On 30 August, 9th Brigade, led by the Stormont, Dundas, and Glengarry Highlanders, cleared the river line into Rouen. Patrols pushed into the city and beyond. The next day the brigade moved through the city in a triumphal procession, leading the division towards the Channel coast at Le Tréport. The only resistance was dealt with by troops of 7th Recce Regiment (17th Duke of York's Royal Canadian Hussars), who reported heavy fighting in their long-awaited role as divisional reconnaissance, positioned well out in front of the infantry. The 4th Division moved out of its Seine bridgehead, reaching Buchy on the morning of 31 August. The division was still operating at 50 per cent below its authorized tank strength, and 10th Brigade was short 25 per cent of its infantry establishment. A 'promised' four-day halt for rest and reorganization raised spirits to a new high, but at 2200 hours the mood was rudely shattered by orders to move out for the Somme.[81]

Crerar had been called to Montgomery's headquarters and there informed of the spectacular night march of the 11th Armoured Division, which had resulted in the seizure of the Somme bridges at Amiens. Montgomery now told him that 7th Armoured Division would be moving west to capture Point Remy and Abbeville the next morning and that he required 2nd Canadian Corps to press on through the night to take over this extension of the Somme bridgehead. Crerar climbed back into his Auster airplane and flew to Simonds's headquarters, where the necessary orders were promptly issued. The 4th Division set off shortly after midnight for the Somme. At midday the vanguard was approaching Airaines when it collided with elements of 7th Armoured Division. The traffic congestion and German resistance in Airaines slowed the march, and not even the Manitoba Dragoons, attached to the division for deep reconnaissance, reached the Somme on 1 September.[82]

On the morning of 1 September, Crerar issued a new directive formalizing his verbal instructions of the previous night. Simonds, believing that the Abbeville crossings would be handed over intact, ordered Polish Armoured Division and 3rd Infantry Division to take up the pursuit while 2nd and 4th Divisions absorbed replacements. Given the limited crossing points available to the corps and the narrowness of the Canadian sector, it did not seem likely that more than two divisions would be able to move north abreast. When the reconnaissance regiment (10th Mounted Rifles) of Polish Armoured Division arrived at Abbeville on the night of 1 September, it saw no sign of British troops waiting to hand over a bridgehead. Instead it exchanged shots with a small enemy rearguard force that was holding the bridge approaches on the river's south bank. The defenders, from 245th Division, were panicked by the arrival of the Poles. Despite stand-fast orders they retreated across the river, destroying the Abbeville bridges. Harassing artillery fire demonstrated that the Germans held the north bank in strength.[83]

On the evening of 2 September, while the Poles were preparing to establish a bridgehead west of Abbeville, Montgomery sent a signal to Crerar expressing his dissatisfaction with Canadian efforts:

Second Army are now positioned near the Belgian frontier and will go through towards Brussels tomorrow. It is very necessary that your two Armd. Divs. should push forward with all speed towards St. Omer and beyond. Not rpt not consider this the time for any div. to halt for maintenance. Push on quickly.

Crerar replied that he was

delighted to learn that Second Army is now positioned near Belgium frontier but would advise you that until late this afternoon Second Army troops have not been within five miles Abbeville and that all bridges R. Somme blown with enemy in considerable strength holding north bank. Not a case of more divs. on line R. Somme but of securing one main route crossing of river. In any event 2 Can Inf Div bns down to average strength 525 and in my opinion a forty-eight hour halt quite essential in order it can absorb approx. one thousand reinforcements arriving today. You can be assured that there is no lack of push or of rational speed Cdn. Army. St. Omer and beyond will be reached without any avoidable delay.

This exchange may well have provoked an angry row between Crerar and Montgomery, ostensibly over Crerar's absence from Montgomery's conference the next day. Crerar had gone to Dieppe to take part in ceremonies there and had missed the meeting. Arriving after it was over, he was subjected to a blistering attack that included Montgomery's declaration, 'Our ways must part.' The Canadian commander stood his ground, replying that he 'could not accept this attitude and judgment' and that he would 'never consent to being pushed about by anyone.' Montgomery quickly calmed down when Crerar spoke of dealing with the issue 'through official channels.'[84] Montgomery would have been happy to replace Crerar, whom he had never wanted as one of his army commanders, but he was not prepared to risk a political row.

Crerar's determination to attend the ceremonies in Dieppe reflected his personal involvement in the events of August 1942 as well as his belief that the commander of Canada's national army ought to be present.[85] As soon as he learned that the city had been liberated he authorized a series of commemorative activities. If Operation Fusilade, the assault on the defences of Dieppe, had gone forward, and if Bomber

Command as well as artillery had hammered the city, the mood of the population would have been very different. Fortunately, 8th Recce Regiment had brushed aside opposition and raced through the night to the outskirts of the town. It quickly became apparent that the Germans had abandoned Dieppe and that it was possible to call off the scheduled heavy bomber attack. As the Canadians entered the city the streets filled with people determined to welcome their liberators. At the Great War Monument in the central square most of the citizenry gathered to witness an impromptu ceremony and to sing 'La Marseillaise,' 'God Save the King,' and 'Tipperary.' Similar scenes were repeated throughout the day as battalions that had participated in the 1942 raid reached the city.[86]

The celebrations in Dieppe had no impact on the pace of Canadian operations at the Somme. The river was more than sixty metres wide at Abbeville, and with the bridges blown, some delay was inevitable. The Poles succeeded in getting patrols across shortly after midnight on 2 September, and a footbridge was working before dawn, but Abbeville was not cleared until mid-morning. Polish engineers worked all day on 'Lwov Bridge,' and the division's armoured brigade crossed late that night. Early on 4 September the Polish vanguard moved north towards Hesdin, encountering well-organized units of 15th Army.[87]

The Germans had used the delay at the Somme to good advantage. The commander of 67th Corps recalled that 'the defense of the Somme, and the possibility thereby tendered to officers to exert their influence on units, once again gave these units the feeling of a certain planned order.' Of equal importance to 67th Corps was the addition of a regiment of anti-aircraft guns from the Somme sector. Ten batteries of 88s and twelve 37 or 20 mm light AA batteries were made mobile under the command of 'a very energetic AA regimental commander and his staff.' This regiment was to provide 67th Corps with a vital anti-tank and artillery element during its retreat north. On 4 September it played a crucial role in preventing Polish Armoured Division from getting beyond Hesdin, just twenty-five miles north of the Somme.[88]

On 4 September, 3rd Division followed the Polish forces out of the Abbeville bridgehead northeast towards Boulogne and Calais. The recce regiment led the way with the same elan as had marked their operations beyond the Seine. The regiment discovered secondary crossings of the rivers Authie and Canche, and its lead squadrons drove relentlessly forward, shooting up a convoy and destroying an enemy blocking force at Samer by charging into the centre of town with all guns blazing. They were at the outskirts of Boulogne that night.[89]

The Polish Division also got into gear, catching up with the tail end of the retreating German columns and taking prisoners from 245th Division. They reached St-Omer to find the bridges across the Neuf Fosse canal blown and an enemy covering force entrenched on the north bank. The Poles rushed the defences with their rifle brigade, and the engineers spent the night building a new, eighty-foot bridge.[90] The two lead divisions of First Canadian Army had moved forward quickly once across the Somme, but 15th Army was still retreating in good order. On 6 September, as Polish Armoured Division prepared to move north from St-Omer, 4th Division began its delayed move forward. Its armour had followed 10th Infantry Brigade across the Somme on 3 September and all units had spent the next two days in rest and reorganization. Two mixed battlegroups, 'Moncel' and 'Stewart' (named after the commander of 4th Armoured Brigade and the acting commander of 10th Infantry Brigade) were created for the advance north.[91]

The task assigned to 4th Division on 6 September was expressed simply as 'to pursue the enemy to the area of Eecloo.' The corps' armoured car regiment, 12th Manitoba Dragoons, attached a squadron to 4th Division for deep reconnaissance; its other squadrons felt out the area along the corps front, keeping contact with Polish Division on the right flank and the coastal situation on the left. The assumption behind these orders was that although the enemy would try to hold the Channel ports, the presence of 2nd British Army in Antwerp left 15th Army with no alternative except a hasty evacuation across the Scheldt. No one at army, corps, or divisional headquarters believed the Germans would make a stand south of the Scheldt. First Canadian Army intelligence gleefully reported: 'We have in the bag three divisions for sure, plus stragglers; the total bag is now probably 50,000.'

This intelligence summary, issued on 5 September, echoed the general mood of exhilaration that had infected all levels from SHAEF on down, but at the leading edge of the corps' advance there were signs that the Germans were still capable of interfering with easy assumptions. Polish Armoured Division had encountered larger groups of the fleeing enemy as well as stronger rearguard actions as they entered Belgium. It fell to the Polish forces to liberate Ypres, the focal point of so many First World War battles. The Poles continued their march across the historic Flanders battlefields, fighting briefly for Passchendaele before meeting stubborn resistance at Rouleres and Thielt. By midnight on 9 September they were twenty miles southwest of Ghent. During their drive north they had captured more than 3,000 prisoners and inflicted heavy casualties on the retreating enemy, but there own casualties were considerable.[92]

The 4th Division also found that its easy march north was ending. On 6 September, 'Moncel Force' encountered determined resistance in Bergues, an outpost of the Dunkirk perimeter. When the garrison there refused a surrender demand, General Foster decided to bypass the town and move into Belgium. The next day both 4th Division battlegroups reached the line of the Ghent Canal and found the enemy strongly positioned behind the water barrier. Von Zangen had ordered his corps commanders to hold the canal line as a 'barricade' while 15th Army's evacuation across the Scheldt was organized.[93]

One unit of 2nd Canadian Corps was able to continue to move forward. The Manitoba Dragoons, travelling as much as fifty miles ahead of the rest of the corps, occupied Nieuport and with the aid of the Belgian resistance, cleared the town. They moved on to Ostend, arriving on the heels of the retreating Germans. Ostend was a small but important port, and its capture without a siege was an unexpected bonus. The Dragoons then probed north to Zeebrugge, the western bastion of the German defences, but the town and canal line were held by an ad hoc formation of naval and artillery units that showed every intention of holding their positions.[94]

On the afternoon or evening of 7 September all Allied headquarters down to army level were informed that ULTRA had decrypted a day-old message from OKW to 15th Army adding 'Fortress South Scheldt' to the list of areas to be defended to the last man. Little is known of First Canadian Army's use of ULTRA except by inference. The daily summaries issued by Lieutenant-Colonel Peter Wright's intelligence section do indicate that for a brief moment, ULTRA's information on German intentions was taken seriously. On 9 September the summary noted: 'It can be expected that the Germans will retain a force south of the

Scheldt, a force which will take considerable pressure to dislodge.' The next day, however, the summary, reflecting the news of 4th Division's crossing of the Ghent Canal, contended that the Germans would now be forced to withdraw across the Scheldt. From 10 September to 21 September, First Canadian Army intelligence supported the estimate of 21 Army Group that the enemy would not defend the 'Breskens Pocket' for any length of time.[95] Given that ULTRA had reinforced its 7 September decrypt with a series of specific messages to 15th Army detailing corps and divisional assignments, this faulty analysis must be attributed to an unwillingness to allow hard intelligence to interfere with preconceptions.

The optimism of senior commanders was much in evidence on 8 September when Major-General Harry Foster ordered 'Stewart Force' to seize a crossing of the Ghent Canal north of Oostcamp at the village of Moerbrugge. No detailed plan was developed, nor was time taken to arrange artillery support. The Argylls crossed the canal in two boats borrowed from a nearby mooring. The lead company got across in good order, but artillery and mortar fire rained down on the rest of the battalion, and by dark the three companies were holding a narrow perimeter under constant fire. In the early hours of the morning the Lincs crossed to join their comrades 'under heavy fire from the flanks.' Daylight on 9 September found both battalions virtually cut off, short of ammunition, and facing repeated counter-attacks. Enemy fire prevented the divisional engineers from bridging the canal until late that night. Not until the morning of 10 September did the first South Alberta tanks arrive to support the final clearance of Moerbrugge. Casualties in this encounter had been very heavy, and the position was consolidated only after the main body of German troops were ordered to withdraw behind the Leopold Canal, leaving the remaining defenders of Moerbrugge to their fate.[96]

'Moncel Force' confronted a very different problem. Their advance had brought them directly to the ancient city of Bruges with its treasures of Flemish history. The mayor had pleaded with the German commander to avoid damaging his city, but when the motorized companies of the Lake Superior Regiment approached they found the bridges blown and the crossroads mined, with anti-tank guns covering the roads. The suburb of St-Michelle was occupied, and patrols set out to

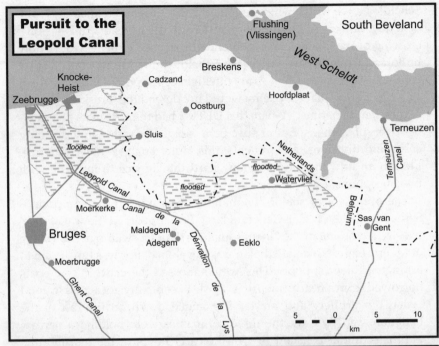

Pursuit to the Leopold Canal

Flushing (Vlissingen)

South Beveland

West Scheldt

Breskens

Knocke-Heist

Zeebrugge

Cadzand

Hoofdplaat

Oostburg

Terneuzen

Sluis

Netherlands

flooded

flooded

Watervliet

flooded

Leopold Canal

Moerkerke

Canal de la Dérivation de la Lys

Maldegem

Adegem

Eeklo

Belgium

Sas van Gent

Bruges

Moerbrugge

Ghent Canal

5 0 5 10
km

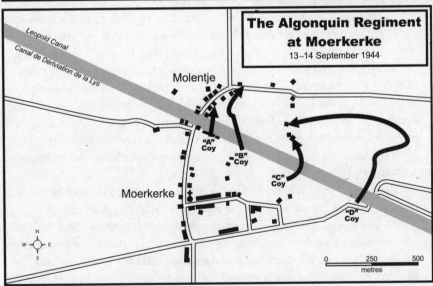

The Algonquin Regiment at Moerkerke
13–14 September 1944

Leopold Canal
Canal de Dériviation de la Lys

Molentje

"A" Coy

"B" Coy

"C" Coy

Moerkerke

"D" Coy

W—E N S

0 250 500
metres

locate the enemy's positions. On the evening of 9 September the Lake Superiors mounted a three-company attack, only to find that the enemy had moved its defences forward to the railway line. No one was anxious to carry out a street-by-street battle after 'Stewart Force' reported success at Moerbrugge and rumours of a German withdrawal from Bruges reached the forward companies. Much to the chagrin of the Lake Superiors, the Royal Hamilton Light Infantry and the Royal Regiment of Canada arrived to take over the city while the motor battalion cleared the area to the east. The next morning, 12 September, the RHLI and the Manitoba Dragoons entered the city and Major-General Foster made a triumphant entry, signing the guest book at the town hall and receiving 'an autographed set of reproductions from the famous Flemish artist Memling.'[97]

The battle for the Ghent Canal had been surprisingly difficult; even so, success there reinforced corps' and division's view that the Germans were in full retreat. Foster now ordered 'Moncel Force' – more precisely, its infantry battalion, the Algonquins – to undertake an immediate crossing of the double canal line at Moerkerke, Belgium. Here the Leopold Canal and the Canal de Dérivation de la Lys run side by side, separated by a sixty-foot-wide dyke. Foster acted 'in the expectation that a sudden surprise crossing would keep the enemy on the move.' No serious resistance was expected, and bridging equipment was quickly moved forward. Forty assault boats manned by men from the Lincoln and Welland Regiment were provided, and the entire divisional artillery as well as the mortars and medium machine guns of the New Brunswick Rangers were sited to assist the crossing. The armoured regiments provided indirect fire.[98]

Today the road that runs beside the canal in the village of Moerkerke carries the name 'Algonquinstraat.' Forty years ago this quiet country lane was the start line for a battle that was to reveal just how committed the enemy was to the defence of the Breskens Pocket. Shortly before midnight on 13 September, all four companies of the Algonquins were ferried across the two ninety-foot canals under heavy harassing fire. By dawn it was evident that the Algonquins were defending three isolated pockets with dangerous gaps between them.

The engineers began construction of a bridge, but small arms fire stopped the work. At first light the situation was growing desperate.

Enemy artillery and mortars prevented bridging, and enemy shellfire, which seemed to be directed by an enemy agent, struck battalion head-quarters and the regimental aid post in Moerkerke. The shelling was so intense that it was impossible to get supplies of ammunition across the canal to the rifle companies, which were now reporting shortages. There were no additional infantry available to reinforce or extend the bridgehead, nor was there air support. Lieutenant-Colonel Bradburn's request for an air drop of supplies was denied because no aircraft were available.

At 1200 hours the inevitable order to withdraw was issued. With the aid of an enormous barrage and smoke screen, the Algonquins with-drew, fighting their way through pockets of enemy troops, who had infiltrated as far as the island between the two canals. With most of the boats destroyed by shellfire, many of the men had to swim back to the south bank, abandoning their equipment. Of the 240 men who had crossed into the bridgehead, twenty-eight were dead, forty wounded, and sixty-six taken prisoner.[99]

The enemy's view of this encounter was expressed by the com-mander of the German forces, General Erwin Sanders:

The Canadians succeeded in forcing a bridgehead at Moerkerke which, if it had been allowed to develop, would have not only cut short a further evacuation through Breskens, but would have secured the vital ground south of the Scheldt which commanded the estuary and which at this stage the Germans were determined not to give up. When news reached the Corps Commander, he came down personally to Gen. Sanders at Lapscheure giving him strictest instructions that the bridgehead must at all costs be eliminated, promising him the Corps reserve to help him achieve his task. During this time the division was making every effort to eliminate the bridgehead without extra aid but despite every attempt, the Canadians maintained their precarious foothold.

After the meeting between Corps and Divisional commanders and before the Corps reserves could arrive, the Canadians withdrew under cover of the most incredible artillery barrage that Sanders had ever seen. No one was more surprised than he when at the conclusion of this prodigious effort, instead of a renewal of the conflict which he consid-ered was imminent as a result of this fire, he found the enemy had retired and had used this form of cover to evacuate his troops. Not all the Canadians, however, were evacuated and his Division succeeded in taking 60 prisoners.[100]

Clearly, neither side understood the position its opponent was in. The 4th Division had followed orders to rush a canal crossing in the belief that no significant enemy resistance would be met. The Germans were geared up for a major battle, which was not to come until early October. They would have ample time to complete the evacuation of 15th Army.

The thrust to the north by 2nd Canadian Corps had been stopped cold at the Leopold Canal. Since low priority was given to 'pursuing an enemy who may be retreating,' 4th Division was ordered to turn east, masking the Leopold while the area between the Terneuzen Canal and Savajaards Plaat was cleared. The division was delighted to hear that operations against the Breskens Pocket were more properly work for an infantry division.

While 4th Division liberated Belgian Flanders, 2nd Division began the siege of Dunkirk. After the difficult and costly struggle to clear the enemy from the Fôret de la Londe, 2nd Division had reached Dieppe without difficulty on 3 September. After the celebrations in Dieppe, Crerar had arranged for the division to pause and reorganize before continuing north. More than 1,000 reinforcements – enough men to restore many of the rifle companies to something approaching full strength – had arrived in France to join the division at Dieppe. Fifth Brigade, which had been allotted 320 replacements, led the division to Dunkirk on 6 September.[101] The Black Watch began by seizing a bridging site south of Bourbourgville and establishing a base for the advance. There was heavy rain all morning with a high, cold wind. The Germans had flooded much of the area 'by blowing the canal banks ... the ditches were full of water and the ground very spongy.'[102]

The battle for Bourbourgville proved to be the first of a series of battalion-level actions intended to compress the Dunkirk perimeter while Montgomery made up his mind about a full-scale assault. The men who had to carry out these attacks would long remember the battles for Coppenaxfort, Loon Plage, Bray Dunes, and La Panne as especially nasty engagements later rendered pointless by the decision to mask Dunkirk and send the divisions to Antwerp. Brigade and battalion commanders saw it differently, arguing that the ten days of carefully controlled combat provided a much needed opportunity to integrate reinforcements and prepare the rebuilt battalions for their part in operations to clear the approaches to Antwerp.[103]

One of the striking characteristics of a victorious army is that its units advance with all their baggage, pursuing an enemy that has lost much of its equipment in battle. In modern warfare, living off the land is rarely possible and the pursuing army expends great amounts of energy creating long lines of communication along which the desired amounts of fuel, ammunition, and supplies may flow. The retreating army, forced by circumstance to distinguish between the essential and the desirable, simply keeps going: without transportation, it marches; without food, it does not eat.

The pursuit of the German armies in France after the breakout from Normandy was a contest between a largely motorized Allied army and a horse- or foot-powered German army, 'horse-power against horses,'[104] as one intelligence report put it. Yet the Allies failed to trap and destroy large remnants of the German army, which were able to re-establish themselves on the borders of their homeland. Despite losses, which were estimated at more than 600,000 men, and despite the reduction of German armour in the west to one hundred battleworthy tanks,[105] the fact remains that elements of all five German Armies escaped without leaving huge gaps in their defensive perimeter – or at least no gaps that the Allies were able to exploit.[106]

2

Siege Warfare: Boulogne and Calais

While First Canadian Army's two armoured divisions fought their way towards the Scheldt, its infantry divisions peeled off to carry out their allotted tasks along the French coast. General Sir John Crocker's corps had been assigned the capture of Le Havre in mid-August. The decision to commit two infantry divisions, two tank brigades, most of the army's artillery, and large elements of specialized armour 'gadgets' of Major-General Sir Percy Hobart's 79th Armoured Division to the capture of a single port may seen excessive, but Crerar had been ordered to ground the corps after the capture of Le Havre. The battle for the city, Operation Astonia, was a model of combined operations, one that involved close cooperation between army, navy, and air force. More than 4,000 tons of bombs were aimed at the fortifications before the infantry attack was launched, and on D-Day, 10 September, a further 4,719 tons were dropped. The monitor HMS *Erebus* and the battleship HMS *Warspite* added the weight of their 15-inch guns to the attack. Two days later Le Havre surrendered.[1]

In the meantime, Montgomery's debate with Eisenhower over strategy had heated up. Montgomery, desperate for supplies that would make his 'single thrust' policy feasible, signalled to Crerar on 6 September asking him to estimate the chances for an early capture of Boulogne. 'I want Boulogne badly,' he told Crerar.[2] By 9 September 'Monty' had convinced himself that with 'one good Pas de Calais port,' additional transport, and an increased air lift he could make it to the Ruhr. He knew that 15th Army had begun withdrawing across the Scheldt on 6 September, and ULTRA told the full story of the German orders to garrison the coastal 'fortresses,' but his reaction to all this was to accept a long delay in the opening of Antwerp and to leave the escaping 15th Army to the tactical air force.[3] It is worth noting that 'one good Pas de Calais port' would have helped 21 Army Group but would have done nothing to alleviate the supply problems of the American armies. If a Channel port were opened and the Antwerp problem ignored, only Montgomery's armies would have enough supplies to mount a major offensive. Without Antwerp, the Arnhem adventure was the only game in town for which stakes were available.[4]

Very little has been published about the operations to secure the Channel ports, but the 562 Canadians buried at the Calais Canadian War Cemetery are reason enough for us to examine these battles. Also, those events tell us a good deal about the strengths and weaknesses of the Canadian approach to war after Normandy. The outline plans for both operations were developed by Guy Simonds, but he left the details and the command decisions to 3rd Canadian Division. Simonds was reluctant at first to believe that a full-scale assault on Boulogne would be necessary; but as patrol reports, photo reconnaissance, and information from the French resistance developed a detailed picture of the defences, he began making plans for a deliberate and massively supported attack. The Operational Research Section, which worked closely with 3rd Division during the battle, described Boulogne as

> well-prepared for all round defence. Around the town is a ring of high ground, with Fort de la Creche, Bon Secours, St Martin de Boulogne to the north, the highest ground of all, Mont Lambert, in the centre and Herquelinque, St Etienne and Noquet to the south. Each of these features was heavily wired with mines and provided with emplacements, some heavily concreted, giving crossfire between themselves and the adjoining feature. Well to the north, centred on la Trésorerie, were more defences, while inside the main ring are further hills on which the enemy artillery is concentrated.

More than ninety enemy guns, ranging from 75 mm to 350 mm, were available to the garrison of some 10,000 men,[5] and Lieutenant-General Ferdinand Heim, the overall commander, was determined to hold the port for as long as possible.[6]

Simonds decided to avoid the obvious approach to Boulogne along the valley of the River Liane; instead he concentrated the two available brigade groups to the east of the city. If the German fortress at Mont Lambert could be neutralized, an aggressive advance astride the main east–west road might break through the defensive perimeter and allow the other fortified positions to be attacked from the rear. To achieve a quick penetration, Simonds proposed the use of armoured columns composed of tanks and other armoured vehicles, including the Kangaroos of the newly formed 1st Canadian Armoured Personnel Carrier Regiment.[7] Much would depend on the scale of artillery support and on the degree of accuracy the gunners would obtain. Simonds did not hesitate to delegate such matters to his artillery commanders, Brigadiers Bruce Matthews and Stanley Todd. Both men were militia officers in an army that favoured regulars for senior command positions, but Simonds recognized competence when he saw it.

The artillery plan for Operation Wellhit was a complex and sophisticated document that coordinated 368 guns. These were to include 'heavies' as well as two anti-aircraft regiments firing airbursts in a ground support role. The guns were supposed to neutralize the enemy's forward positions and strongpoints as well as its artillery. More than four hundred targets were to be engaged by predicted fire, with air observation pilots in Auster aircraft available for correction. A system of 'stonks and concs on call' was established; in this way, Forward Observation Officers (FOOs) – or company commanders if necessary – would be able to call down linear or pinpoint concentrations on pre-designated targets, which had been assigned code names.[8]

The plan assumed that Bomber Command would offer support, and an elaborate counter-flak program was devised, but the Channel ports seemed to have a low priority until Simonds went to Versailles to plead his case at Eisenhower's headquarters. According to the corps War Diary, the discussions were going badly when 'Air Marshals Tedder, Harris and Leigh-Mallory arrived for another meeting.' Simonds seized the opportunity and presented his air support requirements. 'The Air Marshals agreed without hesitation that if Boulogne and Calais were to be captured forthwith and air support was necessary, then it should be given in full measure.'[9]

Air Marshal Harris returned to his headquarters in England, where it was reported to him that large parts of Le Havre had been destroyed; thousands of civilians were rumoured to have died there. Officers from Bomber Command were sent to investigate;[10] in the interim, it was decided to limit the use of heavy bombers at Boulogne to clearly defined target areas around the defensive perimeter, especially Mont Lambert. Arrangements were made for an RAF officer on the ground to communicate directly with the master bomber to ensure that the markers put down by the pathfinders were on target.[11]

Simonds was also having problems obtaining tactical air support ('tacair'). The 1st British Corps had first call on 84 Group until Le Havre capitulated; after that, attacks on the ferries evacuating 15th Army across the Scheldt and several days of rain limited the tacair contribution. In the end, forty-nine missions were flown in support of the Canadians, including two ninety-plane attacks by medium bombers.[12] Experience in Normandy suggested that little could be expected from this scale of attack. To make the most of its contribution, 84 Group established a Forward Control Post (FCP) at 3rd Division headquarters, promising that once the battle began, Typhoons would deliver rockets on target 'within 30 minutes of calling for them.' The problem of 'friendly fire' that had plagued the army–air force relationship in Normandy was tackled directly by selecting likely targets and briefing pilots with the aid of air photographs. Targets of opportunity were only to be hit if they were well beyond the bomb line separating Canadian and German troops.[13]

The role of a divisional commander in a corps commanded by Simonds was normally a limited one, but Major-General Dan Spry was determined to place his own stamp on 3rd Division. Spry, a thirty-one-year-old Permanent Force infantry officer, had been selected to replace Major-General Rod Keller largely because Crerar was determined to promote an infantry officer and his first choice, Brigadier Sherwood Lett, wounded in Normandy, hesitated when offered the job. Brigadier Ken Blackader, a militia officer who had served as acting commander in late August, was considered too old.[14]

Spry had little opportunity to get to know his senior officers during the pursuit to the Seine, but on 3 September he brought his staff officers, brigadiers, and heads of services together to discuss problems and opportunities. Captain J.R. Martin, the Historical Officer assigned to 3rd Division, was present at the conference and was 'most impressed with General Spry's able advice and ready decisions.' His summary of the discussion indicates that Spry was determined to exercise command and provide leadership. He drew from his experience in Italy without hesitation or apology. He reminded everyone that commanders at all levels must always be in a position to read the battle and employ their resources to influence the outcome – advice that everyone would need to remember once the siege of Boulogne began.

Spry held a separate meeting with his staff officers, an exceptionally competent group of men who were also gaining a reputation for arrogance. Spry reminded them that their function was to assist him and the fighting formations, adding that 'no staff officer may refuse a request … [He] cannot say no without first referring the matter to the divisional commander or GSO 1.' This was supposed to be standard practice in the Canadian Army, but evidently the staff needed a reminder.[15]

Spry established his headquarters in a chateau at Le Fresnoy east of Boulogne and began preparing for the assault. One immediate problem was the fate of the civilian population; this was largely solved when the fortress commander, Lieutenant-General Heim, proposed a truce while the civilians were evacuated. Martin witnessed the 'extraordinary procession of refugees streaming out of the city':

> [When] the civilians first reached our lines they glanced at our uniforms and murmured 'Canadians.' Moving slowly, their brightly coloured clothes in sharp contrast to their unhappy expressions, these people all bore enormous burdens; some said nothing and looked almost sullen though a few appeared exuberant and made confident gestures of violence concerning 'les Bosches.' Small dogs, some in baskets and some peeping from brief cases, and others straining at leashes were plentiful. Few if any of these people realized that food, shelter and transport is to be provided for them. To most it seemed only that the besieging forces were indirectly responsible for their eviction and flight into the countryside.[16]

Weather, and delays in the arrival of the specialized armour, led Simonds to postpone the attack on Boulogne until 17 September. This gave 3rd Division time to make arrangements for spectators; many were finding reasons to visit Boulogne to witness twentieth-century siege warfare. Divisional Headquarters issued an instruction – unique in the annals of the campaign – directing visitors to a spectators' stand, which had been erected on high ground overlooking the battlefield. 'The naval, military and air force personnel as well as press correspondents' were reminded that 3rd Division 'accepts no responsibility for spectators.'[17]

Planning for the movement of artillery and armour resources to Boulogne was started well before the launching of Astonia. On 8 September, Simonds met with Major-General Hobart (GOC 79th Armoured Division) and Brigadier Churchill Mann, the Chief of Staff of First Canadian Army, to discuss Boulogne. In a memorandum dated simply

September 1944, 'Church' Mann described the resulting 'Lift of Special Equipment':

> On completion of Astonia time was at a premium in moving the special devices necessary for Wellhit. It was urgent that the limited transportation resources be utilized at maximum capacity to place the devices at the disposal of 2 Can. Corps in sufficient time.
>
> The problem was to provide in four days a lift of 119 equipments with 63 transporters (including eight provided by 79 Armoured Division). This move entailed a distance of 200 miles.
>
> The problem resolved itself onto the necessity of all transporters doing one turn around and covering 600 miles in four days. This could be accomplished only if the transporters drove continuously using relief drivers to enable drivers to get a maximum amount of sleep.[18]

Hobart, at least, was impressed with this effort and wrote Crerar a letter commending the tank transport and Service Corps companies involved.

The detailed plan for Wellhit left little room for improvisation. It soon became clear that Cap Gris Nez and Calais could not be attacked until the artillery and armour committed to Boulogne were released. This placed particular pressure on Lieutenant-Colonel J.A. Anderson's North Shore (New Brunswick) Regiment, which was to capture the northern bastion of the fortified area at La Trésorerie while the enemy continued to occupy the coastal gun positions a few kilometres away. Spry ordered 7th Brigade to actively contain the enemy, but since La Trésorerie was not one of the heavy bomber targets, the North Shores faced a difficult challenge.

The battalion moved into position on 6 September, which left ample time for active patrolling and for liaison with the French resistance. Like other battalions, the North Shores had created a scout platoon made up of volunteers, who actually seemed to enjoy probing the enemy defences. Lieutenant Victor Soucesse and his men were able to provide detailed reports that identified, for example, a number of dummy gun positions.[19] Unfortunately, his reports also indicated that the Wimille–La Trésorerie–Wimereux sector was heavily fortified, with the defenders vastly outnumbering the Canadians. Repeated air attacks provided encouragement, but every experienced soldier knew this would be a costly and difficult job.

The North Shores were a well-led battalion with a full compliment of officers and men, including many experienced leaders. Like all battalion battlegroups, they included a platoon of combat engineers, a mortar platoon from the Cameron Highlanders of Ottawa, and a battery of 3rd Anti-Tank Regiment M10s. When the scout platoon reported that the village of Wacquinghen had been abandoned, Anderson ordered a company to occupy it. Once in the village, Major Otty Corbett 'began to get worried' because a hill known as the Pas de Gay 'looked high and menacing in the starlight.' Corbett was unable to contact battalion headquarters, but he knew that with daylight the enemy would have direct observation of the village, so he sent one of his platoons 'around the north side of the ridge to see if we could obtain surprise.' The enemy discovered the platoon and after a brief exchange of fire forced it to ground. Corbett was convinced the hill was a key feature and decided to gamble that his men could take it that night. Leaving one platoon in the village, he directed the third platoon to move around the left flank. The enemy, focused on the original threat, 'left themselves wide open to this attack,' and by 0800 hours Corbett's men had captured 'a beautiful observation post which gave control of the ground right to the seacoast.' The 205 mm guns of La Trésorerie, 800 metres to the south, were also in clear view.[20]

Anderson ordered the position reinforced and consolidated so that it could be used to provide covering fire for a cross-country attack on the northeast side of La Trésorerie. A thirty-minute preliminary barrage and support from 'D' Company got the two North Shore companies onto the feature despite losses suffered in a minefield. The problem now was how to break into the massive concrete gun positions. Enemy artillery and anti-aircraft guns were preventing armoured support from reaching the forward companies, which had to rely on hand grenades and PIAT bombs. The officer commanding the battery of M10s discovered a location where his guns could take on 'the 20 mm flak pillboxes that ringed the objective' from a range of 1000 metres. This relieved the pressure on the infantry, and that night, 'after much grenade throwing,' half the northernmost casement was captured. The next day the rest of 'the treasury' was cleared with PIATs and 'phosphorous bombs.' The

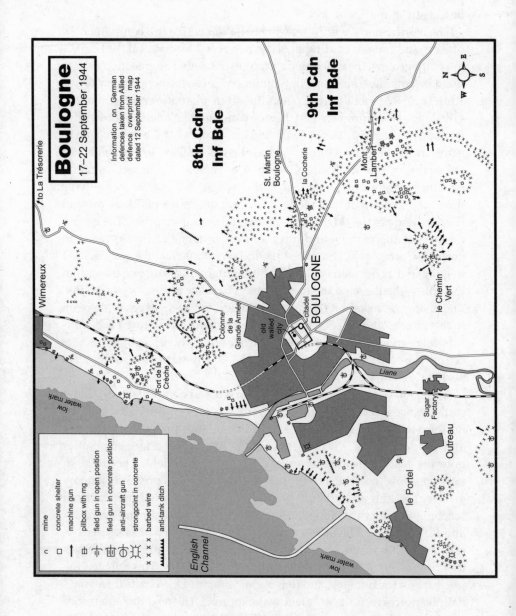

Boulogne
17–22 September 1944

Information on German defences taken from Allied defence overprint map dated 12 September 1944

to La Trésorerie

8th Cdn Inf Bde

9th Cdn Inf Bde

N E S W

Wimereux

St. Martin Boulogne

la Cocherie

Mont Lambert

le Chemin Vert

BOULOGNE

citadel

old walled city

Colonne de la Grande Armée

Fort de la Crèche

low water mark

Liane

Sugar Factory

Outreau

le Portel

English Channel

low water mark

mine
c concrete shelter
□ machine gun
↑ pillbox with mg
field gun in open position
field gun in concrete position
anti-aircraft gun
strongpoint in concrete
x x x x barbed wire
anti-tank ditch

War Diary notes that 'the cost had not been light. Both companies had gone into the attack at strength; at its conclusion "A" Company numbered about 70 men, "B," 60 men. They had taken around 450 prisoners of war.'[21]

The battalion's task was far from complete: it had been ordered to secure Wimille and the costal town of Wimeureux. Anderson decided to allow his assault companies to rest and recover while his reserve companies and the invaluable M10 battery attacked Wimille and Auvergne. Both villages were cleared on 20 September, yielding another 465 prisoners. This left Wimereux, a much larger coastal town, for the next day. Worried that Wimereux might be full of civilians, Anderson declined the offer of fire support from medium regiments. With one field regiment and a number of captured German 20 mm flak guns, which 'made a terrific noise … without smashing the town extensively,' the two company-sized battlegroups liberated Wimereux in an aggressive pincer movement. The town was packed with civilians, who 'warmly greeted' their liberators.[22]

The actions fought by the North Shore Regiment are an outstanding example of what a well-led battalion battlegroup could accomplish even with minimal support. No doubt most of the German defenders lacked the will to resist once they were in personal danger, but this required the infantry to close with an enemy that was still capable of bringing large volumes of direct and indirect fire to the battlefield. The detailed accounts of the battle gathered by the regimental historian leave little doubt that the enemy stubbornly resisted the initial stage of each attack. M10s and – in the last phase of the battle – Crocodiles and AVREs played an important role, but the battle was fought and won by a first-rate infantry battalion.

Three kilometres to the south, Le Régiment de la Chaudière had built up a detailed picture of the enemy defences through active patrolling. To reach their primary objectives – the Bon Secours feature and the Marlborough strongpoint – the 'Chauds' first had to clear the village of Rupembert with its fortified radar station. Lieutenant-Colonel Paul Mathieu decided to take the village with just one company and the battery of M10s allotted to his battalion. To succeed at this, his men would have to be on the move as soon as the medium bomber attack finished and while the artillery was still striking the defences. Even though the Forming Up Place (FUP) was under enemy fire, the attack began on time, with the M10s targeting each blockhouse. The Chaudière *fantassins* (riflemen) were on top of the enemy before it could man its defences. As a consequence, the Chauds were able to hand over an intact radar station to a team of RAF and Royal Navy technicians.[23]

The capture of the high ground overlooking the route to Bon Secours proved more difficult. Captain Michel Gauvin's company encountered a minefield, where it lost two men from the lead platoon before two of the lightly wounded charged a machine gun post, allowing the rest of the company to secure the objective.[24] Fifty enemy soldiers surrendered, adding to the seventy taken at the radar station. In 1944 Bon Secours was a cluster of houses on the Boulogne–Wimille road just 800 metres east of the Colonne de la Grande Armée, a 54 metre tower topped with a statue of Napoleon that provided an 'ideal observation post.'[25] The entire area was wired and the ground sown with land mines. Carefully sited light machine gun positions added to the defences, but the really serious problem was a battery of 88s behind Napoleon's column. Firing in a ground support role, these guns controlled the approaches to Bon Secours and the entire fortified zone.[26]

The next morning, 19 September, the Chauds launched a two-company set-piece attack with artillery support, but no progress could be made. That night a single platoon worked its way round the enemy's right flank, and by dawn a Chaudière company was dug in at Le Poterie, ready to provide fire support for a second assault on the position. This attack was quickly aborted when the enemy responded with even heavier fire. It was evident that neither medium bomber nor Typhoon attacks had significantly degraded the German defences; all the Canadian artillery could do was keep the Germans' heads down. On the morning of 21 September a third attempt, using slow infiltration tactics, was launched from La Poterie. The German garrison did not surrender until the evening of 22 September, when direct short-range fire and the threat of flame persuaded the German marines that further resistance was likely to prove fatal. The Chauds' casualties were sixty-two, including eleven killed in action.[27] This was light, considering the nature of the battle.

The Queen's Own Rifles had been assigned to clear the village of St Martin Boulogne, then turn north to capture the enemy strongpoint at

Fort de la Crèche. The scout platoon provided detailed reports, which included the information that a minefield some 600 metres deep was barring the approach route. Fortunately, the QOR battlegroup included a squadron of Flail tanks as well as a squadron of the Fort Garry Horse. St Martin was within the zone targeted by the heavy bombers, so the riflemen, who 'had enough of being bombed by our own air force,'[28] stayed well back. The sight of 250 bombers passing and repassing over the battalion area while waiting for the pathfinders to mark the targets made for a nervous ten minutes, but then the bombs dropped with good accuracy.

After the Flail tanks cleared two narrow paths through the minefield, the Queen's Own took their first objectives quickly. The enemy had fortified the local jail, and while one of the lead companies dealt with this obstacle, a reserve company advanced to the railway station in St Martin. It took two-and-a-half hours of close combat to subdue the enemy in the village; the street fighting ended only after the battalion 6-pounders, firing over open sights, took out the last enemy mortar and machine gun positions. The night was spent evacuating the wounded and patrolling for enemy locations.[29]

After a brief orders group, two companies began advancing into the northern sector of St Martin. In the course of a tense, difficult day more than one hundred prisoners were captured and a wide swath of the town cleared. The next morning the lead company came under fire from the Marlborough strongpoint, a fortified position with six 75 mm guns and eight 20 mm flak guns.[30] The battalion soon reported that they could neither capture nor pass the position until the medium artillery had given it 'special treatment.'[31] The position finally fell on 21 September. The attack on Fort de la Crèche began that afternoon, with forty-six Mitchell and sixteen Boston medium bombers achieving an accurate strike with 500-pound bombs. As soon as the M10s began to fire on the fort, a white flag went up and the garrison of five hundred surrendered. The Queen's Own entered the fort and liberated a good deal of 'luxury loot.'[32] The actions carried out by the Chaudières and Queen's Own Rifles were demonstrations of what could be accomplished by well-traineed battalions commanded by officers who were conscious of their responsibility to the soldiers fighting at the sharp end. Careful reconaissance, good communications, all-arms battlegroups, supported by observed artillery fire and and controlled use of air power, produced results without incurring heavy casualties. Brigadier Ken Blackader and his battalion commanders had much to be proud of.

Brigadier John Rockingham, inevitably known as 'Rocky' to his troops, had assumed command of 9th Brigade in late July. A tall, handsome, seemingly fearless warrior who often ventured well forward to see the battle for himself, Rockingham had won the respect and affection of his men. Their task in Wellhit was to capture Mont Lambert and the city of Boulogne, including the heavily fortified zone west of the Liane. Mont Lambert was a primary target for the heavy bombers, since only direct hits stood any chance of destroying standard enemy pillboxes. Bomber Command's real objective was the enemy's morale.[33]

Rockingham decided to try and take Mont Lambert with just one battalion, the North Nova Scotia Highlanders, while the Stormont, Dundas, and Glengarry Highlanders advanced directly into the city on the main road. This allowed Rockingham to keep the Highland Light Infantry in reserve for the later stages of the battle. The rifle companies of the North Novas would have to move quickly to take advantage of the bombing and artillery barrage; otherwise they would find them-selves advancing up a thirty-degree slope under enemy fire. Lieuten-ant-Colonel Don Forbes and his men had ample opportunity to consider the problem. Mont Lambert rises some 40 metres above the fields designated as the North Nova's start line. The chateau and village of Mont Lambert, on the narrow road below the crest of the hill, was a potential obstacle, and beyond it were numerous bunkers and pill-boxes. A minefield added strength to a position that was garrisoned by more than 1,500 men.[34]

The North Novas were the main part of a battlegroup that included a squadron of Fort Garry Shermans, mine-clearing Flail tanks, AVREs, Kangaroo armoured personnel carriers, and the usual allotment of divisional support troops. Forbes decided to attack three companies up; the mobile columns were to advance some 3000 metres to capture the eastern spur, the saddle, and the crest of the hill. Dog Company, headed for the spur, came within a few hundred metres of its objective but could not consolidate until the high ground on either side was secure. The men dug in, using convenient bomb craters. They had no difficulty fending off tentative enemy counter-attacks, but their own efforts to advance were just as fruitless. Able Company's advance was delayed by the slope and some accurate fire, but by the evening of 17 September they were firm on their objective. Unfortunately, Charlie Company found the minefield and well-camouflaged pillboxes near the Chateau intact and suffered seventeen casualties – one-fifth of their strength – before a troop of Crocodile flame-throwing tanks worked their way into the village and dealt with the pillboxes. Movement during the night was restricted by mines as well as by uncertainty about where everyone was, but Forbes was able to establish contact with his companies and coordinate a renewed advance at first light.[35]

Major M.G. Clennett's Dog Company, with good support from the Garries, had completed its tasks by the morning of 18 September. Among their prizes was a mortar positioned on a hydraulic lift that could disappear into the ground. Success brought its usual reward: Clennett was told that his company was now in the best position to assault the crest. A twelve-minute artillery concentration ended with the company still 70 metres short of its first objective, so there was nothing to do but 'make a run for it.' Suddenly, the artillery fire resumed, and Clennett was among those wounded by 'friendly fire.' The junior leaders now took control, using fire and movement to reach the pillboxes. The regimental history records one such example: 'Pte. Clyde Moraes leaped [sic] up in the open and stood, not over thirty yards from the pillbox, with his Bren forced the Germans down and kept them down while Pte. N.E. Smith, No. 2 on the gun, stood out in the open with Moraes and kept his gunner supplied with full magazines for the Bren.'

This courageous action allowed the rest of the platoon to reach the position, which was fiercely defended. Five other pillboxes and six gun positions were captured, and more than three hundred prisoners taken. The final assault had full armoured support, which included Crocodiles. Enemy resistance collapsed, and the prisoner total rose to 1,800 men. The North Novas took nearly one hundred casualties, including thirty killed.[36]

The North Novas paid a heavy price in capturing Mont Lambert, but they had accomplished what Rockingham had hoped, and drawn fire that might otherwise have slowed the advance into the heart of Boulogne. As it was, the Glens, mounted in thirty Kangaroos and supported by armour and a section of Wasp flame-throwers from 7th Recce Regiment, moved quickly to the edge of the city before craters and mines forced them to proceed on foot. Phase I was complete by 1040 hours. The right flank company had been assigned to capture La Cocherie Woods; this meant having to cross 1000 metres without armoured support, which it did without hesitation.[37]

Despite intermittent fire from Mont Lambert and the high ground to the north, the engineers of 18th Field Company established routes through the minefield and cleared the roads, mostly by hand. Phase II began in the late afternoon, and by dusk – which came an hour earlier now that the army had abandoned Double Summer Time – the two armoured-infantry columns were well into the upper city. Spry postponed a further advance until daylight.[38]

The next morning the battalion's lead column reached the walled Old City and the Citadel. 'D' Company used the cover of smoke to approach the bastion gate in preparation for employing a modern equivalent of a battering ram. Meanwhile there took place 'a strange drama of a medieval siege mingled with modern warfare.' A civilian offered to show the company commander a secret entrance into the Citadel. While an AVRE with a 'Petard' heavy mortar was preparing to blow the gate, Major John Stodhard and a platoon of eager soldiers used that tunnel to enter the Citadel. The two groups converged in the courtyard. Some two hundred prisoners, many of them very drunk, were marched back to the PW enclosures.[39]

While the drama at the Citadel was unfolding, the other Glengarry companies pressed on to the Liane, clearing the way for the Highland Light Infantry to cross the river and establish a bridgehead. The area west of the river, including the port of Boulogne, was a key part of the Atlantic Wall, with seven separate gun positions capable of 360-degree fire.[40] Under other leadership a new set-piece attack would have been called for, but Rockingham ordered his reserve battalion to 'move now' and get across the river. Rockingham went forward to organize fire support for the crossing: 'He moved up every available tank, armoured vehicle, anti-tank gun, PIAT etc. as close to the river as possible ... Their task was to plaster the enemy in the building on the opposite bank whilst the infantry crossed ... The artillery was used on deeper targets and counter-battery.'[41]

The infantry got across, but there was no bridge to allow supplies and armoured support to reach them, so little could be accomplished. The sappers decided the best hope was to repair a bridge with scavenged timber. Unfortunately, the available engineers were an assault team equipped to blow things up and were without hammers and nails: 'So being good sappers they set to work fitting the timbers together with good healthy air. At 0415 hours 19 September the first vehicle crossed the river.'[42]

All battles create personal tragedies as men are killed and wounded, but for the Highland Light Infantry, Boulogne was a particular nightmare. Two young, energetic company commanders, who were also brothers, were killed in action within a day of each other. The Kennedys, Doug and Paul, had enlisted in 1940. Both had fought in Normandy as platoon commanders and had been promoted to replace fallen comrades. The younger brother was killed instantly by a direct hit on company headquarters. His runner and signaller died with him. The next night, Major Paul Kennedy's company was engaged in house clearing in the Liane bridgehead when he was killed by machine gun fire.[43] The toll of young lives continued the next day as the rifle companies fought to clear the built-up area.

The HLI reorganized into three battlegroups, each with armoured support, including Flail tanks. Brigadier Todd arranged for full-scale artillery support, but the enemy apparently escaped injury, countering with heavy and accurate fire. Air burst 88 mm shells were a particular hazard, and so was a gun described as 'something really big.' Those, along with 40 mm and 20 mm anti-aircraft batteries, which the Germans used as super-heavy machine guns, prevented any advance. The HLI suffered forty more casualties, and four Flail tanks were destroyed before the attack was called off.[44]

The siege of Boulogne, which had been expected to end quickly, was now entering its fourth day. The spectators had left, and at 21 Army Group the usual complaints about the slowness of the Canadians were being heard. Montgomery's nightly report noted: 'There is no definite news that Boulogne has been captured but there cannot be very much more resistance in the town and we hold most of it.'[45] Montgomery had assumed that the Boulogne garrison would give up as quickly as their counterparts at Le Havre, and he was growing impatient. In his mind, the Channel ports were a minor obstacle; the real battle was being fought at Nijmegen and Arnhem, where he believed a breakthrough to Apeldoorn was imminent.[46]

The view from 3rd Canadian Division was different. Their intelligence summary for 19 September described the resistance in Boulogne as 'surprisingly tenacious,' and attributed this to the 'thick concrete defences [that] minimize the effect of our fire power' and to the 'very low percentage of foreigners within the garrison.' More than 4,000 enemy soldiers had surrendered, but thousands more were manning the remaining fortifications. Pressure from senior commanders led Spry and Rockingham to send the North Novas as well as the Glens across the river to join the battle for the coastal fortifications.

The Glens took over the left flank, which allowed the HLI to concentrate on le Portel and the harbour area. By the time the Glens' lead company reached the foot of the hill below the Outreau position, a battery of 88s was targeting the HLI advance to le Portel; it failed to notice either the Glens or the Fort Garry tanks that accompanied them. Under the system of 'concs and stonks' on call, the FOO called for target 'Norway' – the code word for the position. The men charged the hill, following the bursting fire as closely as possible, and captured the first three gun batteries intact. The other battery commander had time to destroy his guns before surrendering. The Glens also cleared a chateau, which yielded prisoners and a meal of chicken and French fries.[47]

The North Nova objective, a strongpoint near Nigles, was intact despite the best the artillery and Typhoons could do. Its guns covered the open ground towards Outreau, and Rockingham agreed to let the North Novas loop around the position and attack from the south. Fortunately, the Fort Garries had captured an enemy position at St-Etienne after a troop of tanks charged 'the crest with all guns blazing.' This gave the North Novas a firm base and tank support for their circuitous advance. After a sharp fight for the radar station at Ecault, they reached the coast near Noquet. Patrols established that the Nigles strongpoint was heavily defended with both barbwire and a wide anti-tank ditch, so a set-piece attack with full artillery support was organized for the next day.

The HLI had continued to press forward in their sector but the massive le Portel coastal guns were protected by a battery of 88s and a fortified field gun position in Henriville. Typhoons were unable to silence either them or the single 88 mm gun at the end of the breakwater. At nightfall the enemy was still holding positions near the harbour. The next day Rockingham decided to try another form of persuasion, broadcasting an ultimatum to the fortress commander:

> You have lost the battle for Boulogne. Over 7,000 prisoners have been taken and all forms of resistance have ceased except this position. You are completely surrounded by a large force of all arms.
>
> If you surrender now no further casualties will occur on either side and you and your garrison will be treated as prisoners of war and eventually return to your families. If, however, you do not surrender with all your garrison we will attack you with every means at our disposal, during which time we will incur some casualties but there is no way of assessing how many you will incur.
>
> You have one hour to make up your mind. Come out with a white flag flying, your hands above your heads and unarmed, within one hour. If this does not occur we will commence at once to destroy you and your garrison. You have had your warning, surrender or die from flames.[48]

Perhaps it was the threat of flames that worked, because shortly after the ultimatum expired, the enemy began to wave white flags.

The garrison commander, Heim, was one of those who gave himself up. He ordered the holdouts, including the gun crew at the end of the mole, to surrender. By late afternoon the guns were silent and civilian refugees were streaming back to see what was left of their ruined city. Canadian Civil Aid detachments moved quickly to open medical facilities for civilian casualties as well as soup kitchens and water points. Within days, the city was alive again and on the road to recovery.[49] From the Allied point of view it was the port, roads, and railway lines that mattered. Army engineers of a Port Construction and Repair Group began work on 23 September, but with ships sunk across the entrance channel and mines offshore as well as in the harbours, it took until 12 October to open part of the port. By the time the work was finished, Antwerp was available.[50]

The Canadians were not involved in port reconstruction. On the morning of 23 September, 8th Brigade began to redeploy to Calais while 9th Brigade prepared to capture the cross-Channel gun batteries at Cap Gris Nez. Crerar was under pressure from Montgomery to open the Port of Antwerp, and he pressed the navy to decide whether Calais would have to be secured before Boulogne could be used as a port. Admiral Bertram Ramsay thought that as long as Cap Gris Nez was occupied, Calais would be ignored; Crerar decided that if Calais could not be captured quickly, 'he was prepared to mask it.'[51]

This decision was not communicated to Spry or to the artillery commanders, who had begun preparing for Operation Undergo while the fighting still raged in Boulogne. Photo reconnaissance had identified forty-two heavy gun batteries in the 30 kilometre coastal zone around Calais, and the Corps Survey Regiment installed a five-microphone sound-ranging base and extensive flash-spotting posts to help pinpoint locations. Two batteries of 7.2-inch howitzers and two regiments of heavy anti-aircraft guns moved into position on 21 September and began to register the enemy batteries. Since the air observation planes were committed to Boulogne, serious counter-battery work did not take place until the operation began. By then the full weight of the available artillery – eight medium regiments plus the divisional artillery – were on grid and ready to support the attack.[52]

The 7th Brigade had been investing Calais since early September. Just as it began to tackle the enemy's elaborate defences, the Regina Rifles seized the village of Wissant, thus isolating Cap Gris Nez from Calais.[53] This success led Spry to try and clear the entire 'Cap Gris Nez rectangle.' But when the two available battalions began to close on the first of the 38 cm batteries, it became apparent that the enemy, to repel any landward approach, had wired and mined a large area and studded it with pillboxes. Spry ordered the Reginas and Royal Winnipeg Rifles to hand over the area to 7th Recce Regiment until the entire division, Bomber Command, and all the artillery were available.

The approaches to Calais provided a sharp contrast to those of Boulogne. The hills and forests of the Boulanais region give way to flat, open countryside criss-crossed with canals and drainage ditches. In May 1940 these obstacles and the fortifications surviving from wars of other centuries had helped the Rifle Brigade hold Calais for six precious days in aid of the Dunkirk evacuation. By 1944 the thirty-kilometre Calais–Cap Gris Nez sector of the Atlantic Wall contained six major fortified zones, including a two-kilometre 'bristling mass of wire, guns and mines,' which provided all-around protection to the Noires Mottes battery's 40 cm cross-Channel guns.[54]

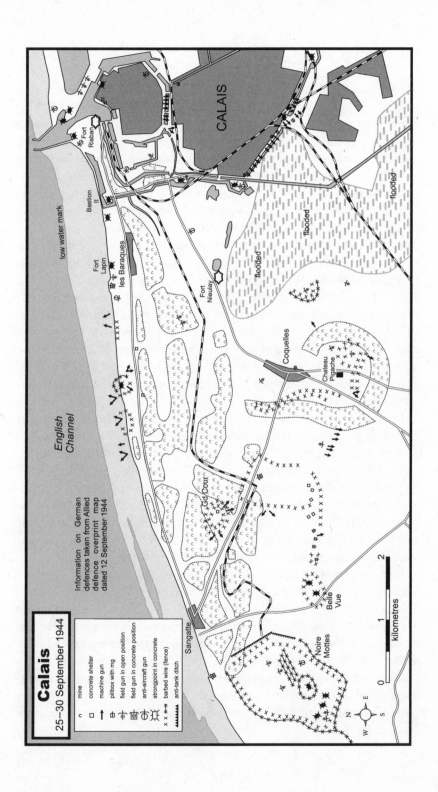

Calais
25–30 September 1944

Information on German defences taken from Allied defence overprint map dated 12 September 1944

Legend:
- c — mine
- □ — concrete shelter
- machine gun
- pillbox with mg
- field gun in open position
- field gun in concrete position
- anti-aircraft gun
- strongpoint in concrete
- x x x x — barbed wire (fence)
- anti-tank ditch

English Channel

low water mark

CALAIS

Fort Risban
Bastion II
Fort Lapin
les Baraques
Fort Nieulay
Coquelles
Chateau Pigache
Gd. Cour.
Sangatte
Belle Vue
Noire Mottes

flooded
flooded
flooded
flooded

N
W   E
S

0   1   2
kilometres

Lieutenant-Colonel Don Mingay, 3rd Division's tireless senior staff officer, had begun work on an outline plan for Undergo before he knew what resources would be available, so the plan had to be repeatedly amended. The final order, issued on 22 September, required 7th Brigade to 'attack and capture or destroy' the garrison of Calais, including the Bellevue Ridge and Coquelles fortified areas. The 8th Brigade was assigned the Escalles–Noire Mottes sector, while 9th Brigade was to deal with Cap Gris Nez. Spry kept the Queen's Own and the Glens in divisional reserve, hoping they would not be needed.[55]

Bomber Command and 2nd Tactical Air Force were 'softening' targets by 20 September, but the battle for Boulogne and rainy weather postponed D-Day until 25 September. This delay allowed Captain J.C. Bond, the Technical Staff Officer at 2nd Canadian Corps, to improvise methods of creating and maintaining a 3-kilometre smoke screen to prevent the enemy on Cap Gris Nez from interfering with the medium and heavy artillery positioned on the reverse slope of Mont Couple, south of Calais. Aided by a Meteorological Officer and men borrowed from 3rd Light Anti-Aircraft Regiment, Bond maintained an effective smoke screen for five days.[56]

Disturbing reports about the survival of almost all the enemy gun positions targeted by the air force at Boulogne led to a much heavier initial bombardment, with Bomber Command committing almost nine hundred aircraft to the attack. Unfortunately, weather conditions made for such poor visibility that only one-third of these planes were able to carry out their mission. Air observation for the artillery was also restricted, and the visitors who assembled at the spectators' stand could see very little. Once again, the armoured-infantry battlegroups found that little damage had been done to the concrete defences.[57]

Fortunately, the Calais garrison was manned largely by Germans who had no intention of dying for their Führer. The Chauds secured Escalles and Cap Blanc Nez, employing 3-inch mortars to generate their own smoke screen. When the first pillboxes were brought under fire, white flags emerged and an officer appeared offering to surrender the entire Cap Blanc Nez position if given two hours to arrange it. The garrison seems to have spent the two hours getting drunk and destroying equipment, but they all appeared on schedule to follow instructions 'to walk directly towards our lines, both arms in the air,' without arms or helmets.[58]

The North Shores relied on Flail tanks to get through the outer minefield at Noires Mottes and on Crocodiles to help them close with the enemy. They also experimented with an explosive-filled hose called a 'Conger,' which could be pushed forward to destroy wire obstacles. Lieutenant-Colonel Anderson had briefed the battalion using an elaborate scale model, and the first phase of the attack went like clockwork, with the enemy abandoning its forward slope positions. But when the North Shores tried to advance over the crest, accurate machine gun fire prevented any further movement. The Crocodile crews tried to move forward, but bomb craters and anti-tank guns barred the way. When darkness fell, no further progress had been made.

A captured German soldier, who spoke English with a Brooklyn accent, helped secure the surrender of troops cut off by the Canadian advance. Major Bill Parker, who 'felt we were riding a wave,' asked for volunteers from among the new prisoners to return and tell the garrison commander to surrender by first light or 'face the consequences.' The next morning white flags could be seen everywhere, including previously unknown positions. One of the most formidable fortified zones on the entire Atlantic Wall had yielded almost three hundred prisoners. It was, a North Shore officer recalled, 'a day to remember.'[59]

The main attack on Calais was carried out by 7th Brigade with the support of 1st Hussars and six squadrons of specialized armour. Brigadier Jock Spragge issued his outline plan on 19 September, so there was ample time for patrols to provide ground checks to supplement the maps and air photos. Lieutenant Louis Bergeron, the Reginas' extraordinary scout platoon leader, made it all the way to Escalles, and reported back that the enemy had abandoned the villages and withdrawn into fortified positions.

The Reginas had exchanged one of their rifle companies for one from the Royal Montreal Regiment that had been serving as First Canadian Army's headquarters defence company. The eager RMRs were introduced to the thrills and terrors of night patrols, and added to the 'full knowledge of the enemy's defence positions' – knowledge that helped build confidence for an attack on the formidable defences of Bellevue Ridge.[60] Meanwhile, the Royal Winnipeg Rifles had developed a detailed picture of the approaches to the Vieux Coquelles strongpoint on the edge of the flooded zone and the formidable-looking Fort Nieulay, their Phase II objective.

When the bombing ended, both battalions crossed the start line with their supporting armour. The Winnipeg battalion, with a squadron of Hussars, followed the Flail tanks through the minefield and rushed the strongpoint before the enemy had fully recovered. White flags began to appear, but intense fire from enemy mortars and 88s slowed consolidation. The Reginas found the ridge defences largely intact, and their two lead companies suffered heavy casualties in overcoming resistance that lasted until 'the flame-throwers got too close.' The RMRs, in their first battle, were brought forward to extend the battalion sector. Spragge decided to commit his reserve battalion to assist the Reginas. The Canscots rode forward in Kangaroos, dismounted on the ridge, and joined the Reginas in clearing the position. The next morning they advanced to Sangatte and began to move towards Calais on the coast road. The Kangaroos proved invaluable, as did the engineers who cleared the road blocks and minefields. The enemy had to be cleared out of 'every house, slit trench and strongpoint,' and this was done cautiously, with the full support of the artillery and armour. That night, Spragge ordered a three-pronged advance to seize Fort Lapin and Fort Nieulay; at the same time, the Reginas were to attempt to cross the flooded fields directly to Calais.[61]

Intense fire from the two forts and other gun positions made for a long and difficult day, but after Bomber Command attacked seven targets on the western side of Calais, good progress was made. Major W.H.V. Mathews, who commanded the lead company of the Canadian Scottish, gave the division's Historical Officer a detailed account of the capture of Fort Lapin and the problems encountered as they continued towards the northern bastion of the Citadel, where the battalion was pinned down by fire so intense that movement was impossible. By dawn on 28 September only one company had any freedom of movement and casualties were mounting. Mathews, in a classic understatement, admitted 'the picture was not a bright one.'[62]

The other two battalions were also encountering serious difficulties. The Royal Winnipeg Rifles captured Fort Neuilay in a carefully controlled action in which 'flame-throwers were again the final argument,' but progress was slow the next day. The Reginas sent one company across the flooded fields, but problems with 'wireless interference' and the morale of cold, wet men who reported they could 'use some rum rations' persuaded Lieutenant-Colonel F.W. Matheson to instruct them to stay where they were. This cautious decision seemed inspired after news arrived that the German garrison commander would cease firing at 1800 hours and talk surrender terms.[63] The next morning Spry discovered that although the garrison commander had agreed to discuss a surrender, his real purpose was to stall for time. Colonel Ludwig Schroeder asked that Calais be declared an open city, and when this was refused he asked for a truce to evacuate the civilian population. Spry agreed to a twenty-four-hour truce to permit the citizens to leave Calais. Then he met his brigade commanders to plan the final assault.[64]

The Queen's Own Rifles were trucked to the east side of Calais to launch an attack from a new direction. Both 7th Recce and the Camerons of Ottawa, who had been holding the sector, were to join this attack. Spry hoped that with the support of medium bombers and Typhoons as well as the available artillery, the Queen's Own would divert enemy resources while 7th Brigade prepared for an all-out assault on the morning of 1 October.

Shortly before the truce was due to expire, a delegation of German officers appeared, claiming that the garrison now wished to surrender and would so do at 1400 hours. Spry saw this as another attempt at delay and replied that 'if they wished to quit they could march out with their hands up, without arms and flying white flags in the normal manner.' At 1200 hours the Canadian artillery began to fire, but Lieutenant-Colonel P.C. Klaehn, CO of the Camerons, sought permission to enter Calais and arrange the surrender.[65] While Klaehn was avoiding fire from his own artillery, the Canscots renewed their attack, seizing the bastion. This aggressive move prompted the surrender of Fort Risban and an agreement to hand over the rest of the port defences once a Canadian officer of high enough rank to satisfy German military etiquette was available.[66]

While the final stages of the seizure of Calais were being played out, 9th Brigade began a classic set-piece attack on Cap Gris Nez. The four cross-Channel gun batteries were housed in large concrete casements, which survive to this day. Each was protected by minefields, barbwire, anti-tank ditches, and pillboxes sited for all-around defence. The Floringzelle battery was able to fire inland, and its 280 mm shells – known to the Canadians as 'freight trains' – had repeatedly tried to hit

Canadian targets. Brigadier Todd's artillery resources included the cross-Channel guns at Dover known as 'Winnie' and 'Pooh,' whose crews were anxious to have one last go at the enemy. With their own air OP overhead, the British guns engaged and damaged the Floringzelle battery, to the great satisfaction of the Canadians, who had feared heavy losses from its guns. The ground attack began after a heavy bomber raid. The North Novas and Highland Light Infantry had little trouble closing with an enemy that had lost all desire to continue a hopeless battle.[67]

Siege warfare along the Channel coast resulted in the capture of three important ports and the surrender of almost 30,000 German soldiers. The Canadian Army had employed overwhelming force at Le Havre; in contrast, the attacks on Boulogne and Calais were carried out by elements of just two infantry brigades assisted by a limited number of armoured squadrons. The soldiers who fought their way into Boulogne and Calais were initially enthusiastic about the air support arrangements and the artillery fire plans, but as the battle wore on it became evident that very little damage had been done to the enemy's defences. The Canadian battlegroups were therefore compelled to improvise means of overcoming the enemy with their own resources, and they could not do this without an intimate knowledge of the ground over which the action would be fought. Maps and air photographs helped, but in the end, they relied on battalion scout platoons to explore the complex terrain. Company commanders quickly learned that Wasp and especially Crocodile flamethrowers were the most effective means of forcing the enemy to abandon fortified positions. The infantry learned that if they could protect the flame-throwers while guiding them into position, a few bursts were usually enough to inspire an enemy surrender. Flame proved to be the ultimate psychological weapon in siege warfare.

The Canadians thought they had accomplished miracles with the limited forces and supplies at their disposal. Montgomery and his acolytes saw it differently. Major-General Hubert Essame put the British view most bluntly in his book *The Battle for Germany*. Echoing Montgomery's complaint that the Canadian Army was 'badly handled and very slow,'[68] he wrote:

That the operations of First Canadian Army during September were slower than they need have been is an unavoidable conclusion. Le Havre did not fall to 1 British Corps until 12 September; Boulogne held out till the 22nd; the Calais area was not cleared until the end of the month; Dunkirk remained in enemy hands; on 1 October the Germans still held a lengthy stretch of the south bank of the Scheldt, the northern suburbs of Antwerp, Walcheren Island and the approaches to the South Beveland peninsula.[69]

All of this was in contrast to the rapid progress of the British army during September.

The British official history is, of course, more cautious, and Major L.F. Ellis is far more aware of logistical and administrative considerations. Yet even he suggests that Crerar did not 'seem to have recognized any great need for haste'[70] in dealing with the Channel ports. Ellis is also critical of the length of time it took to bring 1st British Corps to the Antwerp area to relieve 2nd Army forces needed for the thrust to the Rhine. Two Canadian authors picked up on these themes and concluded that Canadian Army activities were so deficient that had Crerar been a British army commander he would have been sacked.[71] Montgomery's most recent biographer goes one step further, contending that Montgomery dismissed Crerar in September of 1944 and that Crerar's ill health was just a convenient story.[72]

In his official history of the Canadian Army, *The Victory Campaign*, Stacey is critical of Canadian operations in Normandy but avoids directly censuring how the pursuit was conducted; he also avoids any favourable comment. Crerar was moved to suggest to Stacey that he 'wondered whether the official historian had brought out sufficiently ... the difficulties of the coastal terrain, from a tactical and administrative point of view. It seemed to those of us in First Canadian Army that we always had ten more rivers to cross and many, many canals.'[73] Stacey did not disagree, but he was reluctant to criticize Montgomery's decisions and left readers to draw their own conclusions about the achievements of the Canadians at Boulogne and Calais. A reassessment is long overdue. First Canadian Army had faltered badly during the pursuit to the Seine and the Scheldt, but at the Channel ports, Simonds, Spry, and their staffs planned and the soldiers of 3rd Division carried out highly successful operations.

The Forêt de la Londe

Rouen Cathedral among the ruins

Bombing Mont Lambert, 17 September 44

Mont Lambert from the 9th Brigade startline, 17 September 1944

Boulogne

Calais Harbour, 26 September 1944

The Belfry, Hôtel de Ville, Calais, 1 October 1944

Cap Gris Nez, 12 September 44

A 280 mm Cross-Channel Gun, Cap Gris Nez

The Leopold Canal, 6 October 1944

Wasp flame throwers rehearse their role at the Leopold

Esso smoke generators at Terneuzen

Biervliet viewed across a polder, 1946

Carriers in flooded landscape, Breskens Pocket, 28 October 1944

The town of Breskens and Fort Frederik Hendrik, 10 September 1944

Fort Frederik Hendrik, 18 October 1944

Woensdrecht with the railway and road to South Beveland and Walcheren

Funeral service for men of the Black Watch killed in action, 13 October 1944

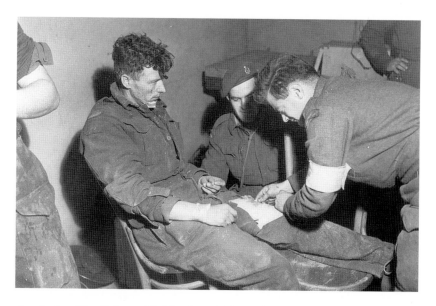

A private of the Calgary Highlanders, 1 November 1944

Field artillery tractor which skidded off the flooded road, South Beveland, October 1944

Sherman tanks of the Fort Garry Horse, South Beveland, October 1944. The lead tank is a Firefly with a 17 pounder gun.

Sherman tanks of the Fort Garry Horse, Beveland Canal, Netherlands, 30 October 1944.

The Walcheren Causeway, 4 November 1944

The Walcheren Causeway, looking east, 1946

Sherman tanks destroyed during the advance to Bergen Op Zoom

Medium artillery in action at Kapelsche Veer, January 1945

Westkapelle, 28 October 1944

3

The Breskens
Pocket

When Lieutenant-General Guy Simonds was told that his corps would be responsible for freeing the approaches to Antwerp as well as securing the Channel ports, he seemed to regard the limitations on the resources available to him as a challenge to his ingenuity rather than a cause for concern. Once the siege of Boulogne was underway, he turned his attention to the Scheldt and the 'Appreciation' drafted by the Plans Section of First Canadian Army. This document, prepared under the supervision of Brigadier Churchill Mann and Lieutenant-Colonel George Pangman, focused on Operation Infatuate, described as the 'capture of the islands of Zuid Beveland and Walcheren.' The army planners did not address the corps-level task of reaching South Beveland from Antwerp and freeing the Breskens Pocket; their task was to develop a method of employing naval and air resources as well as 17th U.S. Airborne Division, which had been promised. The appreciation also noted the availability of a complete regiment of Landing Vehicles Tracked (LVTs), known as Buffaloes, from 79th Armoured Division.[1]

Five possible courses of action were outlined, including two that could be executed if airborne troops were not available. None of the proposals involved an amphibious assault on Walcheren. Simonds was not impressed. He noted that the job of clearing the area between the Leopold Canal and the Scheldt 'may be a major operation,' while the land approach via Beveland 'may well turn out to be an approach down a single stretch of road some five miles in length bordered by impassable ground on either side.' He concluded that an 'assault across water cannot be ruled out if Walcheren Island must be taken,' and he urged an immediate decision to marry up and train the required military and naval forces. While this was taking place, 'bombing operations should be undertaken to break the dykes and completely flood all parts of the island below high water level.' Once this was accomplished the coastal batteries and radar stations should be 'systematically attacked by heavy air bombardment day and night.' When the morale of the garrison was 'sufficiently deteriorated airborne, followed by waterborne troops should be landed.' Given the limited number of forces available, Simonds believed that a brigade from 3rd Division should immediately be earmarked to train for 'seaborne operations against Walcheren.'[2]

The proposal to 'sink' Walcheren by breaching the dykes was already being considered at army headquarters, where Crerar had begun discussions with Montgomery's Chief of Staff, Major-General Francis de Guingand, and the Allied Naval Commander-in-Chief, Admiral Bertram Ramsay. Ramsay backed the plan to bomb the dykes as it would improve the prospects of an amphibious attack by creating a breach through which landing craft might pass. But he insisted that the Royal Navy take over responsibility for any waterborne assault on Walcheren, and he nominated Captain A.F. Pugsley to oversee the arrangements. He also noted that HMS *Warspite* and the monitors *Erebus* and *Roberts* would be available to support a landing. General de Guingand agreed to 'obtain the views of higher authority' on the political dimension of flooding a Dutch island.[3]

Two days later Crerar, Pugsley, and a representative from Bomber Command met to consider the plan. They agreed that the commandos of 4th Special Service Brigade would be used in a seaborne landing; this would allow Simonds to deploy all of 3rd Division to the Breskens Pocket.[4] Despite a report from Crerar's chief engineer, Brigadier G. Walsh, who doubted the dykes could be breached by bombing and who insisted that even if the whole island was flooded the channels created would be too shallow for landing craft, Ramsay and Simonds continued to advocate breaching the dykes. On 1 October 1944 General Eisenhower, apparently without consulting the Dutch government, approved the project.[5] The next day Crerar, who had been coping with a severe stomach ailment, entered hospital, handing over command of the army to Guy Simonds. The senior divisional commander, Major-General Charles Foulkes, became Acting Corps Commander, though in practice Simonds continued to exercise command at the operational level.

While these high-level discussions were underway, Simonds prepared 'preliminary instructions' for Operation Switchback, the plan to clear the area north of the Leopold Canal. On 30 September the Acting Corps Commander issued a draft outline plan based closely on these instructions. Foulkes sketched a two-phase operation: establish a bridgehead, then clear 'the Knocke-sur-Mer fortress area.' The 3rd Division was to break into the pocket in two places 'across the Leopold Canal and across the Savojaards Plaat.' Both attacks were to begin on 6 October, which was less than a week away.[6] This deadline meant that 9th Brigade, which had been selected to carry out the amphibious assault on the northeast corner of the pocket, would have little time for training.

The outline plan did not include paragraphs on 'the enemy,' presumably because intelligence officers were still analysing the available information. Little is known about the use of ULTRA by First Canadian Army, but Crerar and (after 26 September) Simonds were among the select group of senior officers on the list of ULTRA recipients.[7] In addition, Church Mann, the Chief of Staff, Lieutenant-Colonel Peter Wright, the senior intelligence officer, and five other senior staff officers had access to this special intelligence, although they did not have detailed knowledge of its origins.[8] None of the other officers at army or corps were aware that a small group of specialists known as the Signals Liaison Unit, or SLU, were providing the army commander with decrypts of the enemy's most secret communications,[9] including Hitler's orders to defend Walcheren Island and the Breskens area to the last man.[10]

ULTRA provided little assistance when it came to questions of enemy strengths and dispositions, so much depended on photo reconnaissance and patrol reports. Evidence from these sources presented a grim picture. The Algonquin Regiment's attempts to seize control of the Isabella Polder, the only land bridge into the Breskens Pocket, had resulted in heavy casualties and deep frustration; a 'dismal succession of patrol after patrol' confirmed the obvious – the enemy held the area in strength with 'mortar targets registered to within feet' and defensive belts of machine gun fire 'that would sweep the dyke tops at about eight inches height.' It was also evident that 1037th Grenadier Regiment of the Germans' 64th Infantry Division, responsible for the defence of the eastern end of the pocket, was a well-trained force of high-quality troops.[11]

While the Algonquins tried to maintain pressure, the Argylls and the Lincoln and Welland Regiment were adding to the intelligence picture by sending patrols across the Leopold Canal. Typically, a corporal and three riflemen would go, with a section providing covering fire at the crossing point. Mortar and artillery support was available if necessary, but the idea was to observe and to grab a prisoner without attracting attention. The enemy proved elusive, and on 27 September the Lincs were ordered to make an attempt in company strength near the village of St-Laurent. Operation Styx was planned and rehearsed well in advance, and this time fifteen prisoners were captured. The prisoners, from 1038th Grenadiers, confirmed earlier reports that they had orders 'to fight to the last man.'[12]

Canadian intelligence reported that 64th Division had been created in the summer of 1944 from cadres of veteran officers and men on leave from the Eastern Front. The rest of the division was filled with whoever was available, and it was thought that their quality varied widely. The 64th Division had lost much of its artillery at Boulogne and had suffered casualties during the fighting south of the Leopold Canal, and this led intelligence officers to underrate its strength and firepower and to discount the large numbers of naval and air force personnel who were also serving in the pocket.[13] Senior German officers were confident that the division would be able to mount an obstinate defence of Fortress South Scheldt. The 64th was led by General Knut Eberding, an experienced infantry officer. His regimental commanders were regarded as dedicated and effective leaders. General Gustav von Zangen described the 64th as the only division in his army 'still maintaining its full fighting power both as to strength and equipment.'[14]

Major-General Dan Spry and his staff had little time to prepare for Operation Switchback, and 7th Brigade, which had been selected for the assault crossing of the Leopold, did not issue an operational order until 5 October, less than twenty-four hours before the attack was to begin. Brigadier Jock Spragge held a final coordinating conference at 1800 hours that day to confirm timings and arrangements. The plan required the Regina Rifles and Canadian Scottish Regiment to 'assault and seize crossing over Leopold Canal in the area Moershoofd to the Aardenburg.' The brigade was then to enlarge the bridgehead and then, in Phase III, 'mop up in west direction' before advancing to Oostburg and Schoondijke. Divisional engineers were to construct two kapok foot bridges and two road bridges as soon as 'the crossing is secured.'[15] The divisional plan called for 8th Brigade to enter the bridgehead after Phase III was complete to clear the area as far west as the Sluis Canal; meanwhile, 9th Brigade was to advance from its northeast bridgehead to Hoofdplaat and Breskens.[16]

Did the responsible commanders – Simonds, Foulkes, Spry, and Spragge – actually believe that a single infantry brigade without armoured support could cross a canal, overcome large enemy forces in well-prepared defences, advance beyond flooded and saturated ground along a single elevated road, and then clear and defend a 10 kilometre bridgehead? Surely not. The brigade plan provided battalion command-ers with an outline of how they were to proceed in the unlikely event of an enemy collapse or staged withdrawal. The crossing itself – never mind the establishment of the shallow Phase II bridgehead – presented a major challenge that would require elaborate and continuous support.

The battles for Boulogne and Calais had provided convincing evi-dence that the most effective way to overcome an entrenched enemy was with flame-throwers. It was apparent that soldiers who would resist strongly when attacked by infantry, armour, artillery, or air power were quite unable to function when threatened with flame. Since the Germans had disposed their forward troops in slit trenches and pill-boxes along the canal's northern bank, the possibility of using Wasp flame-throwers to support the assault was examined.[17] Experiments proved that if the carrier was placed on the upward slope of the dyke, bursts of flame could carry the thirty metres across the canal, providing several minutes of intense fire and smoke. If all went well, the assault boats, manned by men from the North Shore Regiment, would make it to the north bank, allowing the infantry to overcome the first line of defence before the enemy had recovered.[18] From then on much would depend on the artillery fire plan.

Senior artillery officers were aware of the problems that had been encountered in employing predicted fire at Boulogne, but they believed that great progress had been made. During the siege of Calais, corps artillery headquarters had authorized experiments with a new method of determining wind speed and direction; this involved observing hy-drogen balloons with a radar set able to record data at heights up to 40,000 feet.[19] It quickly became apparent that previous methods of gathering this information – which was so vital to the accuracy of medium and heavy artillery – had failed to provide accurate readings in rapidly changing weather conditions of the kind often experienced in coastal regions. Errors as great as 40 miles per hour and 60 degrees were noted when the existing 'meteors' (meteorological reports) from RAF weather flights were compared to the radar balloon method.[20] For Switchback, two ground stations were established – one near Bruges, the other at St-Nicholas – and observations taken at two-hour intervals. This information was transmitted over land lines to the Met Officers at all levels and should have but didn't play a significant role in increasing accuracy.[21]

Other efforts to increase the effectiveness of the artillery were actively pursued. During the campaign in North Africa, British survey regiments had constructed tall wooden towers to provide observation over the desert. The flat terrain in Belgium and Holland invited imitation, and the engineers constructed five such towers for 2nd Survey Regiment RCA. Each tower was twenty metres tall – the height of the poplar trees used to provide camouflage. All were located along a seven-kilometre east–west baseline just south of the canal. They were originally built to assist in 'flash spotting' – that is, to help visibly locate enemy guns at ranges of up to 3000 metres. However, the enemy's increasing reliance on flashless propellant led the survey regiment to use the towers for correction of fire through airburst ranging and direct observation of enemy movements, especially during Phase I of the battle.[22]

The artillery allocated to Switchback included medium and heavy regiments from 2nd Canadian and 9th British Army Group Royal Artillery. Brigadier Stanley Todd developed the fire plans and exercised control of the guns supporting the assault crossing of the canal.[23] Todd employed the system of 'grouped stonks and concs on call' (linear and pinpoint concentrations) that had first been tried at Boulogne. The task table for 7th Brigade included forty-six likely targets: roads, hamlets, woods, and treelines, each coded with the name of a river. Forward Observation Officers (FOOs), one per company, could call down fire on any of these targets with a single word, as could company, platoon, and section commanders. The predetermined targets could also be used as reference points for observed fire during enemy counter-attacks. Todd retained control of counter-battery and defensive fire tasks, but otherwise the use of the guns rested with the infantry, who were 'given neutralizing fire when they want it for as long as they want it.'[24]

During the Normandy campaign, enemy mortars rather than artillery were responsible for the majority of Allied casualties, and much effort had been expended on creating divisional counter-mortar sections. Forward troops were encouraged to send in 'moreps' (mortar reports) as well as 'shellreps,' and 4th Division was able to supply a good deal of information, allowing the 3rd Division's Counter Mortar

Officer to gain a head start. The most dramatic innovation was the deployment of two sections of No. 1 Canadian Radar Battery, each of which had a GL III set capable of displaying the arc of an individual mortar bomb at ranges of up to 3000 metres.[25] The Radar Battery was able to provide locations for twenty-nine mortar positions, about one-third of the enemy total during Switchback.[26]

One other vitally important support system, tactical air power, was beyond the control of 3rd Division, but Air Vice-Marshal L.O. Brown, the Air Officer Commanding 84 Group, was determined to improve coordination between his formation and the ground troops. Brown commanded a multinational force including British, Dutch, Polish, Norwegian, French, Belgian, and New Zealand squadrons.[27] As the RAF Group Commander assigned to work with First Canadian Army, Brown met daily with the Army Commander and his Chief of Staff to plan air operations. Though the two organizations worked closely, it was not always possible for 84 Group to meet army requests, as it was often employed on priority tasks, these determined by Air Marshal Sir Arthur Coningham at 2nd Tactical Air Force Headquarters.

According to Coningham, Brown and his staff had 'some kind of inferiority complex ... in relations with First Canadian Army' and needed to be closely controlled. Coningham accomplished this by 'overruling group operational directives and working through military channels from 21 Army Group' until he could replace Brown, whom he viewed as 'subservient to the army.'[28] Coningham was determined to preserve the operational autonomy of his tactical air force and to employ its resources in a parallel campaign which was in no way subordinate to that of the ground forces. Brown, in contrast, believed his responsibility was to the Canadian Army, and he was prepared to work closely with Simonds during Switchback, even if it cost him his job.[29]

The air plan for Switchback included attacks by medium bombers on known enemy positions and towns that were judged to be part of the enemy's defences. Besides the coastal batteries at Flushing, Knocke, and Cadzand, the towns of Izjendijke, Biervliet, Oostburg, Schoondijke, and Breskens were targeted during the first week of Switchback in four major attacks. Spitfire and Typhoon squadrons supplemented the mediums, especially at Flushing and Fort Fredrick Hendrik, but they were also employed against towns and area targets selected the previous day. Rocket Typhoon squadrons were on call both for prearranged missions and for emergency close support by forward control methods, including the 'cab rank' system, which allowed for direct contact between the ground forces and aircraft in position over the battlefield.[30] If the weather cooperated, 84 Group would be ready to do its part.

Considering the limited time available, the preparations for Switchback were an impressive example of the flexibility and professionalism of the Canadian Army. There was, however, one serious problem left to deal with. Simonds's original concept of operations, as well as the outline plan issued by the Acting Corps Commander, called for both the attack across the Leopold and the amphibious assault to begin on 6 October. The point was to force the enemy to fight on two fronts. The delay in completing operations at Calais and Cap Gris Nez meant that 9th Brigade did not begin training with 5th Assault Regiment until 5 October. It quickly became evident that the men and equipment for the amphibious assault could not be in position before the evening of 7 October. H-Hour for 9th Brigade was therefore set for 0130 hours on 8 October.[31]

It was now up to Simonds and Foulkes to decide whether to postpone 7th Brigade's attack or allow it to begin as scheduled. In the absence of written records, it is not possible to determine their reasons for committing 7th Brigade to an action that would leave the assaulting battalions on their own for at least forty-eight hours, but there is no doubt that Simonds understood the consequences. The enemy had placed all three of its Grenadier Regiments along the canal, with local reserves positioned to counter-attack. The area selected for the crossing – a long, narrow triangle bounded by flooded or saturated polders – was a carefully prepared killing ground with pre-registered mortar and artillery targets and well-camouflaged machine gun posts with interlocking arcs of fire. From the perspective of the senior commanders, the attack – however costly – would focus the enemy's attention on the canal and greatly improve the prospects for 9th Brigade's risky amphibious landing. Once the decision to go ahead was made, the best the Acting Corps Commander could do was supplement existing plans for elaborate feint attacks using sound effects with a real diversionary effort mounted by the long-suffering Algonquin Regiment. The Algonquins' three-company offensive at the Isabella Polder was intended to focus the enemy's attention to the east in the hours before 7th Brigade's attack. The battalion suffered twenty-eight casualties – about 10 per cent of its rifle companies' strength – in this 'asinine-appearing operation.' After the purpose of its efforts became known, 'many harsh words were recalled.'[32]

Lieutenant-Colonel F.W. Matheson, who had commanded the Regina Rifles in action since D-Day, learned the details of the role his battalion was to play on the morning of 5 October. The Reginas were to attack at the western, broader end of the triangle with two companies up. Once a bridgehead was secure, the assault troops were to push forward to Eede before the reserve companies passed through to seize Middelburg. According to Spragge, the Canscots, crossing at the narrow end of the triangle, would by then be in position to capture Aardenburg, having somehow advanced six kilometres along the narrow road from Moershoofd.

Matheson knew just how unrealistic this scenario was, but there was nothing he could do about it. His decision to employ the detachment from the Royal Montreal Regiment as one of the assault companies became controversial after the battle,[33] but at the time the task of crossing the canal with the aid of flame-throwers did not seem more risky than the ones assigned to the follow-up companies. The RMR company had done well at Calais and was at full strength and eager for action. Captain R. Schwob, the second-in-command, who had been left out of battle at Calais, was especially keen to lead the company. He, like everyone else, thought that a five-minute blast of flame would ensure the success of the initial attack.[34]

As the assault companies married up with boat crews from the North Shore Regiment, the Wasp flame-throwers, grouped in sets of three, were brought onto the slope of the dyke. At 0525 hours, night was turned into 'a semblance of catastrophic day' as the streams of flaming fuel broke up into the smaller ignited blobs that the chemical warfare officers called 'Golden Rain.'[35] The bursts of flame ignited the grass and provided temporary suppression of some positions, but several machine guns on each flank were left untouched. 'Concentrated MG fire' stopped the right-hand company cold by making it impossible for boats to be launched.[36] The large concrete pillbox to the left of the RMR

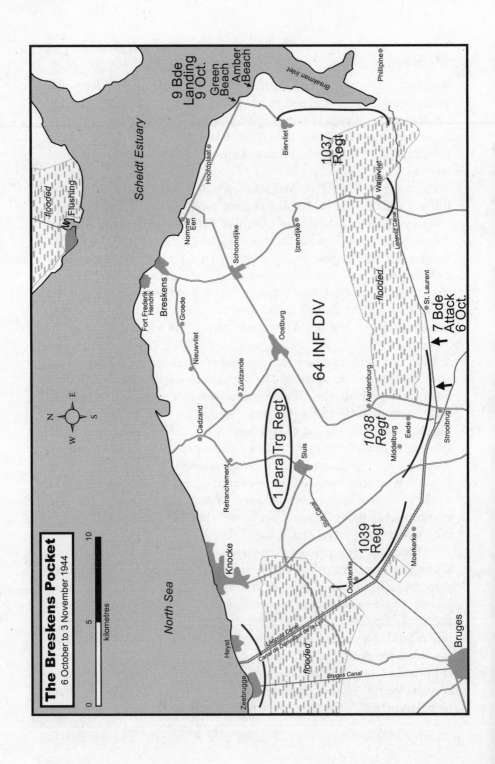

The Breskens Pocket
6 October to 3 November 1944

kilometres
0   5   10

company as well as other machine gun positions survived the flames, and after illuminating the canal with flares, the enemy caught one of the RMR platoons in a cone of fire. Schwob, who had crossed with the other platoon, organized the survivors, and when the rest of the company joined him he sent one platoon north to the first row of trees with orders to advance to the highway.[37] The remaining platoon began to work its way west along the canal. Company headquarters was established in trenches dug into the canal bank. The Germans had dug lines of slit trenches at right angles to the canal to contain the expansion of any bridgehead, and they occupied one such line in strength, blocking the RMR advance.[38]

Matheson ordered one of his reserve companies across into the bridgehead, but before they could go they had to deal with the large pillbox that anchored the enemy defences. Mortar fire was ineffective, and artillery could not be used so close to friendly troops, so PIAT teams fired bombs at the gun slits until the enemy abandoned the position. By 0855 hours the Reginas had secured the pillbox and begun to build up a second small bridgehead under heavy mortar fire.[39] The other reserve company crossed shortly after 1000 hours, strengthening the original bridgehead, which soon incorporated the thirteen survivors of the RMRs. Schwob, who led a charmed life that day, was given command of a Regina company that had lost all its officers.[40] The battalion now faced an impossible situation: any attempt to expand the bridgehead would collapse under the weight of enemy mortar and machine gun fire and force the men to withdraw to their positions along the canal. Fighter-bombers and artillery struck at more distant targets, but the 'enemy was too close for any work by planes.'[41] Matheson, confronted with the possibility that his battalion would be destroyed, sought support from the Canscots, but they too were heavily engaged.

The first moments of what the Canadian Scottish War Diary described as 'one of the bloodiest and dirtiest battles' in the battalion's history began with marked success. The Wasps, including eleven supplied by 4th Armoured Division, were manoeuvred into position, and at 0525 hours the flames shot across the canal, lighting the sky in a scarlet glow and suppressing the canal defences. Both assault companies were across in twelve minutes. They immediately began to expand the bridgehead and secure control of Moershoofd. A kapok footbridge,

assembled by divisional engineers in Middeldorp, was carried forward
and quickly installed. The first infantry to use it were four Germans
desperate to surrender, but the reserve company assigned to the capture of Oosthoek was across and moving west by 0600 hours. The
fighting 'began in earnest' shortly thereafter. The enemy had constructed
a strongpoint at Moershoofd and positioned its main force along the
Graaf Jans dyke, which carried a narrow east–west track west to the
Breskens highway. The Canscots found that their every move brought
down mortar and artillery fire; this forced the lead platoons approaching Oosthoek to take cover in a group of houses. The battle for
Moershoofd was only won after the Canadians 'retired 500 yards to
allow the 25 pounders to have a go.' The village was 'Caenned' by
repeated artillery concentrations, so that when the Canadians secured it
that evening there was little left standing.[42]

By dawn on 7 October two Canscot companies were holding on to a
group of houses along the Graaf Jan dyke, with Germans all around
them. The headquarters section of Charlie Company, cut off and surrounded, was forced to surrender.[43] Canscot casualties in the first thirty-
six hours of Switchback – fourteen killed, forty-eight wounded, fifteen
missing, and nine taken prisoner – were a heavy price for a small,
isolated bridgehead.[44] Spragge reinforced the Canscots with men from
a squadron of 7th Recce Regiment[45] and then committed his entire
reserve battalion, the Royal Winnipeg Rifles, to the task of closing the
gap between the bridgeheads and finding an alternative route to the
main road.

The Royal Winnipeg Rifles had two companies in position across the
canal before first light on 7 October. They advanced about 600 metres
before encountering a 'strong enemy force.' One company began a
frontal attack while the other, 'under cover of a dyke ... reached a point
less than a hundred yards from the enemy.' Using fire from 'every
available weapon including PIATs and 2-inch mortars fired at a low
angle,' the Winnipegs overwhelmed the enemy, capturing sixty-four
prisoners, an entire company of 1038 Regiment's 2nd Battalion. This
very successful action also relieved a Canscot platoon that had been cut
off by enemy counter-attacks.[46] Brigade, on being informed of this first
sign of progress, asked whether this meant the gap had been closed.
The answer it received: there was still a long way to go.[47]

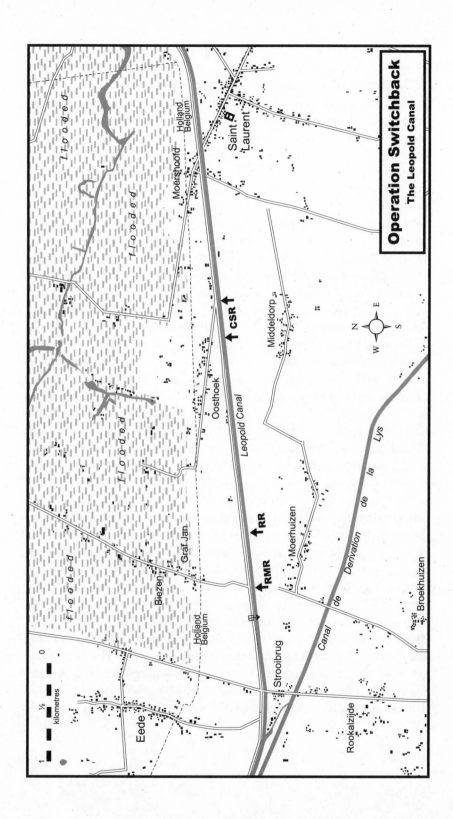

Operation Switchback
The Leopold Canal

The divisional commander, who had spent 6 October at brigade headquarters, was a very worried man. The 9th Brigade's attack was to be postponed for twenty-four hours, which meant that 7th Brigade would be on its own for a third day. It was by no means certain that the Reginas could hold out. Spry was anxious to make greater use of the available air resources before the weather deteriorated. He urged battalion commanders to 'request all possible air targets. The planes are in the air and we can take on targets within ten minutes of receipt of request.' The men on the ground were only too happy to see aircraft overhead, but they were trying to survive in shallow slit trenches within yards of the enemy, and neither close support from Typhoons nor most of the prearranged artillery targets were of much immediate help. Brigade headquarters was able to request Typhoon strikes on two pillboxes '500 metres away,'[48] but otherwise, 84 Group had to search out targets of opportunity.[49] On 7 October it flew 224 sorties.

The first phase of Switchback had not gone according to plan. A frontal attack on an enemy known to be holding the most obvious crossing point in strength could only have succeeded if the combination of flame and artillery had demoralized the defenders. Instead, the soldiers of 1038th Grenadier Regiment, who greatly outnumbered the Canadians in the bridgehead, fought with skill and determination.[50] Eberding was so confident that his division could deal with the attacks that he reported that the eastern bridgehead had been sealed off and the western one 'eliminated.'[51] True, the Reginas were pinned down and unable to advance, but eliminating them would be another matter. Shortly after dark the enemy formed up for a major attack. This was the moment the artillery had been longing for: the enemy were conveniently grouped around 'Skeena,' one of the prearranged medium regiment targets, and the artillery struck hard at them. With this kind of support the Reginas were able to report that 'everything was under control.'[52]

This was the first of a series of counter-attacks carried out by 1038th Regiment reinforced by Eberding's divisional reserve, 1st Para Training Regiment and a battlegroup from 1037th Regiment. The immediate result of this commitment of the best available reserves was a stalemate.[53] The more serious consequences only became apparent when an armada of Buffaloes emerged from the waters of the Scheldt in the early morning of 9 October to open the back door of the Breskens Pocket. This assault, described by the German High Command as 'a decision-seeking attack on the Breskens bridgehead,' caught Eberding without any reserves other than two companies ferried over from Walcheren.[54]

Eberding decided to continue efforts to overwhelm 7th Brigade before dealing with the new threat. Canadian artillery and mortars broke up strong counter-attacks on 9 and 10 October and provided support for the Royal Winnipeg Rifles, who reached the Reginas to close the gap. By the evening of 10 October the Canscots and Winnipegs were ready to take the offensive; however, they failed in their attempts to gain control of Graaf Jan and Biezen. When Graaf Jan was captured on 12 October the enemy launched 'a determined counter-attack which resulted in a house to house battle of great ferocity.'[55]

Conditions in the Leopold bridgehead convinced senior commanders that there was no point in committing 8th Brigade to this sector, and the North Shores, who had remained under Spragge's command, rejoined their brigade. This left Spragge without reserves, so he withdrew a Canscot company and employed it to extend the Reginas' left flank, where the enemy had been infiltrating men across the canal. The Canscots got into position without taking any casualties, but machine guns, firing on fixed lines, blocked any advance beyond the water side of the canal dyke. After grenade warfare erupted, a truce was arranged – this time to evacuate the wounded.[56]

The next day the Canscots and Reginas risked an artillery shoot immediately in front of this position. 'After making a barrage of our own with grenades,' they cleared the enemy to a depth of one hundred yards, taking more than one hundred prisoners. This supreme effort allowed the engineers to construct a bridge at the main road, but no further advance was possible.[57] Combined, the enemy's 1038th Regiment and Para Training Regiment had yielded close to four hundred prisoners, many of them wounded. They had also suffered several hundred fatal casualties.[58] Counter-attacks were no longer a realistic option, but in polder country, static defences based on the 'reverse slopes' of dykes were an effective method of containment. Fortunately, the Canadian commanders understood this, and 7th Brigade was ordered to maintain pressure, not mount new offensives.

The battles for the Leopold Canal made extraordinary demands on the officers and men of 7th Brigade. Lieutenant Robert Gray, returning to the Reginas after hospitalization for pneumonia, took over Charlie Company on the third day. His fifty or so men had a precarious grip on an isolated strip of canal bank. Everyone was 'terribly tired – the fighting had been so intense no one dared relax.' Beyond the canal bank, slit trenches immediately filled with water, and it rained almost every bleak, chilly day. The enemy attacked with 'all the fire power they could muster.' Survival, Gray recalled, depended on artillery SOS tasks 'and the battalion mortars.[59]

The Canadian Scottish war diarist, who was determined to remain optimistic amid the worst of conditions, admitted that

> living conditions at the front are not cosy. Water and soil make mud. Mud sticks to everything. Boots weigh pounds more. Rifles and brens operate sluggishly. Ammunition becomes wet. Slit trenches allow one to get below ground level but also contain several inches of thick water. Matches and cigarettes are wet and unusable. So almost everyone looks for a house. A good house is one which only has a few holes in the walls and not more than half the roof dismantled. They are hard to find after our artillery has lifted its range and after enemy artillery has found its range. Food is sometimes sent forward as raw 'Compo.' Other times it is cooked at 'F' Echelon and sent up in 'hay-boxes.' Carriers are the only vehicles which can use the muddy paths called roads. So the soldier shakes his head, cleans his rifle, swears a good deal and dreams of what he'll do when he gets leave (IF).[60]

The brigade's ordeal can be measured by casualties it took – 533 men in the first seven days of combat. The Regina Rifles and their Royal Montreal Regiment comrades suffered more than half the total losses, including fifty-one men killed. The other battalions each lost more than one hundred men, including fifty fatalities.[61] About one hundred additional casualties were treated at regimental aid posts and at the divisional neuropsychiatric unit for battle exhaustion.[62] Front line soldiers were not the only ones to suffer from combat stress. Lieutenant-Colonel J.M. Meldram, who had commanded the Royal Winnipeg Rifles from D-Day to the Scheldt, was evacuated for medical reasons that were largely the result of stress.[63] Lieutenant-Colonel Matheson's case was more complicated: he was removed from command of the Reginas after openly criticizing senior commanders for sacrificing his battalion. Major Gordon Brown, who talked with Matheson in England in mid-October, thought that however justified Matheson's criticisms were, he was too emotionally distraught to continue in command.[64]

At the army, corps, and division levels the assault across the Leopold Canal was viewed as a great success. Simonds, Foulkes, and Spry had all expected the enemy to fight a staged withdrawal. Instead, Eberding employed his reserves in an effort to wipe out the bridgehead, and this allowed 9th Brigade to carry out a complex and dangerous amphibious attack and to establish a large beachhead before the enemy could react. Combat officers were also surprised by the enemy's determination to overwhelm 7th Brigade. Major A.L. Gollnich, the second-in-command of the Reginas, spoke for many when he told a Historical Officer: 'If the enemy had chosen to adopt a purely defensive role and had withdrawn more slowly all the way to the sea, our casualties would ultimately have been much heavier. Instead he elected to launch many expensive counterattacks, which harsh though our troops found them, eventually weakened him seriously.'

Gollnich believed that the enemy had 'unquestionably spent his best troops in costly counterattacks designed to crush the small but stubborn bridgehead.' This left the defence of the rest of the pocket to 'men of a very inferior sort, many of them odds and sods of poor physical condition.'[65]

The delayed amphibious assault on the northeast coast of the pocket caught the enemy by surprise. Eberding would later tell interrogators he had considered the possibility of an attack across the Braakman Inlet but assumed it could only be on a small scale. He believed that 627th Landeschutzen Battalion – a force of some three hundred combat troops with headquarters at Biervliet – would be able to deal with any such attacks. He could not conceive of a large amphibious landing on the pocket's north coast because he did not know that the Canadians had available a regiment of amphibious vehicles.[66]

The 5th Assault Regiment Royal Engineers had previously operated the ubiquitous Armoured Vehicle Royal Engineers or AVREs, but in

September the arrival of more than one hundred Buffalo LVTs – sur-
plus to American needs in the Pacific – led Major-General Percy Hobart,
the General Officer Commanding 79th Armoured Division, to convert
one of his regiments to LVTs. There was no immediate assignment, so
there was ample time for training.[67] The Canadians, committed to the
coastal flank, were the most likely users, and Hobart informed Crerar
that the regiment would be available by late September. Initially there
was some confusion as to how they could best be employed, but once
the Polish Armoured Division captured the port of Terneuzen, the
regiment was ordered to prepare for Operation Infatuate, the attack on
Walcheren.[68] Simonds decided to use them first in Operation Switchback.

Buffaloes were equipped with 'grousers' attached to their tracks.
These propelled them in water and enabled them to churn through
mud flats and climb slopes up to thirty degrees. The LVT4 was equipped
with a rear ramp and could carry a universal carrier, a 6-pounder anti-
tank gun, or other light equipment as well as a section of men. The
LVT2, which lacked an exit ramp, carried thirty men standing close
together. Each five-man crew included a gunner manning a 30-calibre
Browning machine gun – a useful weapon for suppressing enemy
opposition.[69]

Air photo reconnaissance and reports from Dutch civilians indicated
that if security could be maintained there would be no significant
enemy resistance at either Amber or Green beaches, the selected landing areas. Unfortunately, both sites were in range of the German coastal
batteries at Flushing as well as the gun positions near Breskens, so
much would depend on whether the Chemical Warfare Officers would
be able to provide an effective smoke screen. Smoke could not be
allowed to interfere with the vision of LVT crews, so a screen was to be
created using smoke floats laid out on an 8000-metre dog-leg two
kilometres off shore. Success depended on a westerly wind, which
would prevent the smoke from drifting back onto the beaches.[70] Another related issue, logistical support for the men in the bridgehead,
was the responsibility of the Royal Canadian Army Service Corps,
which was to establish and stock a Beach Maintenance Area. They were
allotted thirty-eight light amphibious vehicles known as Terrapins,
which were to be loaded 'in priority of landing' with ammunition,
water, rations, rum, blankets, fuel, and flame-throwing fluid.[71]

Fire support for the landings would be controlled by Brigadier J.N. Lane, the CRA of 4th Armoured Division. Besides his own field regiments, Lane could employ one medium regiment, one heavy battery of 150 mm guns, and one Heavy Anti-Aircraft Regiment firing air burst in a ground support role. Field regiment FOOs were attached to each company, with a medium regiment FOO for each battalion. The 'Medium FOO' was especially important, for once the bridgehead expanded to Hoofdplaat, the 25-pounders on the east side of the Braakman would be out of range.[72]

Assault companies were reduced to ninety riflemen carrying just enough ammunition, water, and compo rations for forty-eight hours. The men had a day to practise getting in and out of the Buffaloes quickly – no easy task with a two-metre drop over the side. The LVTs were loaded at Ghent, and the entire flotilla began its journey strung out along a canal lined with cheering civilians, who apparently did not include any enemy sympathizers. The engineers had constructed ramps at Terneuzen as the locks had been destroyed, but even with bulldozers to help winch the Buffaloes up the ramps, progress was too slow, and at midnight on 8 October the operation was postponed for twenty-four hours. It was feared that the enemy might hear about the armada,[73] but there was nothing to do except wait for darkness. Finally, just before midnight, the expedition entered the waters of the Scheldt. Buffaloes were powered by very large aero engines. The noise they made could be heard across the estuary, and the Germans soon began firing their anti-aircraft guns into an empty sky.

Originally the two flotillas were to be guided by Dutch river pilots, but none were available on the day and the naval liaison officer at HQ First Canadian Army, Lieutenant-Commander R.D. Franks, offered to navigate, leading in a small boat. He recorded this description of the crossing:

By 0030 hrs we were lying off the sea ramp in our little motorboat showing two dim red lights astern. Well on time the first LVT waddled down the ramp and splashed into the water. We led slowly out of the canal entrance as more and more took to the water and formed up astern. It was a nearly ideal night, calm and quiet with half a moon behind light cloud, but a bit of haze which restricted visibility to a mile at the most. We were quite invisible from the north shore of the Scheldt, where all was quiet ... Just as we cleared the land, our artillery barrage started up, 'plastering' the far beaches and other targets. The noise effectively blanketed our sounds and was generally most heartening ... There was supposed to be a prepared position on the north-east corner of the island and momentarily I expected enemy fire, but we continued unmolested, with the artillery barrage still thundering away ... Our touch down was planned to be on either side of a groyne which proved to be a good landmark and we were able to identify it and then lie off flicking our lamps to guide the LVTs in. They deployed and thundered in past us, looking, and sounding, most impressive. Landing was successful and I could see, through my binoculars, the infantry disembark on dry land and form up and move off. The artillery barrage had by now, of course, ceased and there was silence except for the roar of the engines and an occasional rifle shot.[74]

The North Nova Scotia Highlanders landed on Green Beach, where they waded through 'thick, clinging, slippery mud,' climbed the dyke, and took their first prisoners, nine sleepy German soldiers who thought that all the noise had nothing to do with them.[75] The North Novas moved quickly to establish the initial beachhead; meanwhile, on their left, the Highland Light Infantry ran into several machine gun posts manned by a more determined enemy. By 0900 hours the reserve companies and the brigade command group were ashore and a bridgehead, encompassing several polders to a depth of 1500 metres, had been secured.[76] At dawn the HLI landing area, Amber Beach, came under artillery fire and the first counter-attack began, mounted by 627th Battalion from Biervliet. The enemy seemed determined to retake the bridgehead, 'dashing along the ditches, bouncing out here and there over the culverts, greatcoats flapping and wearing full equipment,' but such attacks were quickly crushed. The arrival of several Wasp flamethrowers allowed the HLI to secure a vital dyke junction, and when a platoon of Camerons arrived, their medium machine guns devastated the enemy's forming-up place in an orchard, allowing the HLI to capture sixty prisoners, including many wounded. The battalion was then able to consolidate its shallow bridgehead, digging in on the reverse side of the dykes.[77]

Enemy coastal batteries on Walcheren, as well as artillery inside the pocket, began shelling the beachhead at first light. Observation from the south was obscured; a northeast wind was carrying smoke from three large Esso generators across the Braakman towards Ijzendijke. The smoke screen in the river was also soon in place, and the enemy obligingly attempted to shell the smoke points and the boats busy replenishing the floats. The enemy soon abandoned this fruitless enterprise and shifted its fire to Terneuzen until a third smoke screen was installed to protect the harbour.[78]

The reserve battalion, the Stormont, Dundas, and Glengarry Highlanders, landed on Green Beach and by noon was ready to begin its planned advance along the coast to Breskens. The Glens' first objective, the fishing village of Hoofdplaat, contained one of the two fortified 'resistance nests' that the Germans had constructed on the northeast coast of the pocket.[79] Lieutenant-Colonel Roger Rowley planned an attack with three companies up. While the right flank company engaged the fortified area near the harbour and the left flank company fought the enemy to the south, the third company was able to reach the village and capture the resistance nest, taking some fifty prisoners. A group of German marines locked themselves into one of the bunkers and called down artillery fire on Hoofdplaat until a section from the battalion's Pioneer Platoon arrived to blast open the door. The reserve company dealt with yet one more fortified position, using a 6-pounder anti-tank gun to force a surrender. This well-orchestrated, carefully controlled battle cost the Glens fourteen killed and forty-six wounded. As was so often the case, platoon commanders accounted for a disproportionate share of the losses, with three killed and two wounded.[80]

The North Novas' advance to the south was supposed to secure a cluster of houses on the Hoofdplaat–Biervliet road known as Driewegen. Their route across the large Wilhemina Polder was swept by machine gun fire, but the lead companies made it to the road dyke and established contact with the Glens. Driewegen was less than a kilometre away, but getting there proved to be very difficult. One attempt, led by a young platoon commander named Lieutenant G.E. Mercer, approached the objective by 'crawling through large culverts' and gradually working up the cross dykes to a junction just north of Driewegen. The enemy was well dug in and strongly supported by mortar and machine gun fire. An attempt to rush the position failed, and Mercer ordered a withdrawal, dropping his equipment to carry a wounded man to safety. Even the most courageous men could not capture such positions without full support, so a new attack was launched at dawn, with Wasp flame-throwers that had been brought forward under cover of darkness and with the field artillery firing at extreme range. The dyke junction was secured, but the enemy held on to the battered village until the next day, when Wasps again proved decisive.[81]

General Spry was now a very worried man. The northeast bridge-head was proving to be almost as difficult and costly as the Leopold. His first new plan was to employ the reserve brigade at the southeast corner of the pocket; he abandoned this idea after Algonquin patrols reported that most of 1037th Regiment was still holding its positions. He then decided to send 8th Brigade into the northeast bridgehead, even though this meant supporting two full brigades with a dwindling fleet of Buffaloes. The division's Commander Royal Canadian Army Service Corps came to the rescue, scrounging enough truck transport to deliver thirty-eight Terrapin light amphibious vehicles to a new mar-shalling area on the east side of the Braakman. The Paulina Polder, just two kilometres across the inlet, was quickly transformed into a supply dump, which was filled on a twice-daily basis.[82]

The men in the bridgehead also benefited from the resourcefulness of the Chemical Warfare Officers, who had originally been asked to pro-vide a smoke screen for just one day. By the late afternoon of 10 October the supply of smoke floats was exhausted and a real crisis loomed. A platoon from 806th British Pioneer Smoke Company was borrowed, along with more storm boats. The 8,000 additional smoke floats avail-able would last little more than a day, so much creativity was required. Rafts were made out of oil drums and large wooden doors and then equipped with large smoke generators. These were towed into place in the estuary. Most of the rafts floundered, so a new solution was impro-vised: LVTs with large Esso generators aboard cruised the estuary supplementing rafts, anchored storm boats, and a generator located on a sand bar.[83]

While staff officers worked to secure and supply the beachhead, Brigadier John Rockingham began to reorganize his stalled operation. Spry agreed to send 7th Recce Regiment to take over the HLI positions in front of Biervliet; this would allow the infantry time to organize a set-piece attack on the village.[84] The field and medium artillery helped the HLI capture the objective, with each company clearing and occupying one-quarter of the village. Since the enemy still seemed fully committed to immediate counter-attacks, the artillery, mortars, and medium machine guns were all given detailed defensive fire tasks.[85] Fortunately, the skies cleared and 84 Group was able to fly a record number of sorties. A number of friendly fire incidents occurred, but the troops were well aware of the possibility of short bombing and target misidentification, and had long since learned to take cover during Allied air attacks, so no casualties were reported.[86]

The troopers of 7th Recce left their armoured cars behind, and though they kept with them some Bren gun carriers for the mortar and anti-tank platoons, they fought as foot soldiers. The regiment's main task was to straighten out the line from Biervliet to Driewegen, and they did so with considerable elan.[87]

Spry sent 8th Brigade into the northeast beachhead with orders to stage a powerful thrust south, attacking the positions held by 1037th Regiment from the rear and opening a land bridge into the pocket. This decision was later questioned by Eberding, who told interrogators that the Canadians failed to exploit their opportunities by advancing into the centre of the pocket,[88] but any further advance west would have taken the infantry battalions – which had already suffered more than seven hundred casualties – out of range of their own field guns. Opening the road through to Watervliet and beyond would permit the artillery to redeploy and establish a supply route beyond the range of the guns on Walcheren.

On 13 October the North Shores led off the brigade advance, with a squadron from 7th Recce Regiment covering the Braakman flank. The enemy had failed to anticipate this move,[89] and both the North Shores and the Queen's Own Rifles encountered only spotty resistance.[90] Eberding ordered 1037th Regiment to withdraw before it was destroyed. On the morning of 14 October, Algonquin patrols discovered that the 'intricate system of defences with their deep concrete dugouts' in the Isabella Polder had been evacuated. The Argylls found a similar situation in Watervliet, and 4th Division engineers were soon at work bridging the canal. The work of clearing mines and booby traps began immediately, and the new divisional maintenance route was functioning on 16 October.[91]

The enemy attempted to counter these developments by establishing a new defensive perimeter running from Hoogeweg on the north coast through Ijzendijke to the Leopold west of Watervliet. Eberding also tried to encourage resistance by issuing his own version of Hitler's infamous 'Kith and Kin,' law, which required retaliation against the relatives of so-called deserters. The order, which was 'to be read to all troops' and 'at once destroyed,' stated that 'where the names of deserters are ascertained their names will be made known to the civilian population at home and their next of kin will be looked upon as enemies of the German people.'[92]

This attempt at emulating the Führer failed to stem the flow of German soldiers into prisoner-of-war cages, because two Canadian brigades were now pressing forward. By 16 October the Queen's Own were poised to seize Ijzendijke; to the north the Glens were fighting their way into Hoogeweg. Once the village was secure, the Glens' reserve company advanced towards a cluster of houses on the dyke between the Hoodfplaat and Oranje polders known as Roodenhoek. The dyke also carried the railway line to Breskens. This formidable barrier was defended by a battery of 20 mm guns as well as LMGs and mortars. Private Gordon Crozier, commanding a section of the lead platoon, 'broke cover and with a Bren gun and nine magazines made a dash for the railway cutting.' Ignoring a wound, he engaged the enemy, neutralizing their fire; this allowed the platoon to secure the position. Crozier then went after five other guns, firing air burst and suffering two more wounds before withdrawing to the regimental aid post.[93]

The next day the OB West Sitrep recorded the official German version of the day's fighting: 'On this front which had already been pushed back in earlier fighting, the enemy succeeded in obtaining several deep penetrations against the tenaciously fighting defenders who were suffering in particular from the ceaseless air attacks ... Enemy thrusts with tanks on the road Hoofdplaat to Nommer Een, from Roodenhoek towards the north-west, as well as on the road Braakman South-Ijzendijke have been intercepted.'[94] Fearing that the situation would soon be irreversible, OB West requested 'two parachute battalions to be used in an attempt to eliminate the penetration west of the Braakman Inlet.'[95]

The steady expansion of the eastern bridgehead forced Eberding to abandon the positions that were blocking 7th Brigade's advance. The Canscots reported that the village of Eede was empty and that the enemy seemed to be establishing a new defensive line along the Bruges–Sluis Canal.[96] Spry ordered both 8th and 9th Brigades to maintain pressure, but he decided it was time to reorganize before launching the assault on the last bastion, an area some twenty kilometres wide and eight kilometres deep that contained the main coastal gun batteries guarding the approaches to Antwerp.

Spry's decision to pause was made in the context of the arrival of 157th Brigade of 52nd (Lowland) Division. The brigade had been brought to France as the ground component of an elite mountain division that had been designated as 'air transportable.'[97] The 52nd had been scheduled to reinforce 1st British Airborne in the Arnhem bridgehead, but with that operation cancelled, Montgomery agreed to use it to reinforce First Canadian Army. The brigade was initially deployed to replace 4th Canadian Armoured Division, but Spry obtained permission to bring it across the Leopold and give the battered battalions of 7th Brigade a brief rest period.[98] Spry was especially concerned about the growing bill of casualties – now averaging more than one hundred men a day.[99] Most of these were from the rifle companies, and it was becoming difficult to find adequately trained replacements. Companies of seventy men and platoons of twenty were now common.

Spry and Rockingham had concluded that the nine well-fortified strongpoints protecting Breskens[100] could only be overcome with the support of the full range of specialized armoured vehicles. General Hobart's division had a well-deserved reputation for innovation, and one of the devices it brought forward for Breskens was a Bren gun carrier modified to carry a small storage tank of nitroglycerine, which could be pumped into a sixty-metre flexible hose after a rocket had stretched the hose across a minefield. The 'Conger' had been used successfully – or at least without loss of Allied lives – at Calais, but on the morning of 20 October an accidental explosion destroyed most of 284th Squadron. Only six of the eighteen AVREs survived, and what was left of the squadron was withdrawn.[101]

This tragic beginning to a difficult battle was largely unknown to the Canadian soldiers, who were briefed on Spry's plans later that day.

With the British brigade holding the southern sector along the Sluis Canal, Spry proposed to concentrate all three of his brigades at the northern end of the enemy's defensive zone. After 9th Brigade captured Breskens and Schoondijke in an elaborate and heavily supported set-piece attack, 7th Brigade was to pass through and 'clean the area west of Breskens as far as Cadzand.' This advance would be paralleled by that of 8th Brigade, whose task it would be to punch a hole in the enemy line at Oostburg before advancing directly to the coast. The formidable fortified area in the northwest corner of Belgium would not be attacked until these operations were complete.[102]

Lieutenant-Colonel Rowley and his Glens were informed that because of the accident, the AVREs that were to be used in crossing the ten-metre anti-tank ditch were unavailable and that neither Flails nor Crocodiles would be accompanying them. This meant Rowley had to formulate a new plan. He recalled: 'What we did was to go in a one-man front. We went along the seawall and used kapok bridging equipment which got us over the anti-tank ditch into Breskens. Of course the Germans never believed that anybody would be so foolish as to put in an attack from there, so we got in with very few casualties. We were on top of them before they knew what had happened and we took 150 prisoners.'[103] It does not diminish the Glens' achievement to mention that ten artillery regiments and the fighter-bombers of 84 Group also contributed to the German surrender.

After Breskens fell, all of the German batteries within range fired on the ruins of the town, hoping to destroy the harbour and inflict casualties. The North Novas' attempts to enter the ruins of Fort Frederik Hendrik were met with streams of machine gun fire from well-concealed positions. In keeping with 3rd Division's emphasis on conserving manpower, preparations were made for a set-piece attack; but before it could be launched, much of the German garrison departed, with the remainder sending out delegates to negotiate a surrender.[104] Three miles to the south the HLI had fought their way into Schoondijke, but they would not attempt to advance beyond it until additional troops were available.

While Spry and his staff were planning the next phase of the battle, 'a splendid limousine with its four stars and Union Jack preceded by a gleaming black jeep' arrived. Montgomery emerged, dressed in cream-coloured slacks and with a green scarf resplendent beneath his flying jacket. According the the divisional historical officer: 'The familiar black beret with its two badges was the sole item of uniform dress.' After the army photographers were gone, Monty met with Spry and Mingay, the division's senior staff officer, in the ops room.[105] Montgomery had come to see for himself why an operation that he had been told would take from four days to two weeks was now in its nineteenth day, with no sign of enemy collapse. Montgomery emphasized the need for speed and seems to have set the end of the month as the latest acceptable date for completing Switchback. His visit was followed by news that must have seemed all too familiar to 3rd Division: it was to press on with all speed, but 157th Brigade was needed elsewhere and would be withdrawn that day. Divisional staff officers spent an anxious night trying to patch together a covering force. Fortunately, 52nd Recce Regiment was allowed to remain with the Canadians, and they could at least patrol the area, which the British brigade had greatly enlarged.[106]

All units now felt intense pressure from 'higher-ups' to move quickly, but the enemy was not yet ready to cooperate. The corps intelligence summary, dated 25 October, identified nine German battlegroups committed to the defence of the western end of the pocket. The summary was properly cautious about the strength of these battlegroups. Almost 5,000 prisoners of war had passed into Canadian hands by 25 October, but no one was prepared to guess how many more German soldiers were still in action.

For the infantry companies the last ten days of the Breskens Pocket would be a time of intense combat and steady casualties. Eberding was determined to conduct an organized delaying action; his plan was to hold strongly at Oostburg and use it as a pivot around which to swing his left flank anticlockwise against the system of concentric dykes in the area of Cadzand–Zuidzande.[107]

The Germans defending the Oostburg sector were able to take advantage of a complex web of dykes and water barriers. To the south of the town a three-kilometre lake known as the Groote Gat split the battlefield. Many of the bridges and culverts on the approach roads had been blown, and enough polders were flooded to limit cross-country approaches to a few well-defended routes.[108] The Canadians had gradually worked out methods for fighting in polder country. If a company went into action with an FOO, one or more M10s, and at least one Wasp, they could visually correct the field artillery, keeping heads down while the sections moved forward in carefully controlled bounds. The flat-trajectory, high-velocity M10s were used to target gun positions dug into the dykes and the pillboxes at strongpoints. Finally a Wasp was brought forward to squirt flame and induce a surrender.

These innovative tactical operations were not always possible, and when the battle for Oostburg began on 24 October, very little went according to plan. The Chauds tried to approach the town from the south. The lead company initially made good progress, capturing a number of dispirited enemy soldiers. Meeting little resistance, the company advanced into a trap and was cut off, suffering twenty-two killed. Only fifteen of the survivors avoided capture.[109] Brigade ordered the Chauds to secure the southern approaches to Oostburg and to prepare to support an attack by the Queen's Own Rifles from both sides of the Groote Gat.

The QORs employed two companies, each formed into a combat team with M10s and Wasps. A smoke screen was used to help the daylight advance, but it took 'a startling exhibition of courage and dash' to win the day. Lieutenant J.E. Burns ordered his platoon to 'fix swords' – the rifle regiment command for 'fix bayonets' – and led them in a wild charge into the town. The regimental history notes that 'theoretically they should all have been killed. Happily none were.'[110] It took another full day of fighting to complete the capture of the Oostburg strongpoint and the town. The enemy was forced to withdraw to Zuidzande.

Charlie Martin, a Company Sergeant Major in the QORs, recalled the situation his men faced in the last weeks of October: 'You'd have two or three farm buildings together and then maybe a half mile of open fields surrounded by dykes. Deep water had collected at the sides of the dykes and it took courage for the men to move along them. There was no cover. It was what we called a section job. Each section – a corporal and a few riflemen usually – would leapfrog forward ... We'd do this five or six times a day – tense, stressful maneuvers.'[111]

The German troops opposing 7th Brigade's advance were able to limit the approach routes available by the usual methods of blowing bridges and flooding fields. They also announced that Groede was the location of a large hospital with many wounded and 'thousands' of civilian refugees. The Canadians agreed to treat it as an open town, but this meant that the only major road – which passed through the village – could not be used. The Royal Winnipeg Rifles had to find an alternate route and bitterly complained that the narrow dyke south of the village was under observed fire from the church tower in Groede. The Canscots, working their way around flooded polders on the coastal flank, also reported an enemy OP in the 'open town,' but there was nothing anyone could do about it.[112]

Montgomery had spent the night at 3rd Division Headquarters. On the morning of 25 October, Spragge and Lieutenant-Colonel Alan Gregory – the new CO of the Regina Rifles – were brought back to give Montgomery a briefing.[113] There was little they could say to reassure the field marshal. Rapid progress was unlikely in such terrain unless enemy resistance collapsed, and all evidence suggested a staged withdrawal to the next concentric dyke. The only good news was that once the Cadzand batteries had been captured there would be no more guns able to reach shipping in the estuary.

The enemy was now defending a small area crowded with mortars and 88 mm guns; this made every movement dangerous. One Canscot company that got too far out in front was overrun on the night of 27 October when 'a well planned counter attack was sent in by Jerry with artillery support.' Total casualties were reported as '4 killed, 4 wounded and 40 missing.'[114] When another company tried to send help, heavy shelling prevented movement. The Canscots' reverse, like the one suffered by the Chauds, had a serious impact on morale. Advancing more quickly, while probing for gaps in the German defences, sounded like a great idea at divisional headquarters, but battalion commanders were loath to move unless they knew their flanks would be protected.

The same kinds of problems plagued 8th Brigade's advance to Retranchement. The North Shores, supported by the armoured cars of 7th Recce Regiment, met 'strong and determined opposition' in the initial stages of each attack, but the enemy quickly raised white flags once they were outflanked or threatened with flame.[115] By 27 October more than 6,000 German soldiers had entered the divisional PW cage and hundreds more were on their way there. That night the Germans evacuated four hundred of their wounded by boat to Flushing[116] and prepared for the final effort.

On 29 October the corps intelligence summary reported growing evidence of an enemy collapse:

> Today at several places south of the Scheldt, our troops lost contact with the enemy who now appears to be withdrawing to the Knocke Sur Mer area behind the canal. The interrogation today of the Adjutant of General Eberding is interesting, even though its absolute accuracy cannot be vouched for. According to the PW the whole front collapsed yesterday as there were not enough men and weapons left to form a line of defence. He went on to say that, in spite of the order of 13 October 44, threatening reprisals for surrender on soldiers' families, there were still many deserters and a lot of the troops did not make use of their rifles any more. He felt that the men were of inferior quality, otherwise the bridgehead would not have fallen so easily. He estimated the remaining garrison to be about 3000. Although it is conceded that this officer was in a better position to make an estimate, it is suggested that his figures are rather high. Up to this evening 104 officers and 7043 ORs have been taken prisoner.[117]

There were in fact more than 3,000 German soldiers left in the pocket, and though their will to resist was not uniformly high, many battlegroups were still able to inflict casualties before appearing, packed and ready, to join their comrades in prisoner-of-war camps. The battalions of 7th Brigade discovered that the enemy in the Cadzand strongpoints 'had to be cut off and slowly extricated from their emplacements or bunkers' by infantry, as the Crocodiles could not be used in the sand.[118] The ammunition for the coastal guns had apparently been destroyed on 27 October, ending any threat to the naval force preparing to assault Walcheren. However, parts of the Cadzand battery held out until 2 November.[119]

During the night of 30 and 31 October, 9th Brigade took over the bridgehead established by the QORs[120] and began pushing north into the Knocke–Heyst–Zeebrugge sector, a fortified area covering 12 kilometres of coast, with strong all-around defences supplemented by extensive flooding.[121] Fortunately, Eberding and most of his officers recognized that their task – delaying the use of the Port of Antwerp – was over. They were located in a bunker on a golf course at Knocke, and the general was brought to divisional headquarters, where Spry politely interviewed the German commander.[122]

The battles fought by 3rd Canadian Division in the Breskens Pocket must surely rank with the most difficult fought by any Allied formation in the Second World War. The casualty total, just under 2,500 men, including 555 killed in action, tells much of the story. What the survivors remembered most was the condition of the battlefield, with its flooded polders and cold, endless rain. Major Robert Gregory, who treated 295 battle exhaustion casualties during Operation Switchback, reported that his patients lacked the will to carry on because it all seemed so hopeless. The only way out of battle was 'death, wounds, self-inflicted wounds and going nuts.' Most of the men, he reported, 'had no insight as to why they were being used to fight so hard and so steadily.'[123]

Everyone who fought in the polders shared these views, but the vast majority found ways to cope with the stress and remain with their comrades until the last enemy soldier surrendered. The next day rumours that the division was to spend a week as guests of the citizens of Ghent were confirmed and the dark mood lifted. After twenty-seven days and nights 'too miserable even for war,'[124] it was time to forget about death and embrace life, if only for a brief moment.

4

North from Antwerp

On 14 September, Field Marshal Montgomery issued a directive outlining the goals of Operation Market Garden: 'Our real objective ... is the Ruhr. But on the way we want the ports of Antwerp and Rotterdam since the capture of the Ruhr is merely the first step on the northern route of advance into Germany.' The task of securing the ports was assigned to First Canadian Army, which was to take over Antwerp on 17 September and begin operations 'to enable full use to be made of the port.'[1]

The 2nd Canadian Division reached Antwerp between 16 and 20 September, with 4th Brigade slated to take over the port's defences. The brigade was now commanded by Lieutenant-Colonel Fred Cabeldu, who had led the Canscots with such conspicuous success in Normandy. One of his company commanders, Major Bob Lendrum, was made CO of the Royals. As their regimental history records, Lendrum proved to be 'a quiet thoughtful man who was utterly unruffled in action ... a thorough and efficient leader.'[2] The RHLI were equally delighted when Lieutenant-Colonel Denis Whitaker, who had been wounded in Normandy, returned to the regiment. The troubled Essex Scottish had found a replacement for Bruce Macdonald, but Lieutenant-Colonel P.W. Bennett was wounded during a 'severe counterattack' on the Essex positions in Antwerp. His replacement, Lieutenant-Colonel J.E.C. Pangman, a Queen's Own Rifles officer, was to have a difficult relationship with the battalion.[3]

The city the Canadians had come to defend was a very strange place in September 1944. The people were friendly enough, but they were busy restoring a normal life and were trying to ignore the war being fought around them. To soldiers accustomed to the dangers of combat and the austerity of wartime Britain, the busy shops full of food and consumer goods made for a strange contrast. The trams were running, and some civilians went about their affairs to the point of crossing over the Albert Canal from the Allied to the German sector and back again. This tranquil mood ended abruptly when Hitler made Antwerp a priority target for his V-1 and V-2 rockets.[4]

The orders issued to 4th Brigade emphasized the preservation of the harbour; meanwhile, the rest of the division was to begin advancing north from Antwerp 'with the resources available' and 'without incurring heavy casualties' until help arrived.[5] Help was supposed to arrive

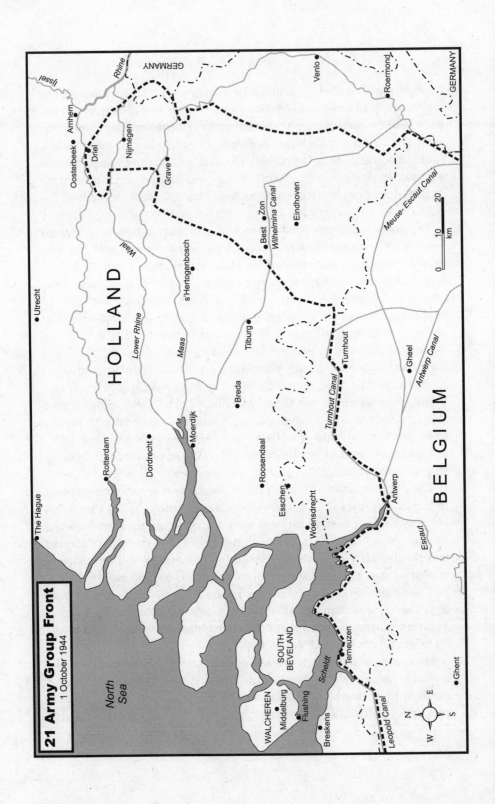

21 Army Group Front
1 October 1944

GERMANY

GERMANY

IJssel

Rhine

Arnhem

Oosterbeek

Driel

Nijmegen

Grave

Venlo

Roermond

Utrecht

HOLLAND

Waal

s'Hertogenbosch

Best

Zon

Wilhelmina Canal

Eindhoven

Meuse-Escaut Canal

Lower Rhine

Maas

Tilburg

Turnhout

Gheel

Antwerp Canal

The Hague

Rotterdam

Dordrecht

Moerdijk

Breda

Roosendaal

Turnhout Canal

BELGIUM

Esschen

Woensdrecht

Antwerp

Escaut

North
Sea

WALCHEREN

Middelburg

Flushing

SOUTH
BEVELAND

Scheldt

Terneuzen

Breskens

Leopold Canal

Ghent

0   10   20
km

N
W   E
S

in the form of a British infantry division brought forward from Le Havre along with General Sir John Crocker's corps headquarters. Crerar instructed Crocker to 'assist the speedy northwards thrust' of the Canadians by committing 49th Division to an advance with its 'main strength on the left' so that it could protect 2nd Division's flank. Crerar agreed to provide a Canadian armoured regiment, the Sherbrookes, to support the division as there was not enough transport or supplies to allow a British armoured brigade to leave Normandy.[6] Had Crerar's orders been carried out, operations north from Antwerp would have achieved much greater and more immediate success; but on 24 September, Montgomery intervened, switching 49th Division's main effort to the northeast in support of the attempt to widen the Nijmegen–Arnhem salient. Before examining Canadian actions in late September and early October, we must try to understand why Montgomery accorded such low priority to operations designed to open the Port of Antwerp. This requires us to suspend our knowledge of the outcome of Market Garden and focus on the day-to-day decisions made by Montgomery and Eisenhower.

D-Day for Market Garden was 17 September, and initially everything seemed to be going well. Montgomery's nightly message to London included this statement: 'I have every hope the Guards Armoured Division will tomorrow get right through to Arnhem and it is to be followed by 43rd Division. The objective of 30th Corps is Apeldoorn and north of Arnhem.' Twenty-four hours later he reported that 'heavy rain' and 'strong resistance' south of Eindhoven had slowed the advance but overall 'operations were going well.' At the end of day three he was still confident that the advance to Apeldoorn would proceed 'once we have captured the bridge at Nijmegen.' Operations to widen the corridor had also begun, with 12th Corps on the left and 8th Corps on the right making 'good progress.'[7]

Optimism was apparently still possible on the night of 20 September, though Montgomery admitted that the situation of 1st British Airborne in Arnhem was 'not good.' With the pending arrival of Polish Parachute Brigade that evening, there was a 'sporting chance of getting the bridge at Arnhem.' But weather forced a twenty-four-hour postponement of the Polish drop, and by the night of 21 September it was evident that the enemy controlled the bridge and had 'rounded up' most of the British parachute brigade. Montgomery still insisted that the general situation was 'satisfactory' and that if sufficient resources were made available, it would be possible to bridge the Rhine west of Arnhem, 'where 1st British Airborne is located using them as a secure bridgehead.'[8]

This was the view of the situation that Monty's Chief of Staff, Lieutenant-General Sir Francis de Guingand, took to a meeting called by Eisenhower for the afternoon of 22 September. Montgomery declined to attend, insisting that he needed to be close to the battle. He wanted 1st U.S. Army to take over the eastern side of the corridor so that General Miles Dempsey's entire army could concentrate 'on attacking the Ruhr from the north.' Eisenhower accepted this proposal and told General Omar Bradley 'to bring up two divisions as quickly as possible to take over the sector now held by 8th Corps.'[9] Montgomery could not ask the Americans for help on his western flank, but he could take resources from First Canadian Army. Specifically, he could order 49th Division to seize a bridgehead at Turnhout, and he could bring Polish Armoured Division – which was out of action trying to replenish its losses in men and equipment – to join 49th Division's drive northeast towards Tilburg.[10] The Poles, like the rest of 1st British Corps, were to draw their supplies from Canadian depots with priority over 4th Canadian Armoured Division, which was confined to a static role.

On 24 September the leading British brigade, along with the Sherbrookes, crossed the Turnhout Canal, established a large bridgehead, and began probing towards Tilburg. Their advance greatly assisted 12th Corps, which was fending off an attack by the enemy's 59th Division, one of the first formations to be evacuated across the Scheldt.[11] That night Montgomery was forced to admit that it might be necessary to 'abandon the attempt to cross the Neder Rijn west of Arnhem' and 'to withdraw 1st Airborne south of the river.' This belated recognition of the plight of the airborne division did not mean an end to offensive action. Instead, Montgomery insisted that 'we can obtain our object equally well if not better by developing thrust lines eastward.'[12]

Montgomery's plan for advancing to the east was fully supported by Eisenhower, who ordered Bradley to meet with Montgomery 'and agree on detail of operational plans,' particularly for 1st Army's part in 'the main effort in the present approved campaign against the Ruhr.'[13] Montgomery issued a new directive on 27 September in which he stated that his intentions were to open the Port of Antwerp and capture the Ruhr, in that order; however, the allocation of resources left no doubt where the priority lay.[14] If any actions to open the Port of Antwerp were to begin in September, 2nd Canadian Division would have to conduct them on its own.

In late September the German forces north of Antwerp were under the command of General Kurt Student and his 1st Parachute Army. General Otto Sponheimer's 67th Corps was now responsible for the area from Antwerp to Turnhout – forty kilometres of flat, marshy country dotted with woods and laced with small canals. In the Antwerp area, where the enemy still held a short stretch of the Albert Canal, 719th Division had developed strong defensive positions. To its left, 711th and 346th Divisions were holding the Turnhout Canal. East of Turnhout, 88th Corps, with 712th, 245th, and 59th Divisions under command, was attempting to regain ground at Eindhoven. Battlegroup Chill, now part of Student's army reserve, was also committed against Eindhoven. German sources describe these divisions as understrength and facing serious equipment and ammunition shortages. Little armour was available to them, and only the army reserve possessed any mobility. Nevertheless, each division deployed between six and eight thousand men, and in the prevailing circumstances a very high percentage were used as combat troops. Attempts to cut the road to Nijmegen had cost 88th Corps large numbers of casualties, but 67th Corps was not involved in heavy fighting until 2nd Division began to attack on 28 September.[15]

The 5th and 6th Canadian Infantry Brigades were transported to the area east of Antwerp over a three-day period. The war diarist of the Calgary Highlanders, Lieutenant Ed Ford, described this 'exhilarating experience': the troop-carrying convoys drove across the First World War battlefields via Ypres and St-Julien, where the 'Brooding Soldier' battlefield memorial loomed at the side of the road. They encountered good roads, pubs like the ones in England, and 'healthy and good looking' women who greeted the convoys with gifts of fruit, bread, and beer. All of this pleased the soldiers, who decided 'that a reasonably lengthy sojourn in the country would not be too great a hardship on the troops.'[16]

Brigadier Bill Megill's 5th Brigade was assigned responsibility for the area immediately east of Antwerp along the Albert Canal. The brigade had used the brief rest period at Dieppe and the limited operations at Dunkirk to integrate hundreds of replacements and rebuild confidence. The Maisonneuves were still short more than two hundred riflemen, and there was no immediate prospect of enough French-speaking reinforcements to change the situation. Lieutenant-Colonel Julien Bibeau and a number of veteran officers and NCOs helped ensure that the 'Maisies' remained a formidable combat unit, but they could not be used as a normal battalion. Thankfully, the soldiers of Black Watch had recovered their confidence and self-esteem, though tensions between their CO and Megill continued. The Calgary Highlanders were commanded by the visibly tired and nervous Donald MacLaughlan. Megill hesitated to remove the Calgary CO because he could not make up his mind about Major Ross Ellis, who had served as a 'battle adjutant' in Normandy. Megill thought Ellis was too young and lacked seniority. Yet the Calgaries were one of the corps' most effective battalions, so Megill left well enough alone.[17]

A Belgian resistance group that had been working with 53rd Welsh Division offered their services, and Megill decided to use them to help him build a picture of the enemy's defences. Divisional headquarters had other ideas. Reports of a German withdrawal to the Turnhout Canal persuaded Major-General Charles Foulkes that 'a more formidable force' should be sent across the canal.[18] Megill wanted to accomplish this by infiltrating a small fighting patrol across a lock gate; the point here was to establish a small bridgehead before launching the main attack. The Black Watch were told to seize the bridgehead, with the Calgaries as the exploitation force.

The operation did not go well. According to the brigade War Diary, 'the RHC fighting patrol got 14 men onto the locks but they were pinned down by machine gun fire and were eventually withdrawn.'[19] Was this a normal mishap or a badly executed action? Megill, who had joined the Black Watch CO to observe the mission, was clearly unhappy with the result, and Lieutenant-Colonel Frank Mitchell reacted with a furious defence of his battalion. Mitchell later claimed that he 'provoked his own dismissal,' presumably in the hope of bringing about Megill's removal.[20] If so, Mitchell lost his gamble.

With Mitchell gone, Megill was anxious to obtain a new commanding officer from outside the list of regimental officers. When told that veteran Black Watch officer Lieutenant-Colonel Bruce Ritchie, who had been commanding the Royal Hamilton Light Infantry, would be appointed, Megill protested strongly. He urged Foulkes to place Vern Stott or Denis Whitaker in command of the Black Watch, but Foulkes would not agree, and Ritchie took up his duties the next day.[21]

The incident quickly faded into the background. On the night of 22 September the Calgary Highlanders got a fighting patrol and then three companies across the canal and rapidly established a solid bridgehead. The Calgaries' success was made possible by the extraordinary coolness and bravery of Sergeant C.K. 'Ken' Crockett, who led a patrol of ten men across the canal on the night of 22 September. Crockett went first and then signalled the others to join him on a small island between the locks. North of the island the lock gates had broken away, and Crockett had to ease himself along a six-inch pipe that stretched to the far bank, where a barricade blocked the path. Returning to the island, Crockett explained the situation and repeated his earlier warning about the need for silence. 'If a flare goes up,' he told his men, 'get as low as you can and don't move ... Nobody fires until I tell you.'

The patrol made it to the north bank of the canal and fought a short, sharp engagement, overcoming three machine gun positions. The rest of the lead Calgary company quickly joined Crockett's group, and by dawn the battalion had dug in and was waiting for the first enemy counter-attack. In the day-long battle that followed, the Calgaries lost forty-nine men including fifteen killed.[22] Evidently the enemy had not withdrawn!

Once the engineers had bridged the canal, the Maisonneuves and the M10 self-propelled guns of 2nd Anti-Tank Regiment joined the Calgaries, forcing the enemy to retreat and allowing 6th Brigade to make an unopposed crossing of the Albert Canal. This very successful action encouraged the divisional commander to order 6th Brigade to seize a bridgehead on the north side of the Turnout Canal before dawn on 24 September. The Fusiliers Mont-Royal made an unopposed crossing but were soon counter-attacked by enemy infantry. The South Saskatchewans, pinned down by machine gun fire, reported that there was 'no opportunity to cross the canal.' With strict limits on the available rounds per gun, the artillery was quite unable to neutralize the enemy.[23]

Brigadier Jacques Gauvreau ordered the South Sasks to make a day-light attempt using smoke. The battalion was able to get all four companies across, but as they began to advance to Lochtenberg it became obvious that the enemy held a barrack-like 'sanatorium' in strength.[24] The Toronto Scottish mortar platoon supported the South Sasks with 'devastating' fire, but the enemy was now employing twenty light Renault tanks in support of their infantry.[25] The main counter-attack, '200 infantry with 12 tanks,' struck the FMRs, who were forced back across the canal. Gauvreau decided to order the South Sasks to retire as well, but Lieutenant-Colonel Stott, who was with the lead company, insisted on waiting until dark. He ordered a staged withdrawal, with the dismounted carrier platoon providing cover.[26]

The unsuccessful battle at the Turnhout Canal was the last action the division fought under the command of Foulkes. When he was appointed Acting Commander, 2nd Canadian Corps, Brigadier R. Holley Keefler, the CRA, assumed command of the division. Keefler, a forty-two-year-old militia officer,[27] had commanded the divisional artillery since 1943, and Simonds was confident that he was the best choice available. His appointment was nevertheless a surprise to everyone, especially the infantry brigadiers.[28]

Keefler's first decision was to take advantage of the bridgehead established by 49th Division near Turnhout. The 146th Brigade, with the assistance of 'Canadian Shermans' from the Sherbrookes, had beaten off enemy counter-attacks and bridged the canal.[29] By the morning of 28 September, 5th Brigade, supported by the Fort Garry Horse, had taken over the left flank of the British bridgehead and begun to move west, rolling up the battlegroups of the Germans' 346th Division.

The Garries had been rushed forward from Boulogne in a convoy of 170 trucks and 35 tank transporters – enough wheeled vehicles to carry the regiment and its tanks. One squadron joined the Maisonneuves, who were working with a troop of armoured cars from 8th Reece Regiment on the first bound. The enemy destroyed the lead tank, but the rest of the troop 'seized the objective in a flank swoop,'[30] much to the delight of the infantry. The Black Watch then took over the advance, capturing the village of St-Leonard in a night attack. Ritchie positioned his four companies along a 1200-metre perimeter, with the 6-pounders of the anti-tank platoon in forward positions.[31] At four in the morning the first of a series of counter-attacks began. Gordon Bourne, then a lieutenant serving with the anti-tank platoon, described the scene: 'Our two flanking companies received a bad mauling but the two centre companies managed to hold out ... When dawn broke and the results of the early morning fighting could be seen, it was apparent the German casualties were very heavy. The sprawling bodies that littered the surroundings were mute evidence of the bitterest tussle.'[32] The Calgary Highlanders attacked through the Black Watch and worked systematically to expand the bridgehead, making contact with the FMRs on the south side of the canal. The Maisonneuves, who had fought their way forward on the north flank, took seventy-four prisoners, but their own casualties – nine killed and thirty-seven wounded – further reduced their combat strength.[33]

The Black Watch were told to plan an attack on Brecht, and Ritchie organized a textbook operation. He was determined not to move until the start line and the approaches to it were securely held. One of the problems confronting Allied commanders in Northwest Europe was the tendency of rifle companies to report that they controlled an area when it was simply in range of their light weapons and under observation by the artillery FOO.

The Calgary War Diary for 1 October 1944 describes a typical situation. During the night the Calgaries had beaten off several counter-attacks, including a wild engagement with a single German tank that 'slipped into a pocket,' making it impossible for the Canadians to use anti-tank guns 'without endangering our own troops.' Major Del Kearn's company engaged the tank with PIATs, and it withdrew. The presence of the tank and the fact that the Calgaries were involved in small firefights all along their front convinced Ritchie that the Calgaries did not control the area, and he insisted that they physically occupy a number of buildings overlooking the start line. MacLaughlan was furious at this implied criticism. The Calgaries' War Diary records his view: 'It became annoyingly evident that the RHC wanted Calgary Highlanders to provide a guaranteed safe approach and passage beyond the start line.' This is exactly what Ritchie *did* want, and he got it! The Calgary forward companies occupied the buildings until the Black Watch were in place, then 'pulled back to their previous positions.'[34]

The attack on Brecht went as planned. The companies moved forward quickly, closely supported by a squadron of Fort Garry tanks. Lieutenant-Colonel E.D. Nighswander, commanding 5th Field Regiment, developed a fire plan that integrated a medium regiment and the brigade's heavy mortars with his own guns: 'Such was the accuracy of the barrage that when the riflemen reached the point where the enemy mortars were sited they found all six of the mortars out of commission and in the area over forty craters from our medium and field artillery shells.' The enemy 'put up a determined resistance' within the town, but the Black Watch, having followed the barrage closely, were in among them quickly, taking prisoners and forcing the Germans to evacuate the farthest edge of the town 'hurriedly,' leaving behind 'stacks of ammunition.'[35]

The next day Ritchie again demonstrated his determination to take no chances with the battalion placed in his charge. A platoon of 'D' Company was cut off by a German force. 'They were in no immediate danger and had suffered no casualties, but plans were made for a full scale attack,' The War Diary notes. 'It was necessary to go from house to house to reach them and in conjunction with the infantry our Universal Carriers, equipped with flame-throwers were used for the first time, while our 17 pounders fired from the flank upon a house known to be occupied by the enemy. B company consolidated the position and the total result was a 300 yard advance, some minor casualties, eight prisoners, and many dead left in the field.'[36]

Ritchie and his battalion took great pride in their conduct at St-Leonard and Brecht.[37] This was the kind of action they had trained for, and the contrast between these battles and the hastily improvised encounters that they and other 2nd Division units had been forced into in the past was obvious to all. But there is a price to pay for tactical successes as well as for failures: the battalion lost twenty-four killed and ninety-six wounded during the week ending 4 October.

The Fort Garry Horse were much less enthusiastic about the battles of late September. Lieutenant-Colonel W.M. Wilson protested the 'spendthrift manner in which brigades and battalions are employing tanks, sending them to attack fortified villages' with infantry following 1,000 yards in the rear. Wilson argued that with the Garries down to thirty-four tanks, his squadrons needed to be under the command of the division, not any lower formation; that way, a tank commander, not an infantry officer, would decide how to employ the available armour.[38] Keefler accepted Wilson's argument, but at the sharp end, compromises were already being worked out between squadron and company commanders. Effectiveness rather than doctrine was what mattered in combat.[39]

By the end of September, constant pressure by the British and Canadians had forced the enemy to concede the Turnhout Canal and to commit all available reserves. General Erich Diestel, who commanded 346th Division, told interrogators that 'in addition to 719th Division which had been on the spot, a regiment of 711th Division, two battalions of 346th Division and battlegroup Schilling' had all been committed to stopping the Canadian advance.[40] Losses were so heavy that a regiment from 70th Infantry Division was brought down from Walcheren to strengthen the defences. A similar situation developed in the sector held by 88th Corps; there, the weakened battlegroups had to draw from Student's armoured reserve, an assault gun brigade, and a heavy (88 mm) anti-tank brigade in order to prevent the British and Polish forces from reaching Tilburg.[41]

Crocker, who now commanded all three divisions in the Antwerp–Tilburg sector, was determined to maintain pressure. Thus on 2 October, 6th Canadian Brigade advanced through Brecht to seize Camp de Brasschaet. The German defenders of the northern suburbs of Antwerp, in danger of being cut off, began to withdraw. The Belgian resistance entered Merxem, and 4th Brigade occupied the village, overcoming rearguards and probing north.[42] That afternoon Simonds issued his first directive as Acting Army Commander; in it he ordered 2nd Division to 'close the eastern end of the Zuid Beveland Isthmus.' He assumed that this might be done quickly, but he did not believe the division could advance through Beveland to Walcheren until 1st British Corps was able 'to cover the eastern flank and rear of 2nd Canadian Infantry Division.'[43] Simonds correctly appreciated the enemy's determination to delay Allied use of the Port of Antwerp, and he was preparing a series of complex amphibious operations designed to defeat the enemy by manoeuvre.

While 2nd Division worked its way forward, the rest of 1st British Corps began attacking out of the Turnhout Canal bridgehead on a northeasterly axis towards Tilburg. With Polish Armoured Division in

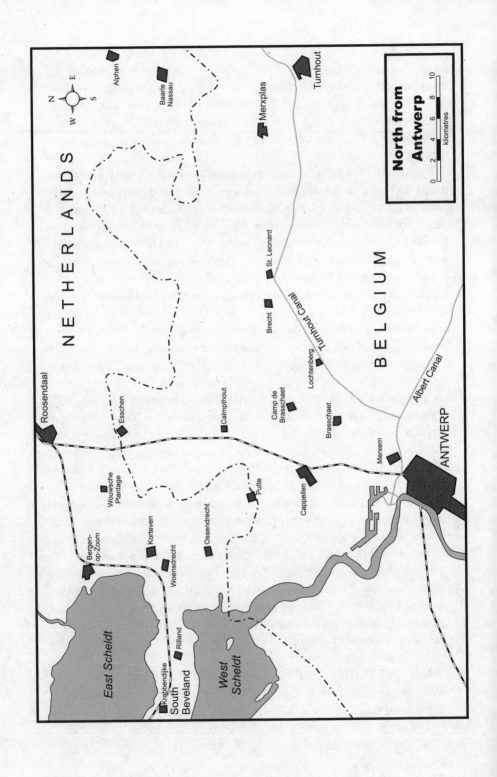

North from Antwerp

0 2 4 6 8 10
kilometres

N E T H E R L A N D S

B E L G I U M

Alphen

Baarle
Nassau

Merxplas

Turnhout

St. Leonard

Brecht

Turnhout Canal

Lochtenberg

Roosendaal

Esschen

Calmpthout

Camp de
Brasschaet

Brasschaet

Merxem

Wouwsche
Plantage

Putte

Cappellen

Albert Canal

ANTWERP

Bergen-
op-Zoom

Korteven

Woensdrecht

Ossendrecht

East Scheldt

Krabbendijke

Rilland

South
Beveland

West
Scheldt

the centre and battalions of 49th Division, working with squadrons from the Sherbrookes, on either flank, progress was steady but also slow and costly. Major-General Stanislaw Maczek's infantry battalions had been partly rebuilt with Polish prisoners of war captured from the Germans in Normandy, but by 4 October losses of over 450 men had once again reduced the rifle companies to half-strength. Maczek reported that lack of infantry training and the consequent need to employ armour in close support was resulting in heavy losses in tanks.[44] The Sherbrooke Fusiliers' experience was similar, especially after Student committed his assault gun brigade and a heavy (88 mm) anti-tank brigade to help slow the corps attack.[45] No such enemy reserves were yet available in the Antwerp sector. After the Essex Scottish overcame a blocking position in the bordertown of Putte, divisional intelligence reported 'definite signs of an enemy withdrawal.' Prisoners included 'many low category personnel' and men from the 70th Infantry Division, a formation made up of men with stomach ailments. German troops were thought to have fallen back to Bergen-op-Zoom, leaving 'outposts which will have to be dealt with in our push forward.'[46]

Back at corps headquarters the same optimism prevailed.[47] The intelligence summary for 7 October boldly insisted that the enemy had 'given up any plan he might have had to stand on the approach to Walcheren.'[48] On the same day that 2nd Canadian Corps distributed this appreciation, General Gustav von Zangen issued an order declaring that 'the defence of the approaches to Antwerp represents a task which is decisive for the further conduct of the war.'[49] Von Zangen did more than offer words: he ordered his army reserve, Battle Group Chill – including 6th Parachute Regiment and several battalions of self-propelled guns – to his right flank with orders to bar access to Beveland.

Diestel, who was commanding a mixed bag of divisional fragments in defence of the area north of Antwerp, described the arrival of the reinforcements when he was interviewed in 1945:

On October 2nd the Canadians attacked north from Merxem and in three days had driven the division's right flank from back to Putte, a distance of some 7 kms ... There was no regular line to hold at this time, but rather a series of tactical points ... The division had lost over 800 men in the battle for the Turnhout and Albert Canals and was in a very tired state. About 7

October, in almost melodramatic-fashion, aid came in the form of the 15 Army Assault Battalion consisting of about 1000 men from the Army Battle School and the von der Heydte Parachute Regiment of about 2500 fanatical and eager young parachutists.[50]

The 15th Army was able to move its reserve to the Antwerp sector because Montgomery had decided to postpone the advance to the Ruhr until 2nd Army was reorganized. The 1st British Corps, reinforced by 51st Highland Division, took over the defence of the western side of the salient and called off attempts to reach Tilburg and s'Hertogenbosch. Montgomery realized that this would leave 2nd Canadian Division on its own with an exposed right flank, but for him the Scheldt was still not a priority. Aware that criticism of his strategy was growing, he told Field Marshal Sir Alan Brooke on 7 October that 'Canadian troops were astride the road leading westwards from the mainland to South Beveland.' He also claimed to 'have examined carefully the whole situation of the opening up of Antwerp with a view to speeding up the matter and it is clear we are using all the troops we can successfully employ.'[51] Montgomery could not possibly have believed either statement, but he was determined to buy time for one more attempt to reach the Rhine.

The actual situation was very different from the one Montgomery described. On 5 October, 2nd Canadian Armoured Brigade, with two of the three Canadian armoured regiments, was committed to support 49th Division's defensive front; this left 2nd Canadian Division with one half-strength armoured regiment for all three of its brigades. Keefler was initially forced to use two of the three Fort Garry squadrons to support an FMR-based battlegroup assigned to protecting the division's exposed right flank. The actions of these squadrons were intended 'to create confusion on the whole brigade front giving the impression to the Hun that he was completely surrounded by tanks.' The battlegroup, code named 'Saint Force,' began operations on 8 October, and by the end of the day it was organizing a defensive front covering the 24 kilometres from Brecht to Huijbergen.[52]

On the morning of 7 October, 5th Brigade took over the lead. Its battalions began to advance, employing an elaborate artillery fire plan that assigned code names to every conceivable target. The company commanders called down fire through the FOO, and when satisfied they 'simply lifted artillery to other positions and watched results.' The Calgaries, with the assistance of tanks, spent most of the day working forward to Hoogerheide by this method. Lieutenant Alex Keller won the Military Cross for his part in one example of infantry–tank coopera- tion. Emerging from a wooded area, his platoon met intense fire from a shrub-covered rise surrounded by open ground. Keller pinpointed the enemy positions and arranged to have the tanks provide covering fire. When the Fort Garry troop opened up, Keller 'with a terse "follow me" proceeded at a fast walk straight across the open ground. His platoon, after a short startled pause, quickly followed.' Sixteen prisoners were captured without a single Calgary casualty.[53]

The Maisonneuves had been ordered to parallel the Calgary advance and secure the village of Huijbergen. There were fewer identifiable targets in their sector, and the whole attack broke down 1500 metres short of the objective when the part of 'C' Squadron of the Garries assigned to the Maisonneuves 'ran into 88 and 20 mm fire: the infantry went to ground and the attack bogged down, never to get started that day.'[54] The night of 7–8 October was a grim one for the Calgaries and Maisonneuves. The shelling and mortar firing was heavy and fairly continuous, and patrols reported enemy movements that indicated a major build-up on the roads north of Hoogerheide. The Maisonneuves attempted to renew their advance the next morning, only to confront an anti-tank ditch strongly defended by 20 mm, small-arms, and mortar fire. Lieutenant Charles Forbes, who had a well-earned reputation for daring, led his platoon in a flanking movement, but they were quickly driven to ground. Forbes charged the position by himself, firing his Sten gun and yelling at his men to follow. He personally 'rushed two posts, killed two crew members and captured five more.'[55] With this position cleared, the Maisonneuves were able to move forward several hundred yards, relieving the pressure on the Calgary flank.

The Black Watch moved into position in Hoogerheide, hidden by an early morning mist. Their task was to move up on either side of the Korteven road to the junction with the Dool Straat. At 1030 hours the advance began, with one company inching its way up the left side of the road and the other on the right. A troop of Fort Garry tanks followed cautiously. Major Alex Popham, a veteran company commander who had fought in every battle since St-André, reported that his company would have to fall back to the start line. Despite the flexible artillery plan the company was taking too many casualties from troops who were 'well dug in, in well-sited positions, and supported by artillery, mortar, heavy machine guns and scores of snipers.' One platoon, under the command of Lieutenant 'Beau' Lewis, actually crossed the Dool Straat and established itself in three houses in the street before receiving orders to pull back. The withdrawal was well executed, and this platoon took up its new position without incurring any casualties. Counter-attacks began before the withdrawal was complete. From the Black Watch War Diary: 'One enemy self-propelled gun charged down the street firing blindly' but was knocked out by a Fort Garry tank mounting a 17-pounder. The Black Watch carrier platoon, with its Bren guns, dealt with a company-size attack, holding fire 'until the enemy was from 50-60 yards away and then they opened up everything they had, killing over fifty.'[56] The Germans pressed along the Canadian perimeter throughout the afternoon, until it finally decided that these encounters were far too costly.

Dutch civilians and air reconnaissance had provided fairly detailed information on the arrival of strong German reinforcements, and both division and corps intelligence accepted an estimate of between 2,000 and 3,000 troops. Keefler reacted to this information by ordering 4th and 5th Brigades to go over to the defensive and prepare for a major attack, which the army intelligence section – probably on the basis of ULTRA decrypts – had predicted for the night of 8 October.[57] The German attack began with intermittent mortaring and shelling, which seemed to be designed to cover the infiltration of patrols. The Black Watch captured one group of twenty-four young soldiers. The War Diary notes that they belonged to parachute battalions, ranged in age from twenty to twenty-six, and were 'fine physical specimens, keen to fight and with excellent morale.' This had not prevented them from advancing into a trap, suggesting that inexperience and overconfidence were also characteristics of the parachutists.

The battle began in earnest around 0400 hours. The Calgaries had just requested help to deal with infiltrators when a general attack began. There were FOOs with each company commander, and for three hours 5th Field Regiment fired a number of prearranged tasks, 'shooting continually upon targets directed by the companies.' In the slit trenches the riflemen fired at anything that moved and drenched the battle zone with Bren guns firing on fixed lines. Shortly before 0800 hours, Major Ross Ellis, commanding the Calgary reserve company, launched a limited counter-attack of his own. A troop of Fort Garry Horse 'put intense fire for ten minutes on a small wood on the west side of Hoogerheide,' and just as this ended 11 Platoon swept through the woods, emerging quickly with '31 walking prisoners and three wounded.'[58]

By midday on 10 October the German counter-attack seemed to be spent. Colonel Frederich von der Heydte's Parachute Regiment had suffered heavy casualties, estimated at 480 men, in addition to more than fifty prisoners of war.[59] Much is made in the secondary literature of the skill of the German officer corps and the fighting power of German paratroopers, yet the battle for Hoogerheide demonstrated serious deficiencies in German doctrine and tactics – deficiencies that were not uncommon in Northwest Europe. Von der Heydte had launched a frontal attack against forces that had gone over to the defensive and had continued to press forward despite heavy losses. To attack in this manner, when reconnaissance would have shown the weakness of the Canadian right flank, suggests overconfidence and doctrinal rigidity. The texture of the battle also indicates that both in their defensive positions and in tactical counter-attacks the Canadians were more than a match for the enemy. In his postwar memoirs von der Heydte recalled a different version of the battle:

It must have come as a considerable surprise to the Canadian Command that after the successful crossing of the Scheldt they should meet with a battle ready and battle worthy reinforced German Command Parachute Regiment. Nevertheless the Canadian Command decided to make an immediate attack on a wide front ... When the first attack shattered as a result of the resistance of the Parachutists, the Canadians, within three hours, attempted to launch a new attack, clearly with fresh troops: this attack also came to a halt immediately before our main positions. I decided to make a counter-attack with limited aims, which brought us to the outskirts of the villages of Woensdrecht and Hoogerheide. The Canadians – I say that as a German – fought brilliantly: to the rank of Brigadier, the officers stood side by side with their men on the front lines.[60]

The 5th Brigade was pulled back into reserve on the evening of 10 October with orders to prepare for another attempt to seal off the Beveland Isthmus. Foulkes, the Acting Corps Commander, had arrived at brigade headquarters during some of the heaviest fighting with new instructions for offensive action. Megill attempted to persuade him that the 'amount of opposition concentrated on this front'[61] meant that this would at least have to be postponed, but Foulkes was insistent: a breakthrough of the German defences had to be achieved as soon as possible. Foulkes informed Keefler that the South Alberta Regiment, 4th Division's armoured recce unit, would come under his command to help protect the still vulnerable flank. Other 4th Division units were promised later that week.[62] This would eventually allow Keefler to use all three of his brigades in offensive operations. Several plans were developed, but the events of the next few days were probably determined by the unexpected success of a company of the Royal Regiment of Canada.

Major D.S. Beatty, a veteran officer, led a powerful composite force: Toronto Scottish machine guns and heavy mortars, anti-tank guns, combat engineers, and troops from 8th Recce Regiment, together with his 'D' Company of the Royals. A detachment of Dutch resistance fighters joined the battlegroup. They moved west from Ossendrecht on a dyke road above the flooded polders and turned north towards the embankment that carried the road and railway line to Walcheren Island. A series of well-supported platoon attacks and a ground mist that obscured observation allowed Beatty's men to consolidate, and that night a second Royals company joined them. The next day 'D' Company fought off a counter-attack and seized a sluice gate and pumping station just 2000 metres south of the road–rail line, the only east–west road that was clear of the flood waters. On 10 October the rest of the battalion joined the lead companies and attacked north, cutting the main road 'by fire.'[63] The next day, 11 October, the German paratroopers struck all across the front in a renewed attempt to overwhelm the Canadians. Foulkes had ordered 4th Brigade, with both the Maisonneuves and the South Sasks under command, to maintain pressure, and as a consequence 4th Brigade and 6th Parachute Regiment flailed away at each other throughout the day. The Royals fought off six separate counter-attacks – 'No ground was given and heavy casualties inflicted'; in turn, its own attempt to seize the railway embankment was beaten back.[64] The RHLI and South Sasks improved their positions in the Hoogerheide–Huijbergen area, but movement attracted well-placed mortar fire and no serious advance was attempted.

Foulkes met with Keefler and Megill that night and outlined a plan that called for 5th Brigade 'to plug the neck' of the isthmus by attacking through the Royals' position. One battalion would seize the railway embankment; the other two would then go through to seal the approaches to Beveland.[65] Megill again protested that the enemy forces in the area were too strong and too well dug in. The terrain, he insisted, offered the defender too many advantages. His battalions had been in action for two weeks and had lost large numbers of experienced officers, NCOs, and men, and there had been no time to integrate the reinforcements. Foulkes had heard all of this before; his only concession was to promise that the attack would have all available support, including whatever ammunition the artillery and mortar units required. The 5th Brigade was given twenty-four hours to prepare.[66]

Foulkes felt he had little choice in the matter. On 9 October, Montgomery had issued a directive that again emphasized offensive action by 2nd British Army in the Nijmegen sector. First Canadian Army was told to use 'all available resources on the operations designed to give us free use of the port of Antwerp.' Montgomery did promise reinforcements. The 104th U.S. (Timberwolf) and 52nd (Lowland) British Division would both be allotted to Simonds, but neither would be available for at least ten days.

When Eisenhower received a copy of Montgomery's directive he had on his desk a report from Admiral Bertram Ramsay, which criticized the pace of operations to clear the Scheldt and noted that the Canadians were being handicapped by an ammunition shortage. Eisenhower was growing increasingly unhappy with Montgomery's conduct of operations, and used this information in a message to him that concluded: 'I must emphasize that of all our operations on our entire front from Switzerland to the Channel, I consider Antwerp of first importance and I believe that the operations to clear up the entrance require your personal attention.' Montgomery was furious at this reprimand; he accused Ramsay of 'wild statements' and denied there was an ammunition shortage. The field marshal also insisted that Eisenhower had agreed to his policy of making the 'main effort' against the Ruhr.[67]

The most important immediate effect of this high-level confrontation was to place enormous pressure on the two Canadian infantry divisions. On the night of 9 October, 2nd Division was informed that 'the limit to artillery ammunition expenditure [which Monty had denied existed] has been removed.'[68] The battle was to be continued with new intensity, and there was little that any brigade or divisional commander could do about it. When, on the night of 11 October, Foulkes allowed Megill to postpone the brigade's attack until 13 October, he went about as far as he could go.

The extra twenty-four hours were put to good use. The first phase of the assault, code-named Operation Angus, would have to be undertaken by the Black Watch; the Maisonneuves were still more than two hundred riflemen short, and the Calgaries had borne the brunt of the fighting at Hoogerheide. The Black Watch had done well since Ritchie had taken charge, and each company was led by an experienced commander. The attack was built around an elaborate scheme to shoot the battalion onto the embankment one company at a time. One medium and two field regiments, as well as the heavy mortars and machine guns of the Toronto Scottish, were to provide the basic firepower. A Royal Marine heavy anti-aircraft regiment with 3.7-inch guns was also available, but it was short of ammunition. The Fort Garry Horse supplied a troop of tanks, but given the field of fire available to enemy anti-tank guns, it could be used only to provide an initial shoot on the dyke junction, code-named Angus 1. The Spitfires and Typhoons of 84 Group would also be participating, weather permitting. Ritchie examined the ground from an artillery spotter plane on the afternoon of 12 October and at 1930 hours called his final Orders Group.[69]

For the Black Watch, 13 October was 'Black Friday,' the second single-day disaster in the history of the Royal Highland Regiment of Canada. It was not so much total casualties, 145, but the ratio of dead to wounded that marked the day's fighting. Fifty-six Black Watch soldiers were killed or died of wounds, and twenty-seven were taken prisoner.[70] What happened? The plan called for 'C' Company, under Captain N.G. Buch, to make the first bound to the dyke junction. The fire plan was meant to neutralize the enemy by targeting positions back to Korteven and drenching the embankment with high explosives. According to the

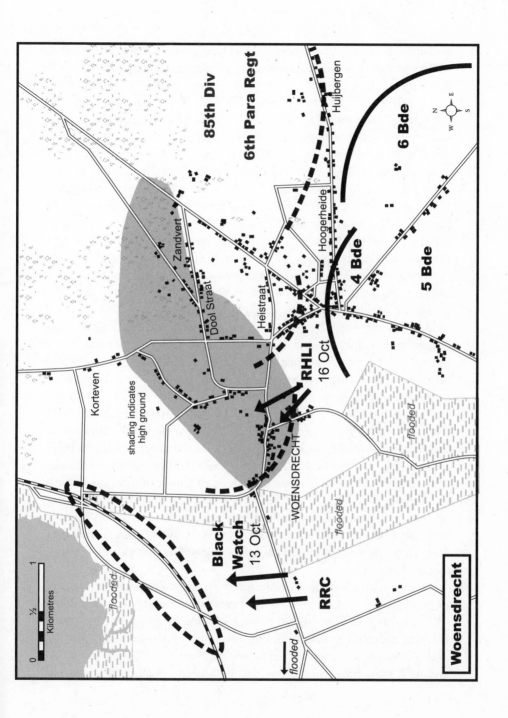

Woensdrecht

divisional artillery commander, much of the effect of this was lost when 'C' Company, 'held up by small-arms fire from dug-in positions,' was thirty minutes late on the start line and lost much of the benefit of the initial artillery program.[71] It was still dark at 0645 hours when the company passed through the Royals' positions, but after less than three hundred yards – perhaps halfway to the objective – the advance faltered in the face of intensive small arms fire. 'B' Company, under Major D.H. Chapman, had moved forward in preparation for the second bound and was heavily mortared while waiting to go in. By 0730 hours both Buch and Chapman had been wounded and other casualties as well as stragglers were filtering back. At first the Black Watch tried to use the mortars and artillery to suppress the enemy fire, but 'owing to the nature of the country it was extremely difficult to indicate a target with any degree of precision.' It was then decided to use smoke to mask the area and get the forward company onto Angus 1 as soon as possible. At 0900 hours the dyke was smoked. Some sections of 'C' Company made it to the objective, only to find themselves pinned against an embankment 8 metres high. As the men tried to dig in, grenades were lobbed over the dyke at them. Most of these men were subsequently taken prisoner, many of them with shrapnel wounds. The balance of 'C' Company withdrew to the start line.[72]

Two attacks had now failed, yet Operation Angus was not called off. Even before the results of the second attack were known, divisional headquarters had issued warning orders for the preparation of a third assault 'led by Wasp flame-throwers.' This could not take place before mid-afternoon, and all that could be done in the meantime was request air support from 84 Group. The records indicate that six requests for air strikes against prearranged targets were forwarded by 5th Brigade and that four were flown. The long, curving dyke between Angus 1 and Angus 2 was a difficult target for fighter-bombers and was not engaged.[73]

Ritchie called his Orders Group for 1500 hours. The battalion was not in good shape. 'C' Company now consisted of twenty-five men while 'B' Company was down to forty-one, including company headquarters. Ritchie concentrated his remaining resources on the task of capturing and consolidating Angus 1. With smoke to screen the right flank, 'A' and 'D' Companies were to move in behind the Wasps, which would flame the embankment from left to right. A squadron of 17-pounder anti-tank guns and a troop of tanks were to engage enemy observation posts. The Wasps moved quickly when the artillery barrage began and were able to complete their task, losing one carrier, which bogged down in the mud. 'D' Company lost its OC in the advance, but Lieutenant Lewis, who had again done a 'marvellous piece of work' in getting his platoon onto the objective, took command, and the rest of the company 'pancaked on the objective.'[74] 'A' Company, which had drawn the more exposed right flank, suffered the heaviest casualties of the day. Lieutenant Alan Mills, who led one of the platoons, described the attack in a letter to his father, written in a hospital in England: 'We formed up behind a dyke and advanced over open ground. When we got practically to our objective (600 yards away) the machine guns and mortars became too hot and we began to drop right and left. Somehow a few managed to get to the objective. Those of us who were hit lay out in an open field with no cover ... The Battalion seems to have horrible shows periodically and this was one of them. A couple of NCOs who lived through May-sur-Orne told me that this was just as bad as that.'[75]

Lewis and his men could be said to have captured Angus 1, but they were quite unable to carry out the order to consolidate. As darkness fell, all jeeps and carriers in the battalion were mobilized to get the wounded out. The Black Watch diary reports that 'many acts of heroism were performed in the dark which will never come to light. No words can pay sufficiently high tribute to those of our men who went out in the dark searching through flooded fields to ensure that all possible had been taken out to proper medical attention.' Shortly after midnight Megill ordered the battalion to withdraw. Operation Angus was over.

The post-mortems on this engagement began almost immediately. Lieutenant William Shea, the battalion intelligence officer, had watched the battle unfold from an observation post. He suggested that the RHC attacks had failed for three reasons: 'first, the great natural defensive strength of the obstacles attacked; second, the determined opposition of the enemy who were paratroops; third, and most important, the poor quality of reinforcements received by the battalion.' According to Shea the reinforcements were 'mainly from the RCASC [service corps] who had little or no infantry training and exhibited poor morale.' They had, he noted, arrived 'a matter of hours before an attack,' and there had

been no time for infantry training. 'Furthermore, most of these reinforcements were not interested in infantry work to begin with, and did
not want to fight.' They did not understand the need to keep up with
the barrage and took cover when their own artillery fired.[76] Shea's
observations are but one example of such complaints from 2nd Division
units in October. With the Minister of National Defence, J.L. Ralston,
visiting corps and divisional headquarters amidst rumours of the possible dispatch of conscripts from Canada for active service, it was
natural that hard-pressed infantry officers would seize on this explanation, but the available evidence does not provide unqualified support
for Shea's interpretation.

The Black Watch, by all accounts including their own, had fought
with conspicuous success in early October at St-Leonard and Brecht,
using reinforcements obtained in September. Casualties – 119 all ranks –
had been evenly spread, and it must be presumed that the fifty-five OR
reinforcements received on 6 October were shared among the companies. The fighting at Hoogerheide, which was also successfully handled,
produced eighty-one casualties, mostly in 'D' Company, which in ordinary circumstances would have received the bulk of the forty-nine
additional replacements who arrived after 6 October. It was normal
practice to leave new men out of battle – especially a battle as difficult
as Angus – but if 'D' Company did take its reinforcements forward,
they must have shared in the day's one considerable success: the one
achieved by Lewis. Many will find this argument difficult to accept, but
it is supported by the available evidence from personnel files and may
be more accurate than impressionistic evidence, even from those who
were there.[77]

The Black Watch were not the only Canadian unit to suffer from
Montgomery's reluctance to assign priority to the Scheldt. Despite a
series of sharp counter-attacks on the South Sasks at Hoogerheide, the
weekend was spent preparing for a new attack, this time to capture the
village of Woensdrecht and the ridge that dominated the battlefield.
Brigadier Cabeldu reluctantly ordered the RHLI to prepare the attack,
and Lieutenant-Colonel Whitaker, with two of his company commanders, carried out an air recce of the battlefield. A sand table model was
constructed, and platoon commanders and their NCOs were brought to
headquarters to study the tentative plan. Whitaker was certain that
only a night attack supported by massive artillery stood any chance of

success. He was confident that his battalion could gain its first objectives; as always, the key question was how to organize to fend off the enemy's counter-attacks. All four companies were given objectives that Whitaker – a well-known quarterback in more peaceful times – code-named after 'Big Four' football teams.[78]

The barrage began at 0330 hours, 16 October, and by 0550 hours all four companies were on their objectives, though a number of enemy positions had been bypassed in the dark and 'would have to be cleaned up.' The two lead companies had pressed north onto the forward slope of the ridge, with one company dug in on the reverse slope and the other tasked with clearing the village. The first enemy counter-attack, a platoon of paras with a self-propelled gun, overran an isolated RHLI platoon. Intense and accurate mortar fire then forced the rest of the company to withdraw. The Canadian gunners were also finding targets, and a steady stream of prisoners of war – including men from the 6th Para Regiment – were dispatched to the PW cage.

Enemy pressure increased as the day wore on. The one available squadron of tanks fired all their ammunition and had to withdraw for more than two hours. The artillery, throwing caution to the winds, fired a 'Yoke' target – all medium and field artillery – to break up one attack, and the tactical air force struck at suspected assembly areas with Spitfires and Typhoons. By evening the RHLI were very thin on the ground, with companies averaging just forty-five men. An Essex Scottish company was brought forward to help out, but as darkness fell, reports that another platoon had been overrun reached battalion headquarters. The next day neither side gained or lost ground; the enemy stopped counter-attacking and the RHLI dug in deeper. The battalion suffered 161 casualties, including twenty-one fatalities, in the first forty-eight hours, and suffered further losses before being relieved by the Queen's Own Cameron Highlanders on 21 October.[79] The enemy continued to hold most of the ridge as well as the road and rail dyke barring access to Beveland.

On 16 October the war diarist at 5th Brigade Headquarters recorded a view that came to be shared by everyone in 2nd Division. 'Cannot understand,' he wrote, 'why they do not put more troops in the area and finish the job once and for all instead of playing about shifting first one battalion and then another. This is beginning to look like a winter campaign unless something breaks soon.'[80]

5

Walcheren

On 5 October the Chief of the Imperial General Staff, Field Marshal Sir Alan Brooke, flew to Versailles to participate in a conference with Eisenhower and his subordinate commanders. Brooke's presence forced Montgomery – who usually sent his Chief of Staff – to attend, and he had to suffer the indignity of speaking as one of Eisenhower's three army group commanders. According to Admiral Bertram Ramsay, Montgomery claimed that he could go to the Ruhr without Antwerp – a comment that afforded Ramsay the opportunity 'to let fly with all my guns at the faulty strategy we had allowed.'[1] Brooke's much quoted diary entry for the day reads: 'One fact stood out clearly, that Antwerp must be captured with the least possible delay. I feel that Monty's strategy is for once at fault, instead of carrying out the advance on Arnhem he ought to have made certain of Antwerp in the first place. Ramsay brought this out well in the discussion and criticized Monty freely. Ike nobly took all the blame on himself as he had approved Monty's suggestion to operate on Arnhem.'[2]

This curious piece of hindsight, from a man who had spent seven crucial days in mid-September fishing in northern Quebec,[3] was not communicated to Montgomery, who left the conference determined to pursue his own strategy.[4]

Brooke's unwavering support for Montgomery encouraged his protégé to begin a new campaign to win back control of the Allied ground forces. He informed Eisenhower 'that the present system of command is most dissatisfying,' and he invited Generals Omar Bradley and Courtney Hodges to 'come and see him' to discuss plans to reach the Ruhr. Bradley, who to put it mildly was thoroughly fed up with his British counterpart, agreed to fly to Eindhoven, but he brought a visitor with him. General George C. Marshall was in Europe to inspect American forces and obtain first-hand information about administrative and logistical problems. His visit to Montgomery, 'the most trying day' of the entire trip,[5] began with Montgomery complaining about Eisenhower's 'lack of grip,' which had led to 'ragged and disjointed' operations. Montgomery realized that Marshall 'entirely disagreed,'[6] but he failed to appreciate the impression he was making on the single most important Anglo-American military leader. From Marshall's perspective, Montgomery had exhibited 'overwhelming egotism' and bad judgment.[7] He went away determined to ignore both Brooke and Montgomery and reinforce Eisenhower's authority.

Marshall's visit and his expression of confidence in Eisenhower may have been the determining factor in the events of the next week. On 9 October, Montgomery issued a new directive that reflected his commitment to continuing the advance to the east. 'We must,' he wrote, 'eliminate certain commitments before we proceed to launch Second Army towards Krefield and the Ruhr.' The priorities were first, the security of the Nijmegen bridgehead; second, the enemy 'west of the Meuse'; and third, 'to open up Antwerp quickly.' The directive did recognize that even if the first 'two things' were dealt with, taking the Port of Antwerp (if it was not yet open) would have to take priority over the advance to the Ruhr. Nevertheless, Montgomery did not intend to let the Antwerp situation interfere with his priorities, and he proposed to reinforce First Canadian Army with two new divisions so that his own plans would not be affected by a diversion of resources to open Antwerp.

The new directive stated that within First Canadian Army, 'Antwerp will take priority over all other offensive operations,' with the exception of the task assigned to 1st British Corps, which was to ensure 'that there is no interference by the enemy' with 2nd British Army's 'supply and communication route running northward through Eindhoven and up to the Rhine at Nijmegen.'[8]

While Montgomery was preparing this directive, Eisenhower was reflecting on information from a joint planning conference of the Royal Navy and the Canadian Army. In a cable marked 'For Field Marshal Montgomery's eyes only from Eisenhower,' the Supreme Commander described the 'severe damage' to the artificial harbour at Arromanches and the Port of Cherbourg caused by a recent gale and noted that this 'reemphasizes the supreme importance of Antwerp':

It is reported to me this morning by the Navy that the Canadian Army will not be able to attack until November 1 unless immediately supplied with adequate ammunition. You know best where the emphasis should be within your army group, but I must repeat we are squarely up against the situation which has been anticipated for months and our intake into the continent will not repeat not support our battle. Unless we have Antwerp producing by the middle of November our entire operation will come to a standstill. I must emphasize that, of all our operations on our entire front from Switzerland to the Channel, I consider Antwerp of first importance and I believe that operations designed to clear up the entrance require your personal attention.[9]

Montgomery replied with an 'eyes only' cable to Eisenhower demanding to know 'by what authority' Ramsay 'makes wild statements to you about my operations about which he can know nothing, repeat nothing.' The 'true facts,' he insisted, were that 'Canadian Army attack began two days ago and tonight is reported to be going much better than at first. There is no shortage of ammunition.' He reminded Eisenhower that the SHAEF conference of 22 September had 'laid down that the main effort of the present operations' is the attack against the Ruhr 'and in your telegram sent here yesterday for Bradley it is again laid down that the first mission of both Army Groups is to gain the line of the Rhine north of Bonn.'[10]

Montgomery was technically right about Eisenhower's orders to reach the Rhine and the beginning of Canadian operations, but there was an ammunition shortage in First Canadian Army and there was absolutely no sign that Montgomery's personal attention was directed towards Antwerp. Eisenhower's Chief of Staff, who drafted the original telegram, had confused the projected date of the assault on Walcheren with the preparatory attack launched by 2nd Canadian Corps, but the essence of the message – 'Antwerp is of first importance' – was clear enough.[11]

Eisenhower replied:

> In everything we do or try to do or to plan our intake of supplies into the Continent looms up as the limiting factor and it is for this reason that no matter how we adjust missions and objectives for both troops in their offensive action towards the east, the possession of the approaches to Antwerp remains with us an objective of vital importance. Let me assure you nothing I might ever say or write with respect to future plans in our advance eastwards is meant to indicate any lessening of the need for Antwerp.[12]

This is vintage Eisenhower: well reasoned, sincere, but lacking a specific order to change priorities. Eisenhower did tell Montgomery that the information on ammunition shortages came from a 'joint planning conference between the Navy and the Canadian Army,' not from Admiral Ramsay; however, he had to accept Montgomery's direct statement that there was no ammunition shortage. Of course there was a shortage of ammunition – and of much else – in First Canadian Army, and both Montgomery and Eisenhower must have known it, and each must have known the other knew it! The immediate effect of Eisenhower's complaint was to bring enormous pressure to bear on 2nd Canadian Division. On the night of 9 October the division was told that 'the limit to artillery ammunition expenditure has been removed.' And as we have seen, the pace of the attacks to seal the Beveland Isthmus was stepped up.[13]

Montgomery's nightly message to Brooke left no doubt about priorities. He announced that the 'operations of Second Army to clean up the area west of the Meuse began on 11 October.'[14] He also reported that 'his maintenance situation was very good' whereas that of 1st U.S. Army was precarious. He proposed to help the Americans, but not by assigning greater priority to Antwerp.[15]

This absurd situation might well have continued for some days had Montgomery resisted the temptation to send Eisenhower a document he titled 'Notes on Command.' This extraordinary memorandum argued for the restoration of a single ground commander, who would be given operational control of all forces allotted to the capture of an objective. 'The current objective,' the note declared, 'was the Ruhr,' and Montgomery suggested that either he or Bradley be given complete authority. He concluded: 'It may be that political and national considerations prevent us having a sound organization. If this is the case I would suggest that we say so. Do not let us pretend we are all right, whereas actually we are very far from being all right in that respect.'[16]

Eisenhower's patience was finally exhausted. After discussing the issues with Marshall, he sent a message to Montgomery which began by noting that Montgomery had avoided the real issue: 'That issue is Antwerp.' If Montgomery continued to believe 'command arrangements' were unsatisfactory, then the problem would have to be 'referred to higher authority for any action they might choose to take, however drastic.'[17]

By the time Eisenhower's hand-delivered letter reached Montgomery on 15 October, German resistance at Woensdrecht had forced Monty to begin paying greater attention to Antwerp. He told Brooke on 14 October that when 8th Corps' operations west of the Meuse were complete, 'I shall turn the Second Army westwards ... this will enable Canadian Army to transfer weight to its left and will thus help to speed up the Antwerp business.' This did not mean abandoning an advance to the Ruhr, as Montgomery intended to group the armies so as 'to regain the ability to operate south-eastwards ... when First U.S. Army is ready.'[18] The next day, after fully absorbing Eisenhower's letter, Montgomery 'decided to make the westerly move of Second Army the main effort of that army.' Warned of Eisenhower's anger, he assured Ike that 'you will hear no more on the subject of command from me ... I and all of us here will weigh-in 100 percent to do what you want ... I have given Antwerp top priority.' This letter, signed 'your devoted and loyal subordinate,'[19] convinced no one that Montgomery was suddenly ready to be a team player, but at least Antwerp might finally get the attention it deserved.

Montgomery's directive of 16 October outlined revised plans for 21 Army Group. 'The use of the Port of Antwerp' was to have 'complete priority,' with the 'whole offensive power of Second British Army' as well as First Canadian Army available. This translated into plans to release 1st British Corps from its responsibilities in the east with its full weight 'pulled over towards Antwerp.' That corps was, however, to transfer 7th Armoured Division, 51st Highland Division, and 34th Armoured Brigade to 2nd British Army,[20] leaving General Crocker with just one infantry and one armoured division until the 104th U.S. Infantry Division was available. Thus, while it is true that once 'the new orders took effect the situation north of Antwerp was transformed,'[21] eight days were to pass before the enemy was forced to abandon Woensdrecht. It is also important to note that the 'whole offensive power of Second British Army' amounted to a very limited advance by 12th British Corps, which did not begin until 22 October.[22]

While his attention was briefly focused on Antwerp, Montgomery lashed out at Ramsay, demanding that he cease dealing directly with General Guy Simonds on operational matters. Ramsay, who was not the least bit intimidated by Montgomery, replied that he had been dealing directly with First Canadian Army 'in all matters concerning Infatuate in view of your apparent reluctance to concern yourself.'

Montgomery promptly backed down, and Ramsay continued to deal directly with Simonds.[23]

Montgomery's directive of 16 October offered Simonds his first opportunity to command a two-corps army since being appointed Acting Army Commander. He decided to reinforce Crocker with 4th Canadian Armoured Division and start the advance on Breda, Roosendaal, and Bergen-op-Zoom without waiting for the promised American division. Plans for Operation Infatuate, the amphibious assaults on Walcheren, were now complete, with 1 November as the target date. To ensure the success of the risky assault landings, Simonds was determined to distract the enemy by launching an attack on the island from the east, and he outlined plans for a new operation code-named Vitality. Vitality I involved the advance of 2nd Canadian Division into South Beveland; Vitality II was to be an amphibious attack on the southeast corner of the Beveland Peninsula designed to outflank the German defences by landing behind the South Beveland Canal.[24] Simonds also revived the army's long-standing request for support from 1st Allied Airborne Army, proposing that 'one para bde drop west of Zuid Beveland related in time to seaborne crossing West Schelde and landward thrust west.'[25] The Airborne commanders saw no reason to change their earlier appreciation that 'terrain characteristics' ruled out the use of paratroops – a view Simonds did not share.

The five distinct operations planned and executed by First Canadian Army in late October and early November 1944 placed an extraordinary burden on army, corps, and divisional staff officers as well as on the combat troops. Shortages of ammunition and fuel continued to plague the army, which depended on Dieppe and Ostend for supplies. The Germans were 'fighting hard ... stubbornly contesting one position after another,' and were evidently determined 'to delay our capture of the Scheldt Estuary at all costs.'[26] Simonds hoped to destroy their will to resist through a series of carefully timed manoeuvres.

The 1st British Corps' long delayed advance could not begin until 4th Armoured Division was fully concentrated, so Operation Suitcase was scheduled for 20 October. The corps commander decided that 4th Armoured Division would lead, advancing 'two brigades up' to seize a crossing of the Roosendaal Canal and secure the town of Esschen. The

49th Division was to 'conform on the right' and 'take over Esschen should 4th Canadian Armoured Division push further north.'[27] This operation was designed to force the enemy to withdraw from the Hoogerheide–Woensdrecht area, allowing 2nd Division to move west. It was not yet clear what part 1st British Corps would be playing in Montgomery's plan to trap the enemy divisions south of the Maas – a task apparently assigned to 12th British Corps.

Major-General Harry Foster employed two mixed brigade groups. Brigadier Robert Moncel, with the Argylls, the Lake Superiors, and two armoured regiments under command, quickly moved north, and by midnight the Governor General's Foot Guards 'were tight against the right flank of the Fusiliers Mont-Royal at Vassenbergen.' Brigadier Jim Jefferson's brigade group, the Lincs and Algonquins with two armoured regiments, kept pace, overcoming isolated enemy positions and scattered mines to reach Kraisstract.[28]

The next morning Moncel's forces reached the Roosendaal Canal, with the Lake Superior Regiment seizing a bridgehead. Foster decided to secure Esschen by sending Jefferson's brigade forward that night. The Algonquins and Lincs moved out in single file on either side of the main road. Bypassing hostile machine gun positions and enemy patrols, the two infantry battalions reached the outskirts of Esschen without arousing the enemy. With 'dawn streaking the sky' the Algonquin rifle companies entered the town and overcame all resistance, aided by a troop of British Columbia Regiment tanks.[29] The next day the Lake Superiors led off at dawn, reaching the Roosendaal Canal at 0930 hours without encountering any opposition except for mines.

The same morning 2nd British Army launched an attack initially designed to capture the bridges over the Maas as far west as Moerdijk. On the German side, O.B. West reported the day's events as follows: 'The situation on 22 October was characterized by the continuation of heavy attacks on the southern front of Fifteenth Army and the launching of an attack from the east towards s'Hertogenbosch ... thus clearly revealing the Allied intention to cut off the German forces south of the Maas ... Orders have been issued for a strengthening of the front in the southern penetration area and the localized withdrawal to prepared positions on the front of 88th Corps [in the east].'[30]

The Germans could give up some ground in the east as they prepared to withdraw onto the Maas bridges, but they would have to stop the advance of 4th Canadian Armoured Division if they were to continue their strategy of blocking access to Beveland and Walcheren. General Otto Sponheimer's 67th Corps had been reinforced by 245th Division, borrowed from the neighbouring corps before the British attack began. The division was supposed to move west in two successive night marches to Wouwsche Plantage and the Woensdrecht area, but the open flank created by 49th Division's advance north proved too tempting, and Sponheimer ordered an attack 'echeloned in depth' with assault guns under command.[31] Major-General G.H. Barker deployed two infantry brigades with 34th British and 2nd Canadian Armoured Brigades, with 9th Royal Tank Regiment's Crocodiles and Flails in support. He knew that the promised American division was arriving and would soon be advancing on his right flank, so he ordered a continuous advance on a one-brigade frontage with controlled bounds. The main weight of 245th Division's attack fell on 56th Brigade at Wuestwezel. After some initial success the German attack 'broke down in the concentrated fire' of British field and medium artillery. Flame-throwing Crocodiles – the first encountered by 245th Division – then forced a withdrawal.[32]

This ill-conceived attack left Battlegroup Chill with the equivalent of two infantry battalions and what was left of 6th Parachute Regiment to hold the ground from Woensdrecht to Nispen, a village just north of Esschen. On the morning of 23 October, Chill collected a small mobile force, built around some self-propelled guns, and ordered it to retake Esschen. This force collided with one of Moncel's battlegroups, which was advancing towards Wouwsche Plantage. The lead squadron of Governor General's Foot Guards lost seven tanks in the encounter, but this temporary check did not prevent a second Canadian battlegroup from advancing north of Hoogerheide and assisting 2nd Division forward to a line three kilometres north of Woensdrecht. On the evening of 23 October, 67th Corps ordered a withdrawal of the entire front to avoid encirclement.[33]

The new German defensive line south of Bergen-op-Zoom included Wouwsche Plantage and the heavily wooded area around it. Three days of bitter fighting were required to overcome these defences. After Jefferson's brigade group was relieved by the British, it moved west to Huijbergen and 4th Armoured Division was able to mount parallel thrusts towards Bergen-op-Zoom and Heerle. Field Marshal Gerd von Rundstedt decided on 27 October to 'forestall an enemy breakthrough and economize our strength' by authorizing 15th Army to withdraw to the general line Bergen-op-Zoom/Roosendaal/Breda,'[34] leaving the severely weakened 70th Infantry Division to fend for itself in South Beveland.

German rear echelon troops had been preparing new defensive positions hinging on Bergen-op-Zoom. When Colonel Frederich von der Heydte ordered the evacuation of the town, the mayor insisted that the refugee-swollen population could not leave. Von der Heydte decided to abandon the city centre, and set up his defences along the River Zoom. The civilians were warned that if they interfered with the army, the city would be burned. The withdrawal was completed on the afternoon of 27 October, and that evening the Lincs and SARs entered Bergen, establishing their headquarters at the Grote Markt, which quickly became the centre of celebrations.[35]

The main goal of the 1st British Corps advance, 'to enable us to operate freely westwards along the Beveland isthmus,' had been accomplished by 24 October, and Montgomery was again turning his attention to the Ruhr. On 25 October, he arrived at Crocker's corps headquarters and visited each division to urge all possible speed in pressing the enemy back to the Maas.[36] With Polish Armoured Division joining in the advance, Crocker would have four divisions available to pursue the enemy. The plan to trap the Germans south of the river by using 'the whole offensive power' of 2nd British Army 'in a strong thrust westwards' was thus abandoned. Two days later, an attack from the eastern side of the Nijmegen salient forced General Miles Dempsey to return units to 8th Corps and limit advances west of s'Hertengobosch.[37] Crocker's divisions were ordered to drive ahead for Moerdijke and the Maas – an advance that continued until 7 November, when the last elements of 15th Army crossed the Maas and blew the Moerdijke bridges.[38]

The decision to force the enemy to withdraw across the Maas as quickly as possible was necessitated by Montgomery's plans to resume the advance to the Rhine by mid-November. This could be accomplished only if First Canadian Army could defend the long left flank, using 1st British Corps to hold the Maas while 2nd Canadian Corps took over the Nijmegen sector. Such a timetable required all four of Crocker's divisions to attack the enemy's new defensive line as soon as possible.

The actions fought by 4th Canadian Armoured Division in the final week of the advance to the Maas were difficult and costly encounters with the best troops available to 15th Army. General Kurt Chill's battlegroup, braced by 6th Parachute Regiment and a number of assault gun companies, fought a series of delaying actions, avoiding the costly counter-attacks that had been employed in the battles for Woensdrecht. The 6th Parachute fought these battles without von der Heydte, who had been transferred to command the Parachute Army Training School on 23 October. His order of the day on leaving the regiment evoked the perverted values of the German officer class in 1944: 'When everything falls apart and wave after wave overcomes our people, a parachutist of my regiment will, despite fate and in the face of the storm, hold high over the flood the flag on which there is written, in glowing letters, only one word: Greater Germany.'[39]

The Parachute Regiment's determined defence of the Zoom line left Jefferson's brigade 'tottering with exhaustion.'[40] Finally, the danger of encirclement from Moncel's force forced the Germans to withdraw. Moncel's brigade began a night advance to Steenbergen. This cross-country attack quickly turned into a bitter struggle for the village of Welberg, which the enemy had selected as its fall-back position. In this polder country a slight rise, like the sand ridge of Welberg, was a vital tactical feature. With most of the approaches flooded or mined, or both, it took a set-piece attack to reach the ruins of the village.[41] During the seventeen days from 20 October, 4th Division suffered close to nine hundred casualties, including 104 men killed in action and 96 listed as missing.[42] The sound of explosions at the Moerdijke bridges was music to the Canadians' ears.

The resolute actions carried out by the German battlegroups at Woensdrecht and then north of Bergen-op-Zoom raise an obvious question: Why was 6th Parachute Regiment withdrawn north, instead of west to assist 70th Division in the far more vital task of defending Beveland and Walcheren? Hitler and his senior commanders had long insisted that the Allies must be prevented from making use of the port of Antwerp, and they had considered committing at least parts of the Parachute Regiment to Beveland. But on 20 October, as 4th Armoured Division began its push north, von Rundstedt issued orders assigning the defence of Beveland and Walcheren to 70th Division. He did this knowing full well that Lieutenant-General Wilhelm Daser's command was now reduced to four battalions of infantry, two battalions of fortress troops, and two engineer battalions functioning as infantry.[43] The senior German naval officer in the Netherlands, Vice Admiral Gustav Kleikamp, protested these orders, arguing that there were insufficient troops to defend the coastal gun batteries and that many of the prepared positions would be left unoccupied.[44] His protest was ignored; von Rundstedt prepared to implement Hitler's orders to hold large bridgeheads south of the Maas – bridgeheads that would be needed if a large-scale offensive to recover Antwerp was launched.[45]

First Canadian Army's plans for the capture of Beveland and Walcheren were shaped by the pattern of tides on the coast of Walcheren Island. The Royal Navy had determined that the most favourable days for an assault landing at Westkapelle were the first and fourteenth of November, and there was enormous pressure on everyone to launch concentric attacks on the island by 1 November. This urgency helps explain why 2nd Division was ordered back into action before the enemy was forced to withdraw from Woensdrecht. On 22 October, while 4th Division's battle for Wouwsche still raged, Major-General Charles Foulkes, the Acting Corps Commander, arrived at Brigadier R. Holley Keefler's headquarters to outline plans for an advance to clear out enemy positions that could interfere with Vitality I, the liberation of South Beveland. Foulkes insisted that 'there would be no discussion of when the operation would take place' as a 'large scale appreciation had been made and all the risks pertaining to the situation were understood.' Whatever the risks, the 'task for 2nd Canadian Division was set so that before the last hour on 23 October some forces would be started out on the South Beveland peninsula.'[46]

Had Foulkes waited twenty-four hours until the full implications of 4th Division's advance were evident to the Germans, the actions carried out by 5th and 6th Brigades would have been relatively easy. As it was, the lead battalions met strong opposition from carefully registered mortar fire as well as from a para battalion, which dominated the area from well-camouflaged machine gun posts. Fortunately, the Canadian battalion commanders behaved sensibly, and the next morning, 24 October, the Calgaries and the Queen's Own Cameron Highlanders reported that the enemy had withdrawn.[47]

With the route into South Beveland open, Operation Vitality I began on the morning of 24 October. In the early hours of a 'rainy, pitch-bleak morning two "Jock Columns" of Essex Regiment infantry, 8th Recce armoured cars and Fort Garry tanks' set out for the Beveland Canal. Captain T.M. Hunter, the Historical Officer attached to 2nd Division, provided a graphic description of the battlefield around Woensdrecht. Scarred by 'deep craters, ruined & flooded farmhouses, together with dead sheep and cattle,' it was littered by the 'usual debris of war' and dotted with 'German dugouts, skilfully sited in the sides of the high dykes.' German graves, 'each marked with a rude cross surmounted by a steel helmet' added to the desolation.[48]

General Daser was to tell Canadian interrogators that his preparations for the defence of South Beveland included the creation of forward positions at the neck of the isthmus near Bath, with the Beveland Canal designated the second line of defence. The town of Goes was fortified as a 'strong point,' and additional field works were built along the south coast. On 24 October, Daser had deployed two companies supported by a heavy machine gun platoon and three gun batteries near Bath, and it was this force that met the initial Canadian advance.[49]

The decision to send an armoured battlegroup along a narrow, dyked road surrounded by flooded or saturated fields was a trifle optimistic, and after 'one 75mm gun had knocked out three recce cars and three tanks,' it was decided that this type of formation was not advisable.[50] The next day a conventional infantry attack with sufficient artillery and mortar fire overwhelmed the enemy position.

Attempts to accelerate the advance were impeded by water, mud, mines, and several surviving anti-tank guns controlling the railway–road embankment, the only passable route across the narrowest part of the isthmus. To outflank the enemy, the infantry had to wade across flooded polders in a cold, continuous rain. All three battalions of 4th Brigade were committed to the battle, and by midday on 25 October some progress had been made.

One key to success in South Beveland was the continuing development of close cooperation between the Fort Garry Horse and the infantry battalions. Since the rest of 2nd Canadian Armoured Brigade was still with 1st British Corps, the weary, understrength Garry squadrons were constantly in action supporting the forward infantry companies. Troop commanders quickly learned that tanks could not lead an advance along the narrow, elevated roads. They soon improvised methods for supporting the infantry from 'hull down' positions behind lateral dykes. These involved firing through holes blown in the dykes, or acting as mobile artillery under the direction of FOOs.[51]

From Foulkes's perspective, this exhausting battle was going according to plan. It must have been so, for at 0245 hours on 26 October, Operation Vitality II began, with the army's indefatigable navigator, Lieutenant-Commander R.D. Franks, guiding a flotilla of landing craft from Terneuzen to the south side of the peninsula behind the canal defences. The task had been assigned to 156th Brigade of 52nd (Lowland) Division, and the Scottish soldiers found the steep and slippery dykes a greater obstacle than the enemy. The terrain and the limited number of available Buffaloes slowed the expansion of the bridgehead, but by first light on 27 October, 4th and 5th Battalions of the Royal Scots Fusiliers had broken the back of the German resistance, capturing more than one hundred prisoners and 'severely punishing' the enemy's counter-attacks.[52]

The success of Vitality II was soon measured by the collapse of enemy resistance at the Beveland Canal. Brigadier J.C. Gauvreau's 6th Brigade was able to cross on the afternoon of 27 October, and the engineers had bridges in place the next morning. Brigadier Gauvreau was one of the many casualties caused by mines, and Lieutenant-Colonel E.P. Thompson, the twenty-three-year-old CO of the Camerons of Canada, took over the brigade. The flooded ground and endless rain continued to hamper operations, but on 28 October contact was made with Scottish troops advancing along the south coast. An officer of the Royal Regiment of Canada described his first encounter with the 52nd Lowland Division:

> I was out with a unit of carriers, maintaining a standing patrol on the left flank of the battalion ... All our men were desperately tired and in a filthy, wet, muddy condition. On our way we were terribly surprised to find a

party of what were obviously Allied troops landing in a small boat. Then forth from the boat onto the shore stepped what seemed to me to be the finest soldier I had ever seen in my life, a fine figure of a Scottish gentleman, carrying the shepherd's crook affected by some senior Scottish officers in place of a cane or a swagger stick. He had a small pack neatly adjusted on his back. (I had absolutely no idea where mine was and couldn't care less.) His gas cape was neatly rolled. (I had last seen mine somewhere around Eterville). He had his pistol in a neatly blanched web holster. (I had mine in my hip pocket.) He had a neatly kept map case. (I had mine stuck in my breast pocket.) He was a Colonel and I was a Captain. His boots were neatly polished and I was wearing turned-down rubber boots. I did manage to salute, although I think it must have been haphazard. He politely enquired if we were Canadians. (Although who else could have looked as we did?) I assured him we were. He asked if I could direct him to battalion headquarters. I did better than that. I escorted him to battalion headquarters. I was taking no chances on losing such a beautiful specimen to the German Army.[53]

It would have been difficult to find a more unlikely partnership than the one circumstance had forced on 52nd Lowland Division and the Canadians. Mobilized in 1939 as a territorial division, the 52nd had been reorganized as a mountain division and subjected to an intense training regime in the hills of Scotland. Those who could not meet the required physical standard joined reinforcement drafts headed for the Middle East and Italy. By late 1943 the division's major role was to lend credibility to the deception plan – known as Fortitude North – that suggested an invasion of Norway.[54]

Major-General E. Hakewill-Smith and most of his senior officers were regular army – professional soldiers who demanded a rigid standard of discipline. Hakewill-Smith boasted that the 52nd 'was the hardest, fittest and best trained division in the army,' and he may have been right. The problem was that the division had not been in combat and was stuck in a backwater. According to Hakewill-Smith, 'every officer and man is still haunted by the fear that the war will end before they have had a good smack at the Boche.'[55]

Brooke responded by ordering the division to 'close down development work on mountain warfare equipment' and transform itself into an 'air transportable' formation able to bring two of its three brigades into action with their light mountain artillery carried in Dakota aircraft.[56] This reorganization, completed in August 1944, led to an assignment to join the airborne troops north of Arnhem if landing fields were secured. The seaborne brigade left for the continent on 12 September, but the balance of the division spent the first days of Market Garden at airfields in Britain waiting for a call that never came.

On 9 October Montgomery asked Brooke to assign the division to First Canadian Army. The divisional recce regiment and 157th Brigade were the first to arrive, reporting on 16 October. They relieved 10th Canadian Infantry Brigade at the Leopold Canal, then sent two battalions into the pocket to take up defensive positions around Aardenburg, relieving the exhausted battalions of 7th Brigade. The Scottish officers were not impressed with Canadian discipline or cleanliness. The CO of 52nd Recce Regiment complained that the 'billets were filthy and looted' and insisted that 'no one in Scotland would ask a pig to lie in the houses on the south side of the canal.'[57] The Canadians in turn were unimpressed with these spit-and-polish soldiers who spent five days north of the Leopold in static positions, mounting patrols.[58] All of this was no doubt unfair, but when 7th Brigade was sent back into battle to clear the coastal area around Cadzand, on passing Scottish troops going the other way, they were not in a generous mood. Both parties would change their minds about the fighting qualities of their counterparts: the Canadians would express grudging admiration for these impressive-looking soldiers, and the Scots would come to admit that the dirty, undisciplined Canadians were tough, relentless fighters.[59]

Simonds had intended to use the Lowland Division to carry out Phase III of Switchback, that is, the clearing up of the last part of the Breskens Pocket. These orders were countermanded in the context of revised plans for Operations Vitality and Infatuate. The Acting Corps Commander, Foulkes, had warned 5th Brigade to prepare for the seaborne assault on Beveland, but continued enemy resistance at Woensdrecht and relative progress at Breskens led Simonds to use 52nd Division for Vitality II and the battle for Walcheren.[60]

After the Beveland Canal defences were breached, the road network allowed Keefler to send two brigades forward. Some veterans of the campaign, as well as the official historian, have maintained that 'to encourage rapid advance,' the acting division commander promised that the 'brigade reaching the area first would hold the near end of the causeway; the other would push across it and form a bridgehead.'[61] Versions of this story may have circulated in November, but there was no race to the causeway. The specific tasks and objectives of each brigade are spelled out in the war diaries, message logs, and operational orders. As might be expected, the divisional plan called for the advance to be made in a series of bounds, with 4th Brigade leading off into the peninsula and 6th Brigade seizing the bridgehead across the Beveland Canal. At that point, 1030 hours 28 October, 5th Brigade was to pass through 'to be directed initially on the town of Goes. If this is successful we are to push on west with an ultimate objective of the causeway linking Zuid Beveland and Walcheren Island.' The 4th Brigade's orders were 'to exploit as far as main road junction and area Eversdijk,' linking up with 157th Brigade, who were to prevent the enemy from forming a 'hardcore of resistance in the southwest corner of Beveland.'[62]

On the morning of 29 October, the day that some suggest Keefler gave the 'race' order, both Canadian brigades were moving steadily west, meeting virtually no resistance. The 5th Brigade's War Diary for 29 October notes: 'Our job has not changed – we are still to go as fast as possible for the causeway. 4th Brigade are pushing out to the west on our left flank and established contact with 157th Brigade during the day.'[63]

The next morning 4th Brigade made rapid progress and reached the west shore of South Beveland. Keefler, responding to unrelenting pressure from corps headquarters, 'asked' Brigadier Cabeldu 'to try and exploit further and push a bridgehead over the causeway.' Cabeldu protested, arguing that only very fresh troops with extensive artillery support could cross a 1200 metre embankment that was less than 40 metres wide in the face of strong enemy resistance. The alternative – a proper assault crossing of the water obstacle – would require some time to mount. Keefler agreed to relieve Cabeldu of responsibility for the crossing, but ordered him to seize the enemy positions at the Beveland end of the Walcheren causeway. The Royals accomplished this task in a finely controlled night action that pinched off all the defenders by moving along the water's edge. They captured 153 prisoners and a great deal of equipment.[64]

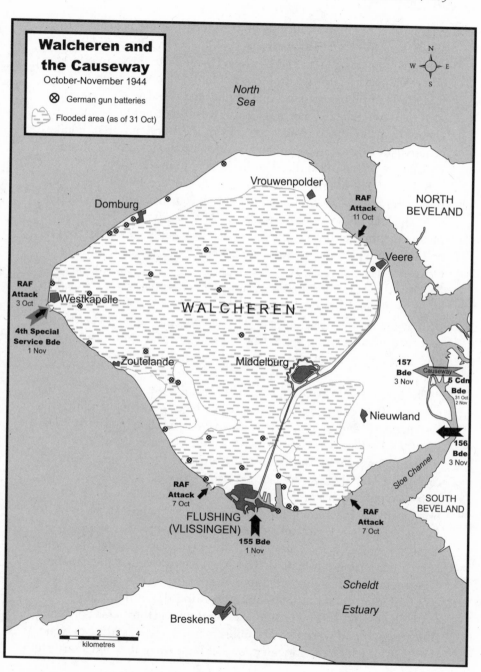

Walcheren and the Causeway
October-November 1944

⊗ German gun batteries

Flooded area (as of 31 Oct)

At 0930 hours on the morning of 31 October, Simonds decided to go ahead with the amphibious attacks on Walcheren Island. Foulkes immediately sent a signal to 2nd Division Headquarters: 'No interference on Walcheren by guns or air. Most desirable we get on with it.'[65] The hazardous amphibious attacks on Flushing and Westkapelle were scheduled for dawn the next morning, and it was important to persuade the enemy that the attack would come from the Beveland area. Foulkes ordered 5th Brigade to begin the operation by seizing a bridgehead on Walcheren, which could then be turned over to the Scots.[66]

Brigadier Bill Megill, whose troops were every bit as weary and understrength as Cabeldu's, accepted his new instructions without protest. He had argued with Foulkes in Normandy and attempted to persuade him that the 13 October attack was badly conceived, but he had no such objections to the task outlined for the brigade early on 31 October.[67] The plan called for the Calgaries – who still had officers and NCOs trained for amphibious assaults – to cross the water obstacle in storm boats and tracked landing vehicles. The Maisonneuves would then be ferried over to join them. This action, coming hours before the seaborne invasion, might prevent the enemy from shifting troops to Flushing or Westkapelle and result in the rapid occupation of Middelburg.[68]

The Calgaries' War Diary records in detail the preparations for the crossing. One company was 'put through its paces in handling the assault boats,' and two privates were given instruction in driving 'Weasel' LVTs, which were to be used to ferry ammunition. While the preparations went ahead, the Black Watch tried to advance along the causeway. Megill asked the Black Watch to conduct a 'quick operation' to try to 'push a strong fighting patrol on to the other side.'[69] Ritchie organized his battalion with all four rifle companies in position to follow up success. Unfortunately, the leading troops were stopped cold some 75 metres before the end of the causeway, leaving the other companies strung out behind. The War Diary describes the situation: 'The enemy had his guns sited to give crossfire on the causeway with one tank dug-in and an anti-tank gun firing down the centre of the road. Enemy snipers had positioned themselves in the marsh bordering the causeway and were very accurate ... The enemy was firing one gun, the shells of which raised water 200 feet high when they fell short. He was also ricocheting A.P. shells down the causeway which was hard on the morale of the war.' The battalion suffered ten killed and thirty-four wounded before it was able to withdraw.[70]

While the Black Watch were digging in, the engineers sent to reconnoitre the water crossing reported that 'there was not sufficient water even at high tide to permit such an operation.' They further reported that 'the ground was too saturated for movement on foot and there were too many runnels in the mud flats to permit "Weasels" to operate.' There was no time for further reconnaissance; if an attack to divert attention from the main landings was to take place, it would have to be across the causeway. The Calgaries' scout officer, Lieutenant Gordon Sellar, who had been detailed to observe the Black Watch attack, was able to provide information on the nature of the enemy resistance and the location of the main defensive line. The newly appointed CO of the Calgaries, Lieutenant-Colonel Ross Ellis, proposed to use the darkness and the barrage to get one company 'to traverse the causeway and fan out north, south and west.'[71] The other companies were to pass through and establish a substantial bridgehead encompassing the village of Arnemuiden. The Maisonneuves would then cross to join the Calgaries. A comprehensive artillery scheme was arranged, with 5th Field Regiment and a medium regiment being joined by a newly arrived field regiment from 52nd Division.

Captain Nobby Clarke got his men moving forward early, as they were 'complaining of sore feet' in the intense cold. At 2340 hours the barrage began. Ten minutes later, battalion headquarters was informed: 'Baker Company reports Merry Christmas' – the attack was underway. The fire plan had been designed to blanket the enemy positions on the island, but with the withdrawal of the Black Watch the Germans had moved well out onto the causeway. Captain Clarke quickly realized the futility of the situation, and Megill accepted the request to withdraw and start again with a new fire plan that would sweep the enemy off the causeway and suppress opposition from the island. The barrage fired by two field regiments was made tight by arranging 'lifts' of just fifty yards every two minutes.[72]

The Calgaries moved out at 0605 hours. It was still very dark, but the men were able to work forward quickly, using the barrage to reach the western end of the causeway. The lead company was held up there for the next several hours, but the FOO directed fire on a succession of targets. By 0930 hours the initial objectives on the island were secure and prisoners were on their way out. Major Bruce Mackenzie advised Ellis that another company could be sent through them, 'although care should be taken because of the high velocity gun firing down the road.' Two other Calgary companies crossed to the island, with the remaining company at the western end of the causeway. Ellis and his scout officer set out across the causeway at 1545 hours. Sellar can still remember the impression Ellis made on him that afternoon. Freshly shaven and neatly dressed, and apparently calm and good humoured, he checked the forward positions, chatting to the men in the slit trenches. Sellar recalls: 'It was amazing to see them brighten up and grin broadly when they saw the Colonel.' Ellis and Sellar then 'slowly walked back down the causeway talking to the men dug in there.'[73]

The Calgaries seemed in control of the bridgehead, but the shelling intensified. One company was hit by a heavy counter-attack and forced to retreat. Able Company's only officer, Captain Wynn Lasher, was wounded, and the situation seemed to be deteriorating. The Brigade Major, George Hees, volunteered to take Lasher's place, and the spare artillery FOO, Captain Walter Newman, asked to go along as second-in-command. Ellis, on his way back to the island to obtain first-hand information, took the two men across and settled them in. The situation had deteriorated further, and it was clear that the enemy was determined to prevent a breakthrough to Middelburg.[74] Ellis once again walked back to Beveland and brigade headquarters. Megill listened to his report but had to tell him to hang on until 'division decided what to do.' At divisional headquarters, Keefler was under considerable pressure from Foulkes. At 1630 hours, corps sent a signal that reported the interception of a German wireless message stating that all German troops in Walcheren were 'ready to surrender.' Foulkes ordered Keefler 'to push on and establish our bridgehead as soon as possible.'[75]

Detailed instructions did not arrive from division until shortly before midnight. The landings at Flushing and Westkapelle were going well after some initial problems, and Megill was told to be prepared to hand over to 157th Infantry Brigade at 0600 hours the next morning. 'It was stipulated however that a further attack would be necessary and the end of the Walcheren causeway firmly controlled before the relief took place.'[76]

Megill had already developed a plan to pass the Maisonneuves through the Calgary position, but Keefler 'ruled that this attack would continue one hour only and relief would take place in the position reached at that time.' In consequence it was decided to commit only two companies of the Maisonneuves, since it was not considered possible to deploy more men along the defile of the causeway in that time. Ellis had withdrawn most of his battalion to Beveland, which meant that no more than fifty men were holding the dyke at the edge of the island.[77]

The lead Maisonneuve company, commanded by Captain Camille Montpetit, was in position at 0400 hours. Unfortunately, the barrage, fired by 52nd Division artillery, began 300 metres short, striking the Calgary positions and delaying the Maisonneuves, who were still 300 metres from the end of the causeway when the guns stopped. Megill ordered the Maisonneuves to dig in where they were and wait to be relieved by the Glasgow Highlanders, but Montpetit's company did not receive the order. They had made contact with the Calgary Highlanders and moved forward onto the island, assuming their comrades were close behind.[78]

The Maisonneuve force consisted of about forty men, including six volunteers from the Belgian White Brigade who had been with the battalion since September. Lieutenant Charles Forbes, heading 18th Platoon, and Lieutenant Guy de Merlis, commanding 16th Platoon, were skilled and aggressive leaders, and the Maisonneuves worked their way forward to a position some 500 metres inland. A farmhouse became company headquarters, with the two platoons deployed back to back along the main road on both sides of the railway underpass. They were, however, totally isolated. For the next eight hours this small battlegroup fought with extraordinary courage. Lieutenant D.G. Innes, an FOO with 5th Field Regiment, maintained contact with Montpetit's men, calling down defensive fire. Rocket Typhoons were also in action, but it was the efforts of individuals that epitomized the day's heroic deeds. Private J.C. Carrière, a signaller, volunteered to stalk a 20 mm gun. After crawling four hundred yards along a shallow ditch partly filled with water, 'he reached a point from which he could bring fire to bear from his PIAT.' Carrière was wounded but managed to knock out the gun and return to his comrades.[79]

Brigadier J.D. Russell, commanding 157th Lowland Brigade, had arrived at Megill's headquarters on the morning of 1 November. He was understandably unhappy at the prospect of sending a battalion into this chaotic situation. His commander had urged him to find an alternative way onto the island, and divisional engineers were searching for a route well to the south of the causeway.[80] This action was expected to take some time, so it is not difficult to understand why Hakewill-Smith challenged Foulkes, the Acting Corps Commander, when the latter ordered 52nd Division to attack across the causeway.[81] This dispute involved an issue quite separate from the decision to commit 5th Brigade on 31 October. Russell agreed to take over the bridgehead on 2 November, but only with a minimum of troops. The Glasgow Highlanders sent two platoons forward, but they were forced to dig in at the western edge of the causeway. Private Charles Ouellet volunteered to contact the relieving troops and with a companion attacked the position holding up the Scottish soldiers. He was able to lead elements of one Scottish platoon to Montpetit's headquarters.[82]

By the afternoon of 2 November the Glasgow Highlanders, with the help of Rocket Typhoons and much artillery, had re-established a narrow bridgehead at the western end of the causeway, allowing the remaining Maisonneuves to withdraw. The Germans continued to do all they could to prevent expansion of the bridgehead and were totally unprepared that night when 6th Cameronians outflanked their position by crossing to the island through the mudflats well south of the causeway. After Canadian engineers, using armoured bulldozers, filled the large crater on the causeway, the bridgehead was firmed up and German soldiers began to surrender rather than counter-attack.[83]

By then 5th Brigade was on its way to Belgium for a long-overdue rest. The causeway had cost the Calgaries seventeen killed and forty-six wounded. The Maisonneuves, with their companies of less than sixty men, had just one fatality and ten wounded. The battle for the causeway was not the ill-conceived disaster as so often portrayed. The Acting Corps Commander's orders to mount an attack and maintain pressure were a necessary part of the overall plan to capture Walcheren Island. The operation itself was carried out with considerable skill and relatively small losses.

The causeway diversion was badly needed. The plans for Operation Infatuate, the clearing of Walcheren Island, placed enormous demands on the assault troops and naval flotillas. The risks taken could only be justified by the urgency to open the Port of Antwerp. The attack on Flushing, carried out with limited air support,[84] required 4th Commando – the unit raised by Simon Fraser, Lord Lovat, that had fought with distinction at Dieppe – to cross the Scheldt from Breskens in Landing Craft Assault (LCAs). They were to seize the harbour as a base for 155th Brigade, which was to pass through and clear the partly flooded streets of the town. The commandos got ashore 'without many casualties' and began the task of overcoming the numerous pillboxes and gun emplacements. The 4th Battalion, King's Own Scottish Borderers (KOSB), joined the commandos, clearing part of the town centre. The Germans withdrew to the northern and western fringes of the town while several thousand Dutch civilians sought safety behind the British lines, where they were ferried to Breskens.

On the morning of 2 November the other battalions of 155th Brigade passed through, with 5th KOSB attempting to reach Middelburg through the flood waters and the 7/9th Battalion Royal Scots Fusiliers advancing west towards the German garrison headquarters at the Hotel Britannia. The Fusiliers worked their way along streets waist deep in water stirred by a tidal current. The Britannia, protected by a network of bunkers and pillboxes and with a four-barrelled 20 mm gun on the roof, fell to a direct assault that led to the capture of six hundred men, including the garrison commander. By nightfall on 3 November, Flushing was secure. The next day General Daser surrendered Middelburg to a flotilla of Buffaloes that had made their way across the floods.[85]

The assault on Flushing was challenging enough for anyone, but its difficulties paled in comparison to those faced by Force T at Westkapelle. The 182 ships involved in this action left Ostend just after midnight on 31 October. Simonds and Ramsay allowed the force commanders to decide whether the operation was feasible when they reached the island.

On 1 November at 0600 hours Simonds signalled, in clear, that it was 'extremely unlikely any air support, air spotting or air smoke owing to airfield conditions and forecast.' Despite this, the naval force commander, Rear Admiral A.F. Pugsley, decided to go ahead with the operation, and at 0820 hours the heavy support squadron, HMS *Warspite* and the monitors HMS *Erebus* and *Roberts*, opened fire. The close support squadron, made up of twenty-seven vessels with firepower ranging from rockets to 17-pounder anti-tank guns, drew most of the enemy fire, permitting the assault craft to pass through the breach in the dyke. Nine support ships were lost and eleven badly damaged, but the commandos were landed and able to begin a three-day battle for the coastal guns.[86] Gale-force winds, driving rain, and mines scattered among the dunes complicated the task of securing the gun positions, but by nightfall on 1 November the troops of 4th Special Service Brigade were safely ashore. The next day the advance along the rim of the flooded island began. First Canadian Army Headquarters was responsible for much of the planning and preparation of Operation Infatuate, but the only Canadian troops directly involved were two Royal Canadian Army Medical Corps surgical teams, which landed with the commandos at Westkapelle.[87] Their story, recalled in Appendix H, was just one episode in a brutal battle that ended on 8 November. By then, minesweepers had cleared the Scheldt as far as Terneuzen.

Two weeks later the Port of Antwerp welcomed the first merchant ship, the Canadian-built *Fort Cataraqui*. A Canadian officer among those watching the arrival of the first ship noted that almost every headquarters was represented except the Canadian Army. Cinderella was back at work.[88] The Port of Antwerp was open just in time to meet the supply needs of Allied armies forced to deal with the Germans' December offensive, an operation designed to recapture Antwerp.

The post-mortems on Operation Infatuate began almost immediately. The heavy casualties suffered by the navy prompted Pugsley to protest the limited commitment of Bomber Command and the failure to silence any of the Walcheren gun batteries. Pugsley, with Ramsay's support, also complained that 'no proper joint plan was ever produced' because the RAF remained the sole judges of what air support could be provided.

Simonds wrote a detailed reply to this report, agreeing with many of Pugsley's comments on the RAF but insisting that a successful 'joint naval and army plan based upon the tasks and outline which had been given to them was produced by the force commanders responsible for the operation.'[89] He concluded his reply with this comment: 'It would be my wish that the operations could have succeeded with much lighter naval casualties, but to keep things in perspective I must point out that these were a mere fraction of the casualties suffered by the army formations involved in the operations for clearing the Scheldt Estuary.'

The Canadian share of those army casualties – more than 90 per cent of the total – included 1,418 men killed in action and 4,949 wounded.[90]

6 〜⌒

Regeneration

On 18 October, two days after Montgomery had taken steps to make the opening of Antwerp a priority, he met with Eisenhower and Bradley to discuss future strategy. Despite concerns about shortages in men and materiel, the three senior commanders agreed on ambitious plans 'to defeat decisively the enemy west of the Rhine; then to seize the Ruhr and, subsequently, to advance deep into Germany.'[1] Montgomery believed that the first phase of these operations could begin as early as 10 November, and he wanted to complete a regrouping of his forces as soon as possible. First Canadian Army was to take over responsibility for the front from the sea to the Reichswald Forest, with 1st British Corps guarding the River Maas and 2nd Canadian Corps relieving American and British forces at Nijmegen.

Montgomery did not envisage a major role for the Canadians; he was determined to attack the enemy in the Venlo area, well to the south of the Canadian sector. This decision, outlined in his directive of 2 November,[2] provided the Canadian army with a much needed opportunity to draw breath after five months of intense combat. The two infantry divisions were given a week-long rest period in Belgium before taking over positions in the Nijmegen salient – an experience that did much to restore the shattered morale of men who had come close to the breaking point.

The operations carried out by First Canadian Army in the autumn of 1944 had placed enormous pressure on front line soldiers. Between 20 September and 7 November, 6,784 men had been wounded and 3,244 reported killed or missing in action. An additional 949 had been treated for battle exhaustion, and 5,008 had been evacuated to hospitals as sick.[3] These losses – 14 per cent of the total strength of the Canadian component of 21 Army Group[4] – were heavily concentrated in the twenty-one infantry battalions. When we use the conservative figure of 70 per cent as the proportion of the losses in infantry units, we arrive at the startling conclusion that 2,250 of the 17,000 men serving with infantry battalions in mid-September had been killed in action in the following seven weeks and that a further 9,000 had been lost to their units for varying lengths of time owing to physical or mental wounds or illness.[5]

Despite these terrible losses, the flow of reinforcements resulted in a gradual increase in the strength of infantry battalions, especially in 2nd Canadian Infantry Division. On 3 September the division reported total deficiencies of 2,645 men. By 16 October the figure was 753, and it remained close to that level for the balance of the month. The 3rd Division reported a shortage of 783 men when the battles for the Channel ports began, and 1,470 when Calais surrendered. Reinforcements brought the division to within 552 men of its complement as Switchback began and 805 by the time it ended. The 4th Armoured Division reported weekly deficiencies as high as 872 in September, but by 2 October that number had fallen to 125, and it was just 141 when Operation Suitcase began on 20 October. Intense combat over the next two weeks would raise the total to 697 by 4 November.[6]

Many of the reinforcements joining infantry battalions in the autumn of 1944 were men who had enlisted and served in the artillery, Service Corps, or Signal Corps. All such replacements had undergone a conversion course to retrain as infantry, but a number of men were said to have reached front line units without adequate training. Battalion commanders protested this situation repeatedly, but it is by no means clear that all of their complaints were accurate or disinterested. The evidence on the issue that is quoted most often comes from a survey conducted by the Black Watch of the training received by all ranks in the battalion's infantry companies as of 19 October 1944. The report claimed that 14 of the 379 men had had no infantry training and 29 of them less than one month. Major A.G. Stevenson, who compiled the report, added the number who had one month of training to these figures and reported that 45 per cent of the men had 'one month or less training as infantry men prior to joining our battalion.'[7] He might equally have concluded that 89 per cent had one month or *more* of recent training and that many of them had served with the battalion through August and September. The service records of the fifty-one Black Watch soldiers killed in action on 13 October show the average length of service as two years and that only fourteen men had been transferred from other corps to the infantry.[8]

The reinforcement question cannot be separated from the politics surrounding the issue of conscription for overseas service. It was no coincidence that the political crisis began in Toronto, where a lively and partisan daily press had been debating conscription for some time. On 18 September, Major Conn Smythe, a well-known figure in Toronto hockey circles, issued a press release accusing the government of sending 'green, inexperienced and poorly trained reinforcements' into battle when 'well trained' conscripts remained in Canada. He reported that 'practically all of the reinforcements have little or no knowledge of the Bren gun' and that their inexperience was resulting in a 'large number of unnecessary casualties.'[9]

Smythe, who was recovering from wounds suffered in Normandy, won a sympathetic audience in much of English-speaking Canada, and his views were widely shared in the overseas army, but this does not mean they were accurate. As the official historian, C.P. Stacey, has noted: 'The main remastering program did not begin until after Major Smythe was wounded and the reports he received in hospital could scarcely have been the results of it.' The more likely explanation is the 'notorious fact of army life that no commanding officer ever admits that the reinforcements his unit receives have been properly trained.'[10]

The reaction to Smythe's press release led the Minister of National Defence, Colonel J.L. Ralston, to travel to Italy and Northwest Europe in search of answers. He found little evidence to support Smythe's claims, but he did conclude that earlier estimates of the adequacy of the reinforcement pool were based on assumptions that the war would end in 1944. Ralston was certain that Canada needed to prepare for a 'prolongation of the war' and that the 15,000 infantry replacements likely to be required in 1945 could only be obtained by 'the extension of the service of N.R.M.A. [conscripts] ... to service overseas.'[11]

Prime Minister William Lyon Mackenzie King was not prepared to accept this recommendation and replaced Ralston with General Andrew McNaughton, who proposed to obtain the necessary reinforcements without compelling the conscripts to serve overseas. After a month of confusion and intrigue it became apparent that few conscripts were willing to volunteer. At that point the government agreed to provide the needed reinforcements by requiring 16,000 conscripts to serve overseas. This belated action ended both the political crisis and the reinforcement issue. Given the much lower casualty rates of November, December, and January, it was possible to rebuild the infantry battalions without conscripts, although once heavy fighting began in February, 2,463 of the 12,908 who were sent overseas joined infantry battalions. This helped maintain units at close to full strength for the balance of the war.[12]

The manpower problem was not the only issue that needed to be resolved in the autumn of 1944. The morale of combat soldiers had declined dramatically in October[13] as attritional warfare in the most miserable conditions yet encountered took its toll. Major Bob Gregory, the psychiatrist attached to 3rd Division, had landed shortly after D-Day and worked closely with Regimental Medical Officers and other Medical Corps personnel throughout the campaign. His psychiatric report for October (reproduced in Appendix E) was based on observations of the 295 exhaustion casualties treated at the division's forward recovery centre. Gregory believed firmly in the principles of proximity, immediacy, and expectancy, so the men who arrived at the field dressing station were not treated as patients but rather as individuals with a 'condition often due to fatigue from which they would recover quickly ... and return to duty.' After a night of sedated sleep, 'the man was allowed passes into town ... Canteen and entertainment services were available.' The purposes of this attempt to approximate 'a normal life' were both therapeutic and observational. At a final interview, Gregory decided who to return to combat and who to send to the Corps Exhaustion Centre in Ghent for further treatment.

Gregory believed that this approach to combat stress had produced good results, allowing large numbers of men to return to their units, but in October his confidence was shaken. He found poor morale and a 'lack of volition to carry on [among] all troops admitted for exhaustion.' His report noted: 'The foremost cause of this seemed to be futility. The men claimed there was nothing to which to look forward – no rest, no leave, no employment, no normal life and no escape. The only ways one could get out of battle was death, wounds, self-inflicted wounds and going "nuts."'

Gregory was so concerned about what he was hearing that he recommended that veteran soldiers not be returned to their units until the fighting in the Scheldt was over to avoid 'completely cracking their morale.'[14]

The 2nd Division did not have its own psychiatrist, but by October medical officers with some psychiatric training were running a divisional recovery centre using the same techniques as Gregory was advocating. On 20 October, as the battle for Woensdrecht resumed, Major Travis Dancey arrived to take over the Corps Exhaustion Unit. Dancey was an experienced psychiatrist with considerable intellectual curiosity. He spent a good deal of time examining the men sent to the unit from the recovery centres and concluded that more and more cases were 'men who had carried on under considerable stress for long periods of time' but who now suffered from what he called 'reverse fatalism' – that is, the feeling that they were 'marked men' waiting for the bullet with their name on it to strike. In Dancey's view, such men could not be sent back into combat.[15]

Senior officers were deeply concerned by the suggestion that men who had recovered from the symptoms of battle exhaustion should not be returned to combat, and the recommendations made by the two psychiatrists were ignored. Instead, attention was focused on various initiatives to improve morale. On 28 October Lieutenant-General Guy Simonds issued a directive outlining policies on the 'Absorption of Reinforcement Personnel,' which listed the proper steps to be taken when receiving new officers and men so that 'they go into action not as individuals but as members of a team.' Simonds emphasized the need for a unit reception school to test and initiate new soldiers. Except in extreme emergencies, reinforcements were to spend from two to five days in such a school before being sent into battle. This was not the first time battalion commanders had been instructed to follow such a procedure, but under the pressure of intense combat with limited resources, many COs had allowed drafts of reinforcements to go forward as soon as they arrived.[16]

Army psychiatrists tackled the morale problem by organizing a series of talks to be given to non-commissioned officers, padres, and – when possible – company and battalion commanders. Major Burdett McNeel, who left the exhaustion unit in September to become adviser in psychiatry at 2nd Canadian Corps, gave most of these talks and led discussions with medical officers after showing the film 'Field Psychiatry For the Medical Officer.'[17] Both McNeel and the Lieutenant-Colonel J.C. Richardson, the senior Canadian psychiatrist in Northwest Europe, were more than willing to devote time to these efforts, but neither had much confidence that education would significantly reduce the number of psychiatric casualties if the army was again committed to prolonged, intense combat. McNeel offered this advice to Regimental Medical Officers:

Judge a man by his record. If he has given good service and is now breaking give him the benefit of the doubt and evacuate him. If he is new and dithery encourage him but hold him to his job. If he is merely a useless type compel him to do his duty as long as it is possible to do so. (The exception to this rule is officers and NCO's who, because of their responsibility for other men must be relieved of their duties when instability becomes evident.)

The cases that benefit most by treatment are the acutely fatigued and those that benefit most by discipline are the young, scared and uninitiated reinforcements, as well as the great borderline group which will be swayed by the general trend of morale in the unit.[18]

Apart from rest and the new policy of forty-eight-hour leaves, the best morale-building device was news of the government's war service gratuities policy. The full program of benefits known as the Veteran's Charter[19] was the product of legislation introduced between 1942 and 1946, but for many soldiers the War Services Grants Act of 1944 was the crucial document. Regimental newspapers like *The Staghound* (published by the Manitoba Dragoons) explained the legislation with simple examples:

A private, who is a married man and has two children, and has served in Canada for one year and two years overseas, will receive:

Basic Gratuity	$450
Increment for Overseas	136
Rehabilitation Grant	108
Clothing Allowance	100
Total	$794

Then there is the re-establishment credit, which is equivalent to the basic gratuity of 450 dollars making the total benefits available on discharge 1244 dollars for the case above. These payments increase with rank.[20]

The prospect of beginning civilian life with the equivalent of a year's wages inspired considerable excitement among the men, who suddenly had reason to be less cynical about their future.

But before the citizen army could resume civilian life, there was a war to be won and a cold, wet Dutch winter to be endured. Infantry battalions and armoured regiments were rotated in and out of the line north and east of Nijmegen, and this small Dutch city was temporarily transformed into a Canadian town. Administrative staffs struggled to deal with coal shortages, the erratic supply of beer, and complaints that rations included too much tea and not enough coffee. A more serious problem was the failure of the existing scale of field rations to provide sufficient calories and bulk for soldiers living 'under arduous and exposed conditions.' This was finally addressed in December with increases in supplies of 'baking powder, flour, dried eggs, pickles or sauces, rice or oatmeal, cheese and jam' sufficient to provide an additional 572 calories a day.[21]

Other measures designed to bolster the morale of the army included the opening of Northwest Europe's 'greatest hamburger emporium,' The Blue Diamond, next door to the Canada Club in Nijmegen. The restaurant, with its ninety-foot counter, served 'beef hamburgers smothered in fried onions, crispy brown doughnuts, light as the proverbial feather, flaky pie, fat baked beans made according to an old habitant formula and coffee black and aromatic – smooth as smoke ... All for free!' The Blue Diamond was for other ranks, not officers, except for nursing sisters, who were specially invited.[22]

The beginning of operations in the Nijmegen salient brought about a number of changes in the command structure of First Canadian Army. Harry Crerar, now fully recovered, returned to army headquarters and was promoted to the rank of full general – a first for a Canadian officer. This gesture of confidence from the Canadian government was not well received by Montgomery, who protested the CIGS, urging Field Marshal Sir Alan Brooke to 'arrange that announcement conveys impression that it is a normal promotion and NOT repeat NOT in any way for distinguished service in the field.'[23] Crerar did not learn of this particular example of the field marshal's attitude towards him, but he had few illusions about his relationship with Montgomery. Crerar was, however, confident of his ability to carry out his responsibilities as Army Commander while Simonds resumed command of 2nd Canadian Corps.

There were other important changes. The temporary elevation of Major-General Charles Foulkes to Acting Corps Commander in October had not altered Simonds's opinion of Foulkes, but Crerar decided to promote his protégé and sent him to Italy to replace Lieutenant-General E.L.M. Burns, another Canadian officer who had failed to impress a British commander.[24] Simonds seized the opportunity to press for the promotion of his senior artillery officer, Brigadier Bruce Matthews, and Crerar agreed that Matthews could take over 2nd Division, with the Acting Divisional Commander, Brigadier R. Holley Keefler, commanding 6th Brigade.

The appointment of two militia gunners to positions that Crerar had tried to reserve for regular force infantry officers was long overdue. Matthews was one of the brightest and most competent officers in the army, with experience dating back to the invasion of Sicily. As a senior artillery officer he had often watched other officers send troops into battle relying on a fire plan he had devised, and he was confident that he knew more about planning proper infantry operations than they did.[25] Under Foulkes, brigadiers had been little more than conduits for passing on orders; Matthews was determined to work with brigade and battalion commanders on all aspects of training and operations.

Matthews believed strongly in the artillery-based battle doctrine employed by the Allied armies. He was confident that men leaning into a barrage could reach their objective and dig in while medium artillery sealed the area with fire, breaking up enemy counter-attacks during the consolidation phase.[26] He knew that it was enemy mortars, not machine guns, that posed the biggest threat, and he was a determined advocate of counter-mortar organization. Together with Major J.M. Watson, the divisional counter-mortar officer, he encouraged cooperation with the Operational Research Section of 21 Army Group and the newly established Canadian Radar Battery, which had begun to experiment with electronic methods of locating enemy mortars. The largest of these trials was a company-level raid carried out by the Black Watch in early December. Code-named Mickey Finn, the raid was intended to test the effectiveness of various methods of locating mortars, including air observation, radar, and sound ranging with four-pen recorders.[27] None of these methods proved especially effective in Mickey Finn, but Matthews was determined to continue the experiments, and by February much had been achieved in this and other areas. A division that had long suffered from poor leadership and manpower shortages was transformed by Matthews and the influx of reinforcements.

The 3rd Canadian Infantry Division's difficult operations in the Breskens Pocket were followed by a week's healing rest in the city of Ghent. Once settled in the Nijmegen area, divisional headquarters had to adjust to the loss of 'Uncle' Stanley Todd, the CRA who had replaced Matthews at corps headquarters, as well as to the departure of both senior staff officers, but their replacements were experienced understudies and the transition was smooth. Brigadier J.A. Roberts, the ultimate replacement for Brigadier Kenneth Blackader at 8th Brigade, was a highly regarded officer who had commanded the Manitoba Dragoons with great success.

Roberts had absolutely no experience commanding infantry, and he stayed out of the way until the fighting in the Breskens Pocket ended. After arriving in the Nijmegen area, he imposed his personality on the brigade, asking General Dan Spry to remove the commanding officers of the North Shores and the Chaudières because they had resisted orders to 'send out patrols on possibly dangerous missions.'[28] The loss of Lieutenant-Colonels J.A. Anderson and Paul Mathieu was keenly felt, but John Rowley, who took over the North Shores, and Gustave Taschereau, who took over the Chaudières, were competent officers who became effective commanders. Roberts also seems to have settled into his new role.

Matthews and Spry initiated brigade and divisional study periods before beginning intense training at the battalion and company levels. The terrain around Nijmegen included flat polder country as well as the vast state forests in the German Rhineland, so a good deal of attention was paid to lessons learned in the Scheldt campaign. Spry was especially concerned about the training of battalions that included hundreds of reinforcements. He declared that all newly arrived replacements should spend seven to ten days training 'under the supervision of the regimental NCO to familiarize themselves with life in the front line and the use of all weapons. Training with flamethrowers, both the Wasp and the Lifebuoy must be emphasized and battle drill ... taught to· everyone ... because the principles have been proven sound in battle.' On the basis of the experience in October, Spry considered it vital to maintain the size of infantry sections so that each would always include a strong rifle group as well as a Bren gun team. If necessary, battalions were to operate with three instead of four companies to ensure that the sections in each platoon could do their job.[29]

The decision to send Foulkes to Italy forced Crerar to bring Major-General Chris Vokes, the energetic, notoriously profane officer commanding 1st Division, to Northwest Europe. In the small pre-war professional army Vokes had friends and admirers, but Foulkes was not one of them, and Crerar knew there would be fireworks if they had to work together.[30] He therefore transferred Major-General Harry Foster to Italy and gave Vokes command of 4th Armoured Division; this solved a personnel problem at the price of disrupting the functioning command relationship that Foster and his two brigadiers had developed in September and October.

Vokes, who described himself as 'a great rough, red hairy bastard,' was determined to impress his personality and ideas on the division. He informed veteran officers that he was 'heartily sick' of hearing about their exploits at 'BuggeroffZoom, Sphitzen-on-the-floor and other places.'[31] Lieutenant-Colonel Dave Stewart, the revered CO of the Argylls, was so incensed with Vokes's behaviour that he wrote to Simonds stating that he had no confidence in the divisional commander. This protest cost Stewart his job, and he was ordered to report to a neuropsychiatric hospital to be examined for nervous strain. Among the symptoms Stewart was supposed to exhibit was 'undue concern for his men.'[32]

Stewart had risked his command because Vokes had agreed to Lieutenant-General Sir John Crocker's proposal to stage another attack on an enemy 'bridgehead' south of the Maas at Kapelsche Veer. The Germans had strengthened their hold on this flat island, formed by a secondary channel of the Maas, in preparation for an advance towards Antwerp, which was to be launched if the major offensive in the Ardennes made good progress. Three earlier attempts to seize the island had failed, and by late January there was no longer any possibility of a German offensive in the area, but Crocker persisted, ordering 4th Division to eliminate the bridgehead 'introducing some new element or method so that surprise can still be achieved.'[33]

Vokes's plan for Operation Elephant violated almost every rule that infantry battalion commanders thought they had learned. The Lincoln and Welland Regiment was to begin the attack 'from three directions simultaneously.' These attacks were to include a sixty-man 'canoe commando,' which was to paddle down the north bank of the Maas, screened by smoke. There were to be no artillery or mortar concentrations on the objective before H-Hour, and when the fire plan began it was to try to neutralize enemy positions on the north bank of the river, not on the island.[34] Predictably, the attack failed, and Brigadier Jim Jefferson was forced to mount a very different operation, seizing limited objectives with artillery and tank support. Kapelsche Veer was finally cleared, but at the cost of 234 casualties, including sixty-five men killed in action.[35] Crocker asked for a post-mortem on the operation to see whether 'valuable lessons' could be learned. At Vokes's request, Jefferson met with officers from the Lincs, the Argylls, and the South Alberta Regiment to review events. Their report emphasized the need for limited objectives, tank support, and neutralization of the enemy with observed artillery and mortar fire. This was simply stating the obvious and did nothing to improve the difficult relationship between Vokes and his division.[36]

The strained command relationships in 4th Division did not seem to matter much in the broader picture, because Montgomery was not proposing to use the divisions of First Canadian Army in major operations. The 2nd British Army's advance to the Maas in the Venlo sector ended on 3 December, nine days before the Americans called off the costly action known as the Battle of the Hürtgen Forest. The limited success of both these operations contrasted sharply with the progress made by 3rd and 7th U.S. Armies to the south, but instead of drawing the obvious conclusion, Montgomery complained that Eisenhower's policy 'of attacking in so many places that nowhere are we strong enough to get decisive results' had led to a 'strategic reverse.'[37] Montgomery's criticisms were endorsed by the British Chiefs of Staff and by Churchill as well, but Eisenhower, with Job-like patience, was able to avoid an open breach with Montgomery and his supporters in London.[38]

This renewal of the broad versus narrow front controversy was temporarily forgotten when on 16 December, in the Ardennes, the Germans launched their last major offensive of the war. While the Battle of the Bulge raged, the Canadian Army guarded against a possible enemy attack across the Maas and continued with routine training and 'aggressive patrol activity.' At army headquarters the planning and administrative (logistics) staff worked long hours in preparation for a major offensive from the Nijmegen area between the Rhine and the Maas. Crerar and his senior officers had assumed that the attack would be carried out by 2nd Canadian Corps. Then on 7 December, Montgomery informed Crerar that 30th British Corps under his favourite general, Sir Brian Horrocks, would temporarily become part of First Canadian Army to carry out Operation Veritable.[39] Army headquarters was to be responsible for engineering requirements, the overall artillery fire plan, the build-up of supplies, and the negotiations for air support.

For security reasons Crerar said little about how the mass of materiel was to be used, but a great deal of effort had gone into preparations for the new offensive. The senior artillery officer at army headquarters, Brigadier H.O.N. Brownfield, had been profoundly disturbed by reports from the Operational Research Section[40] on the accuracy of predicted shooting in Operations Wellhit, Undergo, and Switchback. Both he and his successor, Brigadier E.C. Plow, were determined to address this problem, and staff officers worked closely with the OR scientists in preparation for Veritable.[41]

Infantry and artillery officers at the sharp end knew from experience in Normandy that enemy positions could not always be located accurately and that this negated the value of much counter-battery and counter-mortar fire. More disturbing was the evidence that while 'an accurate concentration on a well-located battery invariably silenced it for the duration of the concentration, the effect seldom lasted.'[42] A detailed ground survey of the Boulogne fortified zone had revealed further problems. The hostile battery list in use turned out to have included a number of dummy positions and fortified sites without guns, while a large number of active batteries were not located.

Major John Fairlie, the Canadian artillery officer who led the OR team at Boulogne,[43] reported that a lack of coordination between the services and within the army had led to problems in compiling an accurate list of hostile batteries and that much better coordination was required. He also noted that the enemy's careful preparation and camouflage of defences meant that vertical air photographs needed to be supplemented by low-level obliques, which were 'the only means of detecting positions screened by overhead cover.' Such photographs had not been available 'due to operational conditions' – meaning, the low priority assigned to Boulogne. Also, the enemy had 'pursued a careful and comprehensive policy of sound ranging deception,' which further complicated efforts to pinpoint battery locations. As a consequence the 350 guns assembled for Operation Wellhit had fired their 80,000 shells without neutralizing many enemy batteries even temporarily. Most of the six hundred Canadian casualties had been due to enemy shelling.[44]

A comprehensive study of the accuracy of predicted fire was carried out as the battle zone moved forward in the Breskens Pocket. Using aerial photographs taken immediately after a counter-battery shoot, supplemented by ground checks, the Operational Research Section determined that on average, only 4.8 per cent of the rounds fired fell within the one hundred square yards around the target. Meteorological errors accounted for part of this, but faulty calibration and 'other sources of error such as command post work, sight testing and gun laying' also contributed to the results. Stated simply, the artillery had to fire 2,000 rounds at a predicted target in order 'to cause 100 rounds to fall in a field 100 yards square.' Since the gunners were operating on the assumption that it took just 170 rounds to achieve this result, the scope of the problem was enormous and was now known to be so. Brownfield was determined to find ways of improving accuracy.[45]

After the fighting to clear the approaches to Antwerp ended, ground observation of weather balloons using radar was taken over by the RAF and used to supplement information obtained by aircraft. This decision, which respected the existing division of labour between the services, was not well received at corps and division because RAF meteors issued at four-hour intervals were deemed inadequate in the kind of changeable weather normally found in Holland and Germany. Canadian Met sections improvised, issuing supplementary meteors at two-hour intervals during operations.[46] On 1 March Major-General M.E. Dennis, the senior artillery officer at 21 Army Group, endorsed the Canadian experiments, requesting authorization for radar equipment to measure wind 'at the rate of one per corps.'[47]

While this debate played out, Brownfield instituted a wide-ranging review of artillery practices in the Canadian Army and issued a series of notes designed 'to pass on any information of interest gleaned from experience.' He insisted that he was proposing not to 'lay down new doctrine' but rather to explore the 'practical difficulties in adhering to doctrine.'[48] Much of the content reiterated fundamental procedures. For example, Forward Observation Officers were reminded that the well-tried rules of ranging had to be followed even in emergencies. If a 'Mike' target was inaccurate – as it often was – the infantry were not helped no matter how rapid the response. Examples of successful engagements with the 3.7-inch guns of the 2nd Heavy Anti-Aircraft Regiment RCA, firing in a ground support role, were cited, and organizational changes allowing the 2nd to function as an additional medium regiment were made.[49]

The value of Air OP flights in their normal role – spotting for the medium artillery – was stressed. However, the notes reported examples of how the light Auster aircraft could be used for other purposes. Squadrons were now equipped with aircraft modified to carry 20-inch cameras, and a small photo processing section was added to the establishment. The Auster pilots flew within the army's Forward Defence Localities (FDLs), photographing the enemy's FDLs and gun areas, 'a result seldom achieved from RAF services with fast aircraft flying in a straight line.' The army's ability to control these seemingly insignificant air assets also paid dividends in traffic control, liaison between formations, and the vital task of registering targets ahead of the ground troops, especially during the consolidation phase of an attack.[50] The Air OP squadrons had also experimented with night flying to observe enemy road movements and predicted fire. Flights were restricted to the eight to ten miles beyond the FDLs, and radar was employed to provide early warning of the approach of enemy night fighters. On one occasion the warning was almost too late as a German aircraft got to within five hundred yards of an Auster. The pilot, following standard procedure, dove from 3,500 to 200 feet, forcing the night fighter to abandon the pursuit.[51]

The Royal Canadian Artillery's wide range of responsibilities included the self-propelled and towed anti-tank regiments, and a good deal of attention was paid to best practices in their deployment. The thin armour and high-velocity gun of the M10 made it unsuitable as an assault gun, but in October, when 3rd Division fought without any tank support, the 3rd Anti-Tank Regiment had to adapt. The 'mere presence of the SPs' inspired our own infantry and demoralized the enemy, so they often became the focus of the plan of attack. 'Troop commanders learned that the principle of "fire and movement" as an axiom of the assault applied as much to the SPs as it did to the infantry. A gun never worked singly but always in conjunction with one or more of its brothers. While one moved the other remained stationary ready to bring covering fire where necessary.'[52] The Allied infantry desperately needed an assault gun with the characteristics of the heavily armoured Stug deployed by the German army, but no such armoured vehicle was available, so the M10 crews had to do their best.

The Canadians were also keen to experiment with a new weapon known as the Land Mattress, which had been developed from a Royal Navy rocket projector used to explode mines during beach assaults. This Allied version of the Nebelwerfer featured twenty projector barrels mounted on a wheeled trailer. The impact of a rocket barrage from each trailer was equivalent to a salvo from a regiment of medium guns, and First Canadian Army planned to use it in the Rhineland offensive. Maintenance problems and the weapon's slow rate of fire led 2nd British Army to reject the weapon; even so, Crerar authorized the formation of No. 1 Canadian Rocket Battery and used the Land Mattress successfully for the balance of the war.[53]

Both the Canadian and British armies were, however, in agreement about the value of Wasp and Crocodile flame-throwers. By the autumn of 1944 most rifle companies in 21 Army Group had direct experience of attacks supported by flame and viewed it as an essential weapon. When a First Canadian Army Technical Officer explained the technique of flame-throwing to a Historical Officer, he began by noting that despite the enthusiasm of the infantry, the Wasp 'must not be expected to win a war by itself.' The key to its effective use was support from infantry weapons, including smoke to bring the Wasp or Crocodile within range of a pillbox, strongpoint, or dug-in position: 'The main use of flame, in any form is for its demoralizing effect ... All experience during operations in this theatre has shown that, when the enemy was confronted with flame, he invariably did one of three things; first he huddled down in his positions; or second he gave himself up immediately or showed a white flag; or third he started to run away. In no case where enemy positions were attacked by flame did they attempt to return fire.'[54]

While the army reflected on the lessons learned in the campaign to date and worked to integrate reinforcements through intensive training, Crerar's Chief of Staff, Brigadier Churchill Mann, and Lieutenant-Colonel Bill Anderson, the Army Operations Officer (GSO 1 Ops), were attempting to deal with the fallout from Air Marshal Sir Arthur Coningham's decision to replace the Air Officer Commanding 84 Group with someone 'less subservient to the army.'[55]

At Crerar's headquarters, senior staff officers of both services worked together in a joint battle room while the army operations room 'provided a filter of information at the next lower level.' The joint battle room was adjacent to the Operations/Intelligence Section of Headquarters 84 Group, which encouraged much greater integration than was possible at 2nd British Army Headquarters. Furthermore, Air Vice-Marshal Leslie Brown had agreed to a remarkable degree of decentralization, including the establishment of air liaison sections at corps and the headquarters of armoured divisions.[56]

Neither Brown nor anyone else could do anything about the procedures for allocating air support. Despite frequent protests from both British and Canadian officers, Air Marshal Sir Arthur Coningham kept to the routine – established before the invasion – of holding a nightly conference at 1730 hours to determine priorities for the next day. From an army perspective this rigidity meant that 'the air effort was therefore sometimes allotted before the requirements for the armies were known and the process of reconciliation was labourious.'[57] First Canadian Army and 84 Group held their meeting immediately after the major decisions were reached, deciding what to do with the resources not required by 2nd Tactical Air Force. At 2nd British Army, evening conferences were seldom held on a daily basis, partly because army headquarters and 83 Group were seldom co-located, but largely because tasks for the group were usually determined at the meeting of 2TAF and 21 Army Group.[58]

The debate over the proper allocation of air resources continued throughout the battles for the Scheldt Estuary, and sharpened as poor flying weather severely limited or cancelled tactical air support for twenty days during October.[59] Despite the weather and the limited air resources available, the work of 84 Group in support of operations carried out by Canadian troops was deeply appreciated. At the conclusion of Operation Switchback, Major General Spry initiated a report praising the cooperative spirit of 84 Group. The division had 'received the maximum air support possible during this period and except when weather conditions made flying impossible allied planes were constantly overhead.' Division staff officers were especially impressed by the rapid response to impromptu requests for close air support through the Forward Control Post system, which included the use of 'cab rank' – that is, the briefing of pilots already in the air over the battlefield.[60]

The report offered only a very general assessment of the damage inflicted on the enemy. Instead, it emphasized the 'breakdown of enemy communications and morale' and the 'encouragement given to our troops,' whose morale was greatly improved whenever air support was available. This emphasis on morale was reinforced when the Operational Research team examined targets in the Breskens Pocket and interrogated prisoners of war about the effects of rocket-firing Typhoons on the battle. The ground survey re-emphasized the difficulty of achieving accuracy with either rockets or bombs and concluded that the 'greatest effect of attacks by rocket firing Typhoons in close support is morale, both on the enemy and our own troops.'[61]

Brown's reward for the achievements of 84 Group was to be dismissal. On 10 November 1944, Coningham replaced him with his preferred candidate, Air Vice-Marshal E.C. Hudleston. The changeover had little immediate impact because First Canadian Army's role in the winter of 1944–5 required minimal air support and because when heavy fighting began in February, Coningham controlled both fighter-bomber groups in support of Veritable, the only offensive underway in 21 Army Group. There is, however, no doubt that Hudleston shared Coningham's view of the proper direction of the air campaign. As a result, relations between the army and 84 Group were greatly strained during April 1945, when Canadian operations again received low priority.[62]

First Canadian Army also found itself on the losing side of the ongoing debate over the role of Bomber Command and the U.S. 8th Air Force. Eisenhower had been required to give up direct control of the heavy bombers in late September, but the Supreme Commander was confident that he could still rely on support for the ground forces 'because of the saving clauses in the Directive regarding support for Overlord and because of the good will of the individuals involved.' Eisenhower was especially confident that RAF Bomber Command would continue to respond to requests because 'Air Chief Marshal Harris had proven to be one of the most effective and co-operative members of this team.'[63] This was a fair assessment of the command relationship under Eisenhower; however, once the new directive took effect it proved to be much more difficult to obtain direct support for army operations. Simonds discovered the new reality when his requests for an extensive bombing program for Walcheren were whittled down in the context of a heated debate over future strategy.[64]

Sir Charles Portal, the Chief of the Air Staff, had led the campaign to end Eisenhower's control and was determined to 'shorten the war' by the 'proper application of the strategic bomber forces to targets behind the front.' He was willing to concede the desirability of bomber support for 'decisive' or essential attacks, but he believed that 'the constant applications of heavy bomber power to the land battle, when it is not essential and when its only purpose is to save casualties, must eventually lead to the demoralization of the army.'[65]

Portal was particularly concerned about a report from Washington that General George C. Marshall was likely to propose 'taking the strategic bomber effort off Germany to some extent at least in order to contribute more to the immediate issue on the battlefield.' Portal wrote to the Deputy Supreme Commander, Sir Arthur Tedder, seeking support for the bombing campaign against 'oil and industry.' Ironically, Portal also expressed concern about a possible diversion of effort 'on some short term transportation plan' – the targeting policy favoured by Tedder.[66]

Tedder chose to ignore this rather serious difference of opinion, replying that he was in perfect agreement that 'the army having been drugged with bombs, it is going to be a difficult process to cure the drug addicts – particularly as the army is getting tired.' The proof of this addiction was 'the repeated calls by the Canadian Army for Heavy Bomber effort to deal with a part-worn battery on Walcheren.'[67] The decision to limit the bombing of Walcheren and the refusal of a request to attack Flushing in advance of the landings clearly demonstrated that the army could no longer rely on full air support. When Major-General Kenneth Strong, Eisenhower's Assistant Chief of Staff for Intelligence, suggested using the strategic air forces 'in close support of the ground forces in the Cologne-Dusseldorf area,'[68] his proposal was also rejected.

Neither Marshall nor Eisenhower was willing to reopen the argument, and for the balance of the war the heavy bombers would concentrate on the destruction of targets in Germany.[69]

One possible method of compensating for the absence of heavy bombers was improving the accuracy of both medium bombers and fighter-bombers. The Army Operational Research Group had worked on this problem for some time and was confident that the deployment of an SCR 584 radar set to track the approach of friendly aircraft, combined with two-way radio communication, would permit more accurate bombing from higher altitudes even in complete cloud cover. Staff officers at First Canadian Army were enthusiastic about the project, and once it was agreed that 2TAF's Operational Research Section would share the resulting the data, No. 1 Mobile Radar Control Post (MRCP) was established. Between 8 February and 8 March the MRCP was used in poor flying weather to control fifty-four separate missions flown by both medium bombers and fighter-bombers. Twenty miles from the target the ground controller took over direction of a formation of up to eighteen aircraft and used his radio to communicate required changes in altitude, course, or airspeed. A computer, 'making due allowance for speed, height, wind and terminal velocity of bombs, calculates the point at which the bombs were to be dropped on a voice order form the ground controller.'[70] Ground checks were carried out on seven targets, and army and air force OR teams agreed that bombing accuracy with an MRCP was 'already comparable with that obtained by visual methods in level bombing,' thus demonstrating that targets could safely be engaged 'closer to our own troops than by any other existing radar means.'[71]

Army officers hoped to use radar to control heavy bombers in support of ground forces, so they were delighted with the results. On 9 February, twelve radar-controlled Spitfires bombed a crossroads in Moyland Woods, destroying two houses. The mean point of impact (MPI) was just 160 yards from the aiming point. A week later, six Typhoons were guided to a second crossroads and achieved a tight concentration of five-hundred-pound bombs right on target. The average displacement of the MPI from the aiming point was 340 yards – about the same as in visual bombing – but because 'no single bomb was found more than 550 yards from the aiming point,' it was possible to imagine using the MRCP to bomb enemy defences with much smaller safety margins.[72]

The Operational Research Sections also worked closely with First Canadian Army and 30th British Corps in the development and analysis of the initial fire plan for Operation Veritable. On the basis of previous studies of the weight of artillery fire required to neutralize enemy positions and destroy line communications, the OR section calculated the number of tons per hundred square yards needed to achieve these goals. The fire plan provided for a four-hour bombardment of the enemy front by field, medium, and heavy artillery, with the forward defences 'peppered' with heavy mortars and any other weapons that could be brought into range. This 'pepper pot' technique was advocated because of indications that the 'number of shells was more important than sheer weight of ammunition.'[73]

The relatively low level of operational commitments in the winter of 1944–5 allowed First Canadian Army to focus on training and on methods of improving combat effectiveness. Professional armies are very conservative organizations, and it is never easy to introduce changes to established doctrine, but the evidence suggests that senior Canadian officers at the army and corps levels were flexible as well as open to innovation.[74] These characteristics would be necessary in the difficult battles of February and March 1945.

The Reichswald Forest, February 1945

3rd Canadian Division vehicles in the Rhine floodplain, 13 February 1945

Stormont Dundas and Glengarry Highlanders, 11 February 1944

The North Shore (New Brunswick) Regiment, moving up past a Buffalo LVT

Lieutenant-Colonel Ross Ellis and the Calgary Highlanders, March 1945. Major-General Bruce Matthews takes the salute; Brigadier W.J. Megill is to his right.

Brigadier John Rockingham (left) and Lieutenant-General Brian Horrocks, March 1945

Harry Crerar, Alan Brooke, Guy Simonds, Winston Churchill, and Bernard Montgomery, the Rhineland, March 1945

Brigadier C.M. Drury, CRA, 4th Canadian Armoured Division, Major-General Dan Spry and Major-General Chris Vokes, Sonsbeck, Germany 6 March 1945

Winston Churchill greeted by Canadian soldiers in the Rhineland

Oblique air photo of Seigfried Line Defences near Cleve, Germany, February 1945

The northern end of the Hochwald Defences

A German position in the Hochwald captured by the Queen's Own Cameron Highlanders of Canada

Wounded soldiers of the North Shore (New Brunswick) Regiment being evacuated by jeep ambulance, 27 February 1944

A kangaroo of 1st Canadian Armoured Personnel Carrier Regiment

Blackfriars Bridge across the Rhine, Rees, Germany, 30 March 1945

Royal Canadian Engineers bypass a damaged bridge at Zutphen, April 1945

Gun positioned to cover bridge crossing, Kusten Canal, Germany, 23 April 1945

A signaler with his 18 set

A section of infantry, the Perth Regiment, April 1945

Engineers of 3rd Canadian Infantry Division prepare storm boats for the attack on Leer, 28 April 1945

Houses damaged in the fighting for Groningen

Lieutenant-Colonel J.A. Dextraze, CO Les Fusiliers Mont-Royal (in sheepskin coat), with Major D.W. Grant, Toronto Scottish (right), planning the next move, 29 April 1945

Frying eggs on the exhaust of a Churchill tank, 1st Canadian Parachute Battalion April 1945

German children, with pockets turned out to show they are unarmed, surrender to Canadian troops in Sogel, Germany, 10 April 1945

The liberation of the Netherlands, Dalfsen, April 1945

Personnel of 12th Field Regiment RCA with the victory issue of the *Maple Leaf*

Food supplies for the Dutch, Wagenlingen, Netherlands, 3 May 1945

The crowd in Trafalgar Square, 8 May 1945

7

Veritable

The year of victory, 1945, did not begin auspiciously for the Allies in Western Europe. In December the enemy's Ardennes offensive had achieved complete surprise and taken the initiative away from Eisenhower's armies. Then on New Year's Eve, Hitler launched another offensive in the south aimed at diverting Allied resources from the Battle of the Bulge.[1] On New Year's Day the Luftwaffe, long absent from the daytime skies, mounted a major offensive, destroying three hundred Allied aircraft, most of them on the ground. This attack, later dismissed as the 'hangover raid,' proved a greater disaster to the German Air Force, which lost two hundred planes, but this was not known at the time, and many feared the revival of an enemy air force that was by then equipped with jet fighters.[2]

The apparent stalemate in the West prompted Eisenhower to send his Deputy Commander, Air Chief Marshal Sir Arthur Tedder, to Moscow to coordinate plans for a future offensive, but before Tedder arrived there, Winston Churchill intervened with a direct approach to Stalin. The British prime minister sought a commitment to 'a major Russian offensive ... during January,' insisting that the matter was 'urgent.' Churchill's appeal prompted an immediate reply from Stalin, who agreed that 'taking into account the position of our Allies on the Western Front,' he had decided 'regardless of the weather' to begin large-scale offensive operations 'not later than the second half of January.'[3]

Churchill's intervention may have prompted Stalin to advance the date of the Soviet winter offensive by a few days, but the price – reinforcing the belief that the Western Allies had lost the initiative – was not worth paying. Tedder had been sent to Moscow to coordinate future actions, not to plead for assistance. However, on arrival Tedder was treated as a supplicant. Given the situation in Poland and the rest of Eastern Europe, this was the wrong moment to ask Stalin for help, and it did nothing to improve an exchange of information on military matters.

Eisenhower's differences with Churchill were minor compared to the problem of coping with Montgomery, who continued to undermine the Supreme Commander's authority in an attempt to regain his position as commander of ground forces. This issue had been largely kept under wraps and dealt with in private correspondence, but on 7 January 1945 Montgomery gave a press conference outlining his personal role in the defeat of Hitler's Ardennes offensive. In both content and tone, Montgomery's statement was deeply offensive to all Americans, but especially to senior U.S. Army commanders. Churchill, who thought Montgomery's 'patronizing tone' was 'most unfortunate,'[4] tried to limit the damage, but the strained nature of Anglo-American military relations was now public knowledge.

The revival of the debate over command and strategy led to open disagreement between the British and American members of the Joint Chiefs of Staff regarding the best approach to pursue in crossing the Rhine and entering Germany. The proposals produced by Eisenhower on 20 January emphasized the advantages of the northern route, favoured by Montgomery, but underlined the necessity of closing to the Rhine along its entire length in order to establish an easily defensible position. Eisenhower also insisted on some flexibility in planning so that he could 'switch my main effort from North to South should this be forced on me.'[5]

Even though Eisenhower was placing the U.S. 9th Army under Montgomery's command for the northern offensive, the British were unhappy with the compromise and carried their protest to the meetings at Malta that preceded the Yalta Conference. The firm hand of General George C. Marshall ended the debate in Eisenhower's favour, but both sides continued to nurse grievances. One other decision taken at Malta was of considerable importance to Canada: it was agreed that all Canadian formations in Italy would join First Canadian Army as soon as possible.[6]

The final outline plan for the invasion of Germany called for 1st and 3rd U.S. Armies to advance to the Rhine before Montgomery's 21 Army Group, with 9th U.S. Army under command, launched Operations Veritable and Grenade, converging attacks designed to destroy the enemy forces remaining on the west bank of the Rhine. Veritable was to begin on 8 February, Grenade two days later. The timing was ambitious. Grenade could not begin until British troops had cleared part of the start line, a strongly defended triangle between the rivers Maas and Roer. Operation Blackcock began on 16 January, and this ten-day struggle in boggy countryside involved some of the fiercest fighting of the war – a fitting introduction to the Rhineland battles.[7] Eisenhower also wanted

1st U.S. Army to seize the Roer dams to prevent the enemy from flooding the river at an opportune moment. This attack, which began on 30 January, turned into another slow slogging match. As American troops approached the dams, the Germans opened the discharge valves, flooding the Roer and increasing the speed of the current so that the river was impassable until the reservoirs were empty.[8] As a result, Grenade had to be postponed for almost two weeks.

General Harry Crerar and the staff of First Canadian Army had been preparing for Veritable since November. The original plan had been to launch the offensive with Lieutenant-General Sir Brian Horrocks's 30th Corps and use 2nd Canadian Corps in a supporting role; this plan was modified under pressure from Lieutenant-General Guy Simonds, who argued that 'to leave the Canadians out of so important and so decisive a battle would be a bitter disappointment to the troops.'[9] The troops were not asked if they agreed with Simonds, but he won his case, and both Canadian infantry divisions were assigned to 30th Corps for the opening phase of the battle.

When Veritable was being planned, the German fortifications at the northern end of the Siegfried Line had none of the formidable character of the main sections farther south. By February the Germans had done a great deal to strengthen the positions. Three defensive belts confronted the Allies, each from 500 to 1000 metres wide. The first, on the edge of the Reichswald Forest, covered the ten-kilometre gap between the Maas and the town of Wyler. North of Wyler the flood plain of the Rhine, covered in several feet of water from the blown dykes, provided another kind of obstacle. Through the heart of the Reichswald and south along the Maas, the Siegfried line itself presented a position that might cause trouble if not quickly breached. A third belt stretched from the Rhine near Rees to Geldern.[10] The extensive 'squares' of forest that made up the Reichswald were an obstacle in their own right, but perhaps the greatest asset the Germans possessed was the weather. When Montgomery first outlined Veritable he had expressed the hope that 'dry or hard ground' would be available. 'If these conditions exist,' he told his commanders, 'then the basis of the operations will be speed and violence. The aim will be to pass armoured columns through to disrupt and disorganize enemy resistance in the rear.' But, he cautioned, 'if the ground is wet and muddy, then a slower and more

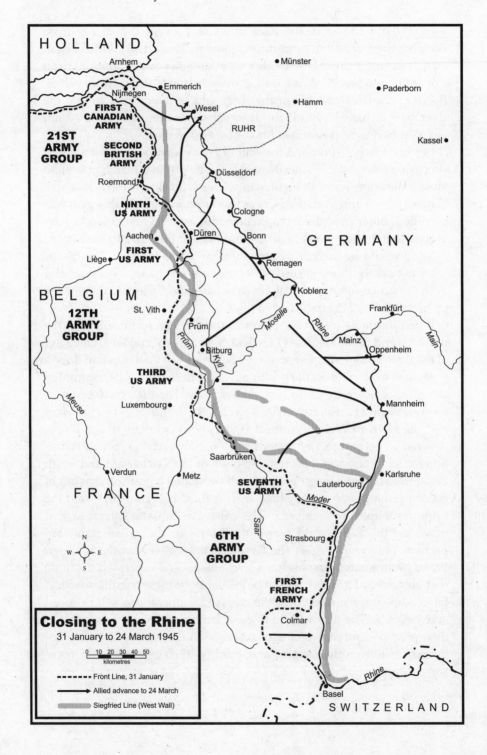

Closing to the Rhine
31 January to 24 March 1945

0 10 20 30 40 50
kilometres

- - - - - Front Line, 31 January

———▶ Allied advance to 24 March

▨▨▨▨ Siegfried Line (West Wall)

methodical progress may be forced upon us.'[11] By February the ground was very wet and very muddy. Rain and grey skies covered the battle-field, keeping air operations to a minimum and promising slow progress.

Terrain, fortifications, and the weather presented major difficulties to the Anglo-Canadian soldiers; the same could not be said for the military forces in their path. Major-General Heinz Fieburg's 84th Infantry Division was known to comprise 10,000 men, with all seven battalions in line across the six-mile front. Interrogations of prisoners and other intelligence had allowed Horrocks to build a detailed picture of a division that had been re-formed after its destruction in Normandy. Manned with inexperienced troops and chronically underequipped, 84th could call upon a single battalion of self-propelled assault guns for immediate support. General Alfred Schlemm, commanding 1st Para-chute Army, was in agreement with Allied assessments and sent a regiment from 2nd Parachute Division to take over the left flank of the defences, thus allowing Fieburg to develop substantial local reserves[12] before Veritable began on 8 February.

The Anglo-Canadian program for Veritable involved the massive application of force to a narrow, constricted battlefield, and First Canadian Army developed an elaborate supply system to make this possible. By 1945 the Canadian Army's engineers and staff officers were among the best the Allies had. Crerar paid tribute to their work during a press conference in which he described the size and scope of the build-up necessary for Veritable:

> 1880 tons of bridge equipment have been used in the construction of the five military bridges which have been thrown across the R. Maas, and lead into the forward assembly area. The Ravenstein 'high level' pontoon bridge – known as the Quebec Bridge, is the longest Bailey bridge yet constructed – 1280 ft. long.
>
> British and Canadian 'Sappers' in the past few weeks have constructed, widened and improved approximately 100 miles of road. For this purpose about 20,000 tons of stone, 20,000 logs and 30,000 pickets have been used.
>
> To move troops and their fighting equipment and supplies into position prior to 'D' Day will involve 35,000 vehicles traveling an average of 130 miles each and using approximately 1,300,000 gallons of petrol.

In order to ensure that convoys reach their appointed destinations, approximately 10,000 route signs were erected, and 1,000 troops have been employed on traffic control duties.

Demands have entailed the production of over 500,000 air photographs and 15,000 enlargements. Over 800,000 special maps, requiring over 30 tons of paper, have been produced.

If the ammunition allotments for the operations, which consists of 350 types, were stacked side by side and five feet high, it would line a road for 30 miles. The total ammunition tonnage, provided for the supporting artillery from 'D' Day, to D plus 3, would be the equivalent in weight to the bomb-drop of 25,000 medium bombers.

1,100 tons of smoke materials, exclusive of artillery, will be used in the ground plan, which will produce what I believe will be the longest smoke screen in the history of this war. At the conclusion of Phase 1, a 20-mile smoke screen should be in operation.[13]

Crerar proposed to use most of this materiel to support a sudden, massive attack by four divisions, each of which would concentrate its energies on an exceptionally narrow front. The Guards Armoured Division and 43rd (Wessex) Division were positioned to be ready to pass through and exploit south in the early stages of the attack. Our focus on the experience of the Canadians in Veritable should not obscure the fact that the overwhelming majority of men involved in the battles of February were British troops under their own leadership in 30th Corps. Casualties to the British forces in February were four times higher than the Canadian total. During the first two weeks of the battle the ratio was ten to one.

Veritable was the first operation carried out by Horrocks under Canadian command. In his memoirs he paid tribute to Crerar, whom he believed was 'much underrated largely because he was the exact opposite of Montgomery.' Crerar 'hated publicity but was full of common sense and always prepared to listen to the views of his subordinate commanders. Every day after the battle started he would fly over the front (a somewhat dangerous operation) in a small aircraft and then come to see me.' Horrocks came to like Crerar 'very much,' especially because Crerar put up with his displays of irritation and bad temper, which Horrocks attributed to a recurrence of malaria.[14]

Canadian officers who met Horrocks at pre-operational briefings encountered a charismatic leader, not a tense, unwell commander. Brigadier J.A. Roberts recalled how deeply impressed he was with Horrocks, whose warm personality contrasted with the cold formality of Simonds and Crerar. Horrocks was 'a born leader such as I never met before.' His briefing 'was strictly to the point, but so overwhelmingly confident and amusing that most of the Canadian commanders felt like cheering when the general completed the outline of his plan and instructions.' When Horrocks visited the sector of the front held by Roberts's brigade, his informal manner and 'personal qualities of leadership ... brought out a respect and affection which made better soldiers of his officers and men.' Roberts wondered why Canadian senior officers behaved with such stiff formality.[15]

Horrocks had assigned the right flank of his attack to 51st (Highland) Division. Here, along the bank of the Maas, there was limited forested area, and although the ground was wet there was no extensive flooding. The choice of 51st Highland for this assignment signalled the acceptance of the division back into the good graces of the British Army. In Normandy, Montgomery had castigated the Highlanders as 'not battleworthy' and sent them in disgrace to be part of Crerar's First Canadian Army. Under their new commander, Major-General T.G. Rennie, the 51st had fought with determination on the Falaise road, during the attack on Le Havre, and in the autumn battles in the Nijmegen salient. Now at full strength and supported by squadrons of 34th Armoured Brigade, the Highlanders were primed to break through the enemy's defensive line and quickly capture Gennep, along with its vital road and rail routes across the Maas. Unfortunately, the area the 51st was to attack had just been handed over to 2nd Para Regiment, and from the first hours of the battle the fighting in the southern corner of the Reichswald was murderous. The young paratroopers neither sought nor gave quarter, mounting repeated counter-attacks before withdrawing to a second defensive line. The Highlanders did not complete the capture of Gennep until 11 February, and on that date the enemy still held the railway line just south of the town as a base for company-strength counter-attacks supported by self-propelled guns. Very limited progress was made in the next three days.[16]

To the left of 51st Division, the 53rd (Welsh) Division was committed to capture the high ground on the edge of the Reichswald and then move through the forest, swinging north towards Cleve. The forest the Welsh encountered seemed to stretch on endlessly, each 'ride' exactly the same as the one before it and the ones beside it. It was a formless battle fought by infantry sections; battalion headquarters, to say nothing of brigade or division, seemed hopelessly remote. In the words of one battalion commander, 'it was Spandau versus Bren the whole way through.'[17] Before the Rhineland battles ended on 6 March the division suffered 3,484 casualties, including 485 men evacuated for battle exhaustion.[18]

The 15th Scottish Division tried to squeeze two brigade groups into the narrow zone between the Reichswald and the flood waters, where 3rd Canadian Division was to operate. The success of this plan depended on the speed with which 2nd Canadian Division could capture the heavily fortified frontier defences at Wyler, thus allowing Canadian engineers to open the Nijmegen–Cleve highway as the maintenance route for the Scottish Division. Major-General Bruce Matthews gave this vital task to 5th Brigade, and Brigadier Bill Megill selected the Calgary Highlanders, with two companies of the Maisonneuves in support, to carry out the attack.

The Calgary Highlanders had come a long way from their difficult experiences in Normandy. Under Lieutenant-Colonel Ross Ellis, one of a number of young Canadian officers who had demonstrated superior leadership skills, the battalion was a consistently effective unit. Ellis possessed a detailed knowledge of the ground – the product of the division's prolonged stay in the area – and he decided to bypass the formidable defences built into the dyke banks of the Wyler Meer.[19] The Calgaries, with the Maisies protecting their right flank, planned a quick thrust through to the Cleve road before turning to attack Wyler from the rear.

Captain T.A. Hunter, the Historical Officer attached to the division, produced this account of the opening of the battle as the initial artillery barrage began:

The weather promised to be fair and the sight of airbursts and tracer in the sky against the yellow light of the rising sun was very impressive. There was a continuous roll of heavy gunfire ... At 0740 hours almost a

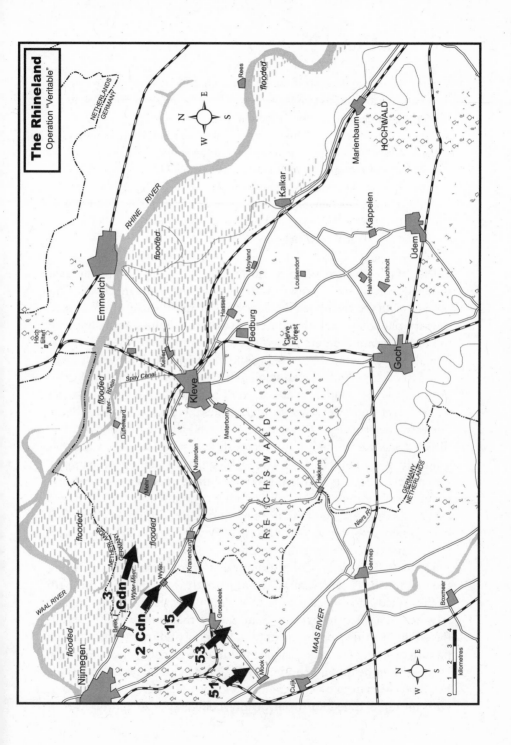

complete silence descended on the entire front.for a period of a full ten minutes ... to enable Flash Spotters and Sound Rangers to locate active enemy batteries not previously known.

A few birds were still flying across the sky in a bewildered manner as the artillery took up their theme again and the tempo accelerated as the full weight of 1000 guns were brought to bear ... As H-Hour approached, if anything, the noise increased and a new note was added by the sound of passing armour moving forward and planes passing overhead. The combined effect produced a vivid picture of a war of machines – a war of calculated and terrible efficiency.[20]

The infantry, called upon to close with an enemy given near total protection from the barrage by deep dugouts, were much less impressed with the calculated efficiency of the machines of war. The lead Calgary platoons encountered a field sewn with mines, some lying on top of the ground, others buried nearby to trap the unwary. Twenty-four men were wounded crossing the minefield, including a number who lost parts of limbs to the small anti-personnel *Schuhmines*. Once in position to carry out their attack, the Calgaries found the Wyler defences intact, and a day-long struggle ensued. Working closely with the Forward Observation Officers (FOOs) of 5th Field Regiment, who also directed the fire of the Toronto Scottish heavy mortars, the Calgaries gradually worked their way forward. Megill asked if more fire support was needed and was told that it was an infantryman's job – what was needed was more men. Ellis sent another company forward; then, just as the light was starting to fade he organized a coordinated attack that ended enemy resistance. The clearing of Wyler cost the Calgaries forty-three casualties, including fifteen killed.[21]

This battalion-level action was entirely typical of the fighting during the first few days of Veritable. The apparently overwhelming strength of the Allied attack meant little to the men spearheading the brigade advance, who had to overcome an enemy that fought from camouflaged and fortified positions until outflanked and overwhelmed. The pattern of strong enemy resistance suddenly collapsing once the choice was between death and captivity was again evident; more than three hundred German soldiers surrendered to the Calgaries. This behaviour, with its rapid transition from deadly belligerence to pitiful cries of

'Kamerad,' presented a real challenge to the soldiers, who were repeatedly cautioned to obey the rules of war with regard to prisoners.

While the Canadians fought to clear Wyler and open the Cleve road, 15th Scottish Division carried out its mission to reach the curved Materborn ridge overlooking the town. The Scottish battalions were supported by 6th Guards Tank Brigade. Their wider-tracked Churchill tanks were thought to be less likely to bog down on muddy ground than Sherman tanks, and so it proved as the Guards led the way to Kranenburg, seizing a crucial bridge and breaking the Siegfried line. However, during the night heavy traffic and flood waters collapsed the road, adding to the traffic problems behind the forward troops.[22]

Despite the growing chaos, Horrocks decided, on the basis of information that part of the ridge had been captured, to 'unleash my first reserve the 43rd (Wessex) Division which was to pass through the 15th Scottish and to burst out on the plain beyond and advance to Goch.' In his memoirs, Horrocks admitted that this was 'one of the worst mistakes I made in the war.' The advance of 43rd Division 'caused one of the worst traffic jams of the war,' greatly complicating the task of taking Cleve.[23] Horrocks's frank admission of error has disarmed historians, but it is hard not to agree that this was a really bad decision taken in the face of a great deal of contrary evidence.

General Dan Spry's 3rd Canadian Division, soon to be known as 'the Water Rats,' was given the task of clearing the area between the Nijmegen–Cleve road and the Rhine so as to protect the left flank of the main advance. During the week before 8 February a thaw had softened the Rhine flood plain, and enemy action to create breaks in two major dykes added to a flood of water that gradually submerged the battlefield the Canadians were supposed to manoeuvre over. The 79th Armoured Division was called on to supply Buffaloes, and the Canadians were reintroduced to the amphibious vehicles that had been so valuable during the Scheldt operations. H-Hour had been set for the late afternoon of 8 February. The assumption was that the main battle for the high ground and the road to Cleve would fully occupy the enemy and allow 3rd Division to move quickly to the line of the Spoy Canal, which linked Cleve to the Rhine. This might have been possible before the flooding, but an amphibious operation launched shortly before dark was likely to be neither sure nor swift.

Brigadier Jock Spragge's 7th Brigade had been assigned to seize the Quer Damm, a natural defensive position that dominated the front. German tunnelling efforts had collapsed the dam, but at either end of it companies of 1052nd Grenadier Regiment were dug in. The Regina Rifles had little difficulty taking the southern section and advanced to the village of Zyfflich with the aid of 'artificial moonlight' supplied by searchlights reflecting off the low-lying clouds. The flood waters had not yet submerged the approaches to the village, and the Reginas were accompanied by a troop of Shermans (13/18th Royal Hussars) and a Flail tank, which led the procession in order to clear mines. Two companies of the Reginas, working with cool, professional caution, had cleared the village by midnight, taking more than one hundred prisoners at the cost of one officer killed and twelve men wounded. The mine-clearing tank had settled the issue, flailing into the village with its guns firing. The Canadian Scottish Regiment attacked the northern end of the dam, sending one company on foot along the face of the dam while two platoons circled around and attacked from the southwest.[24]

On the left or Rhine flank of the divisional sector, 8th Brigade was conducting a well-organized operation, with the North Shore Regiment mounted in Buffaloes for a quick strike to a dyke barrier and the village of Zandpol. Booby traps inflicted most of the casualties while the regiment was clearing the dyke, and when the enemy in Zandpol showed signs of life, 'B' Company asked for a five-minute fire plan on the village to 'quiet it down.' The 13th Field Regiment obliged, and the North Shores entered the village without meeting any resistance. The Régiment de la Chaudière made the next bound to Leuth, but resistance was growing and several small counter-attacks had to be beaten off first. Leuth was taken by 0530 hours; then it was the North Shores' turn again. They pressed forward to Milligan on the south bank of the Rhine, meeting minimal opposition. The Queen's Own Rifles were brought forward, but there was no longer any sign of organized resistance. With the waters still rising, the lead brigades were in danger of being cut off by the flood, so a withdrawal was ordered.[25]

Brigadier John Rockingham's 9th Brigade waited until the afternoon of D + 2, 10 February, to start the Phase II of the operation. The Stormont, Dundas, and Glengarry Highlanders advanced along the southern edge of the flooded area, using Buffaloes to reach the Spoy Canal. By the afternoon of 11 February they had consolidated there, just as elements of British 43rd Division were completing the capture of Cleve. Out amidst the floods the Highland Light Infantry of Canada were involved in a miserable, costly struggle for the village of Duffelward. This Rhineland hamlet was the northernmost position of the Siegfried Line, with fortified houses, pillboxes with overlapping fields of fire, and flood waters swirling in between. 'B' Company of the HLI was mauled badly during its approach, and Duffelward was not taken until the afternoon of 11 February. The weary HLI were pressed forward by a barrage of orders from division, and at midnight on 11 February, two companies were in position on the bank of the Spoy Canal. The North Nova Scotia Highlanders, the brigade's reserve battalion, were ordered to cross the canal and occupy Kellen. 'After wading through knee to waist-deep water in various spots,' they established themselves without meeting any resistance. They waited there, isolated among the floods, facing east towards the Rhine. On 14 February the North Novas conducted the last task of Phase I of Veritable by launching an amphibious attack across the Alter Rhein and capturing the ferry crossing opposite Emmerich. At 1200 hours on 15 February, 3rd Division reverted to the command of 2nd Canadian Corps.[26]

This summary of the difficult tasks carried out by 'the Water Rats' fails to do justice to their extraordinary achievements on this strange battlefield. To operate effectively in such an environment required a high degree of coordination with 79th Armoured Division's specialized armour and flotillas of Buffaloes as well as the field artillery. Reading the War Diaries and especially the message logs reveals just how complex the problem of command and control became at every level.

Once Veritable began, the German High Command (OKW) retained responsibility for the direction of the defence of the Rhineland; this limited the options available to General Schlemm's 1st Parachute Army. Initially OKW was convinced that this was not the main Allied offensive and all that Schlemm could do was dispatch the balance of 7th Parachute Division to the Reichswald. Schlemm also ordered the creation of a new defensive line, Cleve–Kessel–Gennep, but he did not attempt to protest Hitler's predictable demand that no fortified position was to be given up without his personal permission.[27]

On 10 February, OKW accepted that Veritable was the main operation. It sent 47th Panzer Corps, with 116th Panzer and 15th Panzer Grenadier Divisions under command, to an assembly area near Uedem to prepare a corps-level counter-attack designed to regain the high ground west of Cleve. According to a senior staff officer of the corps, 'the dark night ... and strong harassing fire on crossroads and important terrain points by the enemy artillery' made it impossible to assemble the divisions in time, and the attack was not launched until 0930 hours, 13 February. The British 'recognized the German attack, met it energetically and soon were able to commence their own attack.' After a day-long battle the British broke through at the seam between the panzer divisions, forcing a withdrawal. That night both sides, exhausted by the struggle, accepted that a temporary stalemate had developed and ceased to mount new attacks.[28]

The original plan for Veritable had been based on two premises: that the ground would be sufficiently hard (frozen) to permit tank brigades to manoeuvre freely, and that the American attack (Operation Grenade) would be launched shortly after the assault, preventing the Germans from committing enough additional troops to stabilize their northern front. Within forty-eight hours of launching the attack it was clear that the ground was so soggy from the thaw and the deliberate flooding that there would be no breakout of the armoured units. By the afternoon of 12 February Horrocks had been informed that the American attack would have to be delayed for at least another week because the Roer was impassable.

Veritable had not been designed as another slogging match for 21 Army Group's infantry divisions. Churchill's decision of December 1944 to add an additional 250,000 men to the strength of the British Army had promised to solve some of the British reinforcement problems, but the worst shortages were in junior officers, and these could not be overcome with men hastily transferred from other arms.

The British Army had solved its earlier shortage of junior officers by borrowing more than six hundred young Canadians under the terms of the Canloan agreement.[29] By February 1945 all available Canadians were serving with British units and the War Office had been forced to authorize Immediate Emergency Combatant Commissions for the infantry and armoured corps. Outstanding NCOs could be commissioned without attending officer training schools if the operational situation demanded it. By the end of the first week of Veritable, 30th Corps had suffered 2,400 casualties, including 126 officers[30] – a situation that required both emergency commissions and a new operational plan.

Simonds, who had observed the battle while waiting for 30th Corps to release his Canadian infantry divisions, understood the need for a new approach, and he tried to persuade Crerar and Montgomery to reconsider Veritable. He proposed an expansion of Operation Wallstreet, the code name for an idea developed by Major-General G.H.A. Macmillan and the staff of 49th British Division. Since late December, Macmillan's battalions had been patrolling the 'island,' the partially flooded area between Nijmegen and Arnhem. On 18 January, 56th Brigade, working with a squadron of Sherbrooke Regiment tanks, occupied the town of Zetten after a fierce battle with elements of a German parachute regiment. Zetten was just a few kilometres from the Rhine over relatively dry ground, and Macmillan began to think seriously about crossing the river and taking Arnhem.[31]

When Simonds heard about Wallstreet he met with Macmillan and went away to prepare 'an appreciation and plan for a corps-level operation in which both 2nd and 3rd Canadian Infantry Divisions would follow 49th across the Rhine to expand the bridgehead beyond Arnhem.'[32] Corps engineers would build bridges capable of sustaining the advance. Simonds was certain that Wallstreet would force the enemy to respond, thus weakening the resistance in front of 30th Corps and altering the course of the Rhineland battle and perhaps even the war.

Simonds presented an outline to Crerar on 14 February,[33] but it was quickly rejected. Montgomery had visited the Veritable front on 11 February 'to see the conditions for myself.' His nightly message to Field Marshal Sir Alan Brooke suggested that enemy resistance was weakening and that 'the whole problem was one of opening up road centres and developing communications.' He reported that he had instructed Crerar to 'regroup and come up on a two corps frontage ... The postponement of Grenade may be for longer than we think and this makes it very necessary for Veritable to be given all the strength that can be collected.' The next day his message acknowledged that resistance to Veritable was increasing, with most of the available German reserves drawn into the battle, but he remained determined 'to put all the strength into Veritable and go on driving hard to the southeast.'[34] Crerar did ask Simonds to keep Wallstreet 'under consideration so that it might be undertaken without delay once the objectives of Veritable have been secured,'[35] but this was small consolation. Simonds knew that both 6th and 7th Parachute Divisions were firmly committed to the Rhineland battle and that there were few German troops left holding the river west of Arnhem.[36]

It is of course impossible to say what might have happened had Wallstreet been carried out; but it was surely worth trying, given the exhausting character of the Rhineland battle. A plan to seize and defend a bridgehead at Arnhem in February 1945, with full artillery and air support and a secure line of communications, had a much better likelihood of success than the ill-fated airborne venture of the previous September and would almost certainly have been less costly than frontal assaults against prepared defences in the Rhineland.

The rejection of Wallstreet meant that the Canadians were required to take over a front of some 2000 metres on the Rhine flank of the advance. The area was presently occupied by a brigade of 15th Scottish Division, which had been locked in combat with elements of 116th Panzer Division for three days. The Scottish troops were in no condition to continue offensive action after a struggle described as their 'worst experience since landing in Normandy,'[37] but the corps plan required them to advance towards Kalkar, securing Moyland Wood before handing over to the Canadians. This task proved well beyond their capacity, and when 7th Canadian Infantry Brigade arrived almost half of the woods and the village were still in German hands. The next morning, 16 February, 7th Brigade, supported by squadrons of the Scots Guards, took over the task. The Royal Winnipeg Rifles, mounted in Kangaroos, reached Louisendorf and dug in, but the Reginas discovered that the enemy had infiltrated back into the woods previously cleared by the Scottish brigade, so they spent the day clearing the approaches to the start line.[38]

The southern part of Moyland Wood is flat, with regularly spaced conifers, but towards the village a deeply gullied escarpment is cloaked in a mixed, mainly beechwood forest. The Canscots, advancing along the southern edge, had made good progress on 17 February securing

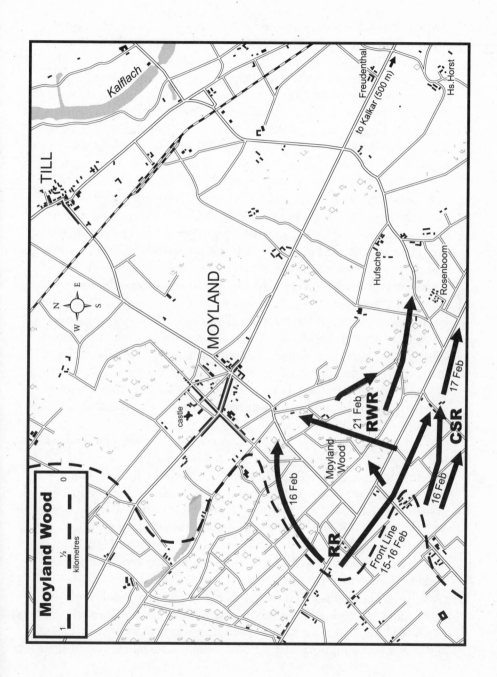

Moyland Wood

the high ground at the eastern end of the woods and holding it despite strong counter-attacks.[39] The Reginas' forming-up place was littered with the bodies of Scottish and German soldiers, which added to the sombre mood; the men could not help but be reluctant to enter a dark forest right out of Grimm's fairy tales. Moyland Wood is little changed to this day; visitors to the battlefield can follow the routes the Reginas and the Canscots took in their first attempt to clear the area. It takes some imagination to picture the noise of the shells crashing into the trees, the sound of concealed machine guns, and the gut-wrenching fear that gripped the riflemen as they worked their way forward. The carefully camouflaged enemy soldiers allowed one Regina company to move deep into the woods before closing in behind them. One Regina platoon was overrun; the others dug in under mortar and machine gun fire. The Canscots, trying to clear the eastern end of the woods, were quickly pinned down by heavy fire.[40]

The next morning, 19 February, the Reginas and Canscots renewed their efforts to clear the woods. It had rained heavily, and everyone was wet and stiff. No one at the sharp end had any confidence that infantry could overcome an enemy holding a wooded ridge with ample machine gun, mortar, and artillery support. The artillery bombardments that preceded the attacks were far too light and brief to do serious damage, and the paratroop battalion that had taken over the defence of the wood was fresh and had little difficulty dealing with the Canadians' attacks.[41]

When Spragge reported that the enemy was too strongly entrenched to be dislodged by his two infantry battalions, Simonds removed the veteran officer and placed the Reginas' commanding officer, Lieutenant-Colonel Alan Gregory, in temporary command. As often happened in such situations, Simonds gave Gregory the time and resources Spragge had lacked. The Royal Winnipeg Rifles left their slit trenches near Louisendorf and moved into position with the Fort Garry Horse south of Moyland Wood. Brigadier E.R. Suttie, who had replaced Stanley Todd in command of the divisional artillery, prepared an elaborate fire plan involving medium and field artillery as well as mortars and machine guns. Suttie knew that simply saturating the woods with fire would do little to help the infantry, and he proposed a system of stonks and linear concentrations instead of a rolling barrage. He hoped that with the target height for shell burst set to just above tree level, no fire would fall short owing to rounds bursting in trees.[42] Gregory and Lieutenant-Colonel Lockie Fulton, the aggressive young commander of the Royal Winnipeg Rifles, devised a plan to clear the eastern end of the wood by combining Wasps with tank support and air attacks. Each of the two lead companies kept three Wasps forward, with three in reserve ready to leapfrog into action when the first three had exhausted the fuel for their flame. This continuous support boosted the morale of the assaulting troops while breaking the will of the enemy.[43] In the day-long battle, which cost more than one hundred casualties including twenty-six killed, the Winnipegs displayed outstanding courage and skill. Major L.H. Denison, who led 'D' Company in the final stages, received the Distinguished Service Order for his inspired leadership. Lieutenant George Aldous, temporarily blinded from grenade fragments, returned to his platoon after first aid treatment and led it in defeating repeated enemy counter-attacks. He received the Military Cross.[44]

Total casualties to the brigade, including battle exhaustion, exceeded five hundred, and the Westerners had to be pulled out of action. When it came time to sum up the lessons learned, the emphasis was on the method of employing flame-throwers, close contact between infantry and tanks, and the hundred sorties flown by 84 Group of 2nd Tactical Air Force.[45] No one mentioned the most important lesson – the enemy was fighting with a new intensity in defence of the Fatherland and would not be overcome through improvised attacks with unfavourable force ratios. Moyland Wood was not Simonds's finest hour. Based on the large number of German prisoners captured, a case could be made that it had been correct to press the initial attacks. That said, the arrival of a fresh para battalion on 18 February demonstrated just how serious the enemy was about holding this position. Firing Spragge and berating Spry was not a substitute for good planning.[46] Fortunately, Simonds calmed down and allowed the division to do its job properly.

While 7th Brigade was fighting to clear Moyland Wood, Brigadier F.N. Cabeldu's 4th Brigade launched a set-piece attack from Louisendorf to secure part of the Goch–Kalkar road. This advance was ordered to support 30th Corps' attack on the heavily fortified town of Goch. The ground was soggy, but the Kangaroos and supporting armour were able to keep pace with the barrage and the two lead battalions dug themselves in astride the road. The parachute battalion defending the area gave up almost one hundred prisoners, most of them stunned from the hurricane of high explosives, but within an hour the expected counter-attacks had begun, launched by platoon-sized groups with assault guns. This was precisely what the bite-and-hold tactics were designed to deal with, and though some ground was given up, the enemy lost yet more men without altering the situation.[47]

General Schlemm must have been tempted to order a withdrawal to the Kalkar ridge and the prepared defences in front of Uedem, but since elements of 2nd Parachute Corps were still holding out in Goch and Hitler's 'no withdrawal' order was in force, he chose instead to launch a strong counter-attack on 4th Brigade's positions. Panzer Lehr, with the equivalent of four battalions of infantry, twenty-two tanks, twelve assault guns, an artillery battalion, and an engineer company, was the only reserve available, and the corps commander, General Heinrich von Lüttwitz, was told to use it for a 'one-time deployment with the 1st Parachute Army.'[48] Lüttwitz decided that an immediate attack on the Canadian positions using the cover of darkness would yield the best results, and two powerful battlegroups began their attacks 'towards 1900 hours.' The Chief of Staff of 47 Panzer would later tell interrogators that 'in retrospect,' a better plan would have been 'to attack from the projecting front of the 6th Para Division into the left wing of the enemy,' but this would have meant waiting until morning.[49]

The Panzer Lehr battlegroup formed up near Kalkar, and by midnight its attack had penetrated as far as the tactical headquarters of the Royal Hamilton Light Infantry, where Lieutenant-Colonel Denis Whitaker was attempting to control the battle. The RHLI reported 'heavy infiltrations of enemy tanks and infantry' but were able to restore the situation by committing a reserve company to their shattered left flank. By 0400 hours Whitaker was in contact with all four of his rifle companies, each organized for all-around defence.[50] The Essex Scottish, advancing on the brigade's right flank, faced the problem of fighting along a divisional and corps boundary. They had been told that 214th Brigade of 43rd (Wessex) Division held the ground west of the Kleve–Üdem road, but the actual British positions left a dangerous gap.

When the first counter-attacks struck the Essex (mounted by a battalion from the Army Parachute Training School), they were forced to yield ground, and as night fell the enemy overran the forward companies.[51]

Brigadier Cabeldu was given command of the Queen's Own Cameron Highlanders, which allowed him to use his reserve battalion to restore the Essex position. A new attack began at 0900 hours, with the Royals and the Fort Garry tanks advancing behind a rolling barrage, and once again the Goch–Kalkar road was reached without difficulty. The commanding officer of the Essex Scottish and his headquarters group were rescued from the farmhouse cellar, where they had escaped their own and enemy shellfire, and they, with other survivors, withdrew. The Royals and Garries closed the gap between their positions and 214th Brigade, gradually establishing a firm position.[52] Cabeldu also sent a squadron of tanks and elements of the Camerons forward to reinforce the RHLI. The barrage that supported the Canadian advance also checked a daylight action mounted by 116th Panzer Division. As the skies cleared after days of rain, 84 Group filled the air, with Typhoons and Spitfires harassing anything that moved. The Luftwaffe responded by sending several ME 262 jet aircraft to the area, but they had little impact on the air or ground battle.[53]

The intense battle fought between 47th Panzer Corps and 2nd Canadian Infantry Division deserves to be examined as an important case study of the limitations of both Allied and German battle doctrine. The Canadians, employing their by now standard procedure, used an elaborate fire plan – including smoke, a rolling barrage, and a carefully planned counter-battery program – to allow tanks and Kangaroo-borne infantry to reach limited objectives, dig in, and repel the initial German counter-attacks. So far so good. As night fell the tanks withdrew to refuel and rearm, leaving the infantry and several troops of 2nd Anti-Tank Regiment to hold positions in farmhouses and orchards scattered across open, flat countryside. General Matthews and Brigadier Cabeldu as well as the RHLI and Essex battalion commanders anticipated a night marked by enemy infiltration tactics; but they also believed the real battle would begin at first light with an attack from the Kalkar ridge on the exposed northern flank. The gunners prepared to fire registered DF (defensive fire) tasks, and the Torscots positioned their 4.2-inch mortars and medium machine guns to provide support. The

Camerons of Canada were attached to 4th Brigade, and the Garries were ready to return to action.[54] If the day dawned fair, 84 Group would have Typhoons overhead waiting in 'cab rank.'[55] Providing all went according to plan, the Canadians would crush another patterned enemy counter-attack.

The Germans had so far proven to be slow learners, but this time General von Lüttwitz, the corps commander, had just been through a daylight counter-attack with British artillery and anti-tank guns. He had no wish to repeat the experience and decided to order an immediate attack. The Germans had a good deal of experience in night actions employing small groups to infiltrate Allied positions, but few commanders had tried to employ large armoured battlegroups in full darkness. The result was a chaotic counter-attack that cost both armies significant casualties without altering the basic situation. Panzer Lehr lost six of its twenty-two available Panthers to the guns of 2nd Anti-Tank Regiment and withdrew into reserve.

The 116th Panzer Division, heavily engaged at Goch, could ill afford further losses unless the corps objective – 'the old main battle line' – was restored. German tank commanders found it impossible to coordinate a night advance, and they withdrew in the face of a 'heavy barrage from artillery of all calibers.' The next morning a renewed attempt collapsed 'after initial successes had to be stopped due to heavy losses.' This proved to be the last major counter-attack by panzer battlegroups in the Rhineland campaign. From 21 February until 9 March, when the remains of 47th Panzer Corps withdrew to the east bank of the Rhine, the armour was used to stiffen resistance and delay the inevitable Allied advance.

Major Paul Krenz, who had served as the second-in-command of the German forces in Goch before being taken prisoner, told Canadian interrogators that 'the principle that no inch of ground shall be yielded under any circumstances' was forcing lower commanders to deceive their superiors, as the orders were impossible to follow. The requirement 'that 85% of all personnel of the unit must at all times be fighting in the line' simply led to falsified strength returns: 'at all levels [commanders] use their reserves to plug holes ... rather than work out an organized plan.' This costly and pointless method of waging war was still possible because the younger German soldiers knew 'nothing better than life at the front' and 'provided they got something to eat and smoke ... would continue to fight.'[56]

The battles for Moyland Wood and the Goch–Kalkar road and the bitter struggle for the town of Goch cost British and Canadian divisions more than 3,000 casualties, including 919 killed, wounded, or missing on 20 February alone. Canadian losses were just over nine hundred men, including fifty-one killed, ninety-nine wounded, and fifty-four taken prisoner from the Essex Scottish.[57] When combined with 'wastage' due to sickness and battle exhaustion, the casualty rate in Veritable was hollowing out the combat power of many battalions. The Canadians could draw upon a replacement pool greatly expanded by the arrival on the continent of reinforcement drafts – which included conscripts – but the British were desperately short of trained men.

Major John Wishart, the psychiatrist attached to 30th Corps, was particularly concerned that up to 50 per cent of the 1,000 British battle exhaustion cases he examined were men who had been wounded and were experiencing 'their first hard battle' since returning to a front line battalion. Most of the other cases were 'young, immature boys experiencing their first action.' Wishart reported that a number of them looked 'younger than their age' and that some had 'never yet had to shave.' None of them were imbued with the intense commitment that characterized the young Germans serving in the parachute battalions, and few seemed likely candidates for returning to their units.

Canadian doctors saw scores of patients who were burnt out emotionally. When the corps psychiatrist, Major Burdett McNeel, reviewed their records, he noted that 'at least one third ... gave a history of being previously wounded or exhausted.' Major Bob Gregory, 3rd Division's psychiatrist, estimated that the rate of repeaters was much higher. Both men agreed that those evacuated as battle exhaustion casualties were too emotionally spent to be returned to their units. Wishart sent less than 20 per cent of the British patients back into combat, and the Canadians, who had always been more cautious, asked fewer than one in ten to face another day with a combat unit.[58]

The horrendous casualty toll in the first two weeks of Veritable was an inevitable product of the enemy's determined defence and the postponement of the American attack. The 1st Parachute Army had drawn upon all available reserves to prevent a breakthrough in the north, turning the Rhineland into a killing ground that weakened the Anglo-Canadian armies while destroying the combat power of much of the Parachute Army. Crerar's Anglo-Canadian Army lost 8,500 men killed, wounded, and missing in just two weeks. Most of these casualties – 6,704 – were suffered by British battalions, but the 1,794 Canadian losses were proportionate to the troops engaged.[59] More than 11,000 German soldiers had surrendered since 8 February, and intelligence estimates, based on decrypted German reports, placed the number of dead and wounded at close to 12,000. Despite these losses, the German army continued to wage war with ruthless determination. Their reward was the continued bombing of the cities of Germany and the deaths of tens of thousands of soldiers and civilians.

8

Blockbuster and the Rhine

General Bill Simpson's 9th U.S. Army had waited impatiently while the battle of the Rhineland was waged by British and Canadian troops. With ten divisions, three of them armoured, 9th Army had more than 300,000 men under command as well as its own tactical air force. Intelligence reports indicated that now that Panzer Lehr had been committed to stemming Veritable, there were fewer than 30,000 German troops, of varying quality, between the Americans and the Rhine. Simpson and his corps commanders were understandably anxious to launch such a promising operation.[1] When U.S. Army engineers calculated that the reservoirs behind the blown dams would be empty by 24 February, Simpson decided to start his attack early on 23 February, while the river was still in flood, in the hope of catching the defenders off guard. There was to be no air bombardment from 'heavies' and no preliminary artillery barrage. More than 2,000 guns – the largest American artillery concentration to that point in the war (one gun per ten yards of front) – would commence firing forty-five minutes before H-Hour.

Engineers, protected by infantry patrols, crossed the Roer before H-Hour, and when the artillery barrage lifted the engineers of 30th U.S. Infantry Division had a footbridge in place. This success story was not, however, typical of this very dangerous assault crossing. Most divisions had a difficult time getting their units over the fast-moving river, and as the day progressed, many footbridges were swept away. The river crossing was the worst part of the first week of Operation Grenade; once the army was established on the east bank of the Roer, the operation went smoothly. The Germans' 59th Division and 363rd Volksgrenadier Division, which met the main weight of the American attack, were pushed back quickly. After twenty-four hours, 9th Army had twenty-eight battalions across the river and seven bridges in operation. The cost was 93 men killed, 913 wounded, and 61 missing. Many of these casualties were combat engineers involved in the river assault and bridge building.[2]

The terrain in front of 9th Army was ideal for a mobile army. The relatively flat farm country was planted mostly in sugar beets and grain, and the road network was extensive. Apart from a number of fortified towns, there were few obstacles in the Americans' path. Before launching Grenade, Simpson wrote his corps commanders an instruction that was reminiscent of orders issued by General Patton: 'If the violence of our attack should cause disruption of the enemy resistance, each corps will be prepared to conduct relentless pursuit in zone, and phases will be abandoned in favour of taking advantage of our opportunity.' By evening of the second day, tank and tank destroyer battalions were across and Simpson was beginning to sense that 'things were breaking up.' There was 'not much in front of Ninth Army,' and it was time to go for the Rhine. The German commander, General Gustav von Zangen, had received reinforcements – 9th and 11th Panzer Divisions, as well as 338th Infantry Division – and as usual, they had to be fed hastily into the defensive perimeter in the hope of maintaining a cohesive line. Counterthrusts then bled their striking power. Thus the best the Germans could do was slow down the American advance.[3] The hammer was well and truly aimed for the anvil of the British and Canadian forces to the north. But the anvil, as we shall see, was not allowed to remain in place until the American hammer had delivered the crushing blow. Instead, frontal attacks on the main German defensive position were ordered, and 2nd Canadian Corps found itself fighting one of its costliest operations of the war.

The decision to pause and mount a new offensive operation to the 'Hochwald Forest and Xanten' was made by Montgomery on 20 February, three days before Grenade began. The eleven German divisions committed to containing the Anglo-Canadian advance were 'sowing the seeds for a successful Grenade,' and Montgomery was determined to maintain pressure and reach the objectives set out in his original orders. Lieutenant-General Guy Simonds's 2nd Canadian Corps, which Montgomery claimed had taken just 400 of the 3,800 casualties suffered in Veritable, was to have primary responsibility for the new offensive on the 'main enemy positions ... while 30th Corps operates from Goch towards Weeze and thence southward.' His nightly message to London noted that he was 'going forward tomorrow to spend two days at TAC HQ Canadian Army ... to examine the battle in detail.'[4]

General Harry Crerar outlined Montgomery's plan to his corps commanders on 21 February. He told 30th Corps to renew its advance the next day, capturing the town of Weeze; if the opportunity arose, it was then to exploit towards Kevelaer. Four British divisions and 1st Commando Brigade were to take part in the advance. The 2nd Canadian

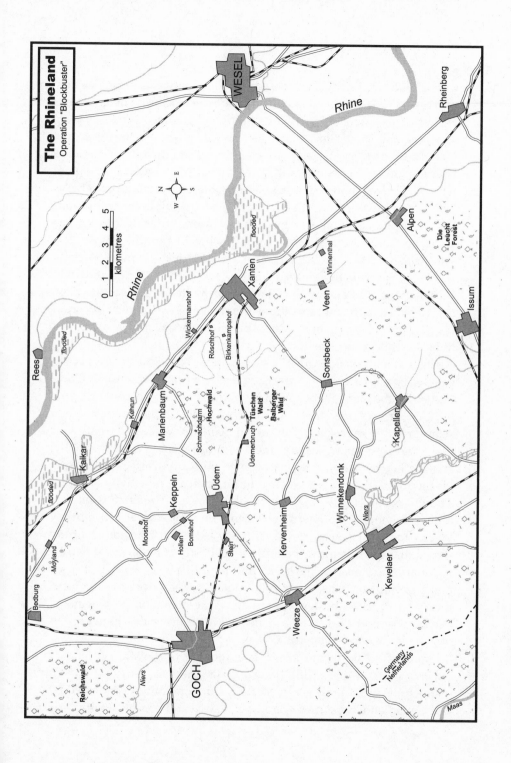

The Rhineland
Operation "Blockbuster"

WESEL

Rhine

Rheinberg

Rhine

flooded

N
W E
S

Alpen

Die Leucht Forest

kilometres
0 1 2 3 4 5

Xanten

Veen Winnenthal

Issum

Rees

flooded

Wickelmanshof

Röschhof

Birkenkampshof

Sonsbeck

Kehrun

Marienbaum

Hochwald

Schmachdarm

Tüschen Wald

Balberger Wald

Kapellen

Kalkar

flooded

Keppeln

Üdem

Üdemerbruch

Winnekendonk

Niers

Mooshof

Hollen Bomshof

Stein

Kervenheim

Mölyland

Kevelaer

Bedburg

Weeze

Germany
Netherlands

GOCH

Reichswald

Niers

Maas

Corps, with two British divisions under command, was to begin a new offensive on 26 February, breaking through the Hochwald defences and exploiting to Xanten.[5] The next day Simonds outlined his corps plan, assigning the name Blockbuster for the Canadian attack. Crerar had placed both 4th Canadian Armoured Division and 11th British Armoured Division under Simonds, and it seems that these added resources tempted him to ignore the problems encountered by armoured vehicles in the first weeks of the battle. He proposed to use his infantry divisions to seize the Kalkar ridge and the defences around Üdem before sending 4th Canadian Armoured through the Hochwald gap towards Xanten. The British 11th Armoured was to parallel this advance, reaching Sonsbeck. Simonds thought that starting the attack in the north would help convince the enemy that the Kalkar–Xanten road was the main axis of his advance and thus draw attention away from the Hochwald Gap and the railway line, which the engineers would tear up and transform into a corps maintenance route.[6]

The next day, after news of the success of the American attack reached Crerar's headquarters, the Army Commander began to reconsider Block-buster. As the intelligence summary put it: 'There is no doubt that the 9th U.S. Army's operations will have an effect on the First Canadian Army front. What form it will take remains to be seen.' Twenty-four hours later, more news arrived: the Americans were advancing rapidly, and the enemy was strongly resisting 30th Corps' attack on Weeze. Furthermore, there was evidence of an 'increase in activity and gun strength in the Hochwald.'[7] All of this prompted Crerar to issue new orders: 'In view of the determined enemy resistance 24/25 Feb, north of Weeze and the consequent inability of 53 (Welsh) Division to firmly secure that town before Operation Blockbuster commences it will be necessary to reconsider the basic draft plan ... If by D + 1 it is obvious that to complete Blockbuster a considerable regrouping is required, then a partial Blockbuster will terminate the operation.' Crerar noted that he was prepared to be satisfied with 'securing this high-ground east of the Kalkar-Uedem road.'[8]

Simonds left no record of what he thought of the strategy behind either a full or a partial Blockbuster. His plans for carrying out his instructions were, however, typical of many operations conducted by 2nd Canadian Corps: they were imaginative and complex, with little allowance for error or the inevitable friction of war. The initial phase called for two brigades of 2nd Division to attack the Kalkar ridge, while 8th Brigade from 3rd Division captured the village of Keppeln. This was straightforward enough, but Simonds proposed to introduce 4th Armoured Division into the battle shortly after first light. The division was divided into two battlegroups: 'Tiger,' including most of the division, and 'Lion,' reduced to the South Alberta Regiment and the Algonquins. Tiger Group was to advance on a narrow axis between 6th and 8th Brigades and seize the centre of the Kalkar ridge. After 2nd Division had come forward to relieve Tiger Group, it was to continue south to the far side of Uedem, which would by then be under attack by a fresh brigade of 3rd Division. Finally, Tiger Group, together with 11th British Armoured Division, was to 'exploit,' breaking through the elaborate defensive lines named by the Germans the 'Schlieffen Position.' In fact, it was more complicated than this. Major-General Chris Vokes organized Tiger Group into five 'mixed forces.' Each was given specific tasks and timings, which seemed unnecessarily complicated to those who had to carry them out.[9]

Major-General Bruce Matthews was not concerned about the broader operational picture. His job was to make sure that 2nd Division was ready to seize the Kalkar ridge and hand over the area to 43rd Wessex Division before advancing to the Hochwald. He was confident that with a smoke screen obscuring observation from enemy artillery on the north bank of the Rhine, with a well-prepared artillery plan, and with a full armoured regiment supporting the lead brigade, his infantry battalions would quickly secure their objectives.[10] His optimism held even though he knew that the Kalkar sector was being defended by the best troops the enemy possessed. The 6th Parachute Division still fielded two close-to-full-strength para regiments, and it was known that 116th Panzer Division had brought its rear elements forward during the brief lull. With a regiment of 2nd Parachute Division also under command, 47th Panzer Corps was a formidable opponent,[11] but Matthews was certain that since ample time had been available to study the objectives, integrate the supporting arms, and brief the troops down to section level, success was all but assured.[12] This was the kind of operation the divisions of 21 Army Group were trained and equipped to carry out, and the enemy had yet to develop a method of defending against such an attack.

During the night of 25 February, as the troops, plagued by an icy rain, began to move to their forming-up places, the enemy launched a spoiling attack on a part of the front line held by 4th Brigade. Brigadier R. Holley Keefler would recall that 'there was a rather tense moment but the RHLI continued to do their stuff and had the front quieted down just 15 minutes before H-Hour.'[13] At 0345 hours all three battalions of 6th Brigade crossed their start lines, with the lead companies mounted in Kangaroos. Overhead tracer fire and other navigation devices, including horizontal and vertical searchlights, inevitably recalled Operation Totalize of the previous summer.

With the equivalent of two squadrons of tanks[14] advancing with each battalion, the brigade quickly reached its objectives. Consolidation was achieved before first light. The South Saskatchewans occupied the high point on the ridge and established a battalion fortress. The first counter-attack did not begin until noon and was channelled through a deep gully, where a troop of Sherbrooke tanks waited in an ambush position. Just thirty-five of the hundred-plus paratroopers who attacked survived to become prisoners of war. The Fusiliers Mont-Royal, in the centre, had little trouble reaching their objective at the scheduled time, but the Queen's Own Cameron Highlanders of Canada ran into a minefield and were forced to change the axis of their advance – no easy task at night in a landscape fitfully illuminated by burning buildings. When Lieutenant-Colonel E.P. Thompson, the young, dynamic CO of the Camerons, was killed by a direct hit on his Kangaroo, Major D.M. Rodgers, the senior company commander, took control and led the battlegroup to its objectives, which were cleared with the help of a FMR company. Rodgers proved to be an inspirational leader, 'personally performing acts of the greatest gallantry,' for which he was awarded a DSO.[15]

The 5th Brigade's task was to protect the division's left flank by seizing the crest of the ridge in front of Kalkar. Only one squadron of tanks was available, and Brigadier Bill Megill decided to keep it in reserve, to be used against the final objective. The Black Watch, advancing on the 6th Brigade's flank, found two of their three objectives untouched by the fast barrage and vigorously defended. Lieutenant-Colonel Bruce Ritchie called off the advance, ordered his men to withdraw, and asked Megill to organize a new attack with armoured support and artillery concentrations on call. This was quickly arranged, and when the battlegroup was four hundred yards from its objectives a second artillery concentration was requested. This lifted at the correct time, and 'heavy fire from all guns and machine guns in the tanks' got the infantry across the open ground and onto their objective.[16] This superb example of all-arms cooperation marked a return to the solid performance the battalion had demonstrated in Belgium.

The Maisonneuves also ran into trouble when one of their companies was caught on open ground and 'shot up from all sides.' Lieutenant Guy de Merlis, commanding the reserve platoon, led his men along a sunken road, bypassing the firefight. They took possession of a house that enfiladed the enemy position, but the platoon lacked the strength to overcome the 'enemy dugouts filled with fanatical paratroops.' Megill waited until the Black Watch were firmly established and then sent two troops of tanks to assist the Maisies. Lieutenant-Colonel Julien Bibeau took direct control of the battle, using the armour to cover the approach of Wasp flame-throwers, which were used to end the resistance in the deeper dugouts. Bibeau, a consistently effective battalion commander, was awarded a long overdue DSO for this action.[17]

The task assigned to 3rd Division in the first phase of Blockbuster was to capture the village of Keppeln as well as the fortified farmhouse and hamlets on the lower slopes of the ridge. Once these outposts were overcome, a fresh brigade would assault the still more formidable defences of Uedem. Brigadier J.A. Roberts decided that his 8th Brigade would advance two battalions up, with the Queen's Own Rifles and Chaudières clearing the flanks and the North Shores in reserve to tackle Keppeln. Roberts was given just two squadrons of Hussars tanks, and he decided to use these initially to support the flank attacks. The North Shores would have to wait until a squadron could be released by one of their sister battalions.[18]

The Queen's Own faced a challenging situation. Lieutenant-Colonel S.M. Lett told the division's Historical Officer that he had been unable to reconnoitre the intermediate strongpoints or the final objectives as the flat open country was 'completely under enemy observation.' When Lett learned that according to the Blockbuster master plan his battalion was simply securing the lower slope of a ridge conforming to the advance of 6th Brigade and would consequently have limited artillery support, he knew there was trouble ahead. He instructed his company commanders to ignore the designated H-Hour and wait until the enemy had begun the counter-barrage. 'Enemy artillery,' he noted, 'is not very flexible. His defensive fire is brought down very accurately. However, once the limitation of the area is determined it can be circumvented with comparative safety.'[19] The delayed start worked perfectly, and the lead companies quickly reached the intermediate objectives. Now the problem was to force the enemy out of their positions. Sergeant Aubrey Cosens was awarded the Victoria Cross posthumously for his extraordinary skill and bravery at one such strongpoint during the close-quarters struggle for Mooshof. By the end of the day the Queen's Own had overcome 'extremely heavy artillery and mortar fire' and the 'determination of the enemy' and had captured more than three hundred paratroopers. Lett was especially generous in his praise of the First Hussars. 'Their support,' he noted, 'was the deciding factor in ousting the enemy from his well dug-in positions.'[20] Lett's recollection was no doubt true for the early stages of the battle, but by mid-morning the Hussars squadron had been withdrawn to support the North Shores' attack on Keppeln.

The New Brunswick batallion used a barrage to advance across the open fields but were forced to the ground before they had covered the first 1000 metres. The Chaudières on the right flank ran into similar difficulties when one of their companies was pinned down by heavy, accurate fire from Keppeln. The other lead company got within one hundred yards of their first objective when 'what appeared to be a white flag was seen.' Taking this as a sign of surrender, the men ceased firing and prepared to gather in prisoners. Suddenly three enemy armoured vehicles emerged from cover and machine-gunned the Canadians, inflicting a number of casualties.[21]

The situation now depended on the North Shores and the thirteen tanks of 'C' Squadron, First Hussars. Roberts had arranged for an artillery concentration on the village; otherwise, the attack plan called for an advance at 'best tank speed' towards a village known to be defended by fixed anti-tank guns and enemy armour. A platoon of North Shores, organized into PIAT teams, rode on the decks of the rear tanks. According to the Hussar's operational report, 'the attack went in

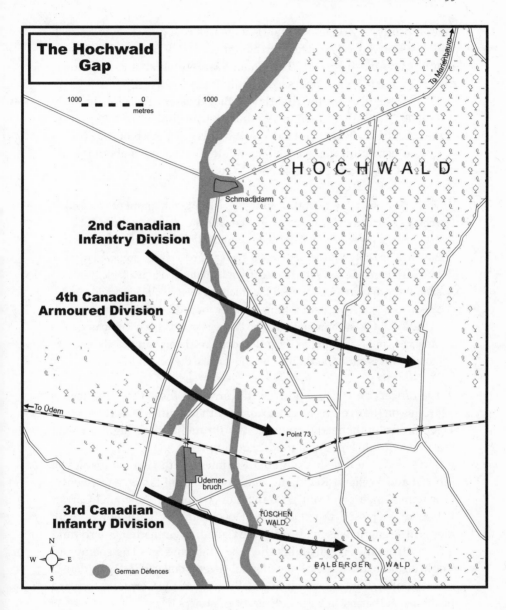

The Hochwald Gap

1000 — — — 0 1000
metres

HOCHWALD

Schmacfidarm

2nd Canadian
Infantry Division

4th Canadian
Armoured Division

To Üdem

Point 73

Üdemer-
bruch

3rd Canadian
Infantry Division

TÜSCHEN
WALD

N
W E
S

German Defences

BALBERGER WALD

To Marienbaum

magnificently.' Two German tanks were destroyed and six were seen withdrawing to Uedem. The North Shores quickly occupied the town, mopping up the survivors. The Chauds were then able to stage their own combined-arms attack, securing all their objectives.[22]

The outline plan for the first day of Blockbuster called for the early intervention of 4th Canadian Armoured Division. Vokes, known to some veterans as 'Blood and Guts Vokes' (his guts, our blood), gave his officers a fist-thumping speech and written instructions about 'tactics and thrust' – typical of his approach to command:

> This will be an all-out effort, strip to the absolute minimum of wheeled vehicles ... The troops must be impressed with the vital necessity to get on and destroy the enemy. Subordinate commanders must act on their own initiative. Do not sit on an objective if you can press on. Be prepared to go hungry but make every effort to see that adequate food is available. Tanks should try to carry extra to feed the infantry. Every vehicle should contain rations and spare petrol. Tanks must be topped up in the forming up place. Do not waste ammunition. The Boche is in a bad way compared to ourselves and is fighting in sheer desperation. He gives up easily when cut off. This is our opportunity – we must make the best of it.[23]

The officers and men who were to carry out these thrusting tactics left Kleve on the evening of 25 February with Brigadier Robert Moncel's Tiger Group in the lead. It poured rain throughout the night, turning the 'Green Route Up' into a muddy quagmire.

'Jerry Force' – British Columbia Regiment with two companies of Lincoln and Welland Regiment, one troop of Flail tanks, and twenty-four Ram Kangaroos from 1st Canadian Armoured Personnel Carrier Regiment – crossed the start line at 0900 hours. 'Snuff Force,' with identical strength, was made up of the Canadian Grenadier Guards and infantry from the Argyll and Sutherland Highlanders. 'The enemy put a fight all along the routes, knocking out several tanks with Panzerfausts and Bazookas, but the armour gradually overran the Germans' forward positions, gathering in large batches of prisoners.'[24]

The two follow-up forces, 'Jock' and 'Cole,' met little direct opposition but suffered a steady drain of casualties from constant mortar and artillery fire. By evening on 26 February the four units had captured and consolidated most of their initial objectives. 'Smith Force,' composed of the Governor-General's Foot Guards and Lake Superior Regiment, along with a troop of SP guns from 5th Anti-Tank Regiment, had been held in reserve for the crucial phase of Tiger Group's action – the capture of the high ground behind Uedem. This assault was to be coordinated with the attack that Brigadier John Rockingham's 9th Brigade was making from Keppeln. Rockingham's two assault battalions, the Stormont, Dundas, and Glengarry Highlanders and the Highland Light Infantry, were in position to move off towards Uedem shortly before midnight. Artificial moonlight created by searchlights cast an eerie glow over the battlefield as the lead companies moved towards the anti-tank ditch that surrounded the town. There was difficulty with 'numerous mines which littered the area,' but progress was remarkably swift. Confused fighting occurred throughout the night, with HLI reporting several counter-attacks, but by 0400 hours the reserve battalion, the North Nova Scotia Highlanders, was in Uedem ready to take the final objectives around the railway yards to the south.[25]

Uedem was the most elaborate enemy position in front of the Hochwald, and the relative ease with which it fell may have been the deciding factor in Crerar's decision to allow Simonds to carry on with a full instead of a partial Blockbuster. Despite heavy casualties (26 February would turn out to be one of the costliest days of the war for the Canadians),[26] the first twenty-four hours of Blockbuster had been a series of successful engagements that resulted in the attainment of all objectives. Crerar and Simonds were aware of the difficulties the tanks were encountering in the boggy terrain, and they knew that the main enemy positions were still in front of them, but no senior commander wanted to call off an operation that showed so much promise. Montgomery's nightly message was especially optimistic: he 'was very well satisfied' and hoped to 'write off or capture the bulk of the Germans west of the Rhine.' He noted that 'this converging operation with two large armies is a tricky business and I have to keep a pretty tight grip on the battle to ensure it goes the way required.' Montgomery hoped that the better weather promised for the next few days would allow the air forces to destroy the Wesel bridges and prevent the withdrawal of the enemy's heavy equipment. The prospect of 'maximum activity of air forces on the Rhine by day and night' added to his confidence that Blockbuster and Grenade would quickly end German resistance.[27]

On the night of 26–27 February, Simonds ordered the next stage of Blockbuster. Despite the difficulties reported by 11th Armoured Division south of Uedem, where boggy ground and numerous enemy anti-tank guns had made for a slow, miserable, costly operation, the advance to Sonsbeok was to continue, with the division's infantry brigade in the lead.[28] The decision to employ the infantry brigade of an armoured division in a slugging match at this stage in the war made little sense, but Simonds, Crerar, and Montgomery were determined to press on. The role of 11th Armoured Division in Blockbuster has not attracted much attention, but something of the nature of its experience may be gleaned by noting that it had the highest battle exhaustion ratio of any British division in the Rhineland battle, with most of the psychiatric casualties suffered by soldiers of the infantry brigade.[29] The divisional historian declined to offer a narrative of those 'painful and depressing' days, which resembled a First World War battle, with gains measured in hundreds of yards. 'Detailed investigation,' the author wrote, 'may be left to the specialists of military science.'[30]

Simonds issued similar orders to 4th Canadian Armoured Division: it was to send Lion Group, comprising the Algonquin Regiment and the tanks of the South Albertas, forward to the western end of the Hochwald gap. 'Lion' was to proceed 'under cover of darkness because there was no protection from the high ground and so that the crest of the hill could be reached before daylight.'[31] The decision to send a small battlegroup forward in these circumstances reflected Vokes's gung-ho approach to combat, but what was Simonds thinking? His troops had overwhelmed the enemy defences on the Kalkar-Uedem ridge in a carefully prepared assault that drew upon virtually every lesson learned in a long, gruelling campaign. All previous experience suggested it was time to pause, deal with any enemy counter-attacks, and either wait for the Americans to force a German withdrawal or organize a new set-piece attack, coordinated with 30th Corps. Simonds knew that 5th Brigade was not yet in position to begin an advance through the woods north of the gap, but he still allowed Vokes to send Lion Group forward on its own.[32]

While preparing for their part in Blockbuster, the Alqonquins and

South Albertas had been briefed on a large sand table that depicted the battlefield in three dimensions. They had been shown how one squadron of tanks and the carrier platoon would cleverly perform a right-hook manoeuvre to place them astride the railway line, in position to support the main advance. This bold action was said to be possible because 11th Armoured Division would be well forward, forcing an enemy withdrawal. But as of midnight on 26 February, British and Canadian troops were still fighting for the southern defences of Uedem and 11th Division was bogged down at the Uedem-Weeze road, well short of the high ground that dominated the objective assigned to the 'right hook' battlegroup.[33]

Lieutenant-Colonel R.W. Bradburn, the CO of the Algonquins, who was in command, hesitated to carry out orders that required him to begin an advance under exceptionally adverse conditions. The rain, mud, and growing confusion caused by the arrival of advance elements of both infantry divisions on the road axis had prevented some of his subunits, including an entire company, from arriving at the forming-up place, so he tried to postpone the attack. But direct orders, relayed by brigade, left him no choice, and the advance began in darkness at 0430 hours. By dawn both the right-hook battlegroup and the main force were reporting some progress, and Bradburn sent his reserve company forward.[34]

As further information became available, Bradburn informed Brigadier Jim Jefferson that 'he was unable to continue his show,' as neither tanks nor infantry could advance against the intense fire in the valley. Brigade, division, and corps message logs for 27 February leave no doubt that the situation was understood by senior commanders. Shortly before noon Simonds arrived at 4th Division Headquarters to confer with Vokes and Jefferson.[35] We do not know if they discussed the obvious solution – to withdraw what was left of Lion Group under cover of smoke or darkness and recommend an end to Blockbuster. It is only possible to record their decision to continue the advance with all available resources.

As a first step, Vokes met with Lieutenant-Colonel Fred Wigle at the headquarters of the Argylls and explained to him the need to secure the eastern end of the Hochwald gap. Wigle was informed that the enemy had received a 'sound drubbing' on the first day of Blockbuster and was 'generally withdrawing towards the Rhine.' He was later to tell the division's Historical Officer that 'he did not anticipate a difficult fight to secure the objective even though only one battalion had been allotted to the task.'[36] Wigle, a former staff officer who was directing his first battle, soon revised this estimate when his battalion was forced to dig in five hundred yards west of the gap owing to heavy, accurate fire. The Argylls and what was left of the original Lion Force could deal with enemy counter-attacks, but any attempt to advance into the gap would have been suicidal.

At 1600 hours, 27 February, Simonds joined Crerar, General Sir Brian Horrocks, and Air Vice-Marshal E.C. Hudleston for the Army Commanders' daily conference. It is unlikely that they knew the details of 9th Army's appreciation – that German resistance on the Roer front was on the verge of collapse – but they were aware that the American bridgehead was secure and that elements of two armoured divisions were across the river. Again, we have no record of their discussions – only of their decision to mount another effort to break through the enemy defences.[37]

The orders that Simonds issued that evening required elements of all his divisions to press forward. To the north of the gap, 5th Brigade was to breach the outer defences and advance into the forest, relieving the pressure on the Argylls; the latter, with a squadron of South Alberta Shermans and an elaborate artillery program, were to secure Point 72 and then fight their way into the gap. The Lincoln and Welland Regiment was to support this thrust by clearing the woods to the south. If these efforts succeeded, 4th Division's armoured brigade would attack through the gap towards Xanten.[38]

The Argylls benefited from a massive artillery program and were able to advance along the fringe of the forest to their objective. But, as the battalion War Diary notes, the battle really began when the enemy began to counter-attack at first light.[39] Unfortunately, 5th Brigade was unable to keep pace. The Calgary Highlanders cleared the anti-tank ditch and dugouts on the western edge of the woods; the enemy withdrew to prepared positions just inside the Hochwald. The Black Watch were unable to locate, never mind subdue, these well-camouflaged enemy posts.[40] The Lincs, advancing across the mouth of the gap shortly after midday, were pinned down by the most intense fire anyone could remember. Despite orders to continue their attack, they dug in and concentrated on surviving. Lieutenant-Colonel Rowan Coleman ignored appeals from Jefferson and Vokes, instructing his young signaller to tell them he was unavailable. Finally, as Coleman recalled in a 1984 interview, the corporal, who was just a few feet away, told him: "'Sir, I just have to tell you this ... Super Colossal Sunray wants to talk to you" ... It was Guy Simonds on the blower. I recognized the unmistakable English accent ... He said "Rowan ... is there anything you can do down there?" I said, "Well I don't think so sir, we are under murderous fire."'[41]

Coleman, who had commanded a rifle company in North Africa and Italy before being appointed CO of the Loyal Edmonton Regiment, had been selected by Simonds to reorganize the Lincs after Kapelsche Veer, and he had no intention of sacrificing his battalion by carrying out a plan that he and his fellow battalion commanders had vigorously protested.[42]

Despite overwhelming evidence of failure, Vokes ordered 10th Brigade to hold its ground and arranged a new effort by squadrons of the British Columbia Regiment and Grenadier Guards. Enemy guns soon put a stop to this attempt, and arrangements were made to relieve the battered units of 4th Division, which were finally to be withdrawn for a brief rest. This did not mean an end to Blockbuster; it did not mean even a pause. Matthews was told to send 6th Brigade to take over the gap and to press the advance of 5th Brigade, committing his reserve, 4th Brigade, to an attempt to break through the northern end of the Hochwald.[43]

Brigadier Cabledu tried to approach this latter task carefully, committing 4th Brigade on a single axis. He hoped to maintain momentum by passing battalions through in bounds. The Essex Scottish led off, encountering soft ground that restricted tank support. The enemy paratroopers were well dug in, heavily armed, and well protected by wire entanglements. Major Fred Tilston was awarded the Victoria Cross for his leadership in overcoming one such position. By nightfall the battalion had penetrated the enemy's forward defences. The 5th Brigade made modest gains in the forest north of the gap, but 8th Brigade, called on to take over the task of clearing the Tüschen Wald, was unable to make any progress against a determined enemy. The situation was very different on 9th Army's front, where, on the afternoon of 1 March, the Americans were less than five kilometres from the Rhine, opposite Düsseldorf and within striking distance of the boundary between the two Allied armies. The weakness of the enemy and the elaborate road network of the Cologne plain invited the bold use of armour, and General Simpson decided to send 'strong armoured punches' towards the Rhine bridges.[44]

Montgomery had visited 9th Army on 28 February and had seen 'the corps commander and many of the divisional generals.' The army, he reported, 'has gained a great victory with very few casualties and this has raised morale to a high level.' The next day he commented on the 'sensational results' in the south and 'the very hard and bitter fighting'[45] in the north. However, he proposed no changes in existing plans to require most of Simpson's 9th Army to cease operations once it reached the Rhine. Eisenhower encouraged Simpson to try and secure an intact bridge across the Rhine. When Simpson met with Montgomery to request permission to operate as far north as the bridges at Wesel, well within the Canadian zone, Montgomery – who must have remembered a similar debate over boundaries at Falaise in Normandy – agreed to extend 9th Army's sphere of action to Rheinberg, ten kilometres south of Wesel. However, he reserved the task of reducing the Wesel bridgehead to First Canadian Army.[46]

This decision left Crerar with few choices. The enemy was known to be busy building a new defensive line around Wesel, but there was no sign of an immediate withdrawal in the Hochwald. Crerar proposed to shift the weight of 30th Corps' attack farther to the south before turning it east to the Rhine; in this way the Sonsbeok-Veen road would be left to the Canadians. Before dawn on 2 March, elements of all three Canadian divisions were plunged into a series of fierce and bloody battles that taxed the capacity of everyone involved.

The 2nd Division renewed its attack, with the Royal Hamilton Light Infantry pressing into the Hochwald through the Essex position. Matthews and Cabeldu were determined to work forward in controlled bounds, and the RHLI carefully bit off 800 metres the first day, with the Royal Regiment of Canada taking a further 800 metres on 3 March. Back in the gap, no such caution was evident. A new battlegroup, composed of the Lake Superior Regiment along with 'D' Company of the Algonquins and armoured squadrons from the Governor-General's

Foot Guards and the Canadian Grenadier Guards, was to undertake Operation Churchill, another night attack, with Kangaroos carrying the infantry forward. Everyone was desperately tired, and when the Kangaroos were late in arriving, the CO of the Lake Superiors, Lieutenant-Colonel R.A. Keane, asked brigade to postpone the operation 'and give the lads a chance to rest.' The Kangaroos did arrive, however, and the attack began just before first light. Major P.A. Mayer described the result:

> A terrific hail of anti-tank fire met the attacking force as it cleared the crest of the Hochwald gap, and within a few minutes the whole area became a veritable hell. Tanks went up in smoke as they were struck by 88-mm fire, and men were machine gunned as they tried to extricate themselves from the burning hulls. Yet despite this fierce opposition, the leading companies of the Lake Superior Regiment (Mot) gained their first objectives by 0715 hours, and the rest of the troops of the Lake Superior Regiment (Mot) and the Algonquin Regiment pressed on. By this time, however, it was broad daylight, and the enemy, thick on the ground and supported by many S. P. guns and Tiger tanks, raked the entire area unmercifully. Soon the forward troops had lost contact and small groups found themselves surrounded. That the Canadians put up a good fight cannot be doubted, for many enemy dead were later found, but there was not sufficient direct support against the well concealed German tanks, and as the day passed, the situation became more desperate.[47]

Vokes ordered the rest of the Algonquins to push out along the axis of the railway to relieve the beleaguered companies; but the enemy, equally strong on either side of the track, put down a devastating fire, inflicting heavy losses.[48]

The 3rd Division had been ordered to attack Sonsbeok after clearing the woods south of the gap and was drawn into in a five-day battle of incredible intensity. Lieutenant-Colonel S.M. Lett described the experience in a post-battle interview which emphasized themes that were familiar to all who survived the fighting:

> The enemy resistance encountered was as determined as any the Battalion has met in the campaign. Their method is to take advantage of every feature the land offers. They did not always cover rides with heavy small

242 / Cinderella Army

arms fire; but they always placed automatic fire on every rise in the ground, when fighting in woods. Their tactics are based on a heavy volume of small arms fire with automatic weapons and few men, willing to withdraw when attacked, to buildings outside the wood. They invariably counterattacked every advance made, and by dark infiltrated into our positions. One morning every Company found itself surrounded and even battalion HQ had to defend itself. The enemy use few men for these tactics; two well-trained soldiers and machine guns generally constitute one of their posts. Both anti-tank and Schumines were plentifully laid throughout the area. Enemy artillery fire supplemented with mortars was intense.

The five days of this battle were most exhausting, there was little rest. For one period of 36 hours the troops had no sleep and only one hot meal. Morale however despite all these difficulties remained high. The casualties for the Battalion for Operation Blockbuster were 65 killed and 135 wounded. The work of the tanks was exceptionally fine; frequently out of touch with their Regiment, [or] troops, out of touch with their Squadron, and, at times, individual tanks fought on with the single object of doing all possible to assist the infantry.[49]

On the night of 2 March, Montgomery reported that 'the general picture in the north is that the enemy is endeavouring to hold with his right in the Hochwald area while he pulls back on his left' to defend a bridgehead centred on Wesel. He recognized that 'to hustle him out of the bridgehead ... may well best done by 9th U.S. Army,'[50] but he did not issue new instructions. Montgomery's failure to order 9th Army to assume responsibility for Wesel is especially difficult to understand, given that Simpson's right and centre corps had almost completed their assigned tasks and had ample resources left to supply and strengthen a thrust north.

Simpson and his corps and divisional commanders turned their attention to plans to 'bounce' the Rhine. The 9th Army Operations Log describes the situation on 4 March: 'Resistance in front of the Army has totally collapsed and all units are racing forward, it is felt the enemy is totally disorganized and has neither defensive forces on this side nor the far side of the Rhine capable of stopping a fast crossing. Plans for the corps crossing were hastily laid and the commanding General planned to ask permission from the Field Marshal the next day to make a try.'[51]

Montgomery vetoed any attempt to cross the river. His decision was later justified in terms of the difficulties of operating in the 'industrial wilderness' of the Ruhr, but no one in 9th Army accepted that explanation. They believed his refusal was based not on military considerations, but rather on 'the effect an impromptu American crossing might have on the Field Marshal's own plans for staging a great set-piece assault to cross the Rhine.'[52] Whatever the reasons, Montgomery's order was definite and Simpson was not Patton. However bitter, he would obey orders.

On the Anglo-Canadian front the day was marked by an enemy withdrawal to positions anchored on Xanten, Veen, and Alphen. First Canadian Army's intelligence summary noted that the enemy 'would now appear to have sufficient troops to cover the front of such a bridgehead.' The summary concluded that the enemy's strategy was designed to 'defeat a breakthrough and extricate an army.'[53] This new, more realistic enemy strategy ought to have persuaded Crerar to pause, reorganize, and launch a new set-piece attack at the most vulnerable section of the enemy perimeter; initially, however, he ordered both corps to maintain pressure everywhere. By 7 March this policy had resulted in a series of bloody engagements that brought Canadian troops to the outskirts of both Xanten and Veen. Under pressure from Matthews, Simonds and Crerar agreed to allow 2nd Division to take the time to prepare a set-piece attack on Xanten, employing a brigade from 43rd British Division to strengthen the advance.[54] No such respite was offered to 4th Division. Its attack on Veen, described as a 'savage slugging match in which every yard of ground became precious in the face of murderous small arms fire, continuous shelling and mortaring,'[55] cost the division another three hundred casualties. On the 9th Army front Simpson's three armoured divisions continued to cut through the enemy, sending thousands more German soldiers to prisoner-of-war camps. Rheinberg fell on 6 March, and the next day a combat command of 8th Armoured Division crossed the boundary to join in the final attempt to reach the Wesel bridges.[56]

The operation to secure Xanten began before first light on 8 March with 4th Canadian and 129th British Infantry Brigades advancing on either side of the main road. The artillery fire plan included elaborate counter-battery resources, and 1st Canadian Radar Battery was moved forward to supplement 2nd Division's counter-mortar resources. An extensive smoke screen prevented the enemy from directing observed fire from the north bank of the Rhine. The Essex Scottish and 4th Somerset Light Infantry made rapid progress, but both the RHLI on the right and 5th Wiltshire Regiment on the left suffered heavy casualties when enemy infiltrations from the flanks cut off the lead companies. Both brigadiers committed their reserve battalions, and by late afternoon British and Canadian troops had made contact in the centre of Xanten.[57]

Matthews now committed 5th Brigade to a night attack designed to seize the high ground overlooking the Alter Rhein before the enemy could regroup. The Maisonneuves, mounted in Kangaroos, led off just before midnight. Megill had persuaded Matthews to place the South Saskatchewans under his command so that he could have troops 'tight against the Xanten forest' to prevent infiltrations from the flank. This precaution proved effective, and the Black Watch were able to secure control of the enemy positions before dawn.[58] Almost half of 2nd Division's casualties in this battle were suffered by the RHLI, a direct result of relying on artillery to protect an open flank.

On 9 March, Montgomery met with his three Army Commanders and issued orders for Operation Plunder, the assault crossing of the Rhine. First Canadian Army was not involved in Plunder; instead it was assigned the task of reducing the Wesel Pocket, which included taking operational command of U.S. 16th Corps.[59] By mid-afternoon on 10 March the last German troops in the shrinking bridgehead had crossed the river and blown the Wesel bridges. The battle for the Rhineland was over.

The Battle of the Rhineland was the last great attritional battle fought by 21 Army Group in the Second World War. It was fought at the sharp end by ordinary young men from Britain, Canada, and the United States who had no ambition to conquer the world or even to save it for democracy. By 1945 all that was left was some personal pride and the feeling that you should not be the one to quit and let your buddies down. The enemy, now fighting on their own soil, seemed to the Allied soldiers to be implacable, bloody-minded bastards, all too ready to die for an evil cause in a war that was already lost; or to surrender minutes after they had killed your best friend and were faced with their own extinction. The politeness of postwar discourse among military historians should not be allowed to obscure the attitudes of 1945; if it does, we will fail to understand what war does to soldiers.

British soldiers were especially bitter about their lot in life. The 21 Army Group's adviser in psychiatry insisted that 'the prospect of further service in south-east Asia is now accepted by troops as in the main inevitable,' but he urged the army to take steps to 'debunk the horror picture many still have of the Far East.'[60] This was official optimism. The initials BLA, for British Liberation Army, now stood for 'Burma Looms Ahead,' and the prospect pleased only those who wished to continue as professional soldiers. The Canadians knew they need not serve in the Pacific unless they volunteered to go, so their future seemed a bit brighter, if only the enemy would face reality.

Every February newspapers around the world mark the anniversary of the bombing of Dresden on 13 February 1945. In almost every article reference is made to the 'fact' that the raid was especially cruel as the war was almost over.[61] Yet Dresden was bombed on the eve of Moyland Wood, four long, bloody weeks before the last surviving German soldier retreated to the east bank of the Rhine. There are no newspaper stories about the agony of the Rhineland battle. Our collective memory of the war has yet to find room for stories of the endurance and survival of ordinary soldiers.

9

The Liberation of Holland

The decision to try to destroy the German Army west of the Rhine and then cross the river in a major operation north of the Ruhr had been made in December 1944, before the Ardennes offensive. The Rhine crossing, code-named Operation Plunder, was to be the major Allied effort to end the war by striking in a 'single thrust' for Berlin. Then, at the Malta Conference in early February of 1945, Eisenhower revised this conception of the invasion of Germany, outlining a plan that allowed for a second major river crossing south of the Ruhr. The British leaders immediately protested that there was insufficient strength for two major operations. The British were still pressing for a single ground commander, so it is possible to sympathize with the growing impatience of American battlefield commanders, who could not understand why so much deference was being paid to British views when they were able to supply less than one-quarter of the troops involved in battle.[1]

The Americans believed that Montgomery had set up the northern crossing to give the glory of taking Berlin to the British Army. This sceptical view of Montgomery's motives was greatly reinforced when it was learned that he wanted to use U.S. divisions for the northern crossing, but under the command of 2nd British Army. Lieutenant-General Bill Simpson, the commander of 9th U.S. Army, was flabbergasted by this proposal, and even Montgomery realized he had gone too far. Instead, one U.S. corps of two divisions, operating under 9th U.S. Army's command, was to cross the river on D-Day. Despite this concession, 2nd Army was to have control of the bridgehead until it was judged secure.[2]

On 7 March, while the battle for the Wesel Pocket raged, troops of the 1st U.S. Army seized the Rhine bridge at Remagen and quickly established a substantial bridgehead on the east bank of the river. Since Montgomery did not plan to cross the Rhine until late March, this success presented the Allied command with a major dilemma. Both the army commander, General Courtney Hodges, and his superior, Omar Bradley, were confident that a breakout from Remagen could be staged whenever permission was granted. Eisenhower, perhaps fearing an even more serious row with the British, ignored intelligence estimates of German weakness and ordered Hodges to limit the bridgehead and use it as a device to draw German reserves away from the north.[3]

The 1st U.S. Army certainly succeeded in this role. By 23 March – D-Day for Operation Plunder – the Germans had moved most of their reserves opposite the Remagen bridgehead and had even attempted a counter-attack. The next day, with the northern Rhine crossing safely launched, 1st U.S. Army was unleashed. Within a few hours it had brushed aside the German defenders and was racing forward into Germany with three armoured divisions in the lead.[4] General George Patton's 3rd U.S. Army also crossed the Rhine before 24 March, but this was a deliberate demonstration of Patton's contempt for Montgomery's elaborate preparations. His staff declared that the Rhine could be crossed at any point without the aid of preliminary bombardment, never mind with airborne divisions. They released the news that they had done so at a time calculated to scrape some of the lustre off reports of Montgomery's crossing.[5] All of this, no doubt, sounds somewhat childish, but the image of feuding generals should not be allowed to obscure the fact that Hodges was right and that Eisenhower's decision to force his American armies to pause for two weeks so that Montgomery could complete preparations for a complex set-piece attack was a stiff price to pay for maintaining unity in coalition warfare. It was a price he would not be willing to pay again.

Montgomery's plan for Plunder called for a series of widely separated assault crossings of the river. First into battle was 51st Highland Division, strengthened by the addition of 9th Canadian Infantry Brigade. The Buffaloes once again proved their value. With 150 available, Major-General Tom Rennie was able to lift four assault battalions, and a bridgehead was quickly established. There were few casualties, but Rennie, who always worked well forward, was fatally wounded.[6] The 15th Scottish Division and 1st Commando Brigade were equally successful, and 9th U.S. Army reported that its assault divisions, the 30th and 29th, got across with 'minor casualties of 16 or 17 men killed per division.'[7]

Despite the evidence of minor German resistance, the airborne part of the crossing, Operation Varsity, was not cancelled. The vast armada of aircraft appeared over the Rhine at 1000 hours on 24 March. The paratroopers of 6th British Airborne and 17th U.S. Airborne made their drop without undue casualties, but by 1030 hours, when the gliders of the air landing brigades were coming in, the German flak gunners had

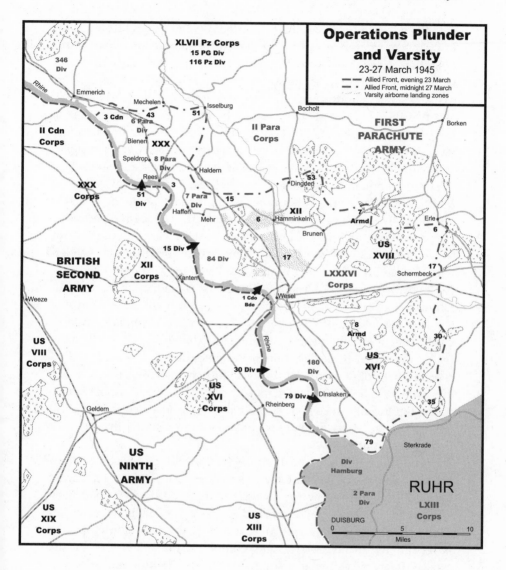

Operations Plunder and Varsity

23-27 March 1945

— — — Allied Front, evening 23 March
– · – · – Allied Front, midnight 27 March
· · · · · · Varsity airborne landing zones

recovered, and a terrible toll was exacted. On the ground the airborne troops were soon involved in the most difficult and costly part of the operation. Casualties were heavy; 6th Airborne lost 1,400 out of a landed strength of 7,220, and one-quarter of the glider pilots were casualties. The paratroopers of 17th Airborne were widely scattered, and two-thirds of the gliders were hit by flak. Out of a force of 9,650 men, 1,300 were casualties. A daring resupply mission, flown at low level by U.S. Army Air Force Liberators, dropped 600 tons of supplies to sustain the division, but at a cost of sixteen bombers shot down.[8]

Senior commanders judged Varsity a great success. Major-General Matthew Ridgeway, the airborne corps commander, contended that the 'airborne divisions at one blow shattered hostile defence and permitted the prompt link-up with the ground troops.' This was no doubt true for some areas of the bridgehead, but Varsity had no impact on the German reserves, which were committed to battle the next day.

The British airborne division included 1st Canadian Parachute Battalion, part of 3rd Parachute Brigade. Their task was to gain control of the wooded area at Schneppenberg. This drop was remarkably well concentrated, and the men moved quickly to their objectives. German resistance varied from determined to demoralized, and the battalion reported control of its area of responsibility by noon on 24 March. The loss of the battalion CO, Lieutenant-Colonel Jeff Nicklin – one of twenty-three fatal casualties – was a serious blow to the small, cohesive battalion, but Major Fraser Eadie took command and directed the defeat of the enemy counter-attacks.[9]

During the battle a medical orderly, Corporal F.G. Topham, earned the Victoria Cross. The citation reads in part: 'Corporal Topham went forward through intense fire to replace the orderlies who had been killed before his eyes. As he worked on the wounded, he was himself shot through the nose. In spite of severe bleeding and intense pain, he never faltered in his task. Having completed immediate first aid he carried the men steadily and slowly back through continuous fire.'[10]

While the airborne troops regrouped, General Alfred Schlemm, who commanded Hitler's 1st Parachute Army, deployed his reserves. Schlemm had recognized that there was little point in trying to defend every part of the river with the limited forces available to him, and he had placed his paratroop divisions between Emmerich and Xanten, where he expected the main Allied attack to take place. His reserve, 47th Panzer Corps, was in the north. The corps, composed of 116th Panzer Division and 15th Panzer Grenadier Division, had taken advantage of the two-week pause in Allied operations to move into Holland. Here, safe from Allied air forces (which were reluctant to bomb Dutch villages), they rested, re-equipped, and absorbed reinforcements. Their determination to defend Germany was said to be stronger than ever. Schlemm waited until noon on 24 March to commit his reserves. He sent 116th Panzer south to slow the American advance and committed 15th Panzer Grenadier to the defence of the northern sector.[11] Since 51st Highland Division was already engaged in a furious battle with two parachute divisions, expanding the bridgehead to the north and east was bound to prove slow and costly. The 9th Canadian Brigade, originally slated to lead the advance to Emmerich, joined in close combat with a powerful enemy.

When the Highland Light Infantry of Canada were ordered to clear Speldrop, the CO was warned that two platoons of a British Black Watch battalion were still holding out in the village and resisting large-scale counter-attacks. Lieutenant-Colonel P.W. Strickland knew he could count on medium artillery to neutralize known enemy positions beyond the village. He was also confident that the field artillery would keep heads down while his men crossed 1000 metres of flat, open ground. However, the village itself would have to be cleared house by house. Strickland decided to use just one company in the initial attack; it would seize the northwest corner of Speldrop and try to identify the British positions. Strickland, like other experienced battalion commanders, knew it was better to stage attacks across open country with fewer men, thus reducing the casualties sustained from both friendly and enemy fire. If one pared-down company – eighty officers and men – could get onto a position and establish a firm base, the rest of the battalion could advance in stages with additional covering fire. This approach worked at Speldrop even though all three platoon commanders were hit. Sergeant Cornelius Reidel led a fixed-bayonet charge on enemy positions in an orchard and then led his men to the objective. The rest of the company joined Reidel, who turned over a number of prisoners as well as three 75 mm guns. Reaching the edge of the village was one thing, clearing it quite another. The enemy had moved a troop of assault guns into Speldrop to support the paratroopers, so Major J.C. King called for battalion 6-pounders and Wasp flame-throwers rather than more infantry. The HLI used this close support to storm the German position and secure the northern edge of the village.[12]

While the HLI was fighting to clear Speldrop, the Stormont, Dundas, and Glengarry Highlanders and the North Nova Scotia Highlanders bypassed the village, moving north towards Bienen, where another British battalion, the 7th Argylls, was waiting for relief. The Argylls had seized a group of farm buildings 300 metres from the village but could go no farther. Lieutenant-Colonel Don Forbes took one look at the terrain and decided to exercise caution. He sent Major Don Learment's 'A' Company forward to 'Argyll Farm' to secure the start line for an attack on the village. Unfortunately, the 15th Panzer Grenadiers had arrived to block the advance, and when the North Novas attacked the village they had to fight for every house, losing 114 men, including 43 killed. The initial advance had been supported by heavy artillery, including the liberal use of smoke, but the companies were brought under heavy enemy fire before the barrage started, and the advance took place under conditions of growing confusion. Brigadier John Rockingham ordered a withdrawal and directed the battalion to 'start from scratch and do the attack over again, using the two remaining companies.' The North Novas' second attack was able to secure the north half of the village. This was not Rockingham at his best: he had seriously underestimated the Germans' strength. That night, after a battery of 3rd Anti-Tank Regiment self-propelled 17-pounders had beaten off an armoured counter-attack, the HLI advanced through the North Novas to complete the capture of the village.[13]

The battles fought by British and Canadian troops in the Rhine bridgehead were as difficult as any in the experience of the two veteran divisions. The decision to stop and organize a set-piece attack instead of 'bouncing' the Rhine allowed Montgomery time to build up resources so that his armies could race to Berlin once the bridgehead battle was won. This reasoned albeit debatable command decision placed an enormous burden on the Allied infantry, which was being sent to attack an enemy that had had ample time to prepare strongpoints and plan a defence-in-depth.

The experience of 9th U.S. Army's assault divisions at the southern end of the bridgehead was dramatically different. Schlemm had guessed that the Allies would avoid the wooded area between the River Lippe and the Ruhr and assigned the sector to a weak infantry division that had been hastily rebuilt after its destruction in the Rhineland. The 104th Division disintegrated under the weight of the American attacks. The 116th Panzer Division, ordered south to block the American advance, had to circle around the airborne landing areas and expose itself to Allied air power before it could counter-attack; this allowed both 30th and 29th U.S. Divisions to create the conditions for a breakout.[14] Unfortunately, enemy resistance in the north prevented the early construction of bridges at Emmerich, and Montgomery gave 2nd British Army priority on the southern bridges, limiting 9th Army to just five hours a day even on bridges built by U.S. Army engineers.[15]

The following extracts from Simpson's Personal Calendar reflect a harsh, impatient, and no doubt unfair judgment of 2nd British Army. They also reflect a good deal of truth and point directly to an important but neglected reason for Eisenhower's decision to remove 9th U.S. Army from Montgomery's command and place the main weight of the Allied attack in the hands of Bradley's 12 Army Group:

26 March. At present Ninth Army is ... in a bottleneck, completely tied down by the slow plodding 2nd British Army. Commanding General [Simpson] explains our need to see Field Marshal who promises early turnover of vital bridge to Ninth Army.

27 March (Tues). Commanding General is very confident, seeing from the light and spotting resistance that an early breakout can be made – if we can successfully fight our way through 2nd British Army. Hard feeling growing here. At 0900 [Simpson] drove to 21 Army Group Tactical HQ for a conference with the Field Marshal and General Dempsey re: the drawing of boundaries all the way to Berlin and the use of the vital Wesel bridge ... Dempsey, with his time-out-for-tea army, was ordered to turn bridge over at 0700 hours on following Saturday.

The British – stopping at night to sleep, for tea and moving slowly at best – are just wasting invaluable time ... The British pace and methods are simply archaic and nerve-racking.

29 March. The Commanding General feels the British are deliberately blocking [Ninth Army's] passage so that they can be first – in their own

good time at that – to get away and grab the glory of a break-through with their Guards Armoured Division.

31 March ... bridge at Wesel ours ... orders to throw off British vehicles. Commanding General was in dead earnest.[16]

On 28 March, in the midst of this quarrel, Montgomery issued a new directive – one that assumed Simpson's army would stay under his command. Without consulting Eisenhower, Montgomery ordered 2nd British and 9th U.S. Armies to advance to the River Elbe, with the British aimed at Bremen and Hamburg and the Americans at Magdeburg and Berlin. The 2nd Canadian Corps was ordered to clear northeastern Holland and the German coast to the Elbe.[17]

These plans were promptly overruled by the Supreme Commander, Eisenhower, who decided to concentrate the Allied offensive in centre of Germany on the axis Erfurt–Leipzig–Dresden and to join hands with the Russians in the centre of Germany. Eisenhower communicated this decision to his Army Group Commanders and to Josef Stalin on 29 March without consulting the British or American Joint Chiefs of Staff. Despite protests from Churchill and Montgomery, Eisenhower stood his ground. The 9th U.S. Army, which had been attached to Montgomery's 21 Army Group since February, was to return to 12 Army Group for operations designed to split Germany in two.

Eisenhower's decision to concentrate his forces in the centre and allow the Soviets to capture Berlin as well as Vienna and Prague was one of the most controversial of the war. He explained it in purely operational terms, insisting that with the Red Army just forty miles from Berlin, it made more sense to divide Germany and concentrate forces to deal with the rumoured 'national redoubt' in the Bavarian Alps before dealing with northern Germany.[18] Neither the British nor the American generals believed that Eisenhower's decision was that simple. Montgomery had repeatedly challenged Eisenhower's authority as Supreme Commander and had conducted a not very secret campaign denigrating Eisenhower's leadership and criticizing his decisions. Eisenhower had endured this chronic insubordination in the hope of preserving Allied unity, but he was aware that his own generals, especially Bradley, were strongly opposed to allowing American troops to continue to serve under British command. The growing rift between the British and American generals had broad repercussions. The U.S. State Department had long favoured a policy of postwar cooperation with the Soviet Union and maintained this view despite Soviet violations of agreements reached at Yalta in February 1945. While Churchill was urging Eisenhower to seize Berlin – a city well within the Soviet zone of occupation – he was also trying to persuade the Americans that this action would have an impact on Soviet policy.[19] But it might also require 9th U.S. Army to be placed under Montgomery's control, and since this was now unacceptable, no serious consideration was given to seizing Berlin.

While the British and Americans were racing to the Elbe, the Canadians were to carry out the much less glamorous task of opening up 'a supply route to the north through Arnhem' and then clearing 'Northeast Holland and the coastal belt eastwards towards the Elbe.' The liberation of the old provinces of West Holland – a task assigned to 1st Canadian Corps, newly arrived from the Mediterranean – was added to the directive almost as an afterthought.[20] Before these operations could begin, Third Canadian Division would have to deal with the substantial enemy forces that were holding the ruins that had once been a town of 16,000 called Emmerich. The 7th Brigade, now commanded by Brigadier T.G. Gibson, was to clear the town, with 8th Brigade passing through to seize the high ground at Hoch Elten.

On 28 March, Gibson sent the Canadian Scottish Regiment down the main road while the Regina Rifles advanced along the river. Reports from Dutch civilians suggested that the enemy was withdrawing, so the lead company decided to cross the Landwehr Canal on an improvised footbridge without waiting for the engineers to bridge the obstacle. The Canscots, who knew their job, fanned out and worked their way up the slope. Machine gun fire forced them to the ground, and Major H.F. Bailey sent out one of his platoons right flanking along the railway line. The platoon was soon pinned down, and it became clear that the enemy, far from withdrawing, was holding the town in strength. Well-directed German artillery fire prevented the engineers from bridging the canal, so the Canadian armour had to stay well back. Lieutenant-Colonel L.S. Henderson decided to expand the battalion bridgehead and borrowed 'D' Company of the Reginas to help out. After a night

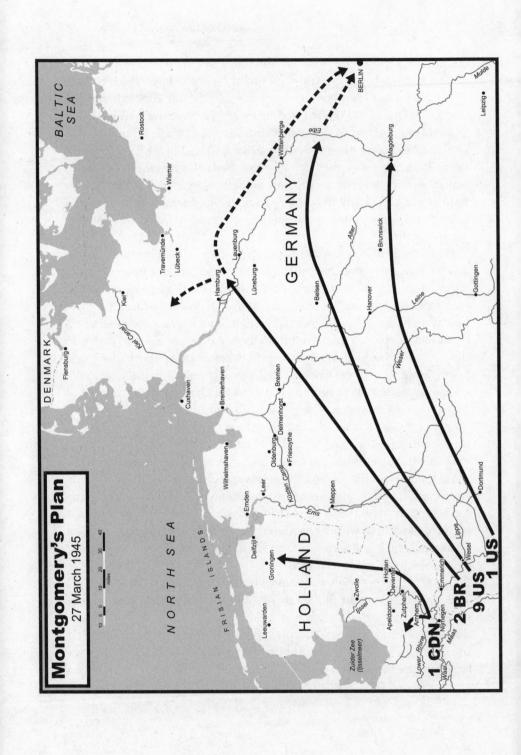

Montgomery's Plan
27 March 1945

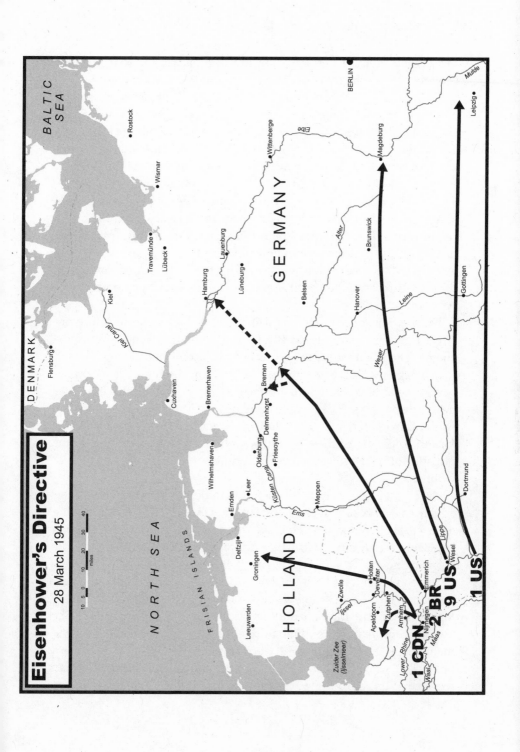

Eisenhower's Directive
28 March 1945

'marked by alternate periods of stealthy approaches and sharp, savage firefights,' the industrial area was secure and the canal bridged.[21]

The extent of German resistance forced 7th Brigade to pause and allow the armour time to marry up with the infantry. The Reginas launched the second phase of the attack with the Sherbrookes and Crocodiles in close support. The battalion broke into the southern sector of Emmerich, but progress was slow. While the Reginas fought their way into the city, the Canscots staged a two-company attack to clear the area north of the railway line. With adequate time for reconnaissance and a good view of the battlefield for the artillery observer, the attack resembled an exercise. The Royal Winnipeg Rifles then captured the nearby village of Leegmeer and moved west to clear a large wood. The Winnipegs' thrust threatened to cut off the forces defending Emmerich; the Germans responded with a wave of counter-attacks on both prairie battalions.

The Reginas, now in the heart of the ruined city, had to improvise street fighting tactics, using PIATs and flame-throwers to repel the enemy. The Winnipegs dealt with several platoon-sized attacks, one of which began with the enemy 'coming at them singing.'[22] The German soldier must have known that defeat was now certain, but if he was desperate he was still deadly. By midday on 30 March most of Emmerich was in Canadian hands. The 7th Brigade was told to secure a start line for 8th Brigade and then go into reserve. In this three-day battle the brigade suffered 172 casualties, including forty-four killed or died of wounds.[23]

Once past Emmerich there was room to deploy two brigades. Their advance was assisted by the arrival of 2nd Division, which was moving on a parallel course into Holland. At noon on 31 March, Canadian engineers began the construction of Melville Bridge, named after the chief engineer of First Canadian Army, Brigadier J.L. Melville. Measuring 1,373 feet in length, the Bailey bridge was open to traffic the next morning. Two other bridges soon followed, guaranteeing adequate logistical support for Canadian operations in the Netherlands.[24] The Canadian victory in the Rhine bridgehead was a remarkable achievement, given the strength of the German forces defending the northern flank. Two Canadian brigades fought the equivalent of three German regiments, inflicted heavy losses, and forced their withdrawal. The artillery and tactical air force played a vital role in the success of both 9th and 7th Brigades, but it was the infantry working closely with armour that won the battle.

Canadian military historians have generally paid slight attention to the operations carried out by First Canadian Army in April 1945. It is almost as if the great battles of February and March in the Rhineland exhausted the historians, just as it wore down the men who fought there in 1945. April is instead remembered as the month of the liberation of Holland, 'the sweetest of springs.' But April was also the cruellest month, for if the war was all but won, the killing had not stopped. The military cemeteries in the Netherlands contain the graves of 1,191 Canadian soldiers killed there in April and of 114 who lost their lives during the last five days of the war in May.[25] Their stories, and the record of the reunited First Canadian Army, are well worth examining.

During the first two weeks of April the Canadians moved swiftly into Holland and Germany. The 3rd Canadian Division began on 1 April, and 7th Brigade soon ran into resistance in the village of Wehl. Lieutenant-Colonel Alan Gregory described the Regina Rifles' pincer attack on the position, providing a clear picture of this type of encounter to 3rd Division's Historical Officer: 'The approach, contact and battle for the town of Wehl was interesting in that of all the operations in Europe, it most closely resembled the textbook procedure for the approach to contact and the elimination of an isolated point of resistance by one of the approaching elements.' Two carrier sections and the scout platoon were sent forward to test the defences, and their probes produced evidence of enemy locations. A fire plan employing artillery and heavy mortars was timed to begin shortly before H-Hour, 0400 hours. Gregory tried to persuade the attached armoured squadron to join in a night attack 'but they refused to play.' The two companies assigned to the first phase took almost two hours to clear to the centre of Wehl; then at dawn the reserve companies, with the tanks, overcame stiff resistance in the north end of the town. The enemy, 'a few average troops with stern NCO leadership, well supported by self-propelled guns and mortars,' imposed a significant delay before they withdrew, having yielded ground and more than one hundred prisoners.[26]

From Wehl, 3rd Division advanced towards Zutphen, a town on the

Ijssel River and the end of the Twente Canal. Intelligence assumed that the city and the canal would be the next major German defensive position, and elements of three Canadian divisions were headed for it. In fact, 2nd Division was able to cross the canal on 2 April after a quick thirty-two-kilometre run. The Royal Regiment of Canada delivered a well-practised attack with assault boats and established a bridgehead, which the Royal Hamilton Light Infantry were soon able to reinforce.[27] Farther east, Lion Force of 4th Armoured Division encountered far more serious opposition and was unable to get over the water obstacle.

Major-General Chris Vokes ordered Brigadier Robert Moncel to use Tiger Force to outflank the enemy by crossing the canal near Delden. The Lincoln and Welland Regiment, with supporting and diversionary fire from the Lake Superiors and Governor General's Foot Guards, were over the canal quickly enough, but before long the bridgehead was heavily counter-attacked and one company was completely cut off. The company commander called the mortars down on his own position and preserved a foothold. Early on the morning of 4 April the enemy withdrew and the Lincs moved into Delden, where the town's citizens went wild with joy and relief. The Twente Canal and Delden may seem like minor affairs compared to the Hochwald, but the Lincs alone took sixty-seven casualties in the day's fighting.[28]

Back on the road to Zutphen, 9th Brigade was in the lead when resistance was encountered at Warnsveld. The North Novas ran into a well-organized position dug in around a hospital. The defenders were using a dual 20 mm gun as a machine gun, and the regiment pulled back until two troops of Crocodiles were available and a new attack organized. After this resistance was overcome the North Novas, Glens, and HLI pressed forward on a three-battalion front with vital support from Sherbrooke tanks. The prisoners taken were described as 'young, about sixteen and seventeen years of age ... When interviewed they still thought Germany would win and their belief in Hitler and Nazism was still unshaken. However there were cases among the prisoners of just badly scared boys.'[29]

The 9th Brigade was routed east of the town, and 8th Brigade was handed the task of clearing Zutphen. The North Shores and Chaudières began a difficult exercise in street fighting. A Chaud lieutenant described the two-day encounter in terms that emphasize the continuing ferocity of German resistance:

> Between the start line and the objective, there was a canal on which both leading companies were stopped for almost two hours ... [because of] well-sited snipers MG nests and bazookas. All enemy positions were dealt with by proper use of infantry on ground supported by tank fire ... During all that time the enemy located on the other side of the Ijssel River held intermittent artillery fire with 88mm ... The enemy which we had to fight were more often first class troops and have shown a bitter fighting spirit ... When they did surrender it was because they were out of ammunition or deprived of any escape.[30]

Zutphen was not completely cleared until the afternoon of 8 April.

The operations of 2nd Canadian Corps during the first week of April were closely tied to the plans of 1st Canadian Corps to capture Arnhem, rebridge the Rhine, and open a major maintenance route for the Canadian and British armies. The battle for Arnhem was the responsibility of 49th Division, which remained with the Canadians to undertake a revised version of Operation Wallstreet when the rest of 1st British Corps rejoined 2nd British Army. The first task was to clear 'the island' between Nijmegen and Arnhem, an area the battalions of 49th Division knew thoroughly from months of patrols. The Ontario Regiment of 1st Canadian Armoured Brigade provided the tank support for this operation, which began on 2 April. The 49th Division was also assisted by 11th Canadian Infantry Brigade, which cleared the left flank as the British advanced.

General Crerar decided to delay the attack on Arnhem until the city and its defenders had been cut off by an advance across the Ijssel from the east. This in turn depended on the success of 3rd Canadian Division in clearing the east bank of the river and the cities of Zutphen and Deventer. While completing these operations the Canadians were confronted by a new set of problems. Reports from the old provinces of Holland, including the cities of Amsterdam and Rotterdam, indicated that the terrible conditions of the 'hunger winter' were continuing and that the people of western Holland were facing starvation. The Nazi governor, Arthur Seyss-Inquart, had deliberately created the food shortage in retaliation for the actions of the Dutch resistance; now he was threatening to flood much of Holland as a defensive measure.[31] If military action was the answer, all possible speed was required.

The 1st Division, which had made the long journey from Italy in March, was placed under 2nd Canadian Corps. Formation patches and divisional signs were removed, and the division was brought north to woods in the vicinity of Gorssel while 3rd Division completed the clearance of Deventer. Major-General Harry Foster held his 'O' Group on 10 April, during which he outlined the plan for the first phase of Operation Cannonshot.[32] Foster selected 2nd Canadian Infantry Brigade (Princess Patricia's Canadian Light Infantry, Seaforth Highlanders of Canada, Loyal Edmonton Regiment) to make the assault crossing of the Ijssel.

Each brigade in 1st Division had one battalion from a Permanent Force (PF) regiment and two militia battalions. This distinction had been of some importance during training in England, but by 1945 very few officers and NCOs who had served in the early years of the war were still around. The battalions were staffed with the products of Brockville and other Officer Training Schools, while senior NCOs were former privates who had proven themselves in action. The Canadians were a citizen army with a thin and spotty veneer of PF regulars. This citizen army had acquired a high degree of professionalism, particularly at the staff level and in supporting arms. Infantry rifle companies suffered such high casualties that the ever-changing mix of officers and NCOs makes generalization about overall combat effectiveness impossible. A battalion that distinguished itself in 1944 might still carry the same proud name in 1945 but it was made up of different men. Sydney Frost, a captain in the Patricias during Cannonshot, noted that just two officers who had landed with the battalion in Sicily were still with the regiment in April 1945.[33] Despite the turnover, regimental traditions and reputations continued.

The 2nd Canadian Infantry Brigade had long been touted as the outstanding brigade in the Canadian Army. During his famous 1942 inspection, Montgomery, who was unimpressed with then divisional commander George Pearkes, and most other senior officers, declared that the 2nd could be the best brigade in all the Commonwealth armies. 'The PPCLI,' he wrote, 'have the best officers, the Seaforths the best NCOs and the Edmontons the best men.'[34] After Sicily and Ortona and the promotion of Brigadiers Chris Vokes and Bert Hoffmeister to divisional commands, the reputation of the 2nd Brigade was set for all time. One result was that it got more than its share of high-profile operations.

Brigadier M.P. Bogert, a veteran of the Italian campaign, was now in command, and he prepared the assault crossing within the framework of a corps artillery plan. The battalions were introduced to the Buffalo and informed that this LVT (Landing Vehicle Tracked) could enter and leave the water on most gradients while providing thirty men with protection from small arms fire. The corps plan called for an elaborate 'smoke box' created by smoke generators as well as concentrations of medium and heavy artillery on prearranged targets, with virtually unlimited artillery available down to company level. Medium bombers were to hit prearranged targets, and Typhoons were on call. For those who had fought in Italy, this was war in a new style. In his memoirs, *Once a Patricia*, Frost writes: 'The more I saw of the orderly, deliberate way the Canadian Army [in Northwest Europe] went about its tasks, the more I liked doing business with them.'[35]

Cannonshot was launched at 1530 hours on 11 April. The enemy seemed totally surprised. Apparently they were unaware of 1st Division's presence and had been assuming that the attack would come from 3rd Division's brigades at Deventer. The initial opposition came from small German battlegroups built around one or two self-propelled guns. The Seaforths and PPCLI used their PIATs until the first anti-tank guns got across the river. By 2100 hours the bridgehead was 'snug.' German reserves had reached the area by midnight, and in accordance with their doctrine counter-attacked immediately.[36] This amazingly predictable behaviour led competent Allied commanders to insist on digging in after an assault rather than exploiting their initial success. Why, they reasoned, risk an encounter battle when your enemies will come to you, allowing your artillery, mortars, and machine guns to destroy them with observed fire? This is precisely what happened in the Ijssel bridgehead. The Seaforths and PPCLI repulsed hastily mounted counter-attacks, taking more than two hundred prisoners and inflicting heavy casualties. The Loyal Eddies joined them, and by dawn the

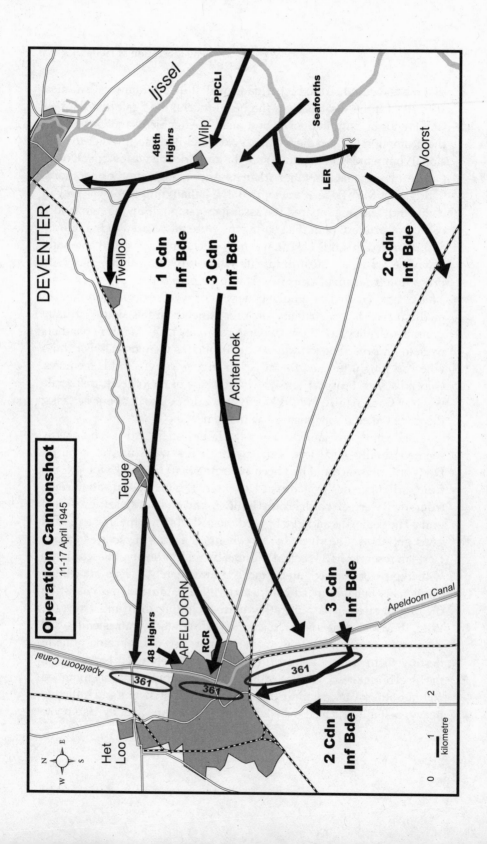

Operation Cannonshot
11-17 April 1945

DEVENTER

Ijssel

48th Highrs

Wilp

PPCLI

Seaforths

Voorst

LER

Twelloo

1 Cdn Inf Bde

3 Cdn Inf Bde

2 Cdn Inf Bde

Achterhoek

Teuge

Apeldoorn Canal

3 Cdn Inf Bde

48 Highrs

APELDOORN

RCR

361

361

361

Het Loo

Apeldoorn Canal

2 Cdn Inf Bde

N
W E
S

0   1   2
kilometre

engineers had a bridge in place. The tanks of 1st Hussars were soon across in preparation for the next phase.[37]

The plan now called for Brigadier J.D.B. Smith's 1st Canadian Infantry Brigade (Royal Canadian Regiment, 48th Highlanders, Hastings and Prince Edward Regiment) to advance east along the axis of the Apeldoorn–Deventer railway to the airfield at Teague while Brigadier J.P.E. Bernatchez's 3rd Canadian Infantry Brigade (Royal 22e Régiment, Carleton and York Regiment and West Nova Scotia Regiment) advanced through Achterhoek, providing flank protection to 1st Brigade. The 3rd Brigade was then to advance south of Apeldoorn to prepare an assault crossing of the canal in the event that 1st Brigade ran into difficulty.[38]

The 1st Brigade, with 48th Highlanders leading, quickly moved west. Resistance was spotty, but one burst of shellfire struck the command group, killing Lieutenant-Colonel D.A. Mackenzie, the Highlanders' CO. The RCR, with 'C' Squadron of 1st Hussars, took over the lead, and by noon on 13 April were less than one mile from Apeldoorn. The plan to pause and prepare a coordinated attack across the canal north of the city was abandoned when the Dutch resistance reported that the main road bridge over the canal, in the heart of the city, was intact. At first light on 14 April the RCR Hussars battlegroups fought their way towards the bridge, which turned out to be well protected by road blocks covered by anti-tank guns. The Hussars lost two tanks, including one that tried a run at a road block.[39] North of the city the bridges were blown. Patrols from the Hasty Ps established that the canal was too strongly defended to be taken on the run.

To the south, 3rd Brigade was held up by a strong enemy position until Bernatchez ordered the lead battalions to bypass the resistance and head for the canal. The Royal 22nd Regiment, as the reserve battalion, were ordered to deal with the enemy, and did so by assaulting the woods from the rear. They then joined their sister battalions along the canal two kilometres south of Apeldoorn.[40] It was now the evening of 15 April. Operation Cannonshot, which had begun with such great promise four days earlier, was in danger of deteriorating into a series of costly piecemeal attacks.

Foster did nothing to help the situation when he ordered 1st Brigade to attack across the canal into the centre of Apeldoorn.[41] To the north and south of the city the enemy had established a thin crust of defences based on the western bank of the canal. A set-piece attack with the kind of assets used in the crossing of the much wider Ijssel would have brought certain success, and would have forced the enemy to abandon the city or risk encirclement. Fighting to clear city streets in a town full of friendly civilians and refugees was not a brilliant idea. No one would use tactical air or heavy artillery fire against a Dutch city, so the infantry and tanks would have to do it one house at a time.

The RCR and 48th Highlanders went about their task carefully. With the BBC reporting that the Red Army was in the suburbs of Berlin, and with the Germans seeking a truce in western Holland, no one wanted to take unnecessary casualties in what appeared to be the last days of the war. The attack quickly turned into a stalemate. The forward companies were 'pinned down by arty, mortar and machine gun fire,' and the supporting tanks were bogged down trying an indirect approach to the canal. A request for Crocodiles to flame the basements of houses along the canal was refused, as none were immediately available.[42]

The best solution seemed to be an assault crossing of the canal south of the city by 3rd Brigade. During the night of 15 April, Bernatchez was directed to plan such an attack. Then, while divisional engineers and artillery were preparing to offer support, the situation suddenly changed. The 2nd Brigade, which Foster had wanted to keep in reserve after the crossing of the Ijssel, had been ordered south by the Army Commander, who wanted protection for the engineers building bridges across the river at Zutphen.[43] Before the infantry brigade arrived, 5th Canadian Armoured Division entered Arnhem and turned east, threatening to cut off the enemy. This manoeuvre allowed 2nd Brigade to do an unopposed crossing of the canal at Diereen and then advance north, turning the enemy positions in front of 3rd Brigade.[44] The Germans withdrew as quickly as they could, abandoning the canal and the city of Apeldoorn. RCR patrols reported that the Germans were gone, and on 17 April the regiment was in the centre of the city.[45] The joy of the Dutch population was boundless. It had looked as if their garden city was about to become a battleground; now, almost miraculously, the fighting had ended. Canadian veterans who return to Apeldoorn for the anniversaries of the liberation know that memories of 1945 are still warm.

First Division had suffered 506 casualties, including more than 100 killed, over the six days of Cannonshot.[46] Most of 1st Brigade's 184 losses came in the fighting for Apeldoorn, a battle that was allowed to continue despite past experience with the costs of clearing urban areas. The contrast between the first phase of Cannonshot, with its careful preparation and full use of the army's skills and resources, and the improvised operations in the suburbs of Apeldoorn, needs to be under-lined. Encouraging subordinate officers to devise and carry out their own measures within the overall framework of their commanders' intentions has always had enormous appeal for professional soldiers and military theorists, but the experience of both the German and the Allied armies in Northwest Europe suggests that success in battle was almost always the result of the carefully coordinated application of all available forces. This required the exercise of command and control at the most senior levels. Cannonshot was no exception.

Since arriving in Holland, Hoffmeister's 5th Armoured Division had been offered little opportunity to use its armoured brigade group. The relatively easy conquest of Arnhem had, however, presented the corps commander with an irresistible opportunity to use the brigade to cut off the retreat of those Germans who were still fighting on the Apeldoorn canal line. British Columbia Dragoons led the way through Arnhem, with 8th New Brunswick Hussars, Westminster Regiment (Motor), and Lord Strathcona's Horse close behind. Enemy blocking positions were shot up or bypassed, and Otterlo was reached by late afternoon.[47]

Brigadier I.H. Cumberland, who commanded 5th Armoured Bri-gade, was not about to pause. The Strathconas were told to take Otterlo and then push northwest to capture Barneveld. If Barneveld was de-fended, they were to bypass it and strike north to cut the Apeldoorn–Amersfort road, the main east–west route of the retreating German forces. The other two armoured regiments were to conform to this thrust, British Columbia Dragoons to the north and 8th Hussars to the south. Otterlo was cleared readily enough, but beyond the town's west-ern limits were many pockets of infantry, some with Panzerfaust or bazooka men, who had to be dealt with by the Westminsters' motorized infantry.[48]

The enemy held Barneveld in strength, and the Strathconas lost three tanks on the edge of town. Bypassing was accomplished quickly, but

2000 metres beyond the north edge of town a well-organized anti-tank gun position, guarded by machine guns, barred the way. The decision was made to stop and organize a proper attack at first light on 17 April. The 11th Infantry Brigade had spent two days following the rapidly moving armoured brigade and had seen little action, so when the Irish Regiment, Governor General's Horse Guards, and elements of the divisional and corps artillery moved into Otterlo, they knew they were well behind the leading troops. The Irish Regiment took up positions on the western perimeter of the village, and the tanks of the Horse Guards found convenient harbours in various corners of the village. Suddenly Otterlo was transformed into a battlefield as hundreds of German soldiers loosely organized into battlegroups stormed through the village, throwing grenades and firing at every shadow. One group bumped into 17th Field Regiment, RCA, and got a warm reception from the enraged gunners. The Regimental Sergeant Major shot two with his Sten gun, and after it jammed he used his bare hands.[49]

The officers of the Horse Guards were at an 'O' Group in the church when the attack began and were forced to stay there until the fighting died down. The regiment's troop sergeants had no difficulty organizing the defence of their positions or the mopping up that followed, leading some to question whether officers were really necessary. The next day the Grebbe Line was reached, and it looked as if 5th Division's war was over. Eisenhower had decided that for 'humanitarian reasons' Allied forces would not continue advancing into the western Netherlands but would begin negotiations to allow urgently needed food supplies to reach the civilian population.[50]

The first major battle fought by 2nd Canadian Division in northeast Holland began on 13 April when lead elements reached the outskirts of Groningen. The division's rapid advance from the Twente Canal bridgehead had been assisted by Special Air Service troops, including seven hundred men of 2nd and 3rd Battalions, Régiment de Chasseurs Parachutistes, and 1st Belgian Parachute Battalion in a ground support role. Their commanding officer, Brigadier J.C. Calvert, had asked General Harry Crerar to allow his highly trained troops to get into action before the war ended; the result was Operation Amherst, a plan to seize bridges in front of the Canadian advance. This costly initiative helped speed the division's advance but did not interfere with the enemy's withdrawal.[51]

The 2nd Division moved north in a series of controlled bounds, passing brigades through one another as objectives were secured. Brigadier Fred Cabeldu's 4th Brigade took over the lead on 12 April, liberating Assen the next morning. The RHLI, with a squadron of Fort Garry tanks, continued north, reaching the outskirts of Groningen later the same day. No one at divisional or brigade headquarters seems to have understood that the city was part of a fortified zone encompassing both flak batteries and coastal gun positions protecting the Ems estuary. The RHLI received no special instructions on how to deal with an enemy holding a large Dutch city with a wartime population swollen to 200,000.[52]

Assumptions about a continued enemy withdrawal to Germany seemed to be confirmed when the first two enemy blocking positions were overcome, but at 1200 hours the lead infantry companies ran up against one of the concrete anti-tank obstacles that had been erected on all roads into the city. German troops were covering the position with machine guns and 20 mm flak guns, firing from trenches in a large city park. The Fort Garries lost two tanks and an armoured ambulance before withdrawing. The RHLI attempted to outflank the position but found that it was part of a well-organized defensive perimeter.[53] As night fell the guns of 4th Field Regiment began to target a sugar factory and other buildings occupied by enemy snipers. By midnight the RHLI, with the aid of a local resistance volunteer, had cleared the Stadspark, but the cost of the day's combat – eight killed and twenty wounded – suggested that Groningen might be a difficult problem.[54]

Major-General Bruce Matthews met with his brigadiers to consider the available options. The most obvious course of action – bypassing the city and continuing north to Delfzijl – was barely considered. Montgomery wanted the Canadians to complete the clearing of northeast Holland and the German coast to the Weser River as quickly as possible so that they could take over Bremen from 2nd Army and protect the British flank during the advance to the Elbe.[55] Leaving a large German garrison behind would require troops to mask the city, and none were available. Matthews decided to commit the entire division, hoping to overwhelm the enemy as quickly as possible. The 4th Brigade was to employ all three battalions to secure the southern approaches, including the railway station; 5th Brigade would circle to the west and enter the city from that direction. Since a Dutch town could not be bombed or shelled indiscriminately, the artillery field regiments were limited to observed fire on identifiable targets.[56]

The Royal Regiment won control of the railway station on the afternoon of the second day and the Essex Scottish used Kangaroos to rush one of the bridges, establishing a foothold inside the ring canal. These tactical victories would not have been possible without the close support of the Fort Garry tanks and the M10s of 2nd Anti-Tank Regiment. The Toronto Scottish machine gun and mortar platoons also adapted quickly to urban warfare, laying down limited smoke screens and hauling a medium machine gun to the roof of the railway station to target windows used by enemy snipers.[57]

Matthews committed his reserve brigade on the morning of 15 April, day three of the battle. The South Saskatchewan Regiment, Fusiliers Mont-Royal, and Queen's Own Cameron Highlanders passed through 4th Brigade and began to work their way forward, supported by tanks. The only sensible course was to clear houses along each of the parallel north–south streets; this turned the battle into a long series of house-clearing actions. The townspeople were eager to help locate the enemy and to offer hospitality to their liberators as each block was cleared.[58] The pressure exerted by 6th Brigade drew enemy reinforcements to the southern section of the city just as 5th Brigade began a three-pronged advance from the west. The Calgary Highlanders secured a canal crossing by swinging a barge into position, 'leaving a gap of about four feet which the men were able to jump with comparative ease.' The next morning the Black Watch advanced into the 'New Town,' a seventeenth-century suburb outside the ring canal. They were held up by machine gun and sniper fire from houses on two sides of a large park. Edging their way through back gardens, the battalion began a two-hour battle, which ended when a mortar barrage and infantry assault with flame-throwers forced the surrender of more than two hundred German soldiers.[59] The heaviest fighting took place around the central market square, where the enemy had fortified the houses along the north side of the largest open space in the inner city. These positions were overcome by manoeuvring tanks into position to destroy the buildings occupied by German troops.[60] More than one-third of the 6,000-man garrison had surrendered by the evening of 15 April, but there were still many pockets of resistance in the northeast quarter of the city. The German garrison commander finally agreed to surrender at noon on 16 April; the next day the last holdouts put down their weapons and joined their comrades in prisoner-of-war cages, which now held 95 officers and 5,117 other ranks.[61]

The 2nd Division reported 43 fatal casualties and 166 wounded in the battle for Groningen. This was a high price to pay at this stage of the war, and the deaths of 110 civilians caught in the crossfire added to the tragedy. German losses were estimated at 300, including 130 killed in action.[62] Despite the civilian casualties and the destruction of 270 buildings, including many of symbolic and historical importance, the citizens of Groningen were determined to celebrate their liberation. The Canadian soldiers willingly joined in, until new orders to move to Germany 'to protect left flank of 30th Corps' were issued. The 4th Brigade led the way east on 19 April.[63]

The battle for Groningen was fought by troops who had no previous experience of urban warfare and no serious training for such a specialized task. The friendly civilian population proved both a hindrance and a help: limitations on the use of heavy firepower were offset by information on enemy locations. The key to success turned out to be common sense and the closest possible cooperation between armour and infantry. The Germans were well equipped with offensive, hand-held, anti-tank weapons, so infantry platoon commanders made certain each block was checked and cleared before the Shermans and M10s moved forward to blast the next enemy positions. When armour was not available the infantry relied on the simple techniques learned in battle drill or on memories of childhood games of Cowboys and Indians.[64]

The battle for Groningen was in its third day when Montgomery arrived at Crerar's headquarters with new instructions. Eisenhower's directive of 15 April required 2nd British Army to seize crossings over the Elbe, secure Hamburg, and advance to Lübeck and the Baltic in preparation for the liberation of Denmark. Operations to clear northeastern Holland and the coastal belt into Germany were also ordered, and Eisenhower assumed this meant the capture of Bremen, scheduled to be the American port of entry into occupied Germany.[65] Bremen was

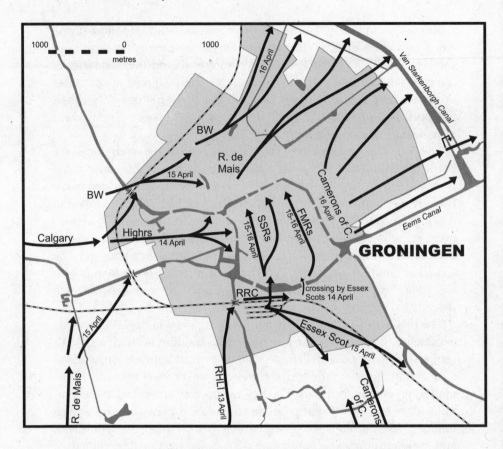

strongly defended, and General Sir Brian Horrocks wanted additional troops, an attack by Bomber Command, and time to build up stocks of ammunition.[66] Montgomery needed a Canadian infantry division to join 4th Canadian Armoured Division on the British flank. Crerar agreed, and both men flew to Simonds's headquarters to work out the details. Crerar also mentioned that he was needed in London and would authorize Simonds to act for him as Army Commander while he was away.[67]

Simonds met with his divisional commanders on 20 April to outline their new tasks. The 4th Division had become embroiled in a costly battle at the Küsten Canal, which the Germans were holding as a defensive line blocking access to Wilhelmshaven. The Algonquins had established a small bridgehead on 17 April, but accurate artillery fire was stopping engineers from bridging the wide canal and the best Brigadier Jim Jefferson could do was feed in more infantry and support them with indirect fire.[68] Vokes was able to report that tanks of the British Columbia Regiment had crossed the canal, but enemy resistance was still strong. Simonds told Vokes to build up the bridgehead before striking east to Oldenburg. If the city was 'too strong for an armoured division to capture,' the division was to seal off the northern exits and advance to the Weser. The Polish Armoured Division was to advance towards Varel and Wilhelmshaven.[69] Simonds did not yet know what role 2nd Division might play, and Matthews was simply told to deploy his division on the left flank of 30th Corps. The most important new task was assigned to 3rd Division: to 'prepare for an infantry brigade assault across the River Leda into Leer ... and advance via Aurich into Emden.' Hoffmeister's 5th Armoured Division was to relieve 3rd Division in northeastern Holland and prepare itself to seize the Dutch port of Delfzijl after Emden was captured.[70]

Before examining the battles for Delfzijl and Emden we need to understand the broad strategic picture as of mid-April 1945. The 9th U.S. Army had reached the Elbe on 11 April; the next day it had secured a bridgehead across the river. Simpson was confident that his troops could reach Berlin quickly – it was just seventy miles away – but Eisenhower was adamant that no lives were to be lost in pursuit of an objective that would only have to be handed over to the Soviets.[71] A rapid advance to Berlin in April 1945 was well within the capacity of the Allied armies, and as Winston Churchill argued, 'As long as Berlin holds out ... German resistance will be stimulated.'[72] Churchill was surely right when he argued that if the Allies had concentrated their forces, they could have reached Berlin quickly and forced the Germans to surrender. He later contended that the war was prolonged for two or three costly weeks because of this decision not to dash for Berlin. But at the time, no American was responsive any longer to Churchill's views.

That night, 13 April, President Franklin D. Roosevelt died, plunging America and the Western world into heartfelt mourning. Newspapers and radio stations focused on stories about Roosevelt, his successor Harry Truman, and the shocking evidence of Nazi death camps – especially Bergen-Belsen – and speculated about an immediate collapse of German resistance. The war, it seemed, was all but over. On 16 April the Royal Air Force and the U.S. Army Air Force suspended the strategic air offensive and prepared to use their heavy bombers to bring relief supplies to Holland. On April 20 in Berlin, Hitler, cornered in his underground bunker, celebrated his last birthday. Two days later he announced his determination to stay despite the advance of Soviet forces, which had all but surrounded the city.

After 9th U.S. Army reverted to Bradley's command, Montgomery's forces for the advance into Germany consisted of 2nd British Army with three armoured and eight infantry divisions, as well as 2nd Canadian Corps with three armoured and two infantry divisions. These forces would be hard pressed to carry out operations all across northern Holland and Germany. The enemy vastly outnumbered 21 Army Group, so much would depend on their morale. Other problems influenced the strategic context in which the last battles of the war were conducted. The Big Three powers – Britain, the Soviet Union, and the United States – had agreed to a policy of unconditional surrender and committed themselves to military operations against Germany until this was achieved. By early April many of the leading Nazis recognized that the war was lost and were seeking to avoid further conflict with the West and to concentrate their forces against the Russians. Proposals for a truce with the Western powers, the possibility of a surrender of German forces in Italy, and offers to capitulate to the West alone were made throughout the final weeks of the war, and rumours of these actions inevitably reached the Soviets. The British and American governments were determined to avoid any appearance of separate negotiations with the Nazi state, and battlefield commanders were instructed to maintain pressure until unconditional surrender was achieved.

Two other factors must also be noted. The British Admiralty were deeply concerned about the increase in U-boat launchings, the threat of new Schnorkel submarines, and the appearance of large numbers of midget submarines. The Royal Navy, therefore, was pressing for the early seizure of the North Sea ports.[73] Since the capture of these ports would also ease the logistical problems of armies provisioned through the Port of Antwerp and permit the entry of food supplies for the civilian population, the ports became a priority for 21 Army Group. Finally, there was the question of Denmark. The adjoining German province of Schleswig-Holstein was slated to be in the British zone of occupation, but what would happen if Soviet forces entered Denmark before the Western armies? Would the Soviets demand a part in the projected campaign against German forces in Norway and a postwar role in Scandinavia? No one wanted to find out, so operations to reach the Baltic and cut off Soviet access to Denmark were viewed as of crucial importance in Washington and London as well as in Eisenhower's headquarters. Montgomery did not see it this way. When Eisenhower sought priority for this operation, offering American troops to carry it out, the request prompted a bitter reply from Montgomery, who declared that if the Russians reached Denmark it would be because of Eisenhower's faulty strategy.[74] Montgomery might ignore Eisenhower, but when Churchill also demanded action the race to the Baltic began.

The last major battles fought by the Canadians in Northwest Europe were carried out in accordance with the strategy of maintaining pressure and securing the North Sea ports. As always, the heaviest burden fell on the infantry, who were required to close with the enemy right up to the last day of the war. Simonds was reluctant to issue the final orders for operations that would cost more Canadian lives. His hesitation was based on two important considerations: the overall military situation, which now pointed to an imminent German surrender; and the limited resources available for what looked to be major battles. There was a birthday dinner for Simonds on 23 April, but the mood was sombre. Bomber Command, which had played a crucial role in the attack on Bremen, was not available for Leer or Emden. Simonds and his staff were even more upset with the uncooperative attitude of Air Marshal Sir Arthur Coningham and Air Vice-Marshal E.C. Hudleston, both of whom insisted that the flak defences of the Emden fortress zone not only prohibited the use of medium bombers but also limited the employment of Typhoons to direct support of the river crossing.[75] Simonds was also surprised to learn that the Buffalo LVTs were needed at the Elbe and that the Canadians would have to rely on storm boats.[76]

On the morning of 27 April, Montgomery reiterated his orders and added the capture of the Frisian Islands to Simonds's list of responsibilities. When a request for commando brigades to assist in these projected assault landings was refused, the low priority attached to Canadian operations was evident to all.[77] The Corps Commander's War Diary entry for 27 April reflects the attitudes expressed at corps and army headquarters: '27 April. Comd had a conference at 1115 hrs with Comds 3 Canadian, 5 Cdn Armoured and 1 Pol Armoured Divs to confirm arrangements for the assault into Leer. It was to carry on irrespective of air sp which by reason of weather and other factors not apparent to this HQ is not likely to extend beyond fighter-bomber attacks.'[78]

Major-General R. Holley Keefler, now commanding 3rd Division, had selected Rockingham's 9th Brigade for the assault crossing into Leer, and 'Rocky' – who always led from the front – conducted a personal reconnaissance of the German defences. Air photos showed numerous slit trenches along the dykes. After he was forced to ground because of small arms fire, he was certain that the positions were manned. Without the familiar Buffaloes, which could handle mud, climb river banks, and bring the infantry ashore, the attack would have to be at high tide, when the storm boats could beach at the base of the dykes. Rockingham was given just enough boats to lift six companies of about eighty men each. He decided on a plan that involved simultaneous attacks on Leer from three directions. The North Novas sent one company directly into Leer, where it was to establish a bridgehead and then build up to battalion strength before advancing into the city centre. The HLI entered the river well away from the city and under cover of smoke, and landed in a lightly defended sector east of the built-up area. The Glens crossed to the west of the city to establish a bridgehead for the engineers.[79]

Success depended on tactical surprise and on neutralizing the enemy during the assault phase. Typhoons, field and medium artillery, and a 'pepper pot' orchestrated by the Camerons of Ottawa kept heads down, and both the North Novas and the HLI were on top of the enemy while the defenders were still under cover. The Glens were confronted with strong enemy positions, which caused havoc during the build-up. They lost fifteen men during the landing as well as three boats.[80]

With three battalions advancing into Leer, Rockingham was more concerned about confusion and losses from friendly fire than about the enemy, who quickly surrendered as soon as their own lives were in danger. At dusk he ordered a halt to operations and turned the battle for Leer over to 7th Brigade, which used the darkness to get its battalions into position for a carefully controlled advance at first light. Only the Reginas encountered organized resistance, and when this was overcome around noon on 30 April, Leer was clear of the enemy. Emden was thirty miles away across polder country, and any movement brought down shellfire from the coastal guns on both sides of the estuary. At 2130 hours 7th Brigade started north, using Wasp flame-throwers to supplement personal weapons. Movement was slow, and when dawn broke everything stopped. Any daylight advance would bring unacceptable casualties.[81]

On 2 May, 8th Brigade took over the advance towards Aurich, a 'key road centre' west of Emden. The next day the Queen's Own Rifles were pinned down by machine gun fire on flat terrain that afforded no cover. Three casualties were suffered before the men dug in along the side of the road. The advance continued on 4 May with further casualties, but during the afternoon a German delegation appeared under a flag of truce, ending further action some hours before the official ceasefire on 5 May.[82]

While 3rd Division was fighting the battle for Leer, Hoffmeister and his infantry brigade commander, Ian Johnston, decided to reinterpret the orders given to 5th Armoured Division. Instead of waiting until Emden was captured before securing the Dutch port of Delfzijl, Johnston's battalions began to compress the Delfzijl perimeter in preparation for the capture of a series of fortified gun positions along the Ems estuary. On 28 April Hoffmeister told Simonds that he proposed to go ahead with an attack on Delfzijl, code-named Operation Canada, because 'three or four days mucking about will cost us more in the end.'[83]

This was an unfortunate decision. Had Hoffmeister waited, the garrison would have surrendered on 4 May with the rest of the Germans in the Emden fortress area,[84] sparing both Dutch civilians and Canadian soldiers. Hoffmeister later explained the decision in terms of preserving port facilities for Swedish ships waiting to enter Delfzijl with relief supplies. He recalled that the corps commander described this task as 'very important ... from a humanitarian aspect.'[85] If this was the reason for mounting the attack, both Simonds and Hoffmeister had been misinformed. No relief ship could reach Delfzijl until the German gun positions on the island of Borkum as well as the coastal guns at Emden had been captured. Liberating Delfzijl would not change the relief

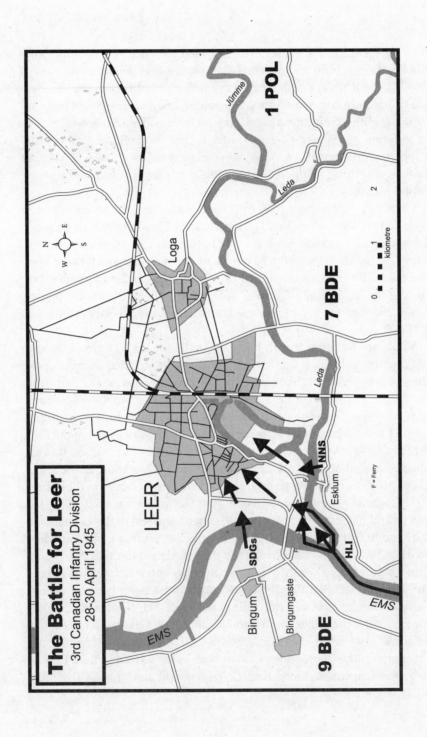

The Battle for Leer
3rd Canadian Infantry Division
28-30 April 1945

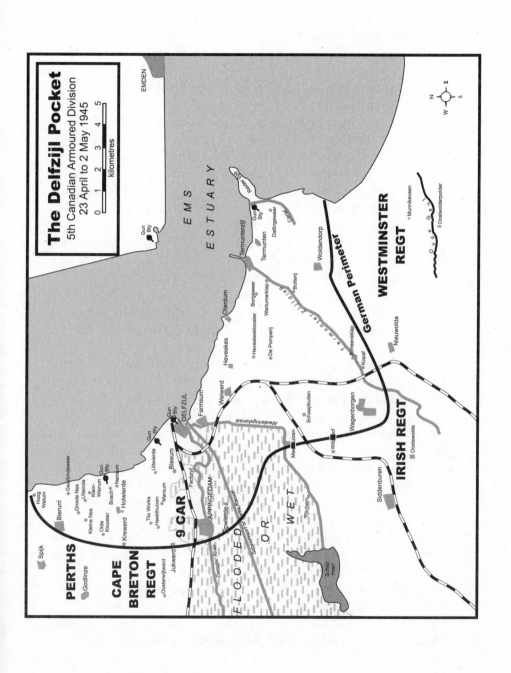

The Delfzijl Pocket
5th Canadian Armoured Division
23 April to 2 May 1945

kilometres
0 1 2 3 4 5

EMDEN

E M S

E S T U A R Y

Radar Stn

Gun Bty

Termunterzijl

Termunten

Dallingeweer

Canal

Woldendorp

WESTMINSTER REGT

Munnikeveen

Oostwolderpolder

Oude Geul

German Perimeter

Borgsweer

Wartumerklap

Botterj

Scheemdekap

Kopef

Nieuwolda

Oterdum

Heveskesklooster

De Pomperij

Heveskes

Weiwerd

Farmsum

Schaapbuilen

Wagenborgen

Oostwolde

IRISH REGT

DELFZIJL

Gun Bty

Gun Bty

Uitwierde

Biesum

Meedhuizen

Wildehof

Siddenburen

Gaarbinderweer

Groote Nes

IJteinde

Klein-Wierum

Bosch

Nansum

Holwierde

The Works

Heekthuizen

Marsum

Kreward

Factorij

Tje Works

APPINGEDAM

Opwierde

Jukwerd

Oosterwijtwerd

Damster River

Scheepvaart of Eemskanaal

Afwateringskanaal

Delfzijlster kanaal

Tjuchem

Tjuchem

Schild meer

F L O O D E D   O R   W E T

9 CAR

CAPE BRETON REGT

PERTHS

Spijk

Hoog Watum

Bierum

Godlinze

Kleine Nes

Olde Klooster

Gun Bty

N
E
W
S

situation, and a battle for the town might result in damage that would restrict the use of the port.[86]

Johnston's three infantry battalions were positioned to advance from two directions, the Perth Regiment and Cape Breton Highlanders from the north and the Irish Regiment from the southeast. The motor battalion, the Westminsters, were dismounted and sent forward to capture the gun batteries south of the town. In this 'flat country with little cover and a complicated system of ditches and canals,' cross-country movement was almost impossible, at least in daylight, so Johnston ordered his men to move only at night and in carefully controlled bounds. Everyone was to be dug in and under cover at first light.[87] This agonizing process continued through to 2 May, when the last defenders of Delfzijl and its gun batteries surrendered. Casualties, including seventy-five men killed in action,[88] were far higher than expected, but 11th Brigade's success was welcome news to the men of 3rd Division, who were attempting to capture Aurich and Emden. Farther to the east, the soldiers of Polish Armoured Division, 4th Canadian Armoured Division, 2nd Canadian Infantry Division, and 2nd Canadian Armoured Brigade were engaged in a series of limited actions to clear the Wilhelmshaven peninsula.

One important task remained – the advance to the Baltic to safeguard Denmark. This operation was carried out by 18th U.S. Airborne Corps, with 6th British Airborne Division under command. Brigadier James Hill's 3rd Parachute Brigade was in the vanguard, and Hill decided to continue north without pause. The columns raced by thousands of armed German soldiers, who along with masses of civilians were fleeing from the Russians. The 1st Canadian Parachute Battalion was in the lead when the Baltic was reached, and it fell to Lieutenant-Colonel Fraser Eadie and his men to confront Soviet forces on the outskirts of Wismar.[89] A fine mixture of determination and diplomacy was required to convince the Soviets that Wismar was going to stay in Canadian hands, but the tough, experienced paratroopers were right for the job. Captain Richard Hilborn, who had jumped into France on D-Day, took on the liaison role with the Russians and managed to smooth over differences with the aid of a generous supply of champagne.[90]

On the morning of 5 May 1945, messages ordering all units to cease offensive operations were issued, and the news spread quickly.

The final days of the war were a tense period for everyone, from the staff officers at corps headquarters, who were denied the support they believed the troops needed, to the men at the sharp end, who were being asked to maintain pressure without taking too many chances. Total casualties in the final two weeks of the war included 490 men killed in action – losses that seemed especially tragic in the circumstances. The ruined cities, ravaged countryside, and forlorn refugees added to the misery. When the news of the ceasefire reached the forward troops on 5 May there were few celebrations, just an overwhelming sense of relief that the war was finally over.

Conclusion

When the official historian C.P. Stacey came to write the conclusion to his book on the campaign in Normandy and Northwest Europe, he put forward the view that the Canadians, after a shaky start in Normandy, developed into a body of 'battle-hardened soldiers' who had 'mastered every aspect of their task.' First Canadian Army, he declared, 'was an exceptionally efficient fighting machine' with 'sound, sure and intelligent command at all levels.'[1] The evidence presented in this study suggests a rather different picture: an army that continued to experience both success and failure at the command, staff, and combat levels. The idea of an ascending learning curve is deeply embedded in military historiography, but an analysis of both Allied and German operations in 1944–5 offers little support for such a view.

At the most senior levels, Allied direction of the campaign was plagued by an increasingly bitter rivalry between British and American commanders. Field Marshals Brooke and Montgomery must bear much of the blame for the deterioration in Anglo-American relations, but Eisenhower's failure to fully exercise the power of supreme command permitted the conflict to develop to the point where too many decisions were influenced by perceptions of national interest or prestige rather than military priorities. The failure to complete the long envelopment at the Seine, the persistent efforts to reach the Ruhr rather than clear the Scheldt after the failure of Market Garden, the pressure to fight through the Hochwald while American troops were advancing to Wesel, the delayed Rhine crossing, the unresolved debate over advancing to Berlin, and the costly battles for the North Sea ports in the last weeks of the war provide reasonable grounds for questioning the generalship of both Montgomery and Eisenhower.

The Allied armies enjoyed much greater success at the operational and tactical levels. Having been compelled to fight with inferior armoured vehicles and inadequate direct-fire weapons of all types – from the Sten gun and PIAT to the 6- and 17-pounder anti-tank guns – the Western citizen armies built on a simple, artillery-based battle doctrine that maximized strengths and minimized weaknesses. They established all-arms battlegroups, learned how to employ flamethrowers and other innovative weapons, and took advantage of total air superiority to concentrate forces and use them at decisive points. Their administrative/logistical systems provided constant support for sustained operations that the enemy could never match.

The Allies were fortunate that the German High Command in the West, from Hitler to Model to von Rundstedt, had embraced ideological and doctrinal concepts that overrode evidence from the battlefield. By late 1944 Hitler's insistence that no position could be voluntarily surrendered without his permission had destroyed what little flexibility the German army possessed. This approach, combined with a commitment to immediate counter-attacks, played to the strengths of the Allied armies, which were equipped and trained to win such battles.

After 15th Army's brilliantly managed withdrawal across the Scheldt estuary, its defence of the approaches to Antwerp was an operational and tactical disaster. The 64th Infantry Division lost the battle for the Breskens Pocket despite a force ratio very much in its favour. German battalions were repeatedly sacrificed in fruitless counter-attacks when common sense dictated a purely defensive role, with staged withdrawals to the vital coastal area. The success of 'Battle Group Chill' at the Albert Canal and the effective employment of this composite force as a 'fire brigade' on the Antwerp–Tilburg front was negated by attempts to roll back rather than contain 2nd Canadian Division at Woensdrecht and by the failure to support 70th Infantry Division in the struggle for South Beveland and Walcheren.

Throughout the Rhineland battles the German Army's parachute and armoured divisions demonstrated dedication and tenacity in defensive warfare while continuing to squander scarce resources in improvised counter-attacks. Employing the last remaining first-class divisions in the West in an aggressive attritional battle made little sense. The purpose of the Rhineland battle was to protect the Ruhr industrial region and the shipping routes along the Rhine and its canals. Committing all available reserves to the British–Canadian front guaranteed that 9th U.S. Army would reach the Rhine quickly. Once this was accomplished there was no point in continuing to fight on the west bank of the river, yet this is precisely what the Germans chose to do. After the war the generals who carried out Hitler's orders blamed him for the debacle, but in the twilight of the Third Reich, as the Allied air forces operated freely over Germany raining down death and destruction, their oaths and their honour were poor excuses for a lack of moral courage and their abdication of responsibility to both soldiers and civilians.

Except for a brief period during the Rhineland battle, First Canadian Army was the smallest to serve under Eisenhower's command. The Canadian component of the Allied armies never totalled much more than 185,000 of the 4 million Allied troops serving in Northwest Europe.[2] It is, however, evident that the divisions of 2nd Canadian Corps played a role out of all proportion to their numbers. Their contribution to operations to secure the Channel ports and open the approaches to Antwerp, together with the part they played in the battles in the Rhineland, place them among the most heavily committed and sorely tried divisions in the Allied armies. By the end of 1944, 3rd Canadian Division had suffered the highest number of casualties in 21 Army Group, with 2nd Canadian Division ranking a close second. Among armoured divisions, 4th Canadian was at the top of the list, as was 2nd Canadian Armoured Brigade among the independent tank brigades. Overall Canadian casualties were 20 per cent higher than in comparable British formations. This was a direct result of the much greater number of days that Canadian units were involved in close combat. The British infantry divisions that ranked third and fourth had suffered heavy losses in the attritional stages of the Normandy battle and had been placed in reserve to allow recovery. Neither 3rd nor 43rd British Infantry Divisions were involved in the kind of operations the Canadian infantry experienced in October 1944. Britain's Guards Armoured Division and 8th Armoured Brigade were committed to action for much shorter periods than their counterparts in 2nd Canadian Corps.[3]

Lieutenant-General Guy Simonds, who commanded the corps throughout the war, can fairly be described as the outstanding corps commander in 21 Army Group. Simonds lacked the human touch that distinguishes great leaders, but no other corps commander displayed such technical competence and flexibility. His analysis of the challenges involved in clearing the Scheldt estuary and his plans for Operations Switchback, Vitality, and Infatuate were brilliant examples of joint and combined warfare that deserve continued study. Simonds also had the good sense to try and turn Montgomery and Crerar away from costly frontal assaults in the Rhineland by proposing an alternative, Operation Wallstreet. On many other occasions Simonds demonstrated a commonsense approach to problems and a genuine concern for preventing the waste of young lives.

The role of General Harry Crerar was much less central to the experience of Canadian combat soldiers. Crerar carried out his primary administrative responsibilities as an army commander and did his utmost to develop and preserve a reasonable degree of autonomy for Canada's national army. Crerar had little to do with purely operational matters, but he managed a highly effective staff that proved capable of meeting the most difficult challenges. The most important staff functions were those related to the use of the Allies' principal weapons – field and medium artillery. Gunners accounted for 18 per cent of the manpower in 21 Army Group as compared to just 15 per cent who wore infantry badges. Effective deployment of the artillery required expertise in survey, meteorology, sound ranging, gun calibration, aerial photo interpretation, radio communication, and air observation. Senior officers of the Royal Canadian Artillery at the army and corps levels worked closely with operational research scientists to analyse and refine methods of improving accuracy; this included the first experiments with radar on the battlefield. This was one part of the military where at first sight one would argue for a positive learning curve.

While it is evident that the gunners did seek to improve their art throughout the war, the results were far less satisfactory than is usually supposed. As part of their study of Operation Switchback, Operational Research scientists were able to demonstrate that under combat conditions mistakes in mathematical calculations were a major contributor to inaccuracies in predicted fire, and that so were calibration and meteorological errors. The result was that both field and medium artillery shoots produced a large 100 per cent zone averaging 1,000 yards in both length and breadth. This meant that just 4.8 per cent of the shells fell inside a hundred-yard square around the mean point of impact, which might or might not be centred on the target. The OR scientists and gunners experimented with a number of methods for improving their effectiveness at neutralizing enemy resilience, but a study of the accuracy of predicted fire in Operation Veritable suggests that after months of effort 'on average not more than 5.1 percent of the rounds aimed at a target fell in an area 100 yards x 100 yards at that target position.'[4]

The OR scientists did not address the effect of such dispersion on Allied infantry. This issue was finally examined in February and March 1945. Brigadier E.C. Plow, the Army's senior gunner, authorized a study of shell fragments collected from both British and Canadian Field Dressing and Casualty Clearing Stations in First Canadian Army. The study, which is reproduced as Appendix G, determined that 7 per cent of the identifiable fragments removed from British and Canadian casualties were from Allied ordnance and that the likely percentage of total casualties from Allied fire might be as high as 19 per cent.[5]

The report, issued on 20 April 1945, was not widely publicized for obvious reasons, but historians need to incorporate its findings when making generalizations about the harsh realities of combat. It may be that casualties from Allied artillery were exceptionally high in the poor weather and wooded terrain of the Rhineland battles, but the evidence suggests that casualties from 'friendly fire' were much higher than is generally supposed. Historians who argue that the Allies won the war by 'shelling and bombing the enemy into submission'[6] might wish to reconsider their view.

Crerar and his staff were also responsible for coordinating the contribution of the tactical and strategic air forces above the land battle. Initially, good relations were developed with Air Marshal L.O. Brown and 84 Group, but neither Crerar nor Brigadier Churchill Mann, the Chief of Staff, were able to maintain this partnership after October 1944, when Coningham replaced Brown and employed 84 Group in the parallel war carried out by 2nd Tactical Air Force. Coningham's actions were deeply resented at army headquarters, but his decision to deploy fighter and medium bombers in tasks that were within their capabilities may have been the correct one. Reports from both air force and army OR sections demonstrated that the kinds of targets selected by the army could only be neutralized if a very large and costly air effort was authorized. Rockets could be delivered with slightly more accuracy than bombs, but even then it took 18 Typhoons firing 140 rockets to achieve a 50 per cent chance of hitting an armoured vehicle or other similar target.[7] Close air support adversely effected enemy morale and greatly increased the morale of Allied troops, but from Coningham's perspective his squadrons had more important tasks to carry out. From late September 1944 to the end of the war, 2nd Tactical Air Force concentrated on cutting German rail communications and attacking other targets in Germany. As early as October 1944 just one-third of all sorties were flown in direct support of the armies; two-thirds were dedicated to other missions.[8] Officers who had come to rely on the Typhoons to maintain the morale of exhausted riflemen found that their requests for close support were increasingly denied for 'reasons not always obvious to the frontline troops' but abundantly clear to pilots, who knew the toll that anti-aircraft guns exacted in aircraft and lives.[9]

The strategic air forces, especially Bomber Command, worked closely with First Canadian Army in August and September 1944. However, reports of excessive and unnecessary civilian casualties in the bombing of Le Havre changed that relationship, as did the new strategic bombing directive that ended Eisenhower's control of the heavy bombers. When Simonds, as Acting Army Commander, sought bomber support for operations against Walcheren Island, he was told that the air force regarded attacks on gun positions as an unnecessary diversion – a position he challenged without success before, during, and after the battle.[10]

Bomber Command was persuaded to provide support to First Canadian Army in Operation Veritable, but apart from the attack on Cleve on the night of 7–8 February – when 769 aircraft bombing from just 5,000 feet destroyed much of the city – only small-scale attacks on other Rhineland towns were authorized.[11] After the Rhine crossing, Bomber Command ceased to provide support for First Canadian Army as it was operating in the Netherlands, but as we have seen, assistance was also denied when a request was made for bombing in the attacks on Leer and Emden. Again it is worth noting that while Canadian senior officers harboured a profound grievance about the loss of direct support from Bomber Command, a good argument can be made that the bombing of German oil and transportation targets was a more effective use of resources. During the last quarter of 1944 and the first quarter of 1945 the strategic bombing offensive destroyed much of Germany's capacity to continue the war – another way of saving soldiers' lives.[12]

The history of Canadian military operations at the battalion, brigade, and divisional levels during the last nine months of the war has been outlined in some detail, and a number of generalizations may be offered. One of the most obvious is that 3rd Canadian Division was the most consistently effective formation – Canadian, British, or Polish – to serve in First Canadian Army. At Boulogne and Calais, in the Breskens Pocket, and during the last weeks of the war, the division made an outstanding contribution to the Allied victory. The division's success in battle was achieved at a high price in casualties, but with the notable exception of Moyland Wood, these losses were incurred during vital operations that were well conceived and carefully planned. A good deal of the credit for the division's performance must go to Major-General Dan Spry and the divisional staff, but it is impossible not to be impressed by the quality of the brigade and battalion commanders in 3rd Division.

The contrast with the experience of 2nd Canadian Infantry Division is striking. Their difficulties in Normandy were compounded by the disaster in the Fôret de la Londe. After a major rebuilding effort in September the division was committed to a series of actions north from Antwerp that were fought without adequate resources. The division's command structure during this period was in constant flux, and while individual battalion commanders were able to achieve outstanding results in October, changes in command and an extensive retraining period were required to prepare the division for action in 1945. Major-General Bruce Matthews and his GSO1, Lieutenant-Colonel P.W. Bennett, provided a new kind of leadership that encouraged consultation, but Matthews's greatest contribution was his effort to ensure that his troops were committed to battle in carefully planned and fully supported operations. The battles fought by the division in the Rhineland – especially the attack on the Kalkar ridge and the capture of Xanten – were superb examples of what well-led, well-supported troops can achieve. Matthews's conduct of the battle for Groningen is also worth much closer study.

The 4th Canadian Armoured Division, under Major-General Harry Foster and Brigadiers Jim Jefferson and Robert Moncel, functioned effectively in the pursuit to the Scheldt and the advance to the Maas. The success of actions carried out by the division in late October deserves to be examined in detail as an illustration of effective tank–infantry cooperation in complex terrain. The division fared badly under the command of Major-General Chris Vokes. At Kapelsche Veer and the Hochwald, Vokes demonstrated that he was unfit to command an armoured division. His ill-considered thrusting tactics simply reinforced failure and led to the heaviest casualties the division experienced during the war. It would be interesting to know why Simonds, who did not hesitate to replace Kitching in Normandy, allowed Vokes to remain in command after his performance in Blockbuster. Within 4th Division the achievements of individual battalions and regiments have been justly celebrated. The Argyll and Sutherland Highlanders and the South Alberta Regiment won widespread admiration for their achievements in battle, and it seems likely that further detailed study will show that other units were equally, though not as consistently, effective.

Anyone who has studied the War Diaries and after-action reports of the Canadian infantry battalions has encountered frequent references to the value of close support by the armoured regiments of 2nd Canadian Armoured Brigade. Numerous examples have been cited in this book, but no subject in the history of 21 Army Group is more in need of evidence-based study than the role played by the independent infantry-support armoured brigades. British historian John Buckley has begun this task in his study of British armour in Normandy,[13] but there is much more work to be done.

One other issue requiring more intensive study relates to the recruitment, training, and combat experience of the thousands of infantry replacements who joined battalions during the campaign. Apart from anecdotal evidence, we know very little about their preparation or performance, yet the army depended on replacements to win the battles of the last nine months of the war.

Lieutenant Walter Keith, a Signal Corps officer who volunteered to retrain as an infantry platoon commander, has provided a detailed account of his own experience that may serve as a starting point. Keith attended a six-week 'Junior Leaders Training Course' in England during the fall of 1944 and was impressed by the 'excellent training staff.' He joined 'D' Company of the Regina Rifles in early March 1945 and was given command of 16th Platoon. His company commander, Gordon Brown, and the second-in-command, Dick Roberts, were both experienced leaders who provided advice and support, but Keith soon discovered that he and his men 'knew nor cared about very little' about life beyond their platoon of thirty-two men 'ranging in age from 19 to 35.'

Only two of the men in 16th Platoon had been with the Reginas in Normandy, and they, with one other, had fought at the Leopold Canal. These three and two November 1944 replacements had survived Moyland Wood. The platoon sergeant, R.S. 'Tommy' Tomilson, who landed on D-Day, survived the entire eleven months without a scratch, remaining 'calm, cool and courageous to the end of the war.' Corporal G. 'Blacky' Turner, the other Normandy veteran, commanded a section when Keith arrived but by March his 'nerves were shot' and he ought to have been evacuated as a battle exhaustion casualty. Turner was killed during the fighting for Emmerich. The other two sections were commanded by the replacements who had joined in November. Keith was the fourth lieutenant to command the platoon, but no one resented the arrival of a green young officer. The platoon sergeant's first words were 'Jesus am I glad to see you sir!' According to Keith, Sergeant Thompson 'never once interfered or showed lack of trust in my limited ability, but was always there if I needed help.'

Keith's memoir is reproduced in full in *Look to Your Front ... Regina Rifles*.[14] It includes the comment that the men of 16th Platoon were very ordinary Canadians, 'mostly fairly small, very young, very quiet and most unwarrior like.' They wore 'heavy Canadian battle dress, good old thick grey wool socks and really short boots.' Everyone except the Bren gunners carried a rifle, water bottle, mess tin and 'a rolled gas cape containing a towel, soap and a razor.' Everything else had been stripped away. 'Rum warmed us when cold, cooled when hot, settled the butter-flies in the belly, calmed nerves and made it possible to function more or less coolly.'

What most impressed Keith was the smooth functioning of the group:

Looking back now I realize that I never once had to cajole or threaten or ever encourage them to do the job they were given, they automatically did it. The section commanders unhesitatingly led their small group of riflemen where they were told to go and the section followed them, stupid though the order may have seemed to be. The 2 inch mortar men ... sited their weapon and delivered bombs where they were needed with no detailed orders from anyone and their accuracy was amazing.

It was with men such as these that the war to liberate Northwest Europe was won.

Appendix A

Deficiencies and Holdings of Canadian Infantry, Other Ranks:
Northwest Europe, 27 August 1944–28 April 1945

Date	Unit Deficiencies						Holdings at 2 CBRG
	1 Cdn Inf. Div.	2 Cdn Inf. Div.	3 Cdn Inf. Div.	4 Cdn Armd Div.	5 Cdn Armd Div.	Total	
1944							
27 Aug		1,999	604	522		3,125	1,726
29 Aug		2,495	836	846		4,177	1,306
30 Aug		2,522	878	846		4,246	1,231
31 Aug		2,612	875	831		4,318	1,354
3 Sep		2,645	752	761		4,158	876
4 Sep		1,960	736	755		3,451	731
5 Sep		1,960	737	761		3,458	1,785
6 Sep		1,450	630	706		2,786	954
7 Sep		1,478	666	706		2,850	882
8 Sep		1,478	770	715		2,963	987
11 Sep		1,794	741	872		3,407	1,841
12 Sep		1,727	759	865		3,351	1,317
13 Sep		1,727	788	729		3,244	1,141
14 Sep		1,550	806	719		3,075	1,781
16 Sep		1,495	733	713		2,941	1,829
18 Sep		1,482	814	641		2,937	1,710
19 Sep		1,553	783	641		2,977	2,746
20 Sep		1,523	711	707		2,941	2,227
22 Sep		1,464	621	624		2,709	2,492
23 Sep		1,299	602	629		2,530	1,535
26 Sep		1,408	673	282		2,363	2,363
27 Sep		1,452	802	318		2,572	2,363
28 Sep		1,442	809	324		2,575	2,288
29 Sep		1,470	761	180		2,411	2,053
2 Oct		1,267	816	125		2,208	2,814
5 Oct		1,165	552	106		1,823	2,028
7 Oct		1,224	540	112		·1,876	1,889
10 Oct		1,058	464	161		1,683	1,160
11 Oct		973	624	182		1,779	2,124
12 Oct		934	646	179		1,759	3,053
13 Oct		979	749	150		1,878	2,181
14 Oct		869	851	94		1,814	2,234
16 Oct		753	747	119		1,619	1,947
17 Oct		820	793	103		1,716	1,858
18 Oct		852	548	119		1,519	3,512
19 Oct		681	566	131		1,378	1,985

Deficiencies and Holdings of Canadian Infantry, Other Ranks:
Northwest Europe, 27 August 1944–28 April 1945 (*concluded*)

| | Unit Deficiencies | | | | | | Holdings |
Date	1 Cdn Inf. Div.	2 Cdn Inf. Div.	3 Cdn Inf. Div.	4 Cdn Armd Div.	5 Cdn Armd Div.	Total	at 2 CBRG
1944							
20 Oct		652	415	141		1,208	2,735
23 Oct		478	410	288		1,176	2,419
24 Oct		474	385	274		1,133	2,352
25 Oct		548	426	294		1,268	2,476
26 Oct		657	533	285		1,475	2,042
30 Oct		679	670	554		1,903	1,921
31 Oct		679	724	557		1,960	1,949
1 Nov		755	768	571		2,094	2,064
2 Nov		815	787	635		2,237	2,070
3 Nov		858	776	615		2,249	2,358
4 Nov		798	805	697		2,300	2,398
6 Nov		803	678	635		2,116	2,748
7 Nov		803	519	639		1,961	2,754
8 Nov		803	424	127		1,354	2,000
9 Nov		632	424	227		1,283	2,153
10 Nov		530	278	262		1,070	1,325
11 Nov		579	278	188		1,045	1,456
13 Nov		424	90	134		648	2,323
30 Nov		325	125	40		490	
29 Dec		205	182	36		423	20
1945							
6 Jan		123	104	57		284	3,131
13 Jan		65	173	51		289	3,414
20 Jan		105	169	211		385	2,650
27 Jan		Nil	Nil	95		95	2,537
3 Feb		Nil	Nil	210		210	2,608
10 Feb		Nil	Nil	Nil		Nil	2,516
17 Feb		Nil	Nil	49		49	3,768
24 Feb		Nil	334	Nil		334	4,221
3 Mar		244	72	105		421	3,704
10 Mar		371	62	254		687	2,715
17 Mar		4	Nil	86		90	2,193
24 Mar	132	9	54	8	28	231	3,979
31 Mar	156	48	191	34	nil	429	5,476
7 Apr	nil	75	Nil	55	nil	130	4,036
14 Apr	74	17	50	14	nil	155	4,022
21 Apr	72	64	25	30	nil	191	3,473
28 Apr	23	193	225	89	108	638	3,728

Source: Library and Archives Canada (LAC) RG 24, vol. 10, 699.

Appendix B

Canadian Army Fatal Casualties, Northwest Europe,
21 August 1944–5 May 1945

Date	Total fatal casualties, all ranks	Date	Total fatal casualties, all ranks	Date	Total fatal casualties, all ranks
Aug. 1944		Sept. 1944		Nov. 1944	
21	48	26	14	1	54
22	21	27	20	2	31
23	51	28	33	3	25
24	20	29	28	4	9
25	17	30	24	5	3
26	67			6	4
27	64	Oct. 1944		7	6
28	116	1	34	8	2
29	70	2	22	9	5
30	14	3	25	10	9
31	11	4	8	11	7
		5	41	12	2
Sept. 1944		6	46	13	4
1	16	7	30	14	14
2	8	8	45	15	6
3	6	9	70	16	–
4	7	10	55	17	7
5	26	11	38	18	6
6	28	12	46	19	8
7	27	13	82	20	7
8	36	14	47	21	13
9	49	15	30	22	4
10	31	16	50	23	13
11	39	17	42	24	7
12	28	18	31	25	5
13	36	19	20	26	12
14	61	20	43	27	2
15	23	21	31	28	5
16	22	22	22	29	5
17	97	23	107	30	2
18	41	24	57		
19	38	25	58	Dec. 1944	
20	25	26	43	1	5
21	14	27	41	2	3
22	42	28	51	3	2
23	17	29	38	4	7
24	38	30	18	5	4
25	51	31	37	6	10

Canadian Army Fatal Casualties, Northwest Europe, 21 August 1944–5 May 1945 (*continued*)

Date	Total fatal casualties, all ranks	Date	Total fatal casualties, all ranks	Date	Total fatal casualties, all ranks
Dec. 1944		Jan. 1945		Feb. 1945	
7	11	14	1	21	41
8	7	15	4	22	18
9	8	16	6	23	11
10	5	17	4	24	30
11	12	18	5	25	6
12	11	19	7	26	214
13	3	20	3	27	74
14	5	21	10	28	56
15	5	22	4		
16	23	23	5	Mar. 1945	
17	14	24	–	1	60
18	7	25	2	2	65
19	7	26	34	3	99
20	16	27	5	4	15
21	4	28	20	5	39
22	6	29	9	6	27
23	3	30	13	7	45
24	8	31	3	8	132
25	11			9	35
26	3			10	11
27	7	Feb. 1945		11	4
28	5	1	3	12	8
29	4	2	7	13	6
30	2	3	1	14	7
31	11	4	1	15	4
		5	3	16	9
		6	4	17	–
Jan. 1945		7	4	18	10
1	11	8	43	19	3
2	3	9	23	20	1
3	4	10	9	21	1
4	1	11	19	22	2
5	3	12	12	23	7
6	6	13	8	24	43
7	4	14	7	25	47
8	11	15	9	26	19
9	3	16	32	27	10
10	3	17	7	28	19
11	4	18	29	29	24
12	9	19	125	30	47
13	11	20	35	31	17

Canadian Army Fatal Casualties, Northwest Europe, 21 August 1944–5 May 1945 (*concluded*)

Date	Total fatal casualties, all ranks	Date	Total fatal casualties, all ranks	Date	Total fatal casualties, all ranks
April 1945		April 1945		April 1945	
1	20	14	66	26	38
2	29	15	51	27	24
3	19	16	38	28	64
4	47	17	55	29	37
5	45	18	30	30	31
6	32	19	19		
7	41	20	22	May 1945	
8	34	21	40	1	43
9	34	22	41	2	29
10	55	23	48	3	9
11	31	24	56	4	21
12	58	25	37	5	12
13	49				

Source: LAC RG 24, vol. 18, 825.

Appendix C

Weekly Incidence of Losses Canadian Army Northwest Europe: All Causes

Date	Exhaustion	Wounded	Killed & missing	Sick	Total
1944					
14 June		1229	217	383	1829
21 June		415	750	586	1751
28 June	66	269	579	368	1282
5 July	40	128	100	313	581
12 July	113	911	342	166	1532
19 July	264	1272	551	409	2496
26 July	107	1661	363	201	2332
2 Aug.	261	1921	942	144	3268
9 Aug.	462	986	721	558	2727
16 Aug.	89	2468	988	109	3654
23 Aug.	39	2490	917	112	3558
30 Aug.	443	1842	1098	1191	4574
8 Sept.	275	1200	595	1031	3101
13 Sept.	52	614	287	409	1362
20 Sept.	70	766	237	682	1755
27 Sept.	110	1066	566	627	2369
4 Oct.	31	580	174	458	1243
11 Oct.	104	1017	568	673	2362
18 Oct.	165	1285	441	815	2706
25 Oct.	152	977	514	634	2277
1 Nov.	217	1052	645	855	2769
8 Nov.	170	807	336	946	2259
15 Nov.	47	150	83	885	1165
22 Nov.	47	152	87	904	1190
29 Nov.	54	125	56	982	1217
6 Dec.	34	152	60	1070	1316
13 Dec.	14	120	52	996	1182
20 Dec.	39	153	74	1236	1502
27 Dec.	13	141	54	737	945
1945					
3 Jan.	30	97	43	1033	1203
10 Jan.	34	82	41	1366	1523
17 Jan.	26	105	43	1100	1274
24 Jan.	19	82	32	1139	1272
31 Jan.	16	239	38	1315	1608
7 Feb.	34	118	105	1097	1354
14 Feb.	36	290	75	1549	1950

Weekly Incidence of Losses Canadian Army Northwest Europe: All Causes (*concluded*)

Date	Exhaustion	Wounded	Killed & missing	Sick	Total
1945					
21 Feb.	35	261	90	1030	1416
28 Feb.	128	951	305	809	2193
7 March	132	1795	591	989	3507
14 March	230	1085	498	1149	2962
21 March	82	111	353	1623	2169
28 March	49	262	60	1434	1805
4 April	62	538	193	1136	1929
11 April	93	957	238	1736	3024
18 April	72	1167	392	1715	3346
25 April	64	677	281	1442	2464
2 May	59	1083	351	1280	2773
9 May	58	518	231	1313	2120
12 May	41	129	130	1288	1588

Source: Report by Lt-Col JC Richardson, Terry Copp Papers, LCMSDS.

Appendix D

Artillery in Operation Switchback

Account by Brigadier P.A.S. Todd, DSO CCRA 2 Canadian Corps (Corps Commander Royal Artillery) formerly CRA 3rd Canadian Infantry Division.

1. Although artillery support for Operation Switchback was rarely limited to divisional resources, still its control was invested in the CRA, 3 Cdn. Inf. Div. rather than in the CCRA. The reasons for this were twofold; (i) it was a single-division front, and (ii) communications with HQ RCA, 2 Cdn. Corps were difficult, owing to its distant location in DESTELBERGEN, east of Ghent.

2. Because the operation included two widely separated assaults, one over the Leopold Canal and one across Savojaard Plaat, with consequent difficulties in deployment and communications, command of 4 Cdn. Armd Div Artillery was further decentralized to the CRA of that formation. Two field regiments (15 and 19 (SP) Cdn. Fd. Regts.) and 10 Med. Regt. RA were nominated to support 9 Cdn. Inf. Bde in its assault landing; for this role they were positioned southwest of NEUZEN, beyond Savojaard Plaat.

3. This was by no means the only problem. In the initial deployment the assault over the Leopold Canal had to be visualized by using two AGRAs (Army Groups Royal Artillery) in enfilade from east to west. 9 AGRA was sited on the right, and 2 Cdn. AGRA on the left, in the vicinity of BRUGES. In order to be able to engage the heavy guns at KNOCKE and CADZAND, which might influence 9 Cdn. Inf. Bde's operation in the BRESKENS area the entire 76 Anti-Aircraft Brigade was deployed between BRUGES and BLANKENBERGHE to function in a ground role ...

15. In such a protracted operation it is not surprising to find several instances of unusual methods in the employment of artillery. On 19 Oct. an Air OP plane fired a very effective shoot on an enemy medium gun position with scale 15 from a battery of 155-millimetre guns. Some days later HQ, RCA fired a Corps target over the little-

used Corps net while on the move. The target, it is reported, was 'effectively neutralized.'

16. A comment on the effectiveness of artillery support was supplied by the enemy commander, Maj-Gen. Eberding when he explained that shelling had made it impossible for his men to blow prepared demolitions in BRESKENS. A distinct disadvantage nonetheless attached to the use of 25-pounders; their fragmentation effect was materially reduced by the wet mud of the polders. The first burst was therefore all-important, for subsequent rounds would find the enemy under cover and hence practically immune from injury.

17. Grouped Stonks and Concs on Call. In addition to the numerous DF (defensive fire) and HF (harassing fire) tasks in readiness, support was given to each infantry attack by fire plans, consisting of stonks and concs on call (linear and pinpoint concentrations). This system has been used so successfully by 3 Cdn. Inf. Div. that it deserves some description. Brig. Todd explained that it is essentially a method of siege warfare, and thus found full development at BOULOGNE and CALAIS, and in the SCHELDT pocket.

18. Its preparation must be worked out after close study of Intelligence maps showing all known or suspected enemy positions. With this detailed knowledge, and taking into account both artillery resources and the infantry plan ... it is possible to assign to every potential source of opposition an appropriate weight of shells, the amount varying according to the nature and importance of the target. This treatment has normally resulted in a combination of numbered medium concs and field stonks, grouped under a code-name.

19. The original task table issued in support of 7 Cdn Inf. Brigade's assault over the Leopold Canal contained 46 such groups, most of them, appropriately, bearing the names of rivers. One of the largest ('Colorado') was scheduled to be of eight minutes' duration, and comprised eight field stonks and three medium concs, to be fired, respectively, by 12 and 13 Cdn. Fd. Regts. at rate slow, and by three medium regiments of 2 Cdn. AGRA at rate normal. The target in this case was a series of enemy positions around the village of DEN HOORN. A smaller one, on the other hand, might consist of only one stonk and one conc, as was the case with 'Richelieu.'

20. It does not follow that each of these groups must be fired according

to a pre arranged, and hence inflexible, timed programme, or even fired at all, should it become unnecessary for any reason. The firing of each one rests with the infantry, for whom they are available on call. The infantry are thus given neutralizing fire when they want it, and for as long as they want it. It is quite in order, for example, to order 'Colorado twice,' which would result in the enemy positions being fired on for sixteen minutes. Once on an objective the infantry can halt if it is deemed desirable, and the area can be marked off by DF tasks. This flexibility means that the fire plan ensures covering fire to meet the infantry's local rate of advance, a factor not found in the timed programme with its rigid stop lines, which may be utterly wasted, should the infantry be held up.

21. The chief advantages of the system are that it will produce quick and effective fire, and that if not abused it is more economical than the too-liberal barrage, since it is confined to those areas alone which can affect the battle. It gives, moreover, much more exact results than the map reference target hastily called for in the heat of battle, for it is based on deliberate calculation, with all that that implies of predicted laying (including angle of sight) and allowance for meteorological conditions. Its preparation also permits adequate time for the proper allotment of weight and natures to each target. Not least important is its simplicity, for the system is readily comprehended by infantry. The distribution of traces (16 per brigade) is sufficiently wide that commanders of sub-units can themselves adjust fire. Even section leaders are able to appreciate fully this method of obtaining artillery support.

22. The possibility of misuse lies in the fact that there is nothing to prevent targets being called for indiscriminately, with resultant waste of ammunition. Grouped concs must not be used in the hope of neutralizing hostile batteries suspected of being in an area ... and covered by them. Such speculation is of no value; the system is only valid when employed on the immediate front of the unit concerned. The neutralization of hostile batteries is much better left to Counter-Battery and Air Op resources, which are equipped to deal with them.

24. Finally, Brig. Todd made it clear that grouped stonks and concs are not to be looked for invariably as standard practice. They are, after

all, a device to be used when the enemy is contained, and when there are only so many points (no matter how numerous) which he can occupy. They cannot be employed over open or unfamiliar country, and naturally they found no place in the approach-to-contact battle across France during late August and early September.

Source: LAC RG 24, vol. 10, 913.

Appendix E

Third Division Psychiatric Report, October 1944

1. The Neuro-Psychiatric (N.P.) casualties for this period are those sustained in the battle of the Scheldt.
2. The breakdown is as follows: (See attached divisional breakdown)

Total N.P. Casualties	Total Reported Casualties*	%N.P. Casualties
295	1957	15%
N.P. Casualties Inf.	Total Casualties Inf.	%N.P. Casualties
268	1626	16.4%
N.P. Casualties RCA	Total Casualties RCA	%N.P. Casualties
3	93	3.2%
N.P. Casualties Div. Tps	Total Casualties Div. Tps	%N.P. Casualties
24	238	10%

3. Disposal

To Corps Reinforcement Centre	199	67.5%
Reboard & Reallocation	52	17.6%
Further Rehabilitation (special employment)	28	9.5%
General Hosp.	16	5.4%
	295	100.0%

4. Of the N.P. cases occurring during this battle about 90% had three months or more of battle experience. Because of the length of time in contact with the enemy (93 days to the end of the battle of the Scheldt) and because of the fighting conditions which were severe, the N.P. casualties rate was high.
5. Very few troops on arrival at the Field Dressing Station (FDS) showed outward signs of nervousness. Most were markedly fatigued. A man was kept three nights and was assessed from first interviews, observation over a period of 48 hrs. and final interviews and history.

*Total reported casualties do not include killed and missing.

Treatment consisted of moderate sedation up to and including the first night, light sedation the second night and no sedation the last day or night. After his first 24 hrs. the man was allowed passes in town from 1400 to 2200 hrs. Pay services were made available, canteen and entertainment services were provided and the man was given every opportunity to lead as near as could be approximated a normal life. The man was in no way treated as a patient. He was informed that the condition was often due to fatigue, from which he would recover quickly and for which the Army granted him 48 hrs at this unit. Following this he was expected to return to duty. The freedom which the man was given was of value in two ways; first as therapy which he fully enjoyed and appreciated and secondly, as a basis for observation. Those who had negative history and reacted normally were considered fit for further service in the line. Those who did not appear to react normally but had negative history were sent to Corps level for further rehabilitation and later weeding. Those who did not react normally and showed positive history were returned for reboard-reallocation.

6. There was one thing of note among all troops admitted for exhaustion – lack of morale or lack of volition to carry on. The foremost cause of this seemed to be futility. The men claimed there was nothing to which to look forward – no rest, no leave, no enjoyment, no normal life and no escape. The only ways one could get out of battle was death, wounds, self-inflicted wounds and going 'nuts.' The second most prominent cause of this lack of volition seemed to be the insecurity in battle because the condition of the battlefield did not allow for average cover. The third was the fact that they were seeing too much continual death and destruction, loss of friends, etc. After these came other minor complaints – lack of use of captured towns, comparisons of treatment received by other forces – non-combatants and higher command not allowing them to enjoy the fruits of conquest – etc. etc. Most of them had no insight as to why they were being used to fight so hard and steadily.

7. Because of the poor morale among what were considered veteran soldiers, it was felt that it was inadvisable to return them to the fighting on the Scheldt for two reasons: first, to avoid completely cracking their morale by fostering their already flourishing opinion

that the Division had no interest in them except to 'get blood from a stone' in order to bring glory to others and secondly, because these men were considered valuable as veteran soldiers, to lead newcomers in the fighting to come. The men who are considered for return to duty were, therefore, sent to advance reinforcement company to be held until the battle of Scheldt was completed after which they were to be returned to their original unit. This block of men were to be followed on return to their units. Without notification, however, these were sent along to Corps Reinforcement Centre; an effort is being made at present to locate them and see if disposal as suggested has been carried out.

8. My attitude regarding exhaustion, although never expressed in writing, has been stated repeatedly in this division. The psychiatrist's work is first to advise on things which tend to lower morale and increase the incidence of exhaustion, thus lessening the possibility of neuro-psychiatric casualties; secondly, to record lessons learned through statistics and other sources; thirdly, to weed and treat cases in the division.

9. With regard to the first point above in (8), the following are necessary:
   a. adequate physical rest
   b. variation in the man's life
   c. periodic stimulation of interest by education
   d. periodic opportunity to lead a normal life
   e. reasonable leave periods.

10d. Periodic opportunity to lead a normal life: it has been shown previously in this theatre of war that a man may retain good efficiency from 18–21 days without rest, in stiff battle with average fighting conditions. At the end of this time his morale begins to drop and his interest begins to wane. He begins to get fed up and to lose his volition. He needs a short change (somewhere between 21–31 days) in which he has a chance to change his entire environment and outlook on life. He needs 24–48 hrs of carefree living as has been supplied by our Brussels leave centre. One merely has to ask a man who has been there to find the result. If he cannot be afforded 48 hrs then his divisional recreation centre should afford him 24. In this present location there is accommoda-

tion for a divisional leave centre which could handle 300–500 men
a day – a man going in late one afternoon and returning to unit the
following day: that is, a half of the reserve battalion of one brigade
could be accommodated 24 hrs and returned to relieve the other
half when they could go to receive the same treatment. Methods
of amusement and handling are well-known in this division and
need not be discussed here.

10e. Reasonable normal leave periods: should be granted if at all possible. A man does not mind losing if he is advised the reason it
cannot at the time be granted. The average Canadian soldier is
reasonable, sensible and has the independence and initiative to
become difficult if he considers he is being treated unreasonably.

11. The ways and means of increasing morale and lessening the incidence of exhaustion have been only partly discussed. The matter
of confidence in weapons, leadership, training, physical condition, belief in the cause and self-confidence do not enter the picture at this phase so much as they do in the training period and
therefore have been avoided. The rest of the subject has been
discussed only in principle as its application is as fluid as the
warfare which we are fighting and as changeable as conditions
under which we fight. Its application is simple, but its administration complicated and difficult. In other words it is an administration and not a medical problem towards which the administration
of this division has been sympathetic and cooperative. It is hoped
that even more may be done in the future.

Respectfully submitted

(Maj.) R.A. Gregory
Neuro-Psychiatrist 3 Cdn. Inf. Div.

Source: War Diary, ADMS 3rd Canadians Infantry Division, November
1944.

Appendix F

Notes on Dyke and Polder Fighting – 3 Cdn Inf Div Study Period
(from Hist Offr 3 Cdn Inf Div)

Trg

(a) *Fire and Movement within the P1*
NCOs are NOT able to give good fire orders and this is especially
important in this type of country where the fire of a few men can be
most influential. In addition, movement into battle was NOT always good and here again, the nature of the ground dictates trg.

(b) In dyke and polder country, there is NO way around selected
routes and therefore, it is essential that inf be well trained in lifting
enemy minefds so that the bn tac routes of adv may be opened up
as quickly as possible.

(c) Battle School practice and principles must be retained; these apply
as much to dyke and polder country as to any other.

(d) In order to meet the immediate need for trg rfts when they arrive at
bn it is necessary to give all new men seven to ten day's trg in the
'A' Ech area under the supervision of the Regt NCO. Here they are
taught to live as they will in the front line and, in addition, to
familiarize themselves with weapons, eqpt, minor tactics, and regt
history.

(e) Trg in the use of flame throwers (both WASP and LIFEBUOY) must be
given and it was generally felt that instr in the tac emp of flame
must be taught in the trg ests in ENGLAND.

(f) The GOC made the following gen points with respect to trg:-

   (i) The size of the sec in battle is vital because it is essential that
   there are both a Bren and a rifle gp. In order to maintain this, it
   may frequently be necessary for bns to consider the possibility
   of temporarily re-organizing on a three coy basis.

   (ii) Battle drill must be taught consistently throughout ops because the principles have been proven sound in battle.

   (iii) In dyke and polder fighting, the clearance of minefds, booby
   traps and rd blocks must be done, more than at any other time,

by inf. Oversize prn pls may frequently be required to train along these lines and such trg must be continued.

EMPLOYMENT OF

Inf

The emp of inf in dyke and polder country conform to the principle of fire and movement.

(a) One feature of fighting on dykes is that it is normally possible to be defiladed on one flank whilst the other can be neutralized by fire.
(b) Operations were usually planned and executed in phases which consisted of an adv from one polder to the next.

Armour

(a) *M-10s*
No enemy tks were encountered during op SWITCHBACK (it is interesting to note that several dummy tks were found during our adv in the SCHELDT pocket). M-10s were used for the close sp of inf during the op, but they were NOT good for this purpose because the gun faces the rear and can only be traversed when the tk is stationary. If there are NO enemy tks, then it was found that the use of M-10s in the close sp role was feasible. For the purpose, it is essential that tps recce posns to be occupied and time allowed for this.

(b) *Tks*
It was felt that tks would have been invaluable for close sp of inf throughout op SWITCHBACK since the 75 mm guns would have been most effective against the dyke posns.

(c) *Penny Packets*
The armour available during Op SWITCHBACK was frequently used in penny packets and this was obviously justified since there was NO other way of using it because of the restricting nature of the ground and space on the rds.

(d) *Flails*
These have a 75mm gun and it was felt that they could have been

used as tks during the op except for their extreme awkwardness on the poor rds. Flails are NOT satisfactory for mine clearances on cobbled rds and had they ran into trouble would have caused bad rd blocks.

(e) *Crocs*

Although it was generally felt that these must be more aggressive, it was realized that hose tks bogged down easily (particularly on the poor rds in dyke and polder country) and would have caused serious difficulties. Essentially, crocs must follow flails in a particular op and the handicaps to both in dyke and polder country are obvious.

Engrs

(a) Many points about the emp of engrs have already been noted:-

 (i) It was felt that one pl should normally be under comd each bde and the balance of the fd coy concerned placed in sp.

 (ii) It is essential that a rep of the fd coy be available at all times to the bde comd to provide engr advice and assistance.

 (iii) Inf are responsible for erecting and handling aslt boats and Kapok bridging, although it is a joint RCE and RCASC responsibility to make these available at the appointed RV when required.

 (iv) It is essential to have the FBE pl in close touch with the aslt fmn at all times during dyke and polder fighting.

 (v) Bulldozers, armd and unarmd, are required to open up routes and the demand for these must be anticipated so that the eqpt can be made available as early as possible. This is essential especially in dyke and polder country where movement is so restricted.

(b) Pnrs – It has already been suggested that bns must develop the activities of pnr pls in dyke and polder country where engr commitments are considerable greater than under normal conditions of terrain and routes. Pnr pl responsibilities for mine lifting, neutralization of booby traps, opening of bn tactical routes and the handling of boats have already been noted.

(c) *AVREs*

Little use was made of these during op switchback. The comments about Flails and Crocs and their employment in dyke and polder country apply equally to the AVREs.

(d) *Route Opening and Maint*

    (i) Pnrs must do more to open routes for bn and bde 'F' Echs because it *is* a bn responsibility to get its 'F' Ech fwd.

    (ii) Bns must attempt more 'scrambling' of 'F' Echs even though this is rendered extremely difficult in dyke and polder country.

    (iii) Individual units must make every possible effort to maintain the routes on which they live so that efficient local maint is NOT disrupted.

    (iv) The guiding principle must be that there are NOT sufficient sprs and eqpt to go around, especially on wide and divergent frontages. Therefore, inf must assume increased responsibility in the opening and maint of their own resources.

Arty

(a) In gen it was felt that the arty had been used extremely well throughout the op and in addition to supporting our own attacks, had broken up many counter attacks.

(b) Co-op between the arty and inf had been splendid throughout and it was agreed that the system of concs and stonks on a code word system had been ideal. This system is readily understood by all inf offrs; pl comds used the arty traces and from their fwd posns were able to correct errors in shoots. In many cases even rfn understood and were able to appreciate the system for obtaining arty sp.

(c) In future ops, it will be normal to issue 16 copies of the arty traces to each bde, one of which will be made available to each bn; this has been the normal practice since the present system of concs and stonks on call was originated.

(d) The destructive or killing effect of the 25 pdr was materially decreased in polder country where the ground is extremely soft. It is, therefore, the first burst which produces the desired effect upon the enemy and only erratic, spasmodic bursts are required to keep him in his dyke bunkers until the inf arrive. Those concerned were asked to consider how long an arty conc should be under these conditions: it is probably only necessary that they be for the period of time which it takes the inf to cover the open ground.

(e) *Smoke* – Smoke is still double-edged weapon and arty smoke was NOT used to any extent during Op SWITCHBACK. We must NOT be afraid to use it, however, and it may be frequently useful for HF when employed on a div scale.

(f) *Harassing Fire* – Special requests for HF tasks must be submitted to div early in the afternoon in order to allow ample time for the necessary orders to be passed down to the guns.

(g) *LAA*

    (i) The absence of any enemy aircraft during Op SWITCHBACK made it possible to employ the LAA regt in an inf role. When the task was that of holding, this employment of the AA guns was feasible and proved helpful during the op which was eventually based on wide frontages. In an offensive role, however, it was realized that the offrs and Ors were NOT sufficiently trained in inf tactics.

    (ii) It was pointed out that it is possible to obtain the effect of air bursts over houses and trees. Comds were asked to consider, for the future, the use of 40-mm in this way.

MMGs (Medium Machine Guns)

(a) *Allotment* – There was gen agreement that MMG coys should be placed under comd of the leading bdes.

(b) *Harassing Fire* – MMG harassing fire is particularly effective in polder country where the nature of the ground makes in possible to take advantage of the long ranges and restricts enemy mov to the dyke rds.

(c) *Direct Sp* – There is NO need for more than a 3° safety angle for employing MMGs in direct sp of inf; if this is realized by all comds it will be possible to give closer sp and also to provide effective fire on the flanks and in rear of inf objectives.

(d) *Gen* – The eventual availability of MK VII barrels and the subsequent increase in an allotment for MMGs was explained to comds.

Mortars

(a) *3-in*

No special pts were brought up about the unusual use of this eqpt in dyke and polder country.

(b) *4.2-in*

(i) Under normal circumstances, hy mortar pls should be placed in sp of bdes so that when possible the whole coy can provide sp fire; if under comd the mortar coy comd, he can then deploy them so as to be able to bring the whole fire effect of the coy to bear on the div frontage.

(ii) The use of phosphorous smoke had been most effective.

(iii) The problem which arose with respect to the bending of base-plates when used consistently with the skirt required in soft ground is now being corrected by modifications in wksps. The base-plate will still pool but NOT so quickly as was the case throughout Op SWITCHBACK.

Source: LAC RG 24, vol. 10, 912.

Appendix G

CONFIDENTIAL
24/AEF/1/3 (Hist)

CANADIAN OPERATIONS IN NORTH-WEST EUROPE

JUNE–OCTOBER 1944

EXTRACTS FROM WAR DIARIES AND MEMORANDA
(SERIES 13)

1. THE EMPLOYMENT OF TANKS IN SUPPORT OF INFANTRY: LESSONS LEARNED ON THE ZUID BEVEIAND PENINSULA, OCTOBER, 1944 (ACCOUNT BY LT.-COL. E.M. WILSON, O.C., 10 CDN ARMD REGT, GIVEN TO HIST OFFR 2 CDN INF DIV, 1 NOV 44).

1. With the return of 'C' Sqn from the CALAIS area, where it had been supporting operations of 3 Cdn Inf Div until 30 Sep 44, the Regiment was once more complete. Thereafter, 10 Cdn Armd Regt worked with 2 Cdn Inf Div from ANTWERP up through CAPPELLEN and putte to the ZUID BEVELAND isthmus, and the unit participated in the actions where stiff resistance was encountered at HOOGERHEIDE and WOENSDRECHT (8-22 Oct). 10 Cdn Armd Regt continued in support of 2 Cdn Inf Div during the period that the ZUID BEVELAND peninsula was being cleared of the enemy (23-31 Oct).

2. The marshy dyke-land WEST of WOENSDRECHT and on into the PENINSULA was not good tank country. Consequently, some variations from normal methods of deployment were necessary. On nearly all occasions the infantry were supported by a squadron or a troop of tanks; the most common formation being one troop with a battalion. Other considerations apart, this formation was necessary because of the restrictions on the choice of available roads.

3. During the operations to the WEST of WOENSDRECHT one troop from 10 Cdn Armd Regt, together with a scout troop of 8 Cdn

Recce Regt, supported one coy of infantry from 4 Cdn Inf Bde along the main road to the WEST (square 5420). On this occasion (24 Oct) the recce cars and tanks were employed together, in advance of the infantry. But, after one 75mm gun had knocked out three recce cars and three tanks, it was decided that this type of formation was not advisable. Accordingly, in later engagements, the infantry pushed ahead with the tanks behind them. When the infantry required armoured support the tanks were then deployed on the flanks, or otherwise, to greater advantage and with less casualties.

4. The experience obtained over this difficult, boggy country indicated also that tanks could be used with considerable effect in 'hull down' positions, if the infantry first blew holes for them in the dykes with grenades. The tanks could then fire through these openings behind the cover of the dykes. Indirect shoots were sometimes employed, using bursts of delayed action H.E. against dykes held by the enemy. In these cases fire was directed by a F.O.O.

5. The Sherman tanks gave an adequate performance and apart from the fact that more 17-pdrs could have been used there was no criticism of equipment. The 75mm projectile will bounce off the front of the Panther tank; but a shot obtained from a flank with this armament has been found to be effective.

6. In a defensive role, the enemy tended to employ his tanks and A tk guns in the following pattern: his armour would reveal itself at different points across our axis of advance, with the intention of enticing our tanks into positions where they would fall an easy prey to A tk guns situated on the flanks. These A tk guns were supported, in turn, by nests of M.G.s.

7. To deal with the German defence tactics, as outlined above, the following methods were employed. As soon as, the A tk guns had been spotted by our troops, our artillery were called upon to knock them out. Thereafter, the tanks moved in on the flanks and cleared a passage for the infantry. Co-operation with the artillery worked very well on all occasions. The lowlands over which these actions were fought had one compensation in that communications by wireless were very good.

8. A system was devised for the speedy evacuation of casualties which seemed to work very well. Usually, a Tac H.Q. was located near the Div or Bde Tac H.Q. and the M.O. was situated there with jeeps at his disposal. If one of our tanks was knocked out, a message was sent at once to the M.O. by wireless and he came forward to attend to any casualties.

9. Probably the most important problem encountered in the course of these operations arose in connection with the question of whether, below a divisional level, tanks should be under command, or 'in support,' of infantry. Below the divisional level, it is essential that a tank commander should have his tanks 'in support,' and not under command, of the infantry. The following reasons were advanced in support of this opinion:

(a) The tank commander is a specialist and knows best how his tanks can be employed.

(b) If tanks are under command of infantry, they are often placed in a position on the ground where they cannot give the maximum support. The infantry commander tends to over-emphasize the 'morale aspect,' in relation to his own troops, when considering where tanks should operate. It is suggested that he should consider where he wishes fire to come down rather than where the tanks themselves should be located ...

(c) When tanks are under command of infantry they are frequently sent into woods and built up areas without support. Tanks cannot hold ground once it has been captured. In some cases, particularly in the woods near HOOGERHEIDE and KORTEVEN, tanks were sent forward and captured the objective, but the infantry were not right behind them to consolidate.

(d) If tanks are under the command of infantry, there is difficulty in getting the former released in time for rest after doing the necessary maintenance on their vehicles. At the end of an action, the infantryman can dig a hole and obtain some measure of rest very quickly. But tank crews require considerable time in order to get their vehicles to a place where maintenance can be done, and the maintenance itself requires further time before rest is possible.

10. Out of the line, at rest, it is very important that armoured and infantry personnel should live together in order to exchange their viewpoints ...

11. Plans for co-operation with aircraft have been made on a number of occasions, although weather conditions have hampered the actual testing of these plans. It is felt that, in an indirect shoot, a flying F.O.O. could very often act as a ranging officer for the tanks. Furthermore, he could fly ahead of tanks and look for enemy movement. It was intended to employ this method of co-operation in connection with 'saint force' (8 Oct), but a heavy mist rendered this impossible. The F.O.O. would be in direct communication by W/T with the squadron commander.

12. As far as reinforcements are concerned, this unit has not experienced any real difficulty. Casualties have been about average and close liaison has been maintained with Brig Rutherford, commanding 'E' Group, C.R.U. This close liaison has prevented any difficulties arising in this connection.

Source: LAC RG 24, vol. 10, 640.

Appendix H

Report of Combined Operations on Walcheren Island from the Viewpoint of #8 Cdn Fd Surgical Unit, RCAMC

This unit entered into this operation quite inexperienced in an assault of this nature and the terrain, weather and conditions under which it has to work. It became immediately apparent that it could not exercise its normal function and that its design of being extremely adjustable to changing situations was going to be tested for the first time. For the first 48 hours the beachead in which the medical units were established was under constant and heavy shell-fire. There were no buildings or shelter available of a safe nature to perform major operations and to properly look after the patient after operation. The area was honey-combed with land mines which could not be detected and removed and the tentage was surrounded by large bomb craters and shell holes containing numerous German prisoners, ammunition, petrol and demolition charges. After the first 24 hours a gale sprang up from the North Sea which, at times, reached a velocity of 50 miles per hour and rain was constant, mingled at times with hail. At all times it was miserably cold and heating of the medical establishment to any adequate degree was impossible. No better conditions could be found as, by the time suitable indoor shelter could be found in the villages to the north and south of the beachead, the major part of the fighting would be over and the mass of the wounded would, as a consequence, be located at the beachead. The problem obviously was one of as rapid evacuation of the wounded to mainland as possible and the role which the Field Surgical Unit should assume was that of 'insurance' in case weather conditions made this evacuation impossible. As a consequence #8 Cdn Fd Surgical Unit was held at the bridgehead and #9 Cdn Fd Surgical Unit was sent forward first to the south, and then to the north to establish an Advanced Surgical Centre as soon as it was feasible. At the beachead conditions entirely justified this move. On the first day of the operation the beachead was under such a constant fire that the FSUs were kept in their amphibious vehicles in the streets of Westkapelle. On the morning of the second day we were brought to the beachead but it was still

considered it was too exposed to fire to set up a surgical centre. This
attitude was completely justified in the early afternoon when a salvo of
shells struck the beachead and set 3 LVT's on fire within sixty feet of the
medical installations. Considerable damage was done and the medical
personnel were trapped in a dugout making it necessary that the Field
Surgical Unit work in the Beach Dressing Station until things quieted
down. Certainly, under these conditions no major surgery could have
been done with justice to the patient. Up to this time evacuation of
patients to the mainland was being carried out in an efficient manner
and it is felt that there was no justification for holding these patients on
the beachead for surgery in view of the dangers and difficulties encountered and the good possibility of a change of weather. This attitude was
also completely justified when in late afternoon a strong North Sea gale
blew up which continued for seven days with very few lulls. Some
hope was still held of getting the patients out who had accumulated, by
the following day. The decision to wait and not operate was made
exceedingly easy by the fact that there were no abdominal cases. At all
times during the second day Major Proctor and Major McCrimmon
talked over the situation with Major Hillsman and the surgical viewpoint was in complete accord with the administrative and evacuation
viewpoint. The morning of the third day found the weather so bad that
it was obvious that no evacuation could take place. Major Hillsman was
asked by Major Proctor and Major McCrimmon to see every wounded
case and report on the surgical situation. This was done and it was
reported that there were three chest cases and four compound fractures
which needed surgery if evacuation could not take place. As for the rest
of the patients it was felt that a break in the weather allowing their
evacuation should be hoped for as the setting up of a major operating
tent in the terrific gale then blowing was virtually an impossibility. As a
consequence the 160 pound tent was set up and these seven urgent
cases were done. The conditions under which this surgery was done
thoroughly justified the wait for a break in the weather for the rest.
Throughout this entire operation the almost miraculous absence of
abdominal wounds made these decisions easy and positive. On the
morning of the fourth day the weather broke to some extent and 2 LCTs
arrived which, unfortunately were loaded and required considerable

time to unload. All patients were got ready for evacuation but before the unloading had proceeded very far these vessels were blown ashore and wrecked. It was decided then in consultation that #8 Cdn Fd Surgical Unit would set up its major canvas and operate upon all cases which had accumulated, both major and minor, as the gamble with the weather did not seem to be going in our favour. The tent was set up in the teeth of a howling gale and surgery was done until about 1730 hours, 24 cases being done using chemical sterilization and jaconette drapes. At 1730 hours strong petrol fumes could be smelt over the entire beachead from wrecked petrol from the LCT's and an order was issued from Brigade that all smoking must stop and fires to be extinguished. Since this included our generator and as we had no lights except open flames we had to close down for the day. However, by taking the most serious cases first this did not do any particular harm as there were only a few trivial cases left and they were entirely German soldiers. This did not mean that the Germans were not being taken care of as well as our men, but by doing the cases in the order of their seriousness it had happened to leave the few Germans. The wind blew all that night and the morning of the 5th day found the weather unchanged. The theatre was opened early and the rest of the cases were done plus the ones who had accumulated during the night, all of whom had been seen by the surgeon upon admission if listed serious cases. Our luck in abdomens still held and there was only one questionable case which we felt justified in waiting upon and this case subsequently turned out not to be an abdomen. Around noon on the 5th day the weather broke and an LCT came in to evacuate the wounded. By this time all surgery had been done except for 3 recent arrivals all of whom were minor cases. The evacuation of all cases was attempted but just before the last nine cases went aboard the gale sprang up again, the hawsers of the LCT broke and it had to hurriedly put to sea to keep from being blown ashore. The evacuation of these cases on this ship was concurred in from the surgical viewpoint as the conditions on the beachead were not satisfactory for post-operative care as the weather was cold and rainy and one could never tell when the tents would be blown down leaving the patients exposed to the most appalling weather conditions. When these cases were put on the LCT the weather was good enough for evacuation. The 9 cases left behind were seen by Major Hillsman and had all been operated upon and needed no further attention. During the night the gale continued to blow. The next day under gale conditions two more cases were done. By this time the cases from #9 Cdn Fd Surgical Unit were coming in and all cases were evacuated through Flushing. Since the fighting was entirely north of the beachead and the attack was not going to develop until the following morning #9 FSU moved up and was covering that. There was nothing left for #8 FSU to do except mine injuries and accidents occurring to the south, locally and a possible overflow from #9 FSU. As a consequence the situation was talked over with Major Proctor and it was decided not to risk any of the equipment of the #8 FSU further except its canvas and generator. #8 FSU closed down and packed its equipment in such a manner that it could immediately set up and work again if it became necessary. No further casualties, however, occurred for it to handle. In all 54 soldiers were operated upon, 22 which were major operations and, by some miracle of chance, none of these were abdomens.

Throughout the entire operation under the most appalling conditions in which there was every opportunity for short tempers and disagreement, the utmost good will and spirit of co-operation existed between three medical installations on the beachead. Major Proctor and Capt Richardson at all times consulted and considered the surgical opinion given by Major Hillsman. Major McCrimmon freely gave supplies and aid to the Field Surgical Unit. At no time was there any disagreement on the manner in which the casualties should be handled and surgical opinion was in complete accord with every decision made by Major Proctor and Major McCrimmon. One cannot end a report of this nature without a few words of intense admiration of the work done by #10 FDS in connection with the #8 FSU. Under the most appalling conditions the post-op care of our patients by this unit left nothing to be desired. No patient in this beachead suffered from lack of care if it was humanly possible by any effort on their part to give it to him. Both officers and other ranks deserve every praise for their efforts. When it was finally decided to do surgery, teams of stretcher bearers, under the supervision of one of their NCOs, were organized. The work of these stretcher bearers in, quickly and efficiently, carrying the patients to and from the operating theatre in the face of a terrific gale, blowing wind, hail, and sand, was one of the brightest of the whole operation from the medical side.

Respectfully submitted.

(Sgd) (JAB HILLSMAN) Major
Officer Commanding
#8 Cdn Fd Surgical Unit, RCAMC.

Source: LAC RG 24, vol. 15, 647.

Appendix I

Canadian Operations in Northwest Europe, June to November 1944: Extracts from War Diaries and Memoranda (Series 17)

Some aspects of the technique of flame throwing: 'Wasp' and 'Lifebuoy' (Account by Lt. George Bannerman, Sask L.I. (M.G.), Tech Offr (Flame), First Canadian Army, given to Historical Officer, 2 Cdn Inf Div, 26 Nov 44).

(a) *The 'Wasp,' MK II and II (C):*

1. The 'Wasp' is another weapon to add to those that the infantry already have, and must not be expected to win a war by itself. If this equipment is properly employed, it will cut down the number of casualties suffered by attacking infantry, but it must be supported by all available fire from infantry weapons, including smoke, and the infantry must follow very closely behind. In this respect the use of flame is similar to that of an artillery barrage and if the infantry do not follow closely behind, the enemy will speedily recover from his initial shock and be in a position to reply.

2. The main use of flame, in any form, is for its demoralizing effect. The success of this aspect has been demonstrated on a number of occasions where the 'Wasp' was effective, in the sense of demoralizing the enemy, without causing apparent physical injury to him. All experience during operations in this theatre has shown that, when the enemy was confronted with flame, he invariably did one of three things; first he huddled down in his positions; or, second, he gave himself up immediately or showed a white flag; or, third, he started to run away. In no case where enemy positions were attacked by flame did they attempt to return our fire. Such casualties as have occurred to 'Wasp' equipments were caused by enemy weapons firing at long ranges, or by reason of the carrier running over mines.

3. In passing, it may be noted that this demoralizing factor applied also in cases where 'Crocodiles,' with similar flame equipment, were used. One striking example occurred during the operations to secure the Channel ports. On this occasion, an operator was

improperly testing the ignition of his weapon, with the result that he produced a short flash of flame approximately 10 feet in length. The sight of this flame was sufficient to induce the immediate surrender of enemy in a strong-point at some distance.

4. Apart from the demoralizing aspect, the physical effect of actual burning was horrible. Enemy who were hit by a sizeable 'shot' of the fuel died almost immediately. If only a few blobs of the burning fuel struck a man it was possible for him to smother the flame. But, if he was struck by a large blob, smothering was practically impossible and in this case the fats in the human body were literally burned up.

5. Two types of 'Wasp' equipment have been used in the northwestern theatre of operations: the 'Wasp' Mk II, and the 'Wasp' Mk II (C). The essential difference between these two equipments is that the 'Wasp' Mk II has two internally mounted tanks carrying 60 and 40 gallons, while the 'Wasp' Mk II (C) has an externally mounted tank of 80 gallons capacity. In other respects these equipments are identical. The main advantage of the Mk II (C) is that the carrier may be used in its normal role, as the carrying space in the rear of the vehicle is still available. Apart from occupying this space, the internally mounted tanks of the Mk II interfere with the maintenance of the carrier's motors, and thus minimize the advantage of the extra 20 galleons of fuel that are carried. Without a strong cross-wind, or head-wind, the maximum range of either type of 'Wasp' is in excess of 150 yards, although the normal effective range is from 120 to 140 yards.

6. To some extent, the accuracy of fire delivered by the 'Wasp' gunner depends on the team work between the driver of the carrier and himself. Although the gunner and driver are not normally interchangeable, in cases where good team work exists the driver is sufficiently aware of the necessity of regulating the speed and motion of the carrier so as to give the gunner the best opportunity for accurate shooting. This co-operation gives a 'Wasp' crew tremendous confidence in their weapon, and builds up their keen interest in the care and preservation of their equipment. Thus, on one occasion, when a 'Wasp' belonging to Essex Scot was knocked out in a village, members of the crew went back at considerable risk to salvage the essential parts of their equipment.

7. The 'Wasp' is particularly useful against enemy positions such as reinforced earth or concrete bunkers, pill-boxes, etc., which cannot be knocked out by other weapons at the disposal of the infantry battalion commander. To get within striking distance of these positions, it is essential for the driver of the carrier to use all available ground as cover, and this cover should be supplemented by the use of smoke and the fire power of the infantry. The 'Wasp' gunner can also assist by firing his gun when still out of range, say 200 yards from the target. Even at that range, the resulting smoke and flame will give additional cover to the advancing carrier.

8. Another use for the 'Wasp' was found, the course of mopping-up operations, when isolated strong-points remained in the hands of the enemy without their former advantage of mutual defence. In these cases, a 'Wasp' could be introduced without fear of fire from the flanks, with the result that these positions were successfully engaged.

9. Where a concrete pill-box is encountered, the flame of the 'Wasp' can only be successfully employed against the slits of the position. It has been found that the 'Wasp' can be fired accurately against these slits at ranges up to 100 yards, and that, in these circumstances, approximately half of one ignited 'shot' (that is, roughly, 2 to 3 gallons) will be sufficient to put the pill-box out of action.

10. The 'Wasp' may also be used against enemy occupying slit trenches in the open, when a technique known as 'Golden Rain,' is employed. The gun is fired at maximum elevation, in the direction of the enemy, with the result that the rod of fuel breaks up in mid air into small, ignited blobs of fuel. Depending on the winds, this 'Golden Rain' will cover a very large area of ground. Under normal conditions the zone covered by the 'Golden Rain' extends from roughly 40 yards to 140 yards in front of the 'Wasp.'

11. In recent operations over the polder country, where a carrier was often the only vehicle that could be moved, with the enemy occupying positions on one side of the dyke and our own troops on the other, the only weapon which effectively winkled out the enemy was the 'Wasp.' The flame was fired over the dyke, and blobs of ignited fuel set fire to straw and wood covered slit

trenches. In almost every case, the enemy was driven out of his positions and was immediately cut down by the fire of supporting infantry or M.G.s mounted on the carriers themselves.

12. P.P.P. (plastic armour) has been found to be a useful accessory to the normal equipment of a 'Wasp' MK II (C). The use of plastic armour gives added protection to the front and to the sides of the carrier as far back as the bulkhead separating the driver's compartment from the rear wells. This armour is a good defence against all types of fire up to 20mm A.P. and it will even stop, or prevent the penetration of 20mm A.P. at anything except point-blank ranges and normal impact. The armour can be used effectively on carriers mounting 'Wasp' MK II (C) equipment for the reason that the 500 odd pounds of P.P.P. tends to balance the weight of the 80 gallon tank on the rear of that type of carrier. If the armour is used on the 'Wasp' MK II, it makes the carrier nose heavy. Being very thick in appearance, P.P.P. also contributes to the feeling of security on the part of the driver and gunner.

13. In the light of past experience, some method of inter-communication between the different members of the 'Wasp's' crew seems necessary, as control is difficult once the 'Wasp' has been committed to action. If some efficient type of inter-communication could be introduced, reciprocal advantages would result to the crew: thus, the driver or the crew commander could indicate targets to the 'Wasp' gunner, and the gunner or driver of the carrier could indicate targets, which have been missed by the flame, to be taken on by the Bren gun in the hands of the crew commander.

Source: Directorate of History and Heritage. (DHH).

Appendix J

Operation Blockbuster – 9th Brigade

Battle Lessons

(a) Exploitation at Night
Although NOT new the principle of rapid exploitation, regardless of the time of day or night, was well brought out. 8 Cdn Inf Bde had broken the crust of resistance in the neighbourhood of KEPPELN 9844. Immediately thereafter, 9 Cdn Inf Bde was passed through. After looking at the ground with its magnificent fds of fire it is very doubtful if such a rapid adv into UDEM could have been made under any other conditions than those that existed at the time.

(b) Flexibility of Plans
Once again it was revealed that plans must NOT be rigidly made to suit one set of conditions. On more than one occasion in this op, plans were made with the thought in mind that, that particular plan would be carried out in daylt. Frequently the op took place at night indicating that the original plan must provide for either light or dark conditions, or two plans must be made. Artificial lighting on night 5/6 Mar was quite inadequate.

(c) Tks in Street Fighting
A tp of tks in close sp of a coy is of great value in house clearing. Drills should be practiced providing for killing the enemy when driven out by tks and the protection of the tks from Bazookas. This method proved effective in UDEM after several other methods had failed and there were no tk cas.

(d) Easily Definable Landmarks
As plans had to be made from maps and out of date air cover, objectives thought to be easily definable were allotted. In the case of the UDEM op which was carried out at night with little daylt recce, it was NOT possible to discover the limits of objectives in the much bombed and

shelled town and when coys arrived in the town they were virtually lost for a good period of time.

(e) Recce
Lessons in two aspects were revealed here:

(i) Woods Recce
It is absolutely vital that very close recce of routes, approaches, FUPs, etc. be made if the whole op is NOT to be slowed down. Prior to the second PHASE in the op, 9 Cdn Inf Bde was ordered to follow closely behind 8 Cdn Inf Bde in the STAATS FORST XANTEN BELBERGER WALD. Valuable time was lost as recce for routes for the brining fwd of vehs and sp arms did NOT follow closely enough behind 8 Cdn Inf Bde fighting.

(ii) Lack of Daylt Recce
Considerable difficulty was encountered as, on at least one occasion, there was NOT the opportunity to recce ground over which an attack was to be made at night. Even though speed was essential it is considered that the results would have been achieved far more rapidly if daylt recce had been possible.

(f) Fire Plan
The Bde Fire Plan should never be completed in detail before bn plans have been finally settled. If so it is inevitable the fire in the required places will, in many instances, NOT be forthcoming. Necessary coordination requires considerable time for planning.

(g) Comns
(i) It is essential that a spare set for use on the Bde A net, carried on a veh other than the bn comds carrier, be readily available. Far too often after the bn comds set goes or is destroyed, bde is out of comm with bn for many hrs, while a spare set is either brought up from bde or rear bn.

(ii) The slowness of passage of infm seems to be from coy to bn and is largely because the 18 set is NOT functioning properly. This cannot be laid to the set itself but conditions gen. It is therefore felt that more frequent employment of runners would result in infm getting back more rapidly.

(iii) Aslt cable and phones could be used to good advantages in towns where progress is slow and R/T always bad.

Source: LAC RG 24, vol. 10, 912

Appendix K

Memorandum of Interview with Lt Col F.E. White,
Officer Commanding 6 Cdn Armd Regt (1 Hussars)
Given to Hist Offr 3 Cdn Inf Div 10 Mar 45

1. The tasks allotted to the Regiment during 'Blockbuster' proved most exacting to both men and equipment. The plan was to keep constant pressure on the enemy by using the nine infantry battalions of the Division. The difficulty arose from the fact that there were only three Squadrons in an armoured Regiment. The result was that Squadrons would barely complete a task with one infantry battalion before they were ordered to assist another. There was frequently no time to maintain the tanks or rest the crews. It was simply a matter of refuelling and restocking with ammunition, a hasty conference with the infantry commander and into action again.

2. The ground the Regiment fought over during this operation varied from flat open country devoid of cover, to closely wooded country and the assaulting of hill features. The weather varied from wet to fine, with good visibility. Muddy going was common throughout the operation. Actions were fought both by day and night.

7. The casualties incurred in reaching KEPPELN were the heaviest in the operation. Personnel casualties were about 30 percent. (N.B. Are actual figures now available?) Throughout the Regiment tank casualties for the day were 33, 14 were knocked out by gunfire, 5 on mines, and 14 were mired. On the credit side the Regiment claim to have knocked out four enemy tanks, the infantry claim we got six, in the capture of KEPPELN alone. This cannot be determined as 4 Cdn Armd Div were in the area and there had been an artillery concentration.

Lessons & Comments

All the normal lessons were applicable to this action however the following are considered to deserve special comment:

(a) The enemy was very clever in his use of SP's and heavy mortars to harass objectives once they were occupied by our troops. A considerable number of casualties were inflicted in this manner consequently it is suggested that a considerable portion of heavy and medium arty should be allocated to CB and CM work and whenever possible medium arty should be placed on call to Tk sub-units involved in the battle for the purpose of dealing with dug in enemy SP's or AFV's.

(b) The use of tanks in support of infantry before 'shooting light' can have only moral effect and it is considered that the difficulty of control, the mental and physical strain on the crew and the vulnerability to Pz fst fire make this undesirable and should only be resorted to on very special occasions and not become the rule.

(c) The situation where a Regt is split up between two Divs is most undesirable as no reserve is available to relieve any critical situation and as happened in this care resulted in the withdrawal of the Sqn in support of Q.O.R. prior to their objectives being attained in order to support the N.S.R. Happily this worked satisfactorily in this case but it has been the experience of this Regt that hurried shows with little or no time in which crews can be briefed usually end in disaster. Also it allows no time for the re-organization within the Squadron necessitated by battle casualties and is extremely exhausting on the crews.

(d) Prior to this OP 22 tradesmen were withdrawn from 6 Cdn Armd Regt (1H) for a special task with 79 Armd Div. 11 Driver Mechanics and 11 Loader Ops. These were partially replaced by reinforcement personnel and it is gratifying that for the most part the replacements fitted in very well, however, in view of the fact that team work is so essential in tank crews this was a great drain on the unit and it suggested that personnel should be trained from RU's during periods when low replacements are required in the field and not drawn from field units.

Leave personnel present a problem especially when battle casualties are encountered in addition. It would seem desirable that when a unit is involved in a battle that the leave personnel be replaced by replacements from T.D.S. The complete crews thus available to be L.O.B but immediately available to replace battle casualties.

(e) Admin functioned quite normally despite adverse conditions and the acquisition of AAC's enabled ammo to be delivered well forward.

(f) Intercomm proved unreliable during this phase of the operation and the links between tks and infantry was not good and broke down completely at times. Relay stations were necessary between RHQ and Bde Tack HQ which in one instance resulted in a message becoming completely garbled during re-transmission. Several breaches of security occurred and these have been brought to the notice of the persons concerned.

Comments & Lessons

In thick woods the enemy is not likely to use his Panzerfauste for he is taking a great risk in having the projectile explode on a tree trunk before it reaches the target.

Similarly the tanks cannot use instantaneous HE and 75 delayed action was not found to have exceptional results. The co-ax and bow gun were the only really effective weapons.

Inf in clearing a wooded area must, or necessity, have a small front and similarly tps cannot work well with more than two tks up.

Although no enemy tks or A/Tk guns were met actually in the woods tks must be prepared to defend themselves in another such attack for the forest does not impede the A/Tk guns AP effectiveness.

It is my opinion that the enemy (as well as ourselves) did not expect us to use tks in such a situation and he will not be caught again.

The enemy seemed to plan his defense around a GHQ and in doing so could switch all his considerable amount of arty to any one suspected FUP or FDL at any time. This would account for the very heavy concentration of arty and mortar fire brought down at all times during the attack and the rest of the day and night.

The enemy used during the day what seemed to be tremendously heavy rocket gun the shrapnel of which knocked out one tk. A large railway gun was also believed to have been used.

Conclusion

Despite all this activity, and the heavy tank losses of the last days' action when we lost 21 tanks, our personnel losses were not as severe as on the first day. This had a tremendous effect on morale. The troops fought till they were exhausted. I found two crews asleep in their tanks, before the area they had helped to capture was mopped up. The Regiment finished Operation 'Blockbuster' with 14 tanks, A Sqn 1, B Sqn 9, C Sqn 4. That the Regiment could continue to fight is an achievement of 54 L.A.D. who in the nine days recovered and repaired over 60 tanks despite enemy action, mines, and booby traps. This could only be done by cannibalisation of tanks, and a supreme effort on the part of the L.A.D. personnel. Repaired tanks were manned by composite crews of knocked out tanks, regardless of Squadron or troop. The resultant team work, thanks to good training was splendid. I have never felt prouder of the Regiment under my command. The total casualties for the operation were:

	Killed	Wounded	Missing	Total
Officers	1	7	1	9
O.R.	10	20	1	31

Source: Directorate of History and Heritage (DHH).

Appendix L

TOP SECRET
A/RCA/TS/7-0

BRA First Cdn Army
20 Apr 45

Chief of Staff
First Cdn Army

Provisional Identification of Shell Fragments

1. Object
   (a) To establish a system of identification of shell fragments in order to study the lethality of various weapons in relation to cas occurring in the field.

2. Examination of Fragments
   (a) Fragments for this examination were gathered over a period extending from 3 Feb 45 until 31 Mar and were collected from cad in FDSs and CCSs within First Cdn Army.
   (b) Identification to date has been based entirely on physical characteristics of fragments such as paint remnants, stampings, took marks, and driving bands.
   (c) A total of 575 fragments have been examined and the provisional identification is as follows:

   (i) *German Origin*
(a) Shell fragments	124	21.6%
(b) SAA fragments	107	18.6%
(c) Rockets	56	9.8%
	287	50.0%

   (ii) *British Origin*
(a) Shell fragments	52	9.0%
(b) SAA fragments	1	0.1%
	53	9.1%

(iii) *Unidentified*		235	40.9%
	TOTAL	575	100.0%

SAA fragments being much more easily identified than shell fragments – it can be assumed that the unidentified fragments are shell, mortar or bomb fragments. This alters the percentage as follows:-

(iv) *German Origin*

(a) Shell fragments	290	50.5%
(b) SAA fragments	107	18.6%
(c) Rockets	56	9.7%
	453	78.8%

(v) *British Origin*

(a) Shell fragments	121	21.1%
(b) SAA fragments	1	0.1%
	122	21.2%

TOTAL	575	100.0%

3. Casualties

(a) During the period that fragments were collected a total of 2,653 pers were cleared through the FDSs and CCSs concerned because of the following types of wounds. Of these pers approximately 2% were prisoners of war.

(i)	Shell wound HE	1429	53.8%
(ii)	Shell wound mortar	408	15.4%
(iii)	GSW Bullet	461	17.4%
(iv)	GSW Rifle	126	4.8%
(v)	GSW MG	87	3.3%
(vi)	GSW Pistol	17	0.7%
(vii)	BW Aerial	14	0.5%
(viii)	BW Mine Grenade	28	4.1%
		2653	100.0%

These figures cannot be absolute as in most cases source of wound is determined by questioning the cas. Combining (i), (ii), (vii) and (viii) above which might be hard to differentiate between as fragments we have 70.7% wounded by these causes. This total compares very closely with the total of 71.6% shell fragments identified in para 2.

(b) During the period under study total cas to the Cdn Forces were as follows

Unit	Killed		Wounded	
	Offrs	Ors	Offrs	Ors
2 Cdn Inf Div	34	429	120	1728
3 Cdn Inf Div	30	377	99	1322
4 Cdn Armd Div	14	175	66	790
5 Cdn Armd Div	–	–	–	2
2 Armd Bde	2	13	15	67
2 AGRA	–	1	–	5
2 Corps Troops	2	46	14	123
Army Troops	–	18	4	66
	82	1059	318	4103

4. Deductions
   (a) As a result of investigations arty fire is by far the most lethal weapon in use by the enemy causing over 50% of cas studied.
   (b) It seems reasonable to assume on the basis of our arty superiority that cas caused to the enemy by our arty fire are an even greater percentage of total cas.
   (c) Present fragment identification shows that 9.0% (21.1%) of fragments were of British origin, whereas only 2% of cas cleared through medical channels during investigation were PW. Assuming fragment ratio holds this indicates that a possible 7% of cas were due to our own arty fire.
   (d) Present methods of fragment identification are not adequate. Investigation should be carried on along chemical or metallographic lines in an attempt to develop a quick field test for identification which is applicable to all sizes and natures of fragments. Present methods are particularly inadequate for small fragments.

Source: LAC RG 24, vol. 10, 673.

Notes

INTRODUCTION

1 These operations are analysed in Copp, *Fields of Fire: The Canadians in Normandy.*

2 Third Ypres produced 2,121 casualties a day over 105 days, Normandy 2,354 casualties a day over 76 days. See Copp, 'First Canadian Army February–March 1945,' in Addison and Calder, *Time to Kill,* 148–9.

3 Stacey, *Arms, Men and Governments,* 422–8.

4 Hayes, 'The Development.'

5 See Appendix A.

6 G.W.L. Nicholson, *The Canadians in Italy* (Ottawa, 1960), 316.

7 Interview, author with Colonel E.A. Coté, June 2004.

8 War Diary, 4th Canadian Infantry Brigade, August 1944.

9 Copp, *The Brigade,* 90–1.

10 Maker, 'Battalion Leadership in the Essex Scottish,' 92–105.

11 Foster, *A Meeting of Generals,* 382.

12 1st Polish Armoured Division, *Operational Report,* LAC RG 24, Vol. 10, 942.

13 Simonds's 'Operational Policy' emphasizing the 'battle of counter-attacks' is reproduced in Appendix A in Copp, *Fields of Fire.*

14 Hastings, *Armageddon,* 135.

1. NORMANDY TO THE SCHELDT

1 Hinsley, *British Intelligence,* 367.

2 Montgomery to Brooke, 18 August 1944, Bernard Law Montgomery Papers (BLMP) 110/46, Imperial War Museum.

3 Eisenhower to Montgomery 19 August 1944, in Alfred Chandler (ed.), *Eisenhower Papers,* 2083.

4 Blumenson, *Breakout and Pursuit*, 573.

5 Directive M519, 20 August 1944, BLMP 107/17.

6 Blumenson, *Breakout and Pursuit*, 573, cites these figures as the estimate discussed at 15th Corps headquarters. No one knew how many vehicles were still south of the river, but this seems like a reasonable estimate.

7 Ibid., 574.

8 Blumenson, *The Battle of the Generals*, 256–8.

9 Stieger, Historical Section (G.S.), Army Headquarters. Report No. 69, 'The Campaign in North West Europe Information from German Sources,' Part III, 5. Directorate of History and Heritage, National Defence Canada (DHH).

10 War Diary, HQ, A.E.A.F., 23 August 1944, PRO Air 37/574.

11 The tactical air force had much less difficulty with such problems because Air Marshal Trafford Leigh-Mallory's Headquarters, Allied Expeditionary Air Force, was able to solve the issues on a daily basis. The senior American air officers believed that 'First U.S. Army should go on and finish the job interdicting the Seine right down to the mouth' and were prepared to work out the details of bomb lines and close air support. Ibid.

12 Blumenson, *Breakout and Pursuit*, 574.

13 Copp, *Montgomery's Scientists*, 191–5.

14 2nd Canadian Corps, Intelligence Summary No. 47, 3 September 1944. The figures are counts of the numbers sent to prisoner-of-war cages by 1st Canadian, 2nd British and 1st U.S. Armies and do not include prisoners taken by 3rd U.S. Army. LAC RG 24, Vol. 10, 809.

15 Copp, *Montgomery's Scientists*, 198.

16 Chandler, *Eisenhower Papers*, 2091–2.

17 Eisenhower to Montgomery, 24 August 1944, ibid., 2090.

18 Directive M520, 26 August 1944, BLMP.

19 These issues are discussed in Copp, *Fields of Fire*.

20 Allied intelligence estimated that 711th Division was a low-category static division in 'good condition' and that the infantry strength of 346th Division was less than 50 percent. The 272nd Division was said to have 'reached the vanishing point.' Historical Section, Army Headquarters Report No. 69, 1951, 5–6. See Zetterling, *Normandy*, for a much higher estimate of the strength of 272nd Division.

21 Historical Section, Canadian Military Headquarters Report No. 183, 1947, 16, DHH.

22 Hart Dyke, *Normandy to Arnhem*, 36. Brigadier Hart Dyke's account of the operations of the Hallamshire battalion, which he commanded in 1944,

includes several references to orders to pause or halt. When interviewed, Brigadier Dyke agreed that progress could have been more rapid, but he did not have an explanation for the orders received. Interview, Copp with Hart Dyke, Sheffield, 1994.

23 Salmond, *The History of the 51st Highland Division*, 172.
24 War Diary, 8th Recce Regiment, 25 August 1944.
25 Lettres, Lt.-Col. Julien Bibeau, 24 August 1944. Archives Le Régiment de Maisonneuve.
26 War Diary, Calgary Highlanders, 24 August 1944.
27 'The Battle of Bourgtheroulde,' War Diary, Black Watch, 24 August 1944.
28 Lt.-Col. F.M. Mitchell, 'Account of the Action at Bourgtheroulde,' DHH.
29 Lt. W. Shea, 'Account of the Battle of Bourgtheroulde,' DHH.
30 War Diary, Le Régiment de Maisonneuve, 26 August 1944.
31 Letter, Crerar to Corps Commanders, 26 August 1944, LAC RG 24, vol. 10, 799.
32 The quotations are from the War Diary, 12th Manitoba Dragoons, 23 August 1944. For the British Columbia Regiment action see 'The Story of the British Columbia Regiment 1939–1945,' NPND Chapter VII. See also Roberts, *The Canadian Summer*, 76.
33 War Diary, Lake Superior Regiment, 24 August 1944.
34 R.A. Patterson, *A History of the 10th Infantry Brigade* (1945), 31.
35 War Diary, Manitoba Dragoons, 24 August 1944.
36 Hayes, *The Lincs*, 43.
37 Simonds to Divisional Commanders, 25 August 1944, LAC RG 24, vol. 10, 799.
38 There are brief descriptions of these battles in the War Diaries, but the best accounts are in the respective regimental histories: Hayes, *The Lincs*; Fraser, *Black Yesterdays*; Cassidy, *Warpath*; and Graves, *South Albertas*.
39 The Brigade War Diary provides an outline account, as do the battalion War Diaries. See McIntyre, 'Pursuit to the Seine,' for an account by a participant that includes photographs of the terrain.
40 The War Diary entries for the Royal Regiment of Canada offer a detailed account.
41 War Diary, South Saskatchewan Regiment, 27 August 1944.
42 War Diary, Royal Regiment of Canada, 27 August 1944.
43 Ibid., 28 August 1944.
44 McIntyre, 'Pursuit to the Seine,' 68.
45 War Diary, Royal Hamilton Light Infantry, 28 August 1944.
46 War Diary, South Saskatchewan Regiment, 28 August 1944.

47 There were 116 fatal casualties on 28 August – the worst day of the battle – and 20 on 29 August. The large majority were in 2nd Division. See Appendix B.

48 Cassidy, *Warpath*, 123.

49 Fraser, *Black Yesterdays*, 254–64.

50 Model to OKW, 24 August 1944, 'Situation Reports German High Command,' DHH, pp. 62–3.

51 CMHQ Report No. 69, 5.

52 Office of the Chief of Military History (OCMH) MS B542, W. Steinmueller, '331 Infantry Division ...,' United States Army Military History Institute (USAMHI).

53 Crerar to Simonds, 29 August 1944, H.D.G. Crerar Papers, vol. 3, LAC MG 30, E157. Crerar agreed to replace Ganong 'by a suitable nominee, *not* a gunner officer.' Lt.-Col. F.N. Cabledu, CO of the Canadian Scottish Regiment, was appointed.

54 Ellis, *Victory in the West*, 21–3.

55 Eisenhower, Messages to Commanders, 29 August 1944, in Chandler, *Eisenhower Papers*, 2100–2.

56 Second British Army Intelligence Summary No. 97, 15 September 1944, LAC RG 24, vol. 10, 577.

57 'Situation Reports, German High Command,' 69.

58 Blumenson, *Breakout and Pursuit*, 679.

59 Moulton, *Battle for Antwerp*, 20–43; Whitaker and Whitaker, *Tug of War*, 13–43.

60 H. Reinhard, 'Report on the Commitment of 88 Corps from the Albert Canal as far as the Lower Meuse, 5 Sept to 21 Dec 1944,' OCMH MS B-156, 5.

61 Moulton, *Battle for Antwerp*, 26.

62 Roberts, *From the Desert to the Baltic*, 209–10; Great Britain Army, *History of the 11th Armoured Division*, 58–60.

63 Reinhard, 'Report,' 6.

64 Horrocks, *Corps Commander*, 72–3.

65 De Groot, 'Escape of the German Army.'

66 Interogation Report, General Wilhelm Daser, Laurier Centre for Military, Strategic, and Disarmament Studies (LCMSDS).

67 Eisenhower, Message to Commanders, 4 September 1944, in Chandler, *Eisenhower Papers*, 2115–16.

68 Eisenhower to Montgomery, 5 September 1944, ibid., 2120.

69 Ellis, *Victory in the West*, 16–17.

70 Eisenhower to Montgomery, 13 September 1944, in Chandler, *Eisenhower Papers*, 2133–4.

71 Stacey, *The Victory Campaign*, 306.

72 Ellis, *Victory in the West*, 29.

73 Love and Major, *The Year of D-Day*, 131–7.

74 Hinsley, *British Intelligence*, 320.

75 Eisenhower to Marshall, 14 September 1944, in Chandler, *Eisenhower Papers*, 2143–4.

76 Powell, *The Devil's Birthday*, 33–7.

77 Brian Urquart, who served as Chief Intelligence Officer of British Airborne Corps Headquarters, has described his efforts to persuade Lt.-Gen. Browning that the presence of II Panzer Corps in the Arnhem areas posed 'a deadly threat to lightly armed airborne troops.' Urquart was 'treated as a nervous child' and sent on leave when he presented air photos of tanks in the Arnhem area to Browning. Urquart, 'The Last Disaster of the War,' *New York Review of Books*, 37, 38.

78 Hinsley, *British Intelligence*, 383–4.

79 Gustav von Zangen, 'The Retreat of 15th Army,' OCMH MSS B249 and 275.

80 Stacey, *Victory*, 324.

81 War Diary, 4th Canadian Armoured Division, 31 August 1944.

82 Copp and Vogel, 'No Lack of Rational Speed.'

83 Polish Armoured Division, Operation Report, LAC RG 24, vol. 10, 942, 20–1.

84 Stacey, *Victory*, 303–6.

85 Dickson, 'Colonials and Coalitions,' 255.

86 War Diary, 8th Recce Regiment, 1 September 1944.

87 Polish Armoured Division, Operation Report, 21–2.

88 '62 Corps from Spring 1944 to September 1944,' OCMH MSS B-596.

89 War Diary, 7th Recce Regiment, 4 September 1944.

90 Polish Armoured Division, Operation Report, 22.

91 War Diary, 4th Canadian Armoured Division, 8 September 1944.

92 Polish Armoured Division, Operation Report, 26.

93 Von Zangen, 'Retreat,' 37.

94 War Diary, Manitoba Dragoons, 4–8 September 1944.

95 First Canadian Army Intelligence Summaries, 8–9 September 1944, LAC RG 24, vol. 10, 659.

96 Fraser, *Black Yesterdays*, 267–80; Hayes, *The Lincs*, 48–51.

97 War Diary, Lake Superior Regiment, 9–10 September 1944; War Diary, 4th Canadian Armoured Division, 12 September 1944.

98 War Diary, 4th Canadian Armoured Division, 12 September 1944.

99 Cassidy, *Warpath*, 138–51.

100 Lt.-Gen. Erwin Sanders, Interogation Report, LCMSDS.
101 War Diary, 2nd Canadian Infantry Division, 2 September 1944; 'Field Returns.'
102 War Diary, Black Watch, 6 September 1944.
103 Interviews, Maj.-Gen. W.J. Megill, Lt.-Col. D.G. Maclauglan, Maj. Jacques Ostiguy.
104 First Canadian Army Intelligence Summary No. 64, 1 September 1944, LAC RG 24, vol. 13, 646.
105 Schramm, *Die Invasion 1944*, 156.
106 Information from Ultra available to SHAEF and Army Commanders indicated that the Germans were scrambling to fill in three 'gaps' – the Low Countries, Aachen, and the Moselle Valley. Bennett, 134.

2. SIEGE WARFARE: BOULOGNE AND CALAIS

1 Stacey, *The Victory Campaign*, 331–6.
2 Ibid., 329.
3 Bad weather interfered with air operations against the Scheldt crossing points, as did demands for assistance with other battles. The Germans were forced to evacuate by night in clear weather but 'about half the days were used as well.' See 'Interrogation General Schwalbe,' LAC RG 24, vol. 10, 617. The 'War Diary G. Int. H.Q. 1 Can. Army' provides daily summaries of air operations. LAC RG 24, vol. 13, 646.
4 After the war, Simonds claimed that the decision to attack the Channel ports instead of masking them and pushing on to Breskens was made by Crerar. Letter Simonds to Stacey, 10 February 1969, quoted in Graham, *The Price of Command*, 177. In an earlier interview with Stacey, 22 December 1954, Simonds had complained that 'so much attention was paid to the Channel Ports instead of surrounding 15th Army.' LAC RG 24, vol. 20, 415. Either Simonds's memory was at fault or he simply did not know that Montgomery's allocation of resources and specific orders determined which operations were undertaken in September.
5 No. 2 ORS, 'Report No. 16: Air and Ground Support in the Assault on Boulogne,' in Copp, *Montgomery's Scientists*, 120.
6 Interrogation Report, Lieutenant-General Heim, 6 December 1945, LAC RG 24, vol. 10, 617.
7 Simonds to formation commanders, 2nd Canadian Corps, 12 September 1944, LAC RG 24, vol. 10, 799. The three armoured assault columns consisted of one troop of Crabs (mine clearing), two troops of Crocodiles (flame), a half-troop of AVREs, and a troop of tanks as well as Kangaroos.

The outline plan divided the operation into four phases, but once the attack was underway, considerable improvisation was required.

8 The artillery plan is outlined in Captain J.W. Monahan, RCA, Canadian Military Headquarters, Historical Section, 'Report No 184: Canadian Participation in North-West Europe, 1944. Part V: Clearing the Channel Ports,' DHH. This summary is based on the War Diary, HQ RCA 3rd Division, and the report prepared by Captain J.R. Martin, *Operation 'Wellhit,'* LAC RG 24, vol. 10, 907.

9 War Diary, 2nd Canadian Corps, 15 September 1944.

10 R.F. Delderfield, 'Confidential Report on the Recent Bombing of Le Havre,' PRO Air 20/5040. The report noted that while British civil affairs officers and French officials spoke of the destruction of entire residential areas and at least 5,000 casualties, the officer commanding 154th Brigade claimed that 'the total was not more than 2,000' and that the bombing saved 'a great number of casualties among combat troops.'

11 Stacey, *Victory,* 339.

12 Copp, *Montgomery's Scientists,* 107–111.

13 Monahan, 'Report No 184,' 40.

14 These issues are outlined in the Crerar Papers, vol. 3.

15 War Diary of J.R. Martin, Historical Officer, 3rd Canadian Infantry Division, 3 September 1944, LAC RG 24, vol. 17, 506; Interview Colonel E. Côte, October 2004.

16 Ibid. See also Major R.B. Little, 'The Evacuation of Boulogne,' Appendix , War Diary, 2nd Canadian Field Historical Section.

17 War Diary, 3rd Canadian Infantry Division, 16 September 1944.

18 Attachment to letter, Hobart to Crerar, 20 September 1944, Crerar Papers, vol. 6.

19 Bird, *The North Shore (New Brunswick) Regiment,* 408.

20 Ibid., 409–12. Major Corbett's account of the attack on the Pas de Gay as well as other first-person accounts are quoted at length.

21 The quotations in this paragraph are from the War Diary, North Shore (New Brunswick) Regiment, 17–18 September 1944.

22 Anderson, 'Account of Operations in the Boulogne Area,' 84–7.

23 Castonquay and Ross, *Le Régiment de la Chaudière,* 289–90.

24 Ibid., 290. Corporal R. Richards received the Distinguished Conduct Medal for this action, and Private J.P.E. Ouellet the Military Medal.

25 The column has an internal stairway and an observation platform. Napoleon is depicted gazing towards England. On a clear day the viewer can see the White Cliffs of Dover and all the Boulonais countryside.

26 Copp, *Montgomery's Scientists,* 130. The Operational Research Section

examined the battery after the battle and concluded that although one 88 mm gun was put out of action by near misses from medium bombers, the other three remained in action.

27 Castonguay and Ross, *Le Régiment*, 291. The Queen's Own Rifles joined in the final attack.

28 Barnard, *Queen's Own Rifles*, 225.

29 War Diary, Queen's Own Rifles, 17 September 1944.

30 Copp, *Montgomery's Scientists*, 128.

31 Monahan, 'Report No 184,' 58.

32 War Diary, Queen's Own Rifles, 21 September 1944.

33 Copp, *Montgomery's Scientists*, 112.

34 For a full description of the battlefield as it appears today see Copp and Bechthold, *The Canadian Battlefields*, 2005.

35 Bird, *No Retreating Footsteps*, 219.

36 Ibid., 220.

37 Rowley, 'The Attack on Boulogne,' 76–83.

38 War Diary, 9th Canadian Infantry Brigade, 17 September 1944.

39 Rowley, 79.

40 Copp, *Montgomery's Scientists*, 129.

41 Monahan, 'Report No 184,' 53.

42 War Diary, 18th Canadian Field Company, September 1944, in ibid., 53–4.

43 Highland Light Infantry of Canada Association, *The Highland Infantry of Canada*, 58–9.

44 Monahan, 'Report No 184,' 57.

45 Montgomery M.216 Personal for CIGS from Commander-in-Chief, 19 September 1944, BLMP.

46 Ibid.; 'Once we have captured the bridge at Nijmegen the advance will proceed to Arnhem and Apeldoorn.'

47 Rowley, 81.

48 Monahan, 'Report No 184,' 65.

49 Operation Wellhit Administrative Order, War Diary, 8th Canadian Infantry Brigade, September 1944; War Diary, 2nd Canadian Field Historical Section, September 1944.

50 Ian Galbraith, 'Operation Wellhit: The Capture of Boulogne,' *After the Battle* 86 (1944): 19–22.

51 Stacey, *Victory*, 345.

52 'Counter Battery Ops Before Calais,' Appendix 1, War Diary, HQ Royal Canadian Artillery, First Canadian Army, LAC RG 24, vol. 14, 306.

53 War Diary, Regina Rifles, 10 September 1944. The Reginas reported that civilians were still in the village that the Germans had just left. Shops and businesses were open, and the seaside resort was undamaged. 'Out to sea

the white cliffs of Dover could be plainly seen, making more than one lad a trifle homesick for our mother country and a step closer to home.'

54 Monahan, 'Report No 184,' 73.

55 Operational Order No. 2, 7th Canadian Infantry Brigade, 23 September 1944, War Diary, 7th Canadian Infantry Brigade.

56 Bond, 'The Fog of War,' 41–58.

57 USAAF, Evaluation Board, *Study of the Effects of the Air Effort in the Capture of Calais*, June 1945. This detailed 170–page study examines all aspects of the battle to provide a context for the analysis of the air effort. LCMSDS Archives.

58 Castonguay and Ross, *Le Régiment*, 295–6. 8th Brigade Operational Instruction, 23 September 1944, War Diary, 8th Canadian Infantry Brigade.

59 Bird, *The North Shore*, 430–2. The day was later marred by the loss of three officers and their driver, killed when a mine exploded under their jeep.

60 War Diary, Regina Rifles, September 1944.

61 War Diary, 7th Canadian Infantry Brigade, 25 September 1944.

62 Mathews, 'Assault on Calais,' 88–95.

63 War Diary, Regina Rifles, 29 September 1944.

64 War Diary, 3rd Canadian Infantry Division, 30 September 1944.

65 Monahan, 'Report No 184,' 88.

66 Mathews, 'Assault on Calais,' 95.

67 Lieutenant-Colonel D.F. Forbes, 'Actions against the Defences of Cap Gris Nez,' DHH.

68 Stacey, *Victory*, 306.

69 Essame, *The Battle for German*, 29.

70 Ellis, *The Victory Campaign*, 60.

71 Douglas and Greenhous, *Out of the Shadows*, 20.

72 Hamilton, *Monty*, 513.

73 Crerar to Stacey, 10 March 1959, Crerar Papers, vol. 3, LAC MG 30, E157.

3. THE BRESKENS POCKET

1 Main HQ First Canadian Army, Operation Infatuate: An Appreciation, 19 September 1944, LAC RG 24, vol. 10, 799. Brigadier George Pangman described the planning process in a series of interviews conducted in 1987–8. Transcript LCMSDS Archives.

2 G.G. Simonds to GOC-in-C First Canadian Army, 21 Sept 1944, LAC RG 24, vol. 10, 799. Stacey, *Victory*, 370–1.

3 Stacey, *Victory*, 371. Love and Major, *Ramsay Diary*, 141. Brigadier C.C. Mann, Operation Infatuate. Notes of Conference 21 September, War Diary, First Canadian Army, 21 September 1944.

4 Crerar made this decision on 22 September 1944, LAC RG 24, vol. 10, 799.

5 Stacey, *Victory*, 375.

6 Operation Switchback, Draft Outline Plan, 30 September 1944, LAC RG 24, vol. 10, 809.

7 There is some controversy over when Simonds was first cleared for ULTRA. This certainly took place on or shortly after 26 September 1944, when he assumed command of First Canadian Army.

8 The 'List of Recipients Ultra' dated March 1945 includes Crerar, Simonds, Brigadier C.C. Mann (Chief of Staff), Brigadier G.E. Beament (Brigadier, General Staff), and Lieutenant-Colonel Peter Wright (GSO I Intelligence), as well as four other senior staff officers. Richard Collins Papers, Archives USAMHI. I wish to thank David Keogh, USAMHI archivist, for bringing this document to my attention.

9 Hinsley, *British Intelligence*, 378–80.

10 Bennett, *Ultra in the West*, 148.

11 Cassidy, *Warpath*, 159–61.

12 Hayes, *The Lincs*, 378–80.

13 2nd Canadian Corps Intelligence Summary, 24 September 1944.

14 Interrogation Report, General Gustav von Zangen, LAC RG 24, vol. 10, 617.

15 7th Canadian Infantry Brigade Operational Order No. 3, Operation Switchback, 5 October 1944; 7th Canadian Infantry Brigade Battlelog October 1944, War Diary, 7th Canadian Infantry Brigade, October 1944.

16 3rd Canadian Infantry Division, Operation Switchback, War Diary, 3rd Canadian Infantry Division, October 1944.

17 Defense Overprint 1:25000 map dated 6 October 1944, LCMSDS Map Collection. A section of this map is reproduced in Copp and Vogel, *Maple Leaf Route: Scheldt*, 84.

18 3rd Canadian Infantry Division, Operation Switchback.

19 Royal Canadian Artillery Branch, Main First Canadian Army to HQ Royal Artillery, 21 Army Group, 5 October 1944, War Diary HQ Royal Canadian Artillery, First Canadian Army.

20 II Canadian Met. Section, Interim Report of a New Procedure for Obtaining More Accurate Meteor Winds using, G.L.3 Apparatus, 15 October 1944, ibid. See also No. 2 ORS Report No. 21, 'Use of G.L.3 in Forecasting Wind for Artillery Meteor'; in Copp, *Montgomery's Scientists*, 325–30.

21 Report No. 24, 'Accuracy of Predicted Shooting,' in Copp, *Montgomery's Scientists*, 311–22.

22 War Diary, HQ Royal Canadian Artillery, First Canadian Army, Appendix I, 44–5. Sound ranging also played an important role in counter-battery, using well-practised techniques, Ibid., 46–47.

23 Interview with Michael Swann, 1990. Lord Swann recalled discussions with Brigadier H.O.N. Brownfield at First Canadian Army Headquarters

after the OR section prepared the report on the 'Accuracy of Predicted Shooting' in Switchback.

24 Brigadier P.A.S. Todd, 'Artillery in Operation Switchback.' Account given to Historical Officer, 9 December 1944, DHH. Reproduced in Appendix D.

25 Ibid. Copp, 'Counter Mortar Operational Research.'

26 War Diary, HQ Royal Canadian Artillery, First Canadian Army, Appendix I, 59.

27 Ellis, *The Victory Campaign*, 390.

28 Letter, Coningham to Breen (Air Ministry), 30 August 1944, PRO Air 37/2.

29 Brown was replaced by Air Vice-Marshal E.C. Hudelston on 10 November 1944. See Air Marshal Sutton to Coningham, 1 November 1944, Ibid.

30 HQ 3rd Canadian Infantry Division, 'Air Support in Operation "Switchback,"' 20 November 1944, LAC RG 24, vol. 10, 672; Bechthold, 'Air Support in the Breskens Pocket.'

31 Combined Operations Headquarters, (COHQ) Bulletin Y/43, Amphibians in Operation Switchback, November 1944, LAC RG 24, vol. 10, 651.

32 Cassidy, *Warpath*, 162–3.

33 Whitaker, *Tug of War*, 272.

34 R.C. Featherstonhaugh, *The Royal Montreal Regiment, 1925–1945* (Westmount: Privately printed, 1949), 183; War Diary, Royal Montreal Regiment, 6 October 1944.

35 Lieutenant George Bannerman, 'Some Aspects of the Technique of Flame Throwing,' 26 November 1944. Canadian Operations in North-West Europe – June–November 1944. Extracts From War Diaries and Memoranda LAC RG 24, vol. 10, 817.

36 War Diary, Regina Rifles, 6 October 1944.

37 The platoon was cut off and the survivors captured. Featherstonhaugh, 188–9.

38 War Diary, Royal Montreal Regiment, 6 October 1944.

39 Battle log, 7th Canadian Infantry Brigade, 6 October 1944. I am grateful to Jeff Nilsson, who provided me with a copy of the 7th Brigade battle log, which he used in his MA thesis, 'Keystone to Victory.'

40 War Diary, Royal Montreal Regiment, 6 October 1944.

41 Battle log, 7th Canadian Infantry Brigade, 6 October 1944.

42 War Diary, Canadian Scottish Regiment, 6 October 1944.

43 For an account of the capture, imprisonment, and escape of Captain Roger Schjelderup, who commanded 'C' Company, see Fowler, 'Roger Schjelderup.'

44 War Diary, Canadian Scottish Regiment, 7 October 1944.

45 The squadron was withdrawn after it became evident that the 'beachhead was much too small for the number of troops already there.' War Diary,

7th Recce Regiment, 8 October 1944.

46 War Diary, Royal Winnipeg Rifles, 7 October 1944.

47 Battle log, 7th Canadian Infantry Brigade, 7 October 1944.

48 Ibid.

49 War Diary, 3rd Canadian Infantry Division, 7 October 1944.

50 Not all German soldiers were committed to the cause. The Canscots reported the surrender of a mortar crew, who stated that their officers 'are keeping them going with pistols' and that they had been notified that if they surrendered their families 'would be taken into custody by the Gestapo.' 7th Canadian Infantry Brigade, Battle log, 7 October 1944.

51 OB West Intelligence Report , 7 October 1944, AHQ Report No. 69, 66.

52 7th Canadian Infantry Brigade, Battlelog, 8 October 1944. Skeena was the responsibility of three medium regiments of 9th British AGRA continuously for four minutes. Task Table War Diary, Royal Winnipeg Rifles, 5 October 1944.

53 2nd Canadian Corps Intelligence Summary, 9 October 1944; 3rd Canadian Infantry Division Intelligence Summary, 11 October 1944.

54 Army Group B Daily Situation Reports, 9 October 1944, AHQ Report No. 69, 64.

55 War Diary, Royal Winnipeg Rifles, 12 October 1944.

56 'Charlie Coy Activities,' War Diary, Canadian Scottish Regiment, October 1944.

57 'Report on C Coy. Oct. 12 44,' ibid.

58 2nd Canadian Corps Intelligence Summary, 11 October 1944.

59 Gray, 'The Leopold Ordeal.'

60 War Diary, Canadian Scottish Regiment, 9 October 1944.

61 Stacey, *Victory*, 395.

62 'Incidence of Rates of Exhaustion/Infantry NP ratios Oct. 1944,' LAC RG 24, vol. 15, 647. Dr Robert Gregory, 'Psychiatric Report October 1944.' Dr Gregory's report is reproduced as Appendix E.

63 Major H.D. Knox, an RWR company commander, described Lieutenant-Colonel Meldram's growing nervous reactions in a 1984 interview, Guelph, 1984.

64 Major Gordon Brown was recovering from a wound when he met Matheson in England. Brown was reluctant to be quoted on his conversation with Matheson but agreed that this statement was factually correct. Gordon Brown Interview, Red Deer, Alberta, 1997.

65 A.L. Gollnich, 'The Bridgehead over the Leopold Canal,' 13 November 1944, 4 pages, DHH.

66 Interrogation Report, Major-General Knut Eberding, War Diary, 3rd Canadian Infantry Division, October 1944.

67 COHQ Bulletin Y/43, 1–2.
68 First Canadian Army, Operation Infatuate, 19 September 1944.
69 79th Armoured Division, Notes for Commanders on LVTs and Terrapins, 14 October 1944, LAC RG 24, vol. 10, 895.
70 W.R. Sawyer, Report on Smoke Screens Carried Out by First Canadian Army, 15 July 1945, LCMSDS Archives, 7. See also Bond, 'The Fog of War.'
71 Turrey, 'Supply Problems in Amphibious Operations.' See 3rd Canadian Infantry Division R.C.A.S.C., *War History*, LAC RG 24, vol. 10, 914, for a full account of RCASC activities August to October 1944.
72 COHQ Bulletin Y/43, 3.
73 Two Dutch historians have suggested that the Germans did recognize the imminent danger of an amphibious landing on 8 October and that they requested artillery support only to be told that Terneuzen was out of range. 'That day Eberding and Aschmann [the naval commander] conferred in Oostburg on the possibility of an attack from the east ... Eberding suspected that such an attack was to be expected in the next few days.' No specific source is cited for this information. Eberding made no reference to such suspicions in his interrogation, and there is no indication that he took any action to alert the defences. Sakkers and Houterman, *Atlantickwall in Zeeland*, 232. English translation by Ralph Dykstra.
74 CMHQ Report No. 188, 96–7.
75 Bird, *No Retreating Footsteps*, 247.
76 War Diary, Highland Light Infantry, 9 October 1944.
77 Major R.G. Hodgins, 'Dyke Warfare,' 26 October 1944, DHH.
78 Sawyer, Report on Smoke Screens, 8–9.
79 The German military distinguished between resistance nests (Widerstandsnester) and larger strongpoints (Stutzpunkte), but the strength of each varied depending on circumstances. Normally a strongpoint included an artillery battery and more extensive fortifications. WN Hoofdplaat included a number of bunkers and fortified houses, but the largest gun was a 20 mm anti-aircraft battery. Sakkers, map enclosed in book.
80 This account is based on Boss and Patterson, *Up the Glens*, 127–9, and War Diary, Stormont, Dundas, and Glengarry Higlanders, 9–12 October 1944.
81 Bird, *North Novas*, 252–6. War Diary, North Nova Scotia Highlanders, 10–12 October 1944.
82 Turrey, 75–8. See 3rd Canadian Infantry Division RCASC, *War History*, LAC RG 24, vol. 10, 914.
83 Sawyer, Report on Smoke Screens, 9–10.
84 War Diary, 7th Recce Regiment, 10 October 1944.
85 Hodgins, 'Dyke WarFare,' 2.

86 84 Group flew 636 sorties, the majority against enemy positions and troop movements in the Breskens Pocket; Bechthold, 'Air Support,' 61.
87 War Diary, 7th Recce Regiment, 12 October 1944.
88 Ibid. Brigadier K.C. Blackader had been relieved of command and sent to England for medical reasons.
89 Eberding interrogation.
90 War Diary, North Shore (New Brunswick) Regiment, 13 October 1944, War Diary, Queen's Own Rifles, 14 October 1944.
91 Cassidy, 104; War Diary, Argyll and Sutherland Highlanders, 15 October 1944; War Diary, 3rd Canadian Infantry Division, 16 October 1944.
92 Document dated 14 October 1944 and signed Eberding. Copies are to be found in several Canadian War Diaries, including that of 9th Brigade.
93 Boss and Patterson, *Up the Glens*, 130.
94 Situation Report OB West, 15 October 1944.
95 War Diary, OB West, 15 October 1944.
96 War Diary, Canadian Scottish Regiment, 16 October 1944, Message log, 3rd Canadian Infantry Division, 15 October 1944.
97 The division was suited for this role because one of its artillery field regiments was equipped with light, air-transportable artillery. The 157th Brigade was supported by a conventional 25–pounder field regiment. Blake, *Mountain and Flood*, 65.
98 Blake does not mention this deployment. Major Kevin Connor, who recently served as second-in-command of 52nd Lowland Regiment and who is writing a new history of the division, has provided me with archival material on the period as well as other assistance.
99 War Diary, Assistant Director Medical Services, 3rd Canadian Infantry Division, 'Casualties Evacuated,' October 1944.
100 Sakkers, 'Einsatzkarte 712 ID,' map pocket.
101 A memorial erected at the farm where the incident took place lists the names of the thirty-one British and ten Canadians who died in the explosion. The Canadians were from 7th Infantry Brigade Company, Royal Canadian Army Service Corps. Copp and Bechthold, *The Canadian Battlefields in Northwest Europe*, 66.
102 War Diary, 9th Canadian Infantry Brigade, 20 October 1944.
103 In Whitaker and Whitaker, *Tug of War*, 303.
104 Bird, *No Retreating Footsteps*, 251.
105 War Diary, Historical Officer, 3rd Canadian Infantry Division, 24 October 1944.
106 War Diary, 157th Brigade, October 1944; PRO WO 171/687.
107 Eberding interrogation.

108 Air photos of this and all other sectors of the Breskens Pocket are available at the Laurier Centre for Military Strategic and Disarmament Studies (LCMSDS) archives at Wilfrid Laurier University in Waterloo, Ontario.

109 Castonguay and Ross, *Le Régiment*, 310.

110 Barnard, *The Queen's Own Rifles*, 135.

111 Martin, *Battle Diary*, 89.

112 Message log, 7th Canadian Infantry Brigade, 25 October 1944. On 28 October, enemy shelling of Groede from Flushing resulted in a stream of refugees, and evidence of further military activity forced Spry to cancel 'open town' status. 7th Brigade occupied the village on 27 October, and the remaining civilians were evacuated. Ibid., 28 October 1944.

113 Ibid., 25 October 1944.

114 War Diary, Canadian Scottish Regiment, 27 October 1944.

115 War Diary, North Shore (New Brunswick) Regiment, 27 October 1944.

116 2nd Canadian Corps Intelligence Summary No. 73, 27 October 1944; CMHQ Report No. 69, 74.

117 Ibid., No. 75, 29 October 1944.

118 J.R. Martin, Battle Narrative: Operation Switchback, Report No 184, Historical Section, CMH, 14; War Diary, 3rd Canadian Infantry Division, November, 1944.

119 Sakkers and Houterman, *Atlantikwall*, 27.

120 Sappers from the Royal Canadian Engineers under the command of Sergeant J.L. Hickman constructed a Bailey bridge across the canal under heavy shellfire. Hickman was mortally wounded. A plaque placed at the bridge site tells the story, and adds: 'In tribute to him and his comrades this bridge was dedicated in his name on 30 October 1989. This simple monument was adopted by the children of the local school.'

121 The 'defense overprint' on the 1:25,000 map of the area locates scores of artillery and infantry positions sited to control the roads rising above the flooded terrain. LCMSDS Map Collection.

122 CMHQ Report No. 188, p. 114.

123 The full text of Dr Gregory's report is reproduced in Appendix E.

124 The phrase is from the War Diary of the Canadian Scottish Regiment, 2 November 1944.

4. NORTH FROM ANTWERP

1 M525, 14 September 1944, BLMP. The main points of the directive relating to First Canadian Army are in Stacey, *Victory*, 359.

2 Goodspeed, *Battle Royal*, 488.

3 Lieutenant-Colonel Bruce Macdonald was relieved of his command at the request of Brigadier H. Young after Operation Atlantic. Essex Scottish officers and men signed a petition affirming their confidence in Macdonald, but Foulkes and Simonds confirmed the dismissal. Maker, *Battalion Leadership in the Essex Scottish*, 92–104. Information on Lieutenant-Colonel Pangman is from interviews with Brigadiers Denis Whitaker and George Pangman. See also Major Mackenzie, 'The Essex Scottish in the Antwerp Area,' Historical Officer Interview, 29 September 1944, and Whitaker and Whitaker, *Tug of War*, ch. 2.

4 Between 12 October 1944 and 30 March 1945, 5,960 rockets fell in the Antwerp area, killing 731 military and 3,515 civilians. 21 Army Group, *Report on Operations June 1945*, LAC RG 24, vol. 10, 536.

5 Messages, 2nd Canadian Corps, 21 September 1944, LAC RG 24, vol. 10, 799.

6 Crerar to Commanders 1st British Corps, 2nd Canadian Corps, 19 September 1944, LAC RG 24, vol. 10, 799.

7 This plan was formalized in Montgomery's directive of 27 September, but 1st British Corps was ordered to begin an advance to Tillburg on 24 September. Stacey, *Victory*, 397.

8 The quotations are from Montgomery's nightly message 'Personal for the CIGS from CinC,' M212, 17 September, M213, 18 September, M216, 19 September, M218, 20 September, M219, and 21 September, BLMP.

9 Minutes, SHAEF Special Meeting, 22 September 1944, BLMP 108/47.

10 Operational Report, Polish Armoured Division, 32; Crerar to Simonds, 24 September 1944, Hinsley, *British Intelligence*, 897.

11 21 Army Group Intelligence Summary, 24 September 1944; Hinsley, *British Intelligence*, 897.

12 M233, 24 September 1944, BLMP.

13 Eisenhower for Bradley and Montgomery, 23 September 1944, BLMP 108/51.

14 Stacey, *Victory*, 379.

15 OCMH MS B798, Battles of 67th Corps, Between the Scheldt and the Maas, 15 September–25 November 1944.

16 War Diary, Calgary Highlanders, 22 September 1944.

17 Interviews, Copp with Megill, MacLaughlan, and Heyland, 1991.

18 War Diary, 5th Canadian Infantry Brigade, 20 September 1944.

19 Ibid., 21 September 1944.

20 Letter, Mitchell to Hutchison, 26 September 1944. Black Watch Archives, Montreal.

21 Megill interview, July 1988.

22 This account is based on Harold's account of the night's events included in the file recommending Crockett for a Victoria Cross. War Diary, Calgary Highlanders, September 1944. The full text of the account is in Copp, *The Brigade*, 127–8. Crockett's own recollections are quoted in Bercuson, *Battalion of Heroes*, 147. Crockett was awarded the Distinguished Conduct Medal (DCM) because 'the importance of the occasion did not warrant a VC'; Bercuson, 151.

23 War Diary, Fusiliers Mont-Royal, 24 September 1944; War Diary, South Saskatchewan Regiment, 24 September 1944.

24 The 'sanitarium' was the regional Depot of Mendicite, 'a combined prison, workhouse and lunatic asylum.' It was later captured by the Hallamshire Regiment. Delaforce, *The Polar Bears*, 158.

25 Van Doorn, *Slag om Woensdrecht*, 24 (English translation by Ralph Dykstra).

26 War Diary, South Saskatchewan Regiment, 24 September 1944.

27 Obituary, R.H. Keefler, DHH.

28 Megill interview.

29 Delaforce, *The Polar Bears*, 155.

30 Morton, *Vanguard*, 75–7.

31 War Diary, Black Watch, 28 September 1944.

32 Interview with Charles Gordon Bourne, *St. Lambert Hometown News*, March 1945, Black Watch Archives, Personnel Files, C.G. Bourne.

33 War Diary, Régiment de Maisoneuve, 30 September 1944.

34 War Diary, Calgary Highlanders, 1 October 1944.

35 War Diary, Black Watch, 1 October 1944.

36 Ibid.

37 Letter, Ritchie to Hutchinson, 7 October 1944, Black Watch Archives. See the Black Watch Letters and Images Project, www.blackwatchcanada.com, for other letters from Black Watch officers.

38 War Diary, 2nd Canadian Armoured Brigade, 1 October 1944.

39 Rushford, 'Attack on an Enemy Strongpoint,' 147–8.

40 Interrogation report, General Erich Diestel, DHH.

41 OCMH MS B798,17.

42 War Diary, 4th Canadian Infantry Brigade, 2 October 1944.

43 Stacey, *Victory*, 380.

44 Operational Report, Polish Armoured Division, 33.

45 War Diary, Sherbrooke Fusiliers, October 1944.

46 Intelligence Summary, 2nd Canadian Infantry Division, 3 October 1944.

47 Ibid., 6 October 1944.

48 2nd Canadian Corps Intelligence Summary, 7 October 1944.

49 The text of the document is reproduced in Copp and Vogel, *Maple Leaf Route: Scheldt*, 27. The original and translation is in War Diary, Toronto Scottish Regiment, October 1944.

50 Interrogation Report, Lieutenant-General Erich Diestel. The text of the report is reproduced in Copp and Vogel, *Scheldt*, 28.

51 M265 Personal for CIGS from CinC, 7 October 1944, BLMP.

52 War Diary, Fusiliers Mont-Royal, 8–10 October 1944.

53 War Diary, Calgary Highlanders, 7 October 1944.

54 War Diary, Régiment de Maisoneuve, 7 October 1944.

55 Honour and Awards File, Régiment de Maisonneuve DHH. See also Forbes, *Fantasin*, 166–8.

56 War Diary, Black Watch, 8 October 1944; War Diary, Fort Garry Horse, 8 October 1944.

57 First Canadian Army Intelligence Summary, 7 October 1944.

58 War Diary, Calgary Highlanders, 9 October 1944.

59 Ibid., 11 October 1944.

60 Von der Heydte, *Muss ich sterben*, 184 (translation by R. Vogel).

61 Copp, *The Brigade*, 144.

62 War Diary, 5th Canadian Infantry Brigade, 10 October 1944.

63 War Diary, Royal Regiment of Canada, 10 October 1944; Goodspeed, *Battle Royal*, 500.

64 Goodspeed, *Battle Royal*, 501.

65 War Diary, 5th Canadian Infantry Brigade, 1 October 1944.

66 Megill interview.

67 The original documents are reproduced in Chandler, *Eisenhower Papers*, 2215 ff., and in the Montgomery Papers. The issue is discussed in Stacey, *Victory*, 387–8.

68 War Diary, 2nd Canadian Infantry Division, 9 October 1944.

69 This paragraph is based on the War Diaries of the division, brigade, battalion, and regiment for 13 October 1944.

70 Stacey, *Victory*, 384.

71 2nd Canadian Infantry Division, Message log, 13 October 1944.

72 War Diary, Black Watch, 13 October 1944.

73 2nd Canadian Infantry Division, Message log, 13 October 1944.

74 War Diary, Black Watch, 13 October 1944.

75 Letter, Lieutenant A.V.L. Mills to Colonel A.V.L. Mills, 22 October 1944, Black Watch Archives.

76 Lieutenant W.C. Shea, 'The Action at Woensdrecht 8–14 October 44,' DHH.

77 The records of the fifty-one Black Watch soldiers killed in action on 13

October show that the average length of service in the army was two years. Only fourteen had been transferred from another corps to the infantry in 1944, and all of these had been through the standard conversion course. Personnel files obtained from National Personnel Record Centre, Library and Archives Canada, Ottawa. I thank Dr Christine Hamelin for her work on this project.

78 War Diary, Royal Hamilton Light Infantry, 15 October 1944.
79 This account is based on the Royal Hamilton Light Infantry War Diary, Denis Whitaker's recollections of the battle recounted in Whitaker and Whitaker, *Tug of War*, 180–4, and 'The Capture of Woensdrecht: Accounts by an Officer of the RHLI,' Historical Officer interview, 22 October 1944, DHH.
80 War Diary, 5th Canadian Infantry Brigade, 16 October 1944.

5. WALCHEREN

1 Love and Major, *Ramsay Diary*, 143.
2 Danchev and Tedman, *War Diaries*, 600.
3 Brooke attended the Second Quebec Conference, leaving England on 5 September and arriving in Canada on 11 September. The conference ended on 15 September, and the next day, Field Marshal Sir Alan Brooke with Air Marshal Sir Peter Portal, Admiral Sir John Coningham, and the Canadian Chief of the Air Staff, Air Marshal Robert Lackie, travelled in two amphibian aircraft 'northwest from Quebec towards Hudson Bay' to a fishing camp at Oriskany Lake. Ibid., 595. Several readers of the original manuscript of *Cinderella Army* suggested that this 'cheap shot' directed at Brooke be removed. My own view is that Brooke's willingness to encourage Montgomery's campaign to undermine Eisenhower is just one of the many reasons to re-evaluate Brooke's reputation.
4 B.L. Montgomery, 'Notes on the Situation 7 October,' BLMP.
5 Bland, *The Papers of George Catlett Marshall*, 624; hereafter *Marshall Papers*.
6 Viscount Montgomery, *Memoirs of Field Marshal the Viscount Montgomery of Alamein* (London: Collins, 1958), 345.
7 *Marshall Papers*, 624. Montgomery's biographer, Nigel Hamilton, describes Marshall as 'not impressed by Monty's assessment of the situation or Monty's solution or Monty.' Hamilton, *Monty*, 108.
8 Montgomery, 'General Operational Situation and Directive 9 October 1944,' M530, BLMP.
9 Chandler, *Eisenhower Papers*, 2215.
10 M268, 9 October 1944, BLMP.

11 Chandler, *Eisenhower Papers*, 2215.
12 Ibid., 2216.
13 War Diary, 5th Canadian Infantry Brigade, 9 October 1944.
14 M269, 9 October 1944, BLMP. 8 Corps advance began on 12 October.
15 M276, 15 October 1944, BLMP.
16 Montgomery's letter is reproduced in Ellis, *Victory in the West*, 85–8.
17 Ibid., 89–91. Chandler, *Eisenhower Papers*, 2221–4.
18 M226, 15 October 1944, BLMP.
19 M281, 16 October 1944, BLMP.
20 M532, 16 October 1944, BLMP. The directive is in Stacey, *Victory*, 635.
21 Stacey, *Victory*, 390.
22 Ellis, *Victory in the West*, 158–9.
23 Montgomery's message, M294, 21 October, and Ramsay's reply, 23 October, are in BLMP.
24 The evolution of plans for Infatuate and Vitality are outlined in CMHQ, Report No. 188. See also War Diary, 2nd Canadian Corps, October 1944, 'Notes on a Meeting at Bde HQ,' 4th Special Service Brigade, 20.
25 Main First Canadian Army to First Allied Airborne Army, 21 October 1944. War Diary, First Canadian Army, October 1944.
26 2nd Canadian Corps Intelligence Summary, No. 21, 21 October 1944.
27 'Operational Order,' 4th Canadian Armoured Division, 19 October 1944, War Diary, 4th Canadian Armoured Division, October 1944.
28 CMHQ Report No. 188, 90–1.
29 Cassidy, *Warpath*, 178–9.
30 CMHQ Report No. 77, 53.
31 Ibid., 50–3.
32 Delaforce, *The Polar Bears*, 165–6.
33 CMHQ Report No. 77, 53. War Diary, Lake Superior Regiment, 23 October 1944.
34 CMHQ Report No. 77, 55.
35 G. Hayes, 'Where Are Our Liberators?'
36 War Diary, 4th Canadian Armoured Division, 25 October 1944; Hoegh and Doyle, *Timberwolf Tracks*, 61.
37 On 28 October Dempsey ordered 15th Scottish Division and 6th Guards Tank Brigade to the east. Two days later 53rd Division was also withdrawn, leaving 12th Corps with just two divisions to compress the pocket of enemy troops, who subsequently retired to the north bank of the river. Ellis, *Victory in the West*, 193.
38 Despite heavy losses in the infantry battalions, the five German divisions, 85th, 245th, 711th, 719th, and 346th, retired across the Maas with much of their artillery and support cadres intact.

39 Von der Heydte, *Muss ich sterben*, 3.

40 Patterson, *History of the 10th*, 47.

41 Cassidy, in *Warpath*, 187–251, offers a full account of the battles for Welberg.

42 Patterson, *History of the 10th*, 48.

43 'Special Interrogation Report Lieutenant-General Wilhelm Daser Commander 70 Infantry Division,' 9, DHH.

44 Hechler, 'German Defence of the Gateway to Antwerp,' 23. Rundstedt even specified how Daser was to employ his six battalions. DHH.

45 On 24 October Hitler informed senior officers of OB West that twenty Infantry and ten Panzer Divisions, with artillery and mortar brigades, would be committed to the Western Front by the end of November or early December, but these forces were intended for offensive action designed to split the Allied armies and regain Antwerp. Seigfried Westphal, *The German Army in the West*, 178, cited in CMHQ Report No. 77, 46.

46 War Diary, Calgary Highlanders, 22 October 1944.

47 War Diary, 6th Canadian Infantry Brigade, 23–4 October 1944; War Diary, Calgary Highlanders, 23–4 October 1944.

48 War Diary, Essex Scottish, 24 October 1944; War Diary, 2nd Canadian Field Historical Section, 26 October 1944.

49 CMHQ Report No. 77, 77–8.

50 Lieutenant-Colonel E.M. Wilson, 'The Employment of Tanks in Support of Infantry: Lessons Learned on Zuid Beveland,' 1 November 1944, Historical Officer interview, DHH, 1. The full report is reproduced as Appendix G.

51 Ibid.,1.

52 Corps Intelligence Officers dismissed the 89th Fortress Battalion as made up of 'old gentlemen and low medical category personnel,' but they would still harass the British troops with machine gun and mortar fire and even mount counter-attacks. 2 Canadian Corps Intelligence Summary, 27 October 1944; War Diary, 156 Brigade, 27–8 October 1944; War Diary, 415th Royal Scots Fusiliers, 27 October 1944, WO 171/1363.

53 Goodspeed, *Battle Royal*, 509.

54 Hesketh, *Fortitude*, 154–7.

55 Hakewill-Smith letters of 4 June and 15 June 1944; Hakewill-Smith Papers, British Army Museum.

56 J.S. Evetts to Hakewill-Smith, 24 June 1944, ibid. Evetts was the responsible staff officer of the War Office.

57 Letters, Lieutenant-Colonel J. Hanky to Hakewill-Smith, 18–19 October 1944, ibid.

58 This view was expressed to me by a number of 3rd Division veterans. During their five days in the pocket the brigade reported one casualty, a

man wounded in a shooting accident. War Diary, 52nd Division, October 1944, PRO WO 171/687.

59 My uncle, Douglas Copp, a Signal Corps CSM in 157th Brigade, first expressed this view to me. In 1986 I had the opportunity to meet with a number of officers of 52nd Lowland Division at the Canadian Studies Centre, University of Edinburgh. It was evident that they shared my uncle's view of the Canadians, both positive and negative.

60 2nd Canadian Corps operational orders, 18 and 23 October 1944, LAC RG 24, vol. 13, 713.

61 Stacey, *Victory*, 402.

62 War Diary, 4th Canadian Infantry Brigade, 28 October 1944; War Diary, 52nd Division, October 1944.

63 War Diary, 5th Canadian Infantry Brigade, 29 October 1944.

64 War Diary, 4th Canadian Infantry Brigade, 30 October 1944; War Diary, Royal Regiment of Canada, 30 October 1944.

65 'Message Log,' War Diary, 2nd Canadian Infantry Division, 31 October 1944.

66 War Diary, 5th Canadian Infantry Brigade, 31 October 1944.

67 Megill, interview.

68 Brigadier W.J. Megill, 'The Capture of Zuid Beveland,' 8 October 1944, 2, DHH. Captain T.M. Hunter, the Historical Officer attached to 2nd Division, was also able to obtain accounts of the fighting on South Beveland from the Acting Divisional Commander, Brigadier R.H. Keefler (11 November 1944); from Lieutenant-Colonel S.H. Dobel, Acting Commander Royal Artillery (15 November 1944); and from a number of infantry officers. DHH.

69 Megill interview.

70 War Diary, Black Watch, 31 October 1944.

71 Megill, 'Zuid Beveland,' 2; War Diary, Calgary Highlanders, 31 October 1944.

72 Ibid.

73 Interview with Brigadier Gordon Sellar; letter, Sellar to Copp, 9 December 1991.

74 Ibid.

75 'Message Log,' War Diary, 2nd Canadian Infantry Division, 1 November 1944.

76 Megill, 'Zuid Beveland,' 3.

77 War Diary, 5th Canadian Infantry Brigade, 1 November 1944; War Diary, Calgary Highlanders, 1 November 1944; Bercuson, *Battalion of Heroes*, 181–189.

78 Megill, 'Zuid Beveland,' 3.
79 Colonel Guy de Merlis, 'Notes,' November 1989; LCMSDS Archives. See also de Merlis, 'The Walcheren Causeway Revisited.' Honours and Awards, Régiment de Maisonneuve, LCMSDS Archives.
80 Brigadier L.B.D. Burns, CRA 52nd Division, who was placed in charge of the two Scottish brigades on Beveland, ordered Brigadier Russell (30 October) to relieve all Canadian units on Walcheren but told Russell 'to carry out the necessary recce and prepare a plan to cross the channel between the two islands [sic]' if the Canadians had not crossed the causeway. War Diary, 52 Division, October 1944.
81 Moulton, *Battle for Antwerp*, 216.
82 De Merlis, 'Notes.'
83 Blake, *Mountain and Flood*, 97; War Diary, Glasgow Highlanders, 2–4 November 1944.
84 The Acting Army Commander, General Simonds, and Admiral Ramsay sought the support of Bomber Command to neutralize the Flushing defences as the weather conditions indicated that only heavy bombers using airborne radar (H2S) could be successfully employed. Air Marshal Harris refused, recalling the heavy civilian casualties at Le Havre, and the British Chiefs of Staff supported Harris. Medium and fighter bombers did participate. PRO Air 37/1060.
85 Moulton, *Battle for Antwerp*, 143–90.
86 Ibid., 192–233. The Close Support Squadron lost 172 killed and 125 wounded. Their sacrifice, which produced higher casualties than those suffered by all naval landing flotillas on D-Day, 6 June 1944, allowed the LCAs to reach the gap with few losses. See AORG Report No. 299, *The Westkapelle Assault on Walcheren*, October 1945, LCMSDS Archives.
87 'Report on Combined Operations on Walcheren Island Made from a Viewpoint of 8 Canadian Field Surgical Unit'; LAC RG 24, vol. 15, 647.
88 Stacey, *Victory*, 424.
89 Pugsley's report and Simonds's reply (dated 1 January 1945) are in BLMP.
90 Calculated from Stacey, *Victory*, 424, and Appendix B.

6. REGENERATION

1 The words are from Eisenhower's Directive of 28 October 1944, Chandler, *Eisenhower Papers*, 2257.
2 Ellis, *Victory in the West*, 104.
3 Lieutenant-Colonel J.C. Richardson, 'Neuropsychiatry with the Canadian

Army in Western Europe – 6 June 1944–8 May 1945,' LCMSDS. The complete figures are reproduced in Appendix C.

4 CMHQ Report No. 63, 'Manpower Problems of the Canadian Army in the Second World War,' 383.

5 A figure of eight hundred has been used to represent the average strength of infantry battalions. The actual percentage of infantry casualties was probably closer to 75 per cent. By the end of the first week of November, total fatal casualties since 6 June 1944 were 9,267, with 24,247 wounded, 3,330 treated for battle exhaustion, and 11,670 hospitalized for various illnesses. These figures are calculated from the data reproduced in the Appendix C adjusted for battle exhaustion estimates for the first two weeks of combat in Normandy.

6 'Unit Deficiencies,' Appendix A.

7 War Diary, Régiment de la Chaudière, October 1944.

8 The personnel records of all 5th Brigade officers and ORs killed in action were examined for Copp, *The Brigade*.

9 Stacey, *Arms Men and Government*, 440.

10 Ibid., 440.

11 Ibid., 445.

12 Ibid., 479. NRMA soldiers suffered 313 battle casualties, including 69 dead. The most complete discussion of the NRMA is in Byers, 'Mobilizing Canada.'

13 The Censorship Report for 15–31 October provides further evidence of problems in morale, though the official summary insists that morale was 'extremely high.' Canadian Army Overseas, 'Censorship Report,' 1, LAC RG 24, vol. 10, 784.

14 Major R. Gregory, 'Psychiatric Report, October 1944,' War Diary, Assistant Director Medical Services, 3rd Canadian Infantry Division, LAC RG 24, vol. 15, 661.

15 Major T.E. Dancey, 'Quarterly Report 2nd Canadian Exhaustion Unit 1 October–31 December 1944,' LAC RG 24, Vol. 15, 569.

16 G.G. Simonds, 'Absorption of Reinforcement Personnel,' 25 October 1944, LAC RG 24, vol. 10, 779.

17 Major B.H. McNeel, 'Quarterly Report of NP Specialist, 2nd Canadian Corps, 1 October–31 December 1944,' LAC RG 24, vol. 12, 583.

18 Ibid.

19 Neary and Granatstein, *The Veteran's Charter*, 85.

20 *The Staghound*, October 1944, War Diary, 12th Manitoba Dragoons.

21 War Diary, 2nd Canadian Corps, DA and QMG December 1944.

22 Ibid., January 1945. The Blue Diamond was built by 31st Canadian Field

Company RCE out of 'six old Nissen huts and some green lumber.' It was designed to serve 2,000 customers a day.

23 Personal and Private for CIGS from Field Marshal Montgomery, 17 November 1944, BLMP 119/135.

24 G.W.L. Nicholson, *The Canadians in Italy* (Ottawa, 1960), 606.

25 These words reflect the comments made by Major-General Matthews after a slightly different version, based on a 1987 interview, was published in Copp and Vogel, *Maple Leaf Route: Victory*. Brigadier N.E. Rodger, Simonds's Chief of Staff, noted that the appointment of Matthews was 'long overdue.' N.E. Rodgers, Personal Diary, LAC RG 24, vol. 10, 798.

26 Interview, Major-General Bruce Matthews, 1987.

27 2nd Canadian Infantry Division, 'Special Report No. 1,' 9 December 1944, War Diary, 2nd Canadian Infantry Division, December 1944.

28 Roberts, *The Canadian Summer*, 104.

29 Historical Officer, 3rd Canadian Infantry Division, 'Notes on Dyke and Polder Fighting – 3rd Canadian Division Study Period.' See Appendix F.

30 LAC, RG 24, Crerar Papers, vol. 3.

31 Vokes, *Vokes*, 189.

32 Fraser, *Black Yesterdays*, 346.

33 HQ I Corps, 'Operation Elephant,' 14 January 1945, LAC RG 24, vol. 10, 943.

34 HQ 10th Canadian Infantry Brigade, 'Op Elephant "Outline Plan,"' 19 January 1945. Ibid.

35 Stacey, *Victory*, 454.

36 'Lessons, Operation Elephant,' 10 February 1945; see also I Corps HQ, 'Lessons from Operation Elephant,' 1 February 1945, LAC RG 24, vol. 10, 943. See Hayes, *The Lincs*, 77–95, for the most detailed account of the action and its aftermath.

37 Montgomery's letter is reproduced in Ellis, *Victory*, 166–7.

38 Eisenhower's letters to Montgomery, Marshall, and Churchill are in Eisenhower Papers, 2320–7. His report to the Combined Chiefs of Staff, 3 December 1944, offers a balanced view of the progress of the campaign, 2328–32.

39 Stacey suggests that Montgomery 'courteously' left the formal decision as to whether 2nd Canadian or 30th British Corps should carry out the operation to Crerar. Stacey notes that logic demanded 30th Corps conduct the offensive. Since Montgomery assigned five divisions to 30th Corps and left 2nd Canadian Corps with just two, there was no doubt about his intentions.

40 The work of No. 2 Operational Research Section is described in Copp, *Montgomery's Scientists*, 6–30.

41 Interview, Michael Swann, May 1990.

42 Copp, *Montgomery's Scientists*, 335.

43 Major John Fairlie, Royal Canadian Artillery, joined the OR section in early 1944. He was invalided home shortly after drafting this report.

44 PRO WO 291/1330, 19.

45 ORS Report No. 24, 'Accuracy of Predicted Shooting'; Copp, *Montgomery's Scientists*, 311–17. Operational Research scientists had long questioned the army's assumptions about the role of artillery. In April 1943 Major Michael Swann, then in charge of a small OR section at the British Army's School of Infantry, circulated a Note on Bombardment based on OR reports from the Army Operational Research Group and his own observations. He warned infantry officers that artillery fire was 'an inefficient method of killing' against troops who were dug in, and he noted that the dispersion of fire was too great to hit small targets without good observation. The report is in PRO WO 32/10375. For a review of the problem prepared in 1945 see L.J. Hudleston, 'The Probability of Hitting Targets with Artillery Fire,' PRO WO 291/1330.

46 During Operation Elephant meteors were issued at two-hour instead of four-hour intervals, and this practice continued in Veritable. First Canadian Army Met Group, 'Report on Phase I of Special Investigation of Accuracy of Artillery Meteors,' February 1945, PRO WO 291/1330. For an account of the RAF system of producing and distributing meteorological data (known as meteors), see Bentley, 'Met.'

47 Accuracy of Predicted Fire Committee, 'Paper "J,"' 15 March 1945. LAC RG 24, vol. 10,654. The paper was a response to a letter from Major-General M.E.Dennis, MGRA 21 Army Group, to the Director Royal Artillery.

48 HQ Royal Canadian Artillery, First Canadian Army, 'Notes No. 1,' foreword. The notes are available as Appendix 6 to the October 1944 War Diary, LAC RG 24, vol. 14, 306.

49 The Army Operational Research Group (AORG) in the United Kingdom was able to obtain radar observation of both ground and air bursts fired by heavy anti-aircraft guns during trials in England, but this does not appear to have resulted in the use of radar for this purpose in the field. AORG, 'Report on Radar,' WO 291/1288.

50 Royal Canadian Artillery, First Canadian Army, 'Notes, No. 2,' 19–20.

51 Ibid., 156.

52 Ibid., 37.

53 Stacey, *Victory*, 408. See British Army Analysis, 'The Role of Rockets as Artillery Weapons 1944–1945,' PRO WO 232/49, for an evaluation of the Land Mattress.

54 The full text of the report is reproduced in Appendix I.

55 Coningham's biographer writes that 'Teddy Hudleston took over 84 Group from Leslie Brown, who had never convinced the Canadians that aircraft were a support, not a substitute for ground action.' Orange, *Coningham*, 220. For a discussion of the challenges of air support of the land campaign see Gooderson, *Air Power at the Battlefront*, especially chs. 7 and 8.

56 'Air Support Organization and Procedure in NW Europe,' PRO WO 233/ 61, ch. 3, 3.

57 Ibid., ch. 2, 4. From the air force's perspective, these meetings allowed time to prepare squadrons for the next day's activities.

58 Ibid., 6. At the height of the battles for the Breskens Pocket and Woensdrecht, Coningham ordered 84 Group to commit additional squad- rons to railway interdiction in northern Holland and Germany. PRO Air 37/639 2A, 14 October 1944.

59 War Diary, G Air Branch HQ, First Canadian Army, October 1944.

60 HQ, 3rd Canadian Infantry Division, 'Air Sp. Op. "Switchback,"' 20 No- vember 1944, War Diary, 3rd Canadian Infantry Division, November 1944. See also Bechthold, 'Air Support in the Breskens Pocket.'

61 No. 2 ORS, Joint Report No. 2 (with ORS 2TAF); Copp, *Montgomery's Scientists*, 223; 2TAF, 'Tactical Employment of Rocket Projectiles,' Tactical Bulletin No. 45, November 1944, PRO AIR 15/721.

62 Stacey, *Victory*, 559.

63 Chandler, *Eisenhower Papers*, 2187.

64 This view was not shared by RAF Bomber Command, which flew 1,694 sorties against targets on Walcheren, making use of every clear day in October. This represented 40 per cent of the daylight effort and 12 per cent of the total sorties in October. Operational Research Section Bomber Com- mand, 'Monthly Report on Losses and Interceptions – October 1944,' LCMSDS Archives.

65 Sir Charles Portal to Sir Arthur Tedder, 22 October 1944. PRO Air 37/1436.

66 Ibid. See also Sir Charles Webster and Noble Frankland, *The Strategic Air Offensive against Germany 1939–1945 Vol III Victory*, 62–74, for a fuller discussion of the controversy.

67 Sir Arthur Tedder to Portal, 25 October 1944, PRO Air 37/1436.

68 Major-General K.W.D. Strong, 'Employment of Strategic Air Forces,' 29 November 1944, ibid.

69 RAF Bomber Command destroyed Cleve and Goch on the eve of Veritable, 7 February 1945, but the Seigfried Line defences and the battlefield
were left to 2TAF, including the medium bombers of 2 Group. RAF Narrative, *The Liberation of North-West Europe*, vol. 5 (first draft), Operation
Veritable, LAC RG 24, vol. 20, 352.

70 Copp, *Montgomery's Scientists*, 273–4.

71 No. 2 ORS/2TAF ORS, Joint Report, 'Note on the Accuracy of the MRCP';
ibid., 275–8.

72 Ibid. I am indebted to the late Lord Swann for drawing my attention to the
implications of the report. Swann interview, 1987. The prospect of using
radar-guided heavy bombers to provide close support of the army was
briefly considered by RAF staff officers. One proposal to employ 'a cab-
rank of heavy-bombers orbiting 25 or 30 miles behind the lines ... being
called up to deal with centres of resistance as they are met' was sent
forward to Bomber Command in April 1945 but no action was taken. PRO
Air 37/1436.

73 Copp, *Montgomery's Scientists*, 359–71.

74 Members of 2 ORS interviewed by the author indicated that First Cana-
dian Army staff was especially cooperative after the investigations in the
Scheldt Estuary. The section had less contact with 2nd British Army
Headquarters. Swann interview, 1987.

7. VERITABLE

1 Hitler explained his current strategic ideas to a number of his generals on
28 December 1944. Heiber and Glants, *Hitler and His Generals*, 544–68. The
impact of Operation Norwind on U.S. 6th Army Group is outlined in
Weigley, *Eisenhower's Lieutenants*, 801–10. See also Fussell, *Doing Battle*,
128–41.

2 Hinsley, *British Intelligence*, 596–602.

3 Gilbert, *Road to Victory*, 1142.

4 Ibid., 1144.

5 Ellis, *Victory in the West*, 209–17.

6 The Canadian government had repeated its request that all Canadian
formations 'be grouped under unified Canadian command' at the Second
Quebec Conference in September 1944 and had rejected British proposals
to employ Canadian troops in the Mediterranean outside of Italy. These
restrictions made the Canadian Corps the obvious choice when the decision to transfer formations from Italy to Northwest Europe was made.
Nicholson, *The Canadians in Italy*, 656–66.

7 Ellis, *Victory in the West*, 241–44.
8 Macdonald, *The Last Offensive*, 143.
9 Personal Diary, Brigadier N.E. Rodger, LAC RG 24, vol. 10, 797.
10 Canadian Military Headquarters Report No. 185, 'Operation Veritable: The Winter Offensive between the Maas and the Rhine 8–25 February 1945,' 19–20.
11 Directive M548, 21 January 1945, BLMP.
12 Stacey, *Victory*, 463.
13 CMHQ, Report No. 185, 25.
14 Horrocks, *Corps Commander*, 157–8.
15 Roberts, *Canadian Summer*, 106–7.
16 Salmond, *History*, 216–19. See also M. Lindsay, *So Few Got Through*, for an excellent first-person account of the battle.
17 Barclay, *History*, 125.
18 Ibid., 179.
19 Copp, *The Brigade*, 172–5; Bercuson, *Battalion of Heroes*, 202–7.
20 War Diary, 2nd Canadian Field Historical Section, February 1945.
21 Brigadier W.J. Megill, 'The Role of 5 Canadian Infantry Brigade in Operation Veritable,' 11 February 1945, DHH.
22 P. Forbes, *6th Guards Tank Brigade*, 95.
23 Horrocks, *Corps Commander*, 155.
24 War Diary, 7th Canadian Infantry Brigade, 8 February 1945; War Diary, Regina Rifles, 8 February 1945.
25 War Diary, 8th Canadian Infantry Brigade, 8–9 February 1945; War Diary, North Shore (New Brunswick) Regiment, 8 February 1945.
26 War Diary, 9th Canadian Infantry Brigade, 10–14 February1945; War Diary, North Nova Scotia Highlanders, 10–14 February 1945.
27 CMHQ, Report No. 185, 23.
28 D.C. Bernsdorf, OCMH MS B-601.
29 Smith, *Code Word Canloan*, 1–9.
30 The War Office Directive is in War Diary, DA 8 QMG, 2nd Canadian Corps, January 1945. Emergency commissions could be offered to British personnel in First Canadian Army. There was no shortage of junior officers in Canadian units. Casualty figures are from CMHQ Report No. 85, Appendix F.
31 Lieutenant-Colonel Trevor Hart Dyke, who commanded the Hallamshire battalion in 49th Division, recalled discussions of Wallstreet and expressed the view that it was doable as a corps operation. Interview, Copp with Hart Dyke, Sheffield, 1986. For Hart Dyke's account of fighting on the 'island' and the battle for Zetten see Delaforce, *The Polar Bears*, 191–4.

32 War Diary, 2nd Canadian Corps, February 1945; GOC's Activities, LAC RG 24, vol. 13, 245.

33 War Diary, 49th Division, Division Commander's Second Outline Plan, 15 February 1945, LAC RG 24, vol. 10, 893.

34 M473 and M474, 10–11 February 1945, BLMP.

35 Crerar to Simonds, 14 February 1945, Crerar Papers.

36 Army Group H, responsible for defending the Maas-Waal line, consisted of 25th and 1st Parachute Army. By February 1945 both the 711th and 712th German infantry divisions had been transferred from 256th Army to the Eastern Front leaving 346th Division and some regimental battle groups to hold the western sector along the Maas. 1st Parachute Army, responsible for the sector Arnhem–Venlo, began committing regiments of 2nd, 6th, and 7th Parachute Divisions to the Rhineland in February. While Allied intelligence officers were uncertain about the location of all elements of these divisions, they knew that the Army Group's mobile reserve, 47th Panzer Corps, had entered the battle in the Rhineland. See First Canadian Army Intelligence Summary, 3 February 1945. See also Special Interrogation Report, General Alfred Schlemm, 23 December 1945, DHH and Special Interrogation Report, General Gunther Blumentritt, 22 May 1946, DHH.

37 H.G. Martin, *History*, 256. See also Woollcombe, *Lion Rampant*, 210–19.

38 Historical Officer, 3rd Canadian Infantry Division, 'The Clearing of Moyland Wood 7–8 March 1945,' DHH, 1.

39 CMHQ Report No. 185, 21.

40 Brown and Copp, *Look to Your Front*, 158–61.

41 For an account of the experience of one Canscot platoon commander see Pearcy, 'Ordered In.' The most detailed accounts of the battle for Moyland Wood are in Roy, *Ready for the Fray*, and Brown and Copp, 158–73. See Special Interogation Report, Lieutenant-General Herman Plocher, Commander 6th Parachute Division, 16 September 1946, DHH.

42 Brigadier E.R. Suttie, 'Report on Operation Veritable,' 2, LAC RG 24, vol. 10, 914. Proximity fuses employed radar in the nose of the shell to send a pulse; the return of the echo was then used to detonate the shell at a predetermined distance from the target. These were made available to artillery regiments in the British and Canadian armies in February 1945. They do not appear to have been used extensively in the Rhineland. See Nicholson, *The Gunners of Canada*, 404. For an account of the Canadian contribution to the development of the device see Avery, *The Science of War*, 98–106.

43 'The Clearing of Moyland Wood,' 4.

44 Norman R. Donogh, 'The Battle of Moyland Wood,' 11. This account was prepared by Norman Donogh of the Royal Winnipeg Rifles from regimental records. I am grateful to Mr. Donogh for allowing me to read this report.

45 'The Clearing of Moyland Wood,' 5.

46 Interview, Brigadier George Pangman with Copp, 1991.

47 Brigadier F.N. Cabeldu, 'The Struggle for the Goch-Calcar Road,' Historical Officer interview, 28 February 1945, DHH.

48 Guderian, *From Normandy to the Ruhr*, 388.

49 Bernsdorf, OCMH, 3.

50 War Diary, Royal Hamilton Light Infantry, 19–20 February 1945; Whitaker and Whitaker, *Rhineland*, 152–73.

51 The War Diary of the Essex Scottish Regiment provides a graphic account of the battle. The 4th Brigade War Diary should also be consulted. See also R.W. Meanwell, 'The Essex Scottish Regiment 1939–1945,' DHH, and J.A. Mouhray, 'The Essex Scottish in the Rhineland, 12 January to 10 March 1945,' MA thesis, Wayne State University, 1966.

52 Morton, *Vanguard*, 99–104. See also Goodspeed, *Battle Royal*, 537–8.

53 First Canadian Army Intelligence Summary, 21 February 1945.

54 This summary is based on the War Diaries of the battalions and brigade for 19–20 February.

55 'The Employment of Support Aircraft During Operations in the S.E. Reichswald Forest,' PRO WO 205/480. The weather was not suitable for air operations on 20 February. See also First Canadian Army, 'Air Support in a Counter Battery Role,' 4 March 1945, PRO WO 205/545.

56 Quoted in First Canadian Army Intelligence Summary, 20 February 1945.

57 CHMQ Report No. 185, Appendix F; Stacey, *Victory*, 484.

58 Copp, 'First Canadian Army February–March 1945,' in Addison and Calder, *A Time to Kill*, 154–6.

59 CMHQ Report No. 185, Appendix F, First Canadian Army Intelligence Reports, 26–7 February 1945.

8. BLOCKBUSTER AND THE RHINE

1 Macdonald, *The Last Offensive*, 139.

2 Ibid., 145–6.

3 Ibid., 154. See also Allan, *One More River*, 141.

4 Personal for CIGS from Commander in Chief, 20/21 February 1945, BLMP 112, M493, M498. The British military historian Major-General H. Essame, who commanded a brigade of 43rd Wessex Division during the Rhineland

battle, has suggested that Montgomery did not approve of Blockbuster but declined to interfere with Crerar's plans. Essame wrote without access to Montgomery's papers.

5 Stacey, *Victory*, 491.

6 War Diary, 2nd Canadian Field Historical Section, February 1945. Major T.A. Sesia, the senior Historical Officer, took detailed notes of the briefing. The corps commander's outline plan is reproduced in Appendix A of Canadian Military Headquarters Report No. 186, *Operation Blockbuster: The Canadian Offensive West of the Rhine 26 February – 23 March 1945.*

7 First Canadian Army Intelligence Summary No. 238, 239, 23–24 February 1945.

8 Crerar Papers, vol. 2, Directives to Commanders, 25 February 1945.

9 Stacey, *Victory*, 491–93.

10 Interview, Copp with Major-General Bruce Matthews, June (1985). Matthews recalled that he was aware of the American advance; however, the tasks demanded of his division required his full attention and he gave no thought to alternative strategies for defeating the enemy west of the Rhine.

11 2nd Canadian Division Intelligence Summary No. 57, 26 February 1945, LAC RG 24, vol. 13, 752. Guderian, *From Normandy to the Ruhr*, 392.

12 R.H. Keefler, 'Operation Blockbuster': Role of 6 Canadian. Infantry Brigade 26 February 1945, 16 March 1945, DHH, 1.

13 Ibid., 2.

14 6th Infantry Brigade was supported by the Sherbrooke Fusilier Regiment, the Fort Garry Horse (less one squadron), 1st Canadian Armoured Personnel Carrier Regiment, and troops of Flail tanks and Crocodiles from 79th Armoured Division.

15 Keefler, 'Operation Blockbuster,' 2. Rodgers was recommended for a Victoria Cross, but this was rejected at 21 Army Group.

16 Copp, *Brigade*, 177–8.

17 War Diary, Régiment de Maisoneuve, 26 February 1945; Guy de Merlis, *Notes*, LCMSDS Archives.

18 CMHQ Report No. 186, Operation Blockbuster, 10.

19 Lieutenant-Colonel S.M. Lett, 'interview with Historical Officer,' 16 March 1945, DHH.

20 Ibid., 2.

21 Major F.J. L'Espérence, 'interview with Historical Officer,' 19 March 1945, DHH.

22 War Diary, 1st Hussars, 26 February 1945; CMHQ Report No. 186, 34.

23 Verbal Instructions GOC 4th Canadian Armoured Division, 22 February 1945, LAC RG 24, vol. 10,937.

24 CMHQ Report No. 186, 18.
25 Ibid., 21–2.
26 There were 214 fatal casualties; see Appendix B.
27 M1005, 26 February 1945, BLMP.
28 Great Britain Army, *History of 11th Armoured Division*, 80–4.
29 D.J. Watterson, 'Quarterly Report of Psychiatrist, 2nd Army,' 31 March 1945, LAC RG 24, vol. 12, 361.
30 Great Britain Army, 82.
31 GS Account of Operation Blockbuster, LAC RG 24, vol. 10, 935. This nine-page document includes the most important decisions recorded in the corps message log.
32 Simonds met with Roberts, GOC 11th Armoured Division, at 0700 hours, 27 February, and with Matthews later that morning. War Diary, 2nd Canadian Corps, February 1945, GOC Activities.
33 The lead elements of 11th Division reached their objective on the morning of 1 March. GS Account, 5. The problems encountered by 11th Armoured Division are outlined in Roberts, *From the Desert to the Baltic*, 223–5.
34 Cassidy, *Warpath*, 254–6.
35 GS Account of Operation Blockbuster, 3.
36 F.E. Wigle, interview with Historical Officer, 24 March 1945, DHH. The interview is reprinted in Fraser, *Black Yesterdays*, 376–80.
37 GOC Activities, 27 February 1945.
38 CMHQ Report No. 186, 24–5.
39 The Argylls' War Diary for 28 February as well as Wigle's interview and other personal accounts are in Fraser, *Black Yesterdays*, 377–80.
40 Copp, *The Brigade*, 179–80.
41 Hayes, *The Lincs*, 104.
42 Ibid., 103.
43 CMHQ Report No. 186, 34–5.
44 These directions are outlined in Macdonald, *The Last Offensive*, 173–4.
45 M1009, 1 March 1945, BLMP.
46 Macdonald, *The Last Offensive*, 175.
47 Copp and Vogel, *Maple Leaf Route: Victory*, 82.
48 CMHQ Report No. 186, 38.
49 Lett, Interview Blockbuster, DHH.
50 M1010, 2 March 1945, BLMP.
51 The 9th U.S. Army Operations Log, 4 March 1945; Simpson Papers, USAMHI.
52 Macdonald, *The Last Offensive*, 178.
53 CMHQ Report No. 186, 47.
54 Matthews recalled discussing the need for a properly prepared attack in a

1987 interview. Whatever the origin of Simonds's decision, a new deliberate attack was planned.

55 CMHQ Report No. 186, 53.

56 The 52nd (Lowland) Division together with a regiment from 35th U.S. Infantry Division dealt with the last defences of the bridgehead. Blake, *Mountain and Flood*, 156–8. See also Weigley, *Eisenhower's Lieutenants*, 900.

57 Stacey, *Victory*, 516–18; Essame, *The 43rd Wessex*, 225–30.

58 Brigadier W.J. Megill, *Account of Operation Blockbuster*, 24 March 1945, DHH.

59 M1023, 9 March 1945, BLMP.

60 Adviser in Psychiatry, 21 Army Group, 'Quarterly Report, 31 March 1945,' LAC RG 24, vol. 12, 631.

61 See Taylor, *Dresden*, for a balanced discussion of the Dresden raid.

9. THE LIBERATION OF HOLLAND

1 Ellis, *Victory in the West*, 209–13.

2 Macdonald, *The Last Offensive*, 295.

3 Weigley, *Eisenhower's Lieutenants*, 915–18.

4 Macdonald, 313–14.

5 D'Este, *Patton*, 212.

6 Salmond, *History*, 239.

7 Macdonald, 308.

8 SHAEF, Report of Allied Air Operations, 28 March 1945. PRO WO 205/251. See also Ellis, *Victory*, 291.

9 Horn and Wyczynski, *Paras versus the Reich*, 200–6.

10 Stacey, *Victory*, 537.

11 Guderian, *From Normandy to the Ruhr*, 412–18.

12 War Diary, Highland Light Infantry, 24 March 1945.

13 Windsor, 'Too Close for the Guns.'

14 Macdonald, *The Last Offensive*, 316–17.

15 Ibid., 318.

16 General Simpson's Personal Calendar, 26–30 March 1945, Simpson Papers USAMHI.

17 M562, BLMP. Stacey, 539.

18 Ehrman, *Grand Strategy*, 131–49.

19 Gilbert, *Road to Victory*, 603.

20 Stacey, *Victory*, 539.

21 War Diary, Canadian Scottish Regiment, 28 March 1945.

22 War Diary, Royal Winnipeg Rifles, 29 March 1945.

23 War Diary, 7th Canadian Infantry Brigade, 29 March 1945; War Diary, Regina Rifles, 29 March 1945; Stacey, *Victory*, 542.
24 Stacey, *Victory*, 543.
25 Appendix B.
26 Lieutenant-Colonel A.G. Gregory, 'Operation Plunder (Capture of Wehl),' DHH.
27 War Diary, 4th Canadian Infantry Brigade, 3 April 1945.
28 Hayes, *The Lincs*, 113–14.
29 War Diary, 9th Canadian Infantry Brigade, 5 April 1945.
30 Lieutenant G. Jean, 'Account of Action at Zutphen,' DHH.
31 Stacey, *Victory*, 581–3.
32 1st Canadian Infantry Division Op Order No. 1, 10 April 1945, LAC RG 24, vol. 10, 896.
33 Frost, *Once a Patricia*, 425.
34 The letters are in the Crerar Papers. See English, *The Canadian Army in the Normandy Campaign*, ch. 6, for an overview.
35 Frost, *Once a Patricia*, 421.
36 Accounts of the battle are contained in the unit War Diaries and battle narratives and summarized in Historical Section (GS), Report No. 79, Operations of 1st Canadian Corps in North West Europe, 15 March–5 May 1945 (Ottawa, 1950).
37 Ibid., 20.
38 Ibid., 22–3.
39 War Diary, Royal Canadian Regiment, April 1945.
40 War Diary, 3rd Canadian Infantry Brigade April 1945; War Diary, Royal 22nd Regiment.
41 Foster's 'Comment on Operation Cannonshot,' recorded by Captain T.J. Allen as an addendum to his 'Report on Operations,' states that 'It had never been my intention to assault Apeldoorn frontally. It was a friendly city filled with refugees and I was not prepared to use arty on it. The plot was to isolate the city by having 1st Canadian Infantry Brigade face up to it and then keep the enemy garrison there occupied, and by putting 3rd Canadian Infantry Brigade across the canal south of Apeldoorn thus coming from the rear.' It is true that the original plan had proposed an envelopment of the city, but it is clear that 1st Brigade was ordered to attack the city with field artillery and that the 3rd Brigade plan developed after this attack failed.
42 Ibid., 22.
43 War Diary, 2nd Canadian Infantry Brigade, 15 April 1945.
44 Ibid., 16 April 1945.

45 War Diary, Royal Canadian Regiment, 17 April 1945.

46 Stacey, *Victory*, 576.

47 Delaney, *The Soldier's General*, 211.

48 Ibid., 212–13.

49 Lieutenant J. Hobson, 'Account of the Battle of Otterlo,' 23 April 1945, DHH.

50 For an account of the negotiations see Van der Zee, *The Hunger Winter*, 170.

51 Stacey, *Victory*, 553–5. The two battalions jumped 690. To date, 492 recovered, 134 missing, 29 wounded, 24 killed.

52 The pre-war population of Groningen, 115,000, had risen to 200,000 by 1945, largely due to the arrival of refugees from the old provinces of Holland. See Ashworth, *The City as Battlefield*, 18.

53 War Diary, Royal Hamilton Light Infantry, 13 April 1945.

54 Dykstra, 'The Occupation of Groningen,' 74–5.

55 War Diary, 2nd Canadian Corps, War Diary Notes, 12–13 April 1945. The entry for 13 April reads: '2nd Canadian Corps to take over Bremen and to clear out Emden-Wilhelmshaven area then cross Weser directed on Hamburg.'

56 War Diary, 2nd Canadian Infantry Division, 14–16 April 1945.

57 War Diary, Toronto Scottish Regiment, 14 April 1945.

58 Ashworth, *The City as Battlefield*, 23–4.

59 Copp, *The Brigade*, 191–2.

60 Ashworth *The City as Battlefield*, 25; Dykstra, 'The Occupation of Groningen,' 110–13.

61 Dykstra, 'The Occupation of Groningen,' 131–2.

62 Ibid.

63 War Diary, 2nd Canadian Corps, War Diary Notes, 17 April 1945.

64 The cowboys and Indians comment was first made by officers interviewed for *The Brigade*, but other veterans have suggested that the infantryman's war was often like a deadly child's game.

65 Chandler, *Eisenhower Papers*, 2611.

66 Horrocks, *Corps Commander*, 177.

67 War Diary, 2nd Canadian Corps, 16–17 April 1945.

68 Cassidy, *Warpath*, 303–7.

69 War Diary, 2nd Canadian Corps, War Diary Notes, 20 April 1945.

70 Ibid. See also Historical Officer, 3rd Canadian Infantry Division, 'Battle Narrative 18 April to 5 May 1945,' LAC RG 24, vol. 10, 986.

71 Pogue, 'The Decision to Halt at the Elbe,' 374–87.

72 Gilbert, *Road to Victory*, 1273.

73 Roskill, *The War at Sea*, 221.
74 Eisenhower to Combined Chiefs of Staff, 14 April 1945, Eisenhower Papers, 2609; Eisenhower to Army Group Commanders, 15 April 1945, Ibid., 2611. Montgomery's response is outlined in Hamilton, *Monty*, 475–500.
75 War Diary, 2nd Canadian Corps, 27 April 1945.
76 Brigadier J.M. Rockingham, 'Operation Duck,' 4 May 1945, DHH.
77 Stacey, *Victory*, 590.
78 War Diary, 2nd Canadian Corps, 27 April 1945.
79 Rockingham, 'Operation Duck,' 2.
80 Boss and Patterson, *Up the Glens*, 259.
81 War Diary, Regina Rifles, April 1945, Battle Narrative 29–30 April 1945.
82 S.M. Lett, 'Operation Plunder, Phase 4,' War Diary, Queen's Own Rifles, May 1945. See also Roberts, *The Canadian Summer*, 140–5, for an account of the surrender.
83 War Diary, 2nd Canadian Corps, April 1945, Notes Chief of Staff, 1 May 1945.
84 Korvetten Kapitan Wolters, who commanded German forces defending the Delfzijl Pocket, told 5th Division Intelligence Officers that he received his orders from Colonel Plessing, the commander of the Emden area. The 5th Canadian Armoured Division Intelligence Summary, 2 May 1945, LAC RG 24, vol. 10, 941.
85 Letters, Hoffmeister to Byers, 18 January 1991 and 1 March 1991. The letters are reproduced in Byers, 'Operation Canada.'
86 The harbour facilities were repaired quickly, but damage to the main lock and a number of bridges prevented use of the Ems Canal until November 1945. I am grateful to Franz Lenselink for sharing the results of his research on Delfzijl with me. Letter, Lenselink to Copp, October 1991, LCMSDS Archives.
87 Brigadier Ian Johnston, 'Report on Operations: 11th Canadian Infantry Brigade,' LAC RG 24, vol. 15, 201. See also 5th Canadian Armoured Division, History of Operations, LAC RG 24, vol. 10, 941. The author of this five- page summary notes that while 'a constant maintaining of pressure might have proved sufficient ... the constant enemy shelling was taking its toll. So it was decided to reduce the pocket immediately.' Byers, 35–45. See also Morrison and Slaney, 'The Breed of Manly Men,' 319–31.
88 Huizanga and Doornbos, *The Battle for the Liberation* (translated for the author by William Jeronimus), lists fatal casualties by name and regiment. Johnston's 'Report on Operations' gives the same total for killed-in-action/missing and lists 180 wounded. It should be noted that 3rd Divi-

sion suffered forty-three fatal casualties in actions in the coastal region of Groningen province before handing over to 5th Division.

89 Stacey, *Victory*, 603–6.
90 Interview with Brigadier James Hill, 1996; interview with Richard Hilborn, 2002. For a fuller account see Horn and Wyczynski, 223–8.

CONCLUSION

1 Stacey, *Victory*, 643.
2 Allied Strengths and Casualties, Northwest Europe May 1945. LAC RG 24, vol. 10, 536.
3 Statistical Section, HQ First Canadian Army, 20 December 1944. LAC RG 24, vol. 12, 631. A brief comparison of Canada and British battle casualties in the Western European theatre follows:

    3rd Canadian Infantry Division (6 June–8 December) 11,376
    2nd Canadian Infantry Division (11 July–8 December) 11,340
    4th Canadian Armoured Division (11 July–8 December) 4,346
    2nd Canadian Armoured Brigade (6 June–8 December) 1,215
    3rd British Division (6 June–8 December) 9,269
    43rd British Division (24 June–8 December) 9,452
    Guards Armoured Division (1 July–8 December) 3,864
    8th British Armoured Brigade (6 June–December) 885

4 Ibid., 298.
5 The report is reproduced in Appendix G. I thank my colleague Marc Kilgour for checking the statistics.
6 Ellis, *Brute Force*, 535. Ellis, who has made an outstanding contribution to the history of both world wars, admitted that he was unfamiliar with evidence about the inaccuracy of Allied artillery and airpower and indicated that he would re-examine aspects of his 'brute force' argument at the Soldier's Experience of War Conference, Edinburgh, September 1995.
7 Copp, *Montgomery's Scientists*, 221.
8 Ellis, *Brute Force*, 154.
9 Copp, *Montgomery's Scientists*, 223. The allocation of 2TAF resources was also affected by the decline in the total number of sorties flown in the fall and winter of 1944–5. Spitfire sorties declined from more than 15,000 per month (August) to 8,000 (October). Typhoon sorties numbered from more than 10,000 (August) to less than 5,000 (October). Of the sorties flown in October, between 10 and 15 per cent were aborted owing to weather. A sortie is a single flight by a single aircraft. SHAEF, *Tactical Air Force Monthly Summary of Operations*, February 1945, DHH.

10 RAF Narrative, 'The Battle for the Approaches to Antwerp,' 53 pages, n.d., DHH, 50–2. See also 'Note of the Bombing of Flushing,' PRO AIR 37/1060.
11 Air Narrative, 'Operation Veritable,' PRO AIR 37/1060, 1–2.
12 O'Brien, 'East versus West,' 107.
13 Buckley, *British Armour in the Normandy Campaign*.
14 Brown and Copp, *Look to Your Front*, 185–204.

Bibliography

Archival Sources

Canada

Library and Archives Canada, Record Group 24
  War Diaries
  Army, Corps, Divisional, and Brigade Files, '200' Series.
  Crerar Papers, MG 30 E157
Directorate of History and Heritage, Department of National Defence
  Biographical Files
  Historical Officer Interviews
Laurier Centre for Military, Strategic, and Disarmament Studies, Archives,
  Wilfrid Laurier University
  Ronnie Shephard Operational Research Papers
  Terry Copp Papers

United Kingdom

Public Record Office
  WO 171 21st Army Group War Diaries
  WO 291 Operational Research Reports
  Air 24, Air 41
Liddell Hart Centre for Military Archives, King's College London
  Alanbrooke Papers
Imperial War Museum
  Montgomery Papers
British Army Museum
  Hakewill Smith Papers

United States

United States Army Military History Institute
  Bradley Papers
  World War II German Military Studies
  Simpson Papers

Secondary Sources

Addison, Paul, and Angus Calder (eds). *Time to Kill: The Soldier's Experience of War in the West, 1939–1945*. London: Pimlico, 1997.
Allan, Peter. *One More River: The Rhine Crossings of 1945*. New York: Charles Scribner, 1980.
Ashworth, G.J. *The City as Battlefield: The Liberation of Groningen, April 1945*. Groningen: University of Groningen, 1995.
Astor, Gerald. *Terrible Terry Allen: Combat General of World War II – The Life of an American Soldier*. New York: Ballantine, 2003.
Avery, D.H. *The Science of War*. Toronto: University of Toronto Press, 1998.
Barclay, C.N. *The History of the 53rd (Welsh) Division in the Second World War*. London: William Clowes, 1956.
Barnard, W.T.T. *The Queen's Own Rifles of Canada, 1860–1960*. Toronto: Ontario Publishing Company, 1963.
Bartlett, Jack F. *1st Battalion: The Highland Light Infantry of Canada*. Galt, ON: n.p., 1951.
Bechthold, Mike. 'Air Support in the Breskens Pocket: The Case of First Canadian Army and 84 Group RAF.' *Canadian Military History* 3 no. 2 (1994): 53–62.
Bennett, Ralph. *Ultra in the West: The Normandy Campaign, 1944–45*. London: Hutchinson, 1979.
Bentley, J. 'Met – The Guiding Hand of the Artillery.' *Journal of the Royal Artillery* 72, no. 2 (1945): 192–7.
Bercuson, David. *Battalion of Heroes: History of the Calgary Highlanders*. Calgary: Calgary Highlanders Regimental Funds Foundation, 1994.
Bidwell, Shelford. *Gunners at War*. London: Arms and Armour Press, 1970.
Bird, Will R. *No Retreating Footsteps: The Story of the North Nova Scotia Highlanders*. Kentville, NS: Kentville, 1954.
– *The North Shore (New Brunswick) Regiment*. Fredericton, NB: Brunswick, 1963.
Blackburn, George. *The Guns of Victory: A Soldier's Eye View, Belgium, Holland, and Germany, 1944–45*. Toronto: McClelland and Stewart, 1996.

Blake, George. *Mountain and Flood: The History of the 52nd (Lowland) Division, 1939–1946.* Glasgow: Jackson, Son & Company, 1950.

Bland, Larry I. (ed.). *The Papers of George Catlett Marshall.* Vol. 4. Baltimore: Johns Hopkins University Press, 1996.

Blumenson, Martin. *The Battle of the Generals.* New York: Morrow, 1993.

– *Breakout and Pursuit.* Washington: Center of Military History, 1961.

– (ed.). *The Patton Papers.* Boston: Houghton Mifflin, 1972.

Bond, James C. 'The Fog of War: Large Scale Smoke Screening Operations of First Canadian Army in Northwest Europe 1944–45.' *Canadian Military History* 8, no. 1 (1999): 41–58.

Borthwick, Alastair. *Battalion.* London: Bâton Wicks, 1994.

Boss, W., and W.J. Patterson. *Up the Glens: Stormont Dundas and Glengarry Highlanders, 1783–1994.* Cornwall, ON: Old Book Store, 1995.

Bradley, Omar. *A Soldier's Story.* New York: Henry Hold, 1952.

Bradley, Omar, and Blair Clay. *A General's Life: An Autobiography by General of the Army Omar N. Bradley.* New York: Simon and Shuster, 1983.

Brereton, Lewis H. *The Brereton Diaries: The War in the Air in the Pacific, Middle East and Europe, 3 October 1941–8 May 1945.* New York: William Morrow, 1946.

Brown, Gordon, and Terry Copp. *Look to Your Front ... Regina Rifles: A Regiment at War, 1939–45.* Waterloo: LCMSDS, 2001.

Brown, John Sloan. 'Col. Trevor N. Dupuy and the Mythos of Wehrmacht Superiority: A Reconsideration.' *Military Affairs* 50 (January 1986): 16–20.

Buchanan, G.B. *The March of the Prairie Men: A Story of the South Saskatchewan Regiment.* Privately published.

Buckley, John. *British Armour in the Normandy Campaign, 1944.* London: Frank Cass, 2004.

Butcher, Captain Harry C. *My Three Years with Eisenhower.* New York: Simon and Schuster, 1946.

Byers, Daniel T. 'Mobilizing Canada: The National Resources Mobilization Act.' PhD thesis, McGill University, 2000.

– 'Operation "Canada."' BA thesis, Wilfrid Laurier University, 1991.

Carrington, Charles. *A Soldier at Bomber Command.* London: Leo Cooper, 1987.

Cassidy, G.L. *Warpath.* Cobalt, ON: Highway Book Shop, 1990.

Castonguay, Jacques, and Armand Ross. *Le Régiment de la Chaudière.* Levis: Régiment de la Chaudière, 1983.

Chandler, Alfred D. (ed.). *The Papers of Dwight D. Eisenhower.* Vol. 4. *The War Years.* Baltimore: Johns Hopkins University Press, 1970.

Clay, E.W. *The Path of the 50th.* Aldershot: Galen and Pole, 1950.

Cooper, Belton Y. *Death Traps*. Novato, CA: Presidio, 1998.

Copp, Terry. *The Brigade: The Fifth Canadian Infantry Brigade, 1939–1945*. Stoney Creek, ON: Fortress, 1992.

– 'Counter Mortar Operational Research in 21 Army Group.' *Canadian Military History* 3, no. 2 (1994): 6–21.

– *Fields of Fire: The Canadians in Normandy*. Toronto: University of Toronto Press, 2002.

– 'Scientists and the Art of War: Operational Research in 21 Army Group.' *RUSI Journal* 136, no. 4 (1991): 65–70.

– (ed.) *Montgomery's Scientists: Operational Research in Northwest Europe, 1944–1945*. Waterloo, ON: Laurier Centre for Military, Strategic, and Disarmament Studies, 2000.

Copp, Terry, and Mike Bechthold. *The Canadian Battlefields in Northwest Europe, 1944–1945: A Visitor's Guide*. Waterloo, ON: Laurier Centre for Military, Strategic, and Disarmament Studies, 2005.

Copp, Terry, and Bill McAndrew. *Battle Exhaustion: Soldiers and Psychiatrists in the Canadian Army, 1939–1945*. Montreal: McGill-Queen's University Press, 1990.

Copp, Terry, and Robert Vogel. *Maple Leaf Route: Antwerp*. Alma, ON: Maple Leaf Route, 1983.

– *Maple Leaf Route: Scheldt*. Alma, ON: Maple Leaf Route, 1983.

– *Maple Leaf Route: Victory*. Alma, ON: Maple Leaf Route, 1983.

– 'No Lack of Rational Speed: First Canadian Army, September 1944.' *Journal of Canadian Studies* (1983).

Danchev, Alex, and Daniel Todman. *War Diaries, 1939–1945: Field Marshal Lord Alanbrooke*. London: Weidenfeld and Nicolson, 2001.

De Groot, S.J. 'Escape of the German Army across the Westerscheldt, September 1944.' *Canadian Military History* 6, no. 1 (Spring 1997): 109–17.

De Guingand, Major-General Sir Francis, KBE, CB, DSO. *Operation Victory*. London: Hodder & Stoughton, 1947.

Delaforce, Patrick. *Churchill's Desert Rats: From Normandy to Berlin with the 7th Armoured Division*. London: Alan Sutton, 1994.

– *The Polar Bears: Monty's Left Flank*. London: Alan Sutton, 1995.

Delaney, D.E. *The Soldier's General: Bert Hoffmeister at War*. Vancouver: UBC Press, 2005.

De Merlis, Guy. 'The Walcheren Causeway Revisited.' *Canadian Military History* 3, no. 2 (1994): 101–4.

D'Este, Carlo. *Eisenhower: A Soldier's Life*. New York: Henry Holt, 2002.

– *Patton: A Genius for War*. New York: HarperCollins, 1995.

De Ward, Dirk Marc. '"Luctor et Emergo": The Impact of the Second World War on Zeeland.' MA thesis, Wilfrid Laurier University, 1983.

Dickson, Paul. 'Colonials and Coalitions: Canadian-British Command Relations between Normandy and the Scheldt.' In Brian P. Farrell (ed.), *Leadership and Responsibility in the Second World War*. Montreal: McGill-Queen's University Press, 2004.

– 'The Hand That Wields the Dagger: Harry Crerar, First Canadian Army Command and National Autonomy.' *War and Society* 13, no. 2 (1995): 113–41.

– 'Harry Crerar.' Unpublished manuscript, 1996.

Douglas, W.A.B., and B. Greenhous. *Out of the Shadows: Canada in the Second World War*. Toronto: Oxford University Press, 1977.

Dupuy, Trevor N. 'Mythos or Verity? The Quantified Judgement Model and German Combat Effectiveness.' *Military Affairs* 50–3 (October 1986).

– *Numbers, Predicitions, and War*. Fairfax, VA: Hero Books, 1979.

Dykstra, Ralph. 'The Occupation of Groningen, Netherlands, September 1944–April 1945 and the Liberation of the City of Groningen by the 2nd Canadian Infantry Division April 13–16, 1945.' MA thesis, Wilfrid Laurier University, 2001.

Ehrman, J. *Grand Strategy*. Vol. 6: *October 1944–August 1945*. London: HMSO, 1956.

Ellis, John. *Brute Force*. London: Viking, 1990.

– *Sharp End of War: The Fighting Men of World War II*. Newton Abbot, Devon: David & Charles, 1980.

Ellis, L.F. *Victory in the West*. Vol. 2. London: HMSO, 1962.

English, J.A. *The Canadian Army in the Normandy Campaign*. New York: Praeger, 1991.

Essame, Major-General H. (ed.). *The Battle for Germany*. London: Batsford, 1969.

– *The 43rd Wessex Division at War, 1944–1945*. London: William Clowes and Sons, 1952.

Farrell, Brian, ed. *Leadership and Responsibility in the Second World War*. Montreal: McGill-Queen's University Press, 2004.

Featherstonhaugh, R.C. *The Royal Montreal Regiment, 1925–1945*. Westmount: Privately Printed, 1949.

Forbes, C. *Fantasin*. Quebec City: Septentrion, 1994.

Forbes, Patrick. *6th Guards Tank Brigade: The Story of Guardsmen in Churchill Tanks*. London: Sampson, Low, Marston & Co., 1946.

Foster, Tony. *A Meeting of Generals*. Toronto: Methuen, 1986.

Fowler, T.R. 'Roger Schjelderup.' *Canadian Military History* 5, no. 2 (1996): 99–105.

Fraser, Robert. *Black Yesterdays: The Argylls' War*. Hamilton, ON: Argyll Regimental Foundation, 1996.

French, David. *Raising Churchill's Army*. Oxford: Oxford University Press, 2000.

Fritz, Stephen G. *Frontsoldaten: The German Soldier in World War II*. Lexington: University of Kentucky Press, 1995.

Frost, C. Sydney. *Once a Patricia: Memoirs of a Junior Infantry Officer in World War II*. St Catharines: Vanwell, 1988.

Fussell, Paul. *Doing Battle*. New York: Little Brown, 1996.

Gilbert, Martin. *Road to Victory: Winston Churchill, 1941–1945*. London: Stoddart, 1980.

Gooderson, Ian. *Air Power at the Battlefront*. London: Cass, 1998.

Goodspeed, D.J. *Battle Royal*. Toronto: Royal Regiment of Canada Association, 1962.

Graham, Dominick. *The Price of Command: A Biography of General Guy Simonds*. Toronto: Stoddart, 1993.

Graves, Donald E. *South Albertas: A Canadian Regiment at War*. Toronto: Robin Brass Studio, 1998.

– (ed.) *Fighting for Canada: Seven Canadian Battles, 1758–1945*. Toronto: Robin Brass Studio, 2000.

Gray, R. 'The Leopold Ordeal.' *Legion Magazine*. October 1987, 6–9.

Great Britain. Army. *A History of 11th Armoured Division*. London, 1945.

Greenfield, Kent Roberts (ed.). *Command Decisions*. Washington, DC: Office of the Chief of Military History, United States Army, 1962.

Grodzinski, John. 'Kangaroos at War.' *Canadian Military History* 4, no. 3 (1995): 43–50.

Guderian, Heinz G. *From Normandy to the Ruhr with the 116th Panzer Division*. Bedford: Aberfona Press, 2001.

Hain, Alistair. 'The Calgary Highlanders: A Profile Based on Personnel Records.' MA thesis, Wilfrid Laurier University, 1990.

Hamilton, Nigel. *Monty: The Field Marshal, 1944–1976*. London: Hamish Hamilton, 1986.

Hart, Stephen A. 'Field Marshal Montgomery, 21st Army Group and North West Europe, 1944–1945.' PhD thesis, University of London, 1995.

– *Montgomery and 'Colossal Cracks': 21st Army Group in Northwest Europe, 1944–45*. Westport, CT: Praeger, 2000.

Hart Dyke, Trevor. *Normandy to Arnhem: A Story of Infantry*. Sheffield: Greemup and Thompson, 1966.

Hastings, Max. *Armageddon: The Battle for Germany, 1944–1945*. New York: Knopf, 2004.

Hayes, Geoffrey. 'The Development of the Canadian Army Officer Corps, 1939–1945.' PhD dissertation, University of Western Ontario, 1992.

– *The Lincs: A History of the Lincoln and Welland Regiment at War*. Alma, ON: Maple Leaf Route, 1986.

– '"Where Are Our Liberators?" The Canadian Liberation of West Brabant, 1944.' *Canadian Military History* 4, no. 1 (1995): 6–19.

Heiber, Helmut, and David M. Glants (eds.). *Hitler and His Generals*. New York: Enigma, 2003.

Hesketh, Roger. *Fortitude: The D-Day Deception Campaign*. London: St Ermins Press, 1999.

Hinsley, F.H. *British Intelligence in the Second World War*. Vol. 3, pt 2. London: HMSO, 1981.

Hoedelmans, Piet. *Jeeps and Klaprosen*. Trans. William Jeronimus. Bergen Op Zoom: Boekhandel Quist, 1990.

Hoegh, Leo, and Howard J. Doyle. *Timberwolf Tracks: The History of the 10th Infantry Division 1942–1945*. Washington, DC: Infantry Journal, 1946.

Hogg, Ian V. *The Guns, 1939–1945*. New York: Ballantine, 1970.

Horn, Bernd, and Stephen Harris. *Warrior Chiefs*. Toronto: Dundurn, 2001.

– *Generalship and the Art of the Admiral*. St Catharines: Vanwell, 2001.

Horn, B., and M. Wyczynski. *Paras versus the Reich*. Toronto: Vanwell, 2002.

Horrocks, Sir Brian, with Eversley Belfield. *Corps Commander*. London: Magnum Books, 1979.

Huizinga, M.H., and H. Doornbos. *The Battles for the Liberation along the Eems and Dollard*. Trans. William Jeronimus. Waterloo: LCMSDS. Original Dutch edition, Groningen: Actief Scheemda, 1985.

Jamar, K. *With the Tanks of the 1st Polish*. Hengelo: H.L. Smith & Son, 1946.

Jarymowycz, Roman. *Tank Tactics from Normandy to Lorraine*. Boulder, CO: Lynne Rienner, 2001.

Kitching, George. *Mud and Green Fields*. Langley: Battleline, 1986.

Kloeke, W. van Ommer. *De Bevrijding van Groningen*. Trans. William Jeronimus. Assen, Netherlands: Van Gorkum, 1947.

Lamb, Richard. *Montgomery in Europe*. London: Buchan and Enright, 1983.

Lindsay, Martin. *So Few Got Through*. London: Collins, 1946.

Lindsay, Martin, and M.E. Johnston. *History of the 7th Armoured Division*. Germany, 1945.

Lindsay, O. (ed.). *A Guards General: The Memoirs of Major-General Sir Alan Adair*. London: Hamish Hamitlon, 1986.

Love, Robert W., Jr., and John Major (eds.). *The Year of D-Day: The 1944 Diary of Admiral Sir Bertram Ramsay*. Hull, UK: University of Hull Press, 1994.

Macdonald, Charles. B. *The Last Offensive*. Washington: Office of the Chief of Military History, 1973.

Maker, John. 'Battalion Leadership in the Essex Scottish.' MA thesis, Wilfrid Laurier University, 2004.

Malone, Colonel Richard Sankey, OBE. *Missing from the Record*. Toronto: Collins, 1946.

Mansor, Peter R. *The GI Offensive in Europe, 1941–1945*. Lawrence: University of Kansas Press, 1999.

Martin, Charles, with Roy Whitestead. *Battle Diary*. Toronto: Dundurn Press, 1994.

Martin, H.G. *History of the Fifteenth Scottish Division*. Edinburgh: William Blackwood, 1948.

Mathews, W.H.V. 'Assault on Calais 25 September–1 October 1944.' *Canadian Military History* 3, no. 2 (1994): 88–95.

McIntire, Douglas M. "Pursuit to the Seine: The Essex Scottish Regiment and the Fort de la Londe." *Canadian Military History* 7, no. 1 (1998): 59–72.

McNorgan, Michael R. *The Gallant Hussars: A History of the 1st Hussars Regiment, 1856–2004*. Aylmer, ON: The 1st Hussars Cavalry Fund, 2004.

Millett, Allan R., and Williamson Murray (eds.). *Military Effectiveness*. 3 vols. Boston: Allen and Unwin, 1988.

Montgomery, Field Marshal, the Viscount Montgomery of Alamein. *Normandy to the Baltic*. London: Hutchinson, 1946.

Morrison, A., and T. Ted Slaney. *'The Breed of Manly Men': The History of the Cape Breton Highlanders*. Toronto: Canadian Institute of Strategic Studies, 1994.

Morton, R.E.A. (ed.). *Vanguard: The Fort Garry Horse in the Second World War*. Winnipeg: Fort Garry Horse, 1945.

Moulton, Major-General J.L. *Battle for Antwerp: The Liberation of the City and the Opening of the Scheldt, 1944*. New York: Hippocrene Books, 1978.

Neary, Peter, and J.L. Granatstein (eds.). *The Veteran's Charter and Post–World War II Canada*. Montreal: McGill-Queen's University Press, 1998.

Nicholson, G.W.L. *The Gunners of Canada*. Vol. 2. Toronto: McClelland and Stewart, 1972.

– *The Canadians in Italy*. Ottawa: Queen's Printer, 1957.

Nilsson, Jeffrey Peter. 'Keystone to Victory: 7th Canadian Infantry Brigade October 1944.' MA thesis, Wilfrid Laurier University, 2003.

O'Brien, Phillips. 'East versus West in the Defeat of Nazi Germany.' *Journal of Strategic Studies* 23, no. 2 (2000): 89–113.

Orange, Vincent. *Coningham*. London: Metheun, 1990.

Owen, Roderic. *Tedder*. London: Collins, 1952.

Patterson, R.A. *A History of the 10th Canadian Infantry Brigade*. Privately printed, 1945.

Pearce, Donald. *Journal of a War: Northwest Europe, 1944–1945*. Toronto: Macmillan, 1965.

Pearcy, R. 'Ordered In.' *Legion Magazine*, February 1997, 18–21.

Place, Timothy Harrison. *Military Training in the British Army, 1940–1944*. London: Cass, 2000.

Pogue, F.C. 'The Decision to Halt at the Elbe (1945).' In K.R. Greenfield, ed., *Command Decisions*. Washington: Center of Military History, U.S. Army, 1962.

Portugal, Jean E. *We Were There*. 7 vols. Toronto: Royal Canadian Military Institute, 1998.

Powell, Geoffrey. *The Devil's Birthday: The Bridges to Arnhem*. New York: F. Watts, 1985.

Rawding, Brian G. 'To Close with and Destroy: The Experience of Canloan Officers.' MA thesis, Wilfrid Laurier University, 1998.

Rawling, Gerald. *Cinderella Operation: The Battle for Walcheren, 1944*. London: Cassell, 1980.

Ritgen, Helmut. *The Western Front, 1944*. Winnipeg: Fedorowicz, 1995.

Roberts, G.P.B. *From the Desert to the Baltic*. London: William Kimber, 1987.

Roberts, James Alan. *The Canadian Summer: The Memoirs of James Alan Roberts*. Toronto: University of Toronto Bookroom, 1981.

Roskill, S.W. *The War at Sea*. Vol. 4. London: HMSO, 1961.

Rowley, Roger. 'The Attack on Boulogne.' *Canadian Military History* 3, no. 2 (1994): 76–83.

Roy, Reginald H. *Ready for the Fray*. Victoria: Canadian Scottish Regiment, 1958.

Sakkers, Hans, and Hans Houterman. *Atlantikwall in Zeeland en Vlaanderen*. Trans. Ralph Dykstra. Middelburg: Citadel, 2000.

Salmond, J.B. *History of the 51st Highland Division, 1939–1953*. Edinburgh: privately published, 1953.

Schramm, P.E. (ed.). *Die Invasion, 1944*. Munich: OKW Kriegstagebuch, 1963.

Shepard, Ronnie. *Readings on Early Military Operational Research*. Shrivenham: Royal Military College of Science, 1984.

Shulman, Milton. *Defeat in the West*. London: Secker and Warburg, 1947.

Sirluck, Ernest. *First Generation*. Toronto: University of Toronto Press, 1996.

Smith, Wilfred L. *Code Word Canloan*. Toronto: Dundurn Press, 1992.

Stacey, Colonel Charles C.P. *Arms, Men, and Governments: The War Policies of Canada 1939–1945*. Ottawa: Queen's Printer, 1970.

– *Six Years of War*. Ottawa: Queen's Printer, 1955.

- *The Victory Campaign: North West Europe, 1944–1945.* Ottawa: Queen's Printer, 1962.

Stewart, Neil S. *Steel My Soldiers Hearts.* Victoria: Trafford, 2000.

Taylor, Frederick. *Dresden.* New York: HarperCollins, 2004.

Thompson, R.W. *Eighty-Five Days: The Story of the Battle of the Scheldt.* London: Hutchinson, 1957.

Tout, Ken. *Tanks, Advance! Normandy to the Netherlands, 1944.* London: Grafton Books, 1987.

Trost, Ralph. *Eine gänzlich zerstörte stadt Nationalsozialismus, Krieg und Kriegsende in Xanten.* New York: Waxmann/Munster, 2005.

Turrey, A.J.S. 'Supply Problems in Amphibious Operations, October 1944.' *Canadian Military History* 11, no. 3 (2002): 75–8.

Urquart, Brian. 'The Last Disaster of the War,' *New York Review of Books,* 24 September 1987, 37–40.

Van Creveld, Martin. *Fighting Power: German and U.S. Army Performance, 1939–1943.* Westport, CT: Greenwood Press, 1982.

Van der Zee, Henri A. *The Hunger Winter: Occupied Holland, 1944–1945.* Lincoln: University of Nebraska Press, 1982.

Van Doorn, J. *Slag om Woensdrecht.* Trans. Ralph Dykstra. Woensdrecht: Boekmandel Quist, 1995.

Verney, Major-General G.L. *The Guards Armoured Division: A Short History.* London: Hutchinson, 1955.

Vokes, Major-General Chris, with John P. Maclean. *Vokes: My Story.* Ottawa: Gallery Books, 1985.

Von der Heydte, F.A. *Muss ich sterben, will ich fallen.* Heidelberg: Vowinckel, 1987.

Webster, Sir Charles, and Noble Frankland. *The Strategic Air Offensive against Germany, 1939–1945.* Vol. 3. *Victory.* London: HMSO, 1961.

Weigley, Russel. *Eisenhower's Lieutenants.* Bloomington: Indiana University Press, 1981.

Weingartner, Steven (ed.). *From Total War to Total Victory.* Wheaton, IL: Cantigny First Division Foundation, 2005.

Whitaker, Denis, and Shelagh Whitaker. *Tug of War: The Allied Victory That Opened Antwerp.* 2nd ed. Toronto: Stoddart, 2000.

- *Rhineland: The Battle to End the War.* 2nd ed. Toronto: Stoddart, 2000.

Williams, Jeffery. *The Long Left Flank: The Hard Fought Way to the Reich, 1944–1945.* Toronto: Stoddart, 1988.

Wilmot, Chester. *The Struggle for Europe.* London: Collins, 1952.

Windsor, Lee. '"Too Close for the Guns!" 9 Canadian Infantry Brigade in the Battle for the Rhine.' *Canadian Military History* 12, nos 1–2 (2003): 5–28.

Woollcombe, Robert. *Lion Rampant.* London: Chatto and Windus, 1955.

Zetterling, Niklaus. *Normandy, 1944.* Winnipeg: J.J. Fedorowicz, 2000.

Illustration Credits

Black Watch Archives: Funeral service

Directorate of History and Heritage, Department of National Defence: The Forêt de la Londe, PMR 82-061; Calais Harbour, PMR 84-19; 280 mm Cross-Channel Gun, PMR94-259; Biervliet across a polder, PMR 82-083; Walcheren Causeway, 1946, PMR 82-078; Harry Crerar, Alan Brooke, Guy Simonds, Winston Churchill, and Bernard Montgomery, PMR 88-071; damaged bridge at Zutphen, PMR 94-284

Laurier Centre for Military, Strategic, and Disarmament Studies: Bombing Mont Lambert, 17 September 44; Boulogne; Cap Gris Nez; Leopold Canal; Breskens and Fort Frederik Hendrik; Fort Frederik Hendrik; Woensdrecht; Walcheren Causeway, 1944; Sherman tanks destroyed during advance to Bergen Op Zoom; Westkappelle, 28 October 1944; northern end of the Hochwald Defences

Library and Archives Canada: Rouen Cathedral, PA 137297; Mont Lambert from the 9th Brigade startline, PA 136245; Hôtel de Ville, Calais, PA 131238; Wasp flame throwers, PA 131240; Esso smoke generators, PA 136818; Breskens Pocket, PA 131252; Calgary Highlanders private, PA 131260; field artillery tractor, South Beveland, PA 138423; Sherman tanks, South Beveland, PA 138428; Sherman tanks, Beveland Canal, PA 138429; Medium artillery at Kapelsche Veer, PA 144708; Reichswald Forest, PA 122934; 3rd Canadian Division vehicles in the Rhine floodplain, PA 143946; Stormont Dundas and Glengarry Highlanders, PA 145774; The North Shore (New Brunswick) Regiment, PA 140424; Lieutenant-Colonel Ross Ellis, Major-General Bruce Matthews, Brigadier W.J. Megill, PA 183996; Brigadier John Rockingham and Lieutenant-General Brian Horrocks, PA 145101; Brigadier C.M. Drury, Major-General Dan Spry, and Major-General Chris Vokes, PA 145969; Winston Churchill greeted by Canadian, PA 47379; Seigfried Line Defences near Cleve, PA 145751; German position in the Hochwald, PA 140885; wounded personnel in jeep ambulance, PA 177595; kangaroo of 1st Canadian Armoured Personnel Carrier Regiment, PA 15920; Blackfriars Bridge, PA 113687; gun, Kusten Canal, PA 146283; signaler, PA 146287; Perth Regiment infantry, PA 145884; damaged houses at Groningen, PA 130945; Engineers prepare storm boats, PA 138285; Lieutenant-Colonel J.A. Dextraze, Major D.W. Grant, PA 146281; frying eggs on the exhaust of a tank, PA 145971; German children surrendering, PA 113697; liberation of the Netherlands, Dalfsen, PA 145972; personnel of 12th Field Regiment RCA with the *Maple Leaf*, PA 15093; Food supplies for the Dutch, PA 134417; crowd in Trafalgar Square, PA 141657

Index